EVE

A BIOGRAPHY

PAMELA NORRIS

———◆———

EVE

A BIOGRAPHY

NEW YORK UNIVERSITY PRESS
Washington Square, New York

First published in the United Kingdom by Macmillan Publishers Ltd in 1998

First published in the U.S.A. in 1999 by
NEW YORK UNIVERSITY PRESS
Washington Square
New York, NY 10003

Library of Congress Cataloging-in-Publication Data
Norris. Pamela.
[Story of Eve]
Eve : a biography / Pamela Norris.
p.   cm.
Originally published: London : Picador, 1998.
Includes bibliographical references and index.
ISBN 0-8147-5812-6 (alk. paper)
1. Eve (Biblical figure)   I. Title.
BS580.E85.N67   1999
222'.11092—dc21   99-34540
CIP

Typeset by SetSystems Ltd, Saffron Walden, Essex
Printed and bound in Great Britain by
Mackays of Chatham plc, Chatham, Kent

For John Senter

CONTENTS

—◆—

ACKNOWLEDGEMENTS

Many people contributed to the writing of this book. My greatest debt is to the many scholars and writers whose work assisted me in the search for Eve's history: their names are recorded in the bibliography and notes. For advice and information, I am grateful to Mark Bostridge, Elizabeth Buchan, Lyndall Gordon, Edith Hall, Tom Healy, Miriel Lenore, Pippa Lewis, Henrietta Leyser, John Pilling, Diane Purkiss and Nicholas Roe. Helen Dunmore kindly shared thoughts on the Garden of Eden; Colin Smith generously provided information about mermaids in English church decoration. Any errors in the text are entirely my own responsibility. Special thanks are due to my agent, Derek Johns, for his calm support and unflagging enthusiasm, and to my editor, Ursula Doyle, for her helpful comments on the manuscript and careful attention to the many details involved in publishing this book. Nicholas Blake was a courteous guide through copyediting and proofs. Suzanne Bailey was indefatigable in the pursuit of illustrations, and their collection on schedule was a tribute to her tact, persistence and powers of persuasion. Staff at the British Library, the University of London Library, the Bodleian Library in Oxford, Rye Library and the Martello Bookshop in Rye were unfailingly helpful. The London Library's wide-ranging collection and excellent postal service were invaluable, and the staff responded with exemplary care to my many enquiries. Friends and family, and, in particular, my parents, Ronald and Patricia Norris, offered welcome encouragement and cheer. The book is dedicated to my dear companion and helpmate John Senter, with thanks for hours of discussion.

PAMELA NORRIS

ILLUSTRATION NOTES

1. Wild animals still peacefully cohabit in the earthly Paradise at the pivotal moment before Adam bites the apple. In Lucas Cranach the Elder's *Fall of Man*, 1526, Eve is characteristically seductive and knowing in contrast to Cranach's unsophisticated Adam.

2. Adam and Eve turn away from one another in shame after the Fall, their hands clutching fig leaves to their genitals. Detail on the fourth-century sarcophagus of Junius Bassus.

3. An agonized Eve torn between desire and repentance, *c.* 1130. Carved by Gislebertus, she probably once reclined above the north portal of the cathedral of St-Lazare, with Adam in the corresponding position on the opposite side of the lintel and the raising of Lazarus, symbol of the Christian potential for spiritual renewal, occupying the tympanum. The creeping figure of Eve, indicative of humanity's inability to stand alone after the Fall, is now in the Musée Rolin, Autun.

4. God performs the first wedding ceremony within a simple fenced enclosure, symbol of the Garden of Eden, while admiring animals and angels look on. Jean Corbechon's beguiling MS illustration of *The Marriage of Adam and Eve*, *c.* 1415.

5. Adam digs while Eve spins, and Cain and Abel play at cudgels; paired with Noah's crowded Ark, symbol of humanity's second chance after years of bad behaviour had called down God's vengeful flood. Illustration to a fifteenth-century Flemish manuscript of the *Speculum Humanae Salvationis*.

6. An energetic serpent with female head and torso confronts Adam in Michaelangelo's *Fall and Expulsion*, 1509–10, on the Sistine Chapel ceiling. Eve's position may indicate that she is about to engage in fellatio, endorsing a sexual interpretation of eating the forbidden fruit, which is further emphasized

by the willingness with which she stretches to take the fig (*fico*), while with her right hand she gestures meaningfully at her genitals (*fica* in contemporary slang).

7. Lucas Cranach the Elder's tempting *Eve*, 1528, is paired with a typically gauche Adam (not shown). The apple she so winsomely offers clearly shows the marks of her teeth.

8. In this sixteenth-century Flemish engraving, Cleopatra stands naked beneath a tree and clutches the asp in a pose that mimics traditional portrayals of Eve, linking the two women in their roles as wicked temptresses.

9. The Watcher angels descend with giant glowing phalluses on one of the daughters of men. William Blake's illustration to *1 Enoch*, *c.* 1824/1827.

10. Humanity's spiritual odyssey, from the sin and death in which all are implicated through Adam and Eve's disobedience to the promise of redemption through Christ's sacrifice and resurrection, is dramatically traced in Hans Holbein the Younger's *Allegory of the Old and New Testaments.*

11. Known as the Burney Relief, this terracotta plaque, *c.* 2300–2000 BC, is generally thought to depict the Sumerian winged goddess Inanna-Ishtar, with attendant lions and owls, but the figure has also been linked to Adam's rebellious first wife, the demoniac Lilith.

12. The newly created Pandora, wearing her decorative crown, is greeted by her husband Epimetheus as she springs out of the earth, while a tiny Eros hovers overhead. Red-figure crater, related to Group of Polygnotos, *c.* 450 BC.

13. The decoration on a cylinder seal showing the mother goddess Tiamat, depicted as a serpent or sea-snake, conquered by the young god Marduk, *c.* ninth–eighth century BC.

14. The butterfly, symbol of transformation, hovers above Psyche's head, a reminder of the long, difficult path she has yet to travel before her joyous reunion with her lover. François Gérard's *Amor and Psyche/Psyche Receiving the First Kiss of Love*, 1798.

15. Mary seems to recoil, as if from a blow, at the news that Gabriel brings. The atmosphere of threat and danger is emphasized by the blood-red curtain to her right, and by Gabriel's scarlet robe and menacingly feathered wings. Matthias Grünewald, *Annunciation*, detail of the Isenheim Altarpiece, *c.* 1512–16.

16. A tranquil Mary sits reading in a medieval enclosed garden, the *hortus*

conclusus recalling Eden and the garden of the Song of Songs, while the infant Jesus plucks at a psaltery held by St Cecilia. See chapter 8 for the symbolism of this intricate painting. *The Garden of Paradise, c.* 1410–20, by an unknown Rhenish artist known as the Überrheinischer Meister.

17. This charming illustration tells the story of Adam and Eve from creation to exile in strip-cartoon form: from the Book of Genesis, in the Moutier-Grandval Bible, Tours, ninth century.

18. In Hieronymus Bosch's *The Earthly Paradise*, God presents Eve to Adam with a gesture of blessing, a marriage that takes place in a landscape dominated by a pink coral edifice, possibly an astrological symbol of Christ's marriage with Ecclesia, the Church. Left wing of the triptych *The Garden of Earthly Delights, c.* 1500.

19. In Bartolo di Fredi's *Creation of Eve*, 1356, in the Collegiata, San Gimignano, a scarlet-winged God, supported by cherubim, draws Eve fully formed out of the sleeping Adam's side into a pleasant flower-stocked garden.

20 and 21. Masolino's *Temptation of Adam and Eve* and Masaccio's *Adam and Eve banished from Paradise* appear on facing pillars at the entrance to the Brancacci Chapel in Santa Maria del Carmine, Florence. Probably painted in the mid-1420s, Masolino's classically beautiful couple, immobilized in primordial grace and dignity on the very brink of catastrophe, are in striking contrast to Masaccio's agonized exiles, bemoaning their fate as the sword-wielding angel drives them out of Eden.

22. Eve is shown as a wrinkled, ancient woman with drooping breasts and leaning on a stick, in Piero della Francesca's *Death of Adam*, from *The Legend of the True Cross* cycle, *c.* 1452–7, in the Basilica di S. Francesco, Arezzo.

23. Eve was frequently identified with the first human woman in Greek mythology, the 'beautiful evil', Pandora, who released suffering and disease from her innocent-looking jar. Jean Cousin the Elder, *Eva Prima Pandora,* 1550.

24. Eve's collusion with the devil's schemes is demonstrated in Hans Baldung Grien's *Eve, the Serpent and Death, c.* 1510–15. Coiling round the tree of knowledge, the serpent provides the intricate link that binds the nakedly seductive Eve to the hideous figure of death, whose flesh peels away to reveal the skeleton beneath as he triumphantly flourishes an apple.

25. Pol de Limbourg's exquisite *Adam and Eve in the Garden of Eden* depicts the Garden of Eden as a circle, an image of wholeness that is broken by the

couple's reluctant egress from the gate. From the *Très riches heures du duc de Berry*, c. 1410.

26. An angry angel pushes Adam and Eve out of Eden, while Mary listens quietly to Gabriel's news. As the Second Eve, she will give birth to the Second Adam, the Redeemer who reverses God's sentence of death in Eden. Giovanni di Paolo di Grazia, *The Annunciation*, detail, c. 1445.

27. Eve, clad in a diaphanous shawl and holding a miniature tree of knowledge, lies at the feet of the enthroned Virgin and Child, in this richly decorated panel by a Florentine artist known as the Master of the Straus Madonna. *Virgin and Child Enthroned with Angels and Saints*, c. 1410.

28. This extraordinary painting forms the left-hand panel of a diptych, and is paired with the Lamentation, the deposition of the body of Christ from the cross, watched by a grieving Mary. Van der Goes' Fall eloquently draws together the threads of present and future: the haggard face and straggling hair of the watching serpent (with two braids caught on top of her head, like demon's horns, or the convenient workaday hairstyle of a busy matron) are a grim warning of Eve's fate once she has committed herself to time; while the iris that so conveniently covers Eve's genitals foreshadows Mary's grief at the Crucifixion of Christ, symbol of the sword that Simeon predicted would pierce her heart (Luke 2:35). Hugo van der Goes, *Adam, Eve and the Serpent*, c. 1470–75.

29. Modest Mary dispenses the host, 'the bread of angels, the food of pilgrims', to a small band of the elect, while a brazenly naked Eve deals death, plucking the forbidden fruit from the serpent's jaws, as a grimacing skeleton looks on. Berthold Furtmeyer, *Tree of Life and Death*, miniature, c. 1478–89, from the Archbishop of Salzburg's missal.

30. By a process of assimilation, Mary Magdalene became the Christian Church's favourite symbol of the reformed whore. In Rogier van der Weyden's portrait (fifteenth century), she is identified by her alabaster pot of costly ointment and her penitent's tears.

31. Dante Gabriel Rossetti's vigorous sketch shows Mary Magdalene as she impetuously abandons her sinful life to follow Christ, who is shown in profile through the window. *Mary Magdalene at the Door of Simon the Pharisee*, 1858.

32. William Blake's illustration of *Satan, Sin and Death: Satan Comes to the Gates of Hell*, 1808, from the Butts series of illustrations to Milton's *Paradise Lost*. Sin, Satan's daughter and lover, is shown with multiple reptilian fanged

tails, guarding the gates of Hell, while their son, the fearful shadow Death, threatens Satan with his dart.

33. A mermaid with a fish in her grasp, symbolizing a human soul caught by the enchantment of evil, on a misericord in Exeter Cathedral, c. 1230–70.

34. A mermaid socializing with the devil, shown with wings and claws, and an evil wyvern, a heraldic winged beast with a serpent's tail and dragon's head, on a misericord in Bristol Cathedral, sixteenth century.

35. The serpent in horrid guise, with leathery wings and claws, and a greedy whiskery nose, eagerly follows the debate as Adam remonstrates with Eve. Rembrandt van Rijn, *Adam and Eve*, 1638.

36. Dante Gabriel Rossetti, 'Buy from us with a golden curl', illustration for Christina Rossetti's *Goblin Market*, first published in 1862. Laura's snipping a curl from her hair may symbolize her loss of sexual innocence when she trades it for the goblins' forbidden fruits.

37. A reptile-tailed girl with reversed hands offers an ambiguous commentary on love's transitory pleasures in Agnolo Bronzino's sumptuous *An Allegory with Venus and Cupid*, c. 1550. See chapter 10 for discussion of the symbolism of this painting.

38. The Hon. John Collier's voluptuous *Lilith*, 1887, lovingly caresses the snake that entwines her naked body, symbol of woman's dangerous eroticism.

39. In Kate Carew's caricature of silent-cinema vamps with their wealthy victim, Annette Kellerman is shown with a mermaid's scaly tail and flowing locks. Early twentieth century.

40. Tamara de Lempicka's moodily erotic *Adam and Eve*, 1932, places the Temptation in an urban landscape, long established as the nerve centre of pernicious glamour and forbidden pleasures.

CHAPTER ILLUSTRATIONS

Intro. Inset illustration to Genesis 3, Coverdale Bible, 1535, Cologne (?).

Chapter 1. Hans Holbein the Younger's dramatic *The Expulsion of Adam and Eve*, woodcut from the *Dance of Death*, 1538.

Chapter 2. The visit of the angels to Abraham's desert encampment. Antonio Tempesta (1555–1630), *Three Men Come to Abraham*, illustration for Genesis 18:2.

Chapter 3. *Eve proffering the forbidden fruit to Adam while the Tempter urges her on*, manuscript drawing, *c.* AD 1000.

Chapter 4. John Flaxman, engraved by William Blake, *Pandora Opening the Vase*, 1817.

Chapter 5. Penelope at her loom, and questioning the stranger (Odysseus in disguise), while the suitors watch suspiciously. Detail from the first page of Tacuino's edition of Ovid, Venice, 1501.

Chapter 6. Joseph Fletcher's *The Historie of the Perfect-Cursed-Blessed Man* demonstrates the connection between the Fall and the Redemption, France, 1629.

Chapter 7. Eve, clad in animal skins, the sign of her Fall, and holding a skull and the death-dealing fruit, in Erhard Schön (*c.* 1491–1542), *Six Old Testament Heroines*.

Chapter 8. A playful infant Christ lifts the Virgin's skirts in Israhel van Mechenem's *Virgin and Child with Apple*, second half of fifteenth century.

Chapter 9. Adam and Eve's crossed arms and legs confirm their sexual entanglement. Albrecht Dürer (1471–1528), *Fall of Man*, woodcut from the *Small Passion*.

Chapter 10. Eve with a female-bodied, winged serpent. From the *Speculum Humanae Salvationis*, 1476.

Chapter 11. Eve's disobedience brought about time and the horror of Hell, symbolized by the falling leaves of the tree of knowledge against which she stands, and the avenging angel in the background, rounding up the damned. Daniel Hopfer (*c.* 1470–1536), *Eve*.

Afterword. Iobst Aman's quasi-rococo *Mother Eve*.

INTRODUCTION

THE STORY OF EVE

Of man's first disobedience, and the fruit
Of that forbidden tree, whose mortal taste
Brought death into the world, and all our woe,
With loss of Eden, till one greater man
Restore us, and regain the blissful seat,
Sing heavenly Muse . . .

JOHN MILTON, Paradise Lost, I:1–6

FROM A FERTILE AND well-irrigated garden, stocked with abundant plant and animal life, to a dusty wilderness of thorns and thistles; from joyous stasis to the laborious movement through time; from life eternal to sickness and suffering and a death unrelieved by the promise of resurrection: the story of Adam and Eve told in Genesis 1–3, the Hebrew account of origins, records a series of metamorphoses. Written down and revised during an extended period of hardship and exile, it is tempting to read the Garden of Eden as a metaphor for Jewish experience – the dream of a secure and prosperous homeland set against the reality of centuries of conflict and the struggle to maintain national identity. But the story of Adam and Eve has other resonances: it is an account of beginnings and endings – where we come from, where we go to, and why – and a narrative that probably originated as a folk tale has had an unprecedented influence on how Western society has defined its moral and spiritual identity. Central to the story is the ambiguous figure of Eve herself.

Genesis is unique among the creation myths of the Ancient Near East. It begins by reversing the natural order of creation: a male god speaks the universe into being and the first woman is 'born' of man, formed from the rib that God takes from the sleeping Adam's side. Later, her biological role is reinstated when she is named by Adam as Eve, 'the mother of all living', although, unlike the mother goddesses of the Ancient Near East religions, Eve's progeny are limited to her human children. The universe of animals and plants, of water and the earth itself from which Adam was formed, remain under the control of God. It is difficult to see Eve as a goddess: the account of her as created simultaneously with Adam and given dominion over all living things is inserted unobtrusively into the first chapter of Genesis and lacks the dramatic appeal of the rib story of Genesis 2, and Eve's history ends with her being condemned to pain in childbirth and submission to her husband, before she is ignominiously thrust out of Eden with Adam. And yet, behind the human form of Eve may hover the image of a mother goddess, from whom all life was believed to issue and into whose capacious and welcoming body it returned. The creation myths that predate or are contemporary with Genesis, the Greek stories and the Babylonian *Enuma Elish*, similarly deal with the establishment of the human status quo, but these narratives are principally concerned with a conflict between generations of deities which is usually resolved by male gods taking control. The sky god Zeus battles with Titans to establish his dominant role in the Greek pantheon and eventually supplants the goddesses' traditional roles. In the Babylonian epic, the young warrior-god Marduk conquers Tiamat, the dragon-mother of all creation, and splits her lifeless carcass to form the sky and earth, and the first human 'savage-man' is a late creation, an afterthought whose role is to wait on the gods. These stories reflect a period of change and adjustment in the cultures that they represent. But, for the God of the Hebrews, there can be no such struggle: it is fundamental to both Jewish and Christian belief that God exists in isolation, and His universe is fabricated, not from His own or the conquered goddess's body, but out of nothing. For these theologies, nature and the divine have become separate.

The movement from a religion where the natural world partakes of and is indivisible from the divine to one that separates God from His creation implies a fundamental change in how the individual perceives his or her own life in relation to deity and specifically to the human condition. When the presence of the god or goddess is perceived as immanent in the natural world, death itself can be accommodated as part of a natural process, a movement back to the earth from which one came and from which one will once again emerge. Separate God from nature and give Him an intellectual or conceptualizing relationship with His creation, and the possibilities for a rhythmic procession of death and rebirth, mirroring the life cycle of plants and the reassuring waxing and waning of the moon, become remote. A harsher view of the finiteness of human life is implied. This at least can seem to be the message of the first books of Genesis, where human beings are ultimately condemned to hard labour, pain and suffering on earth, and where death is simply a return to the dust from which they were made.

There are, however, other ways of interpreting the story of Adam and Eve. It can be seen as a myth about the birth of human consciousness, or the beginning of time or of history. Until Eve tasted the fruit of the knowledge of good and evil and shared it with her husband, she and Adam were ignorant of their human condition. Once they had eaten, they became committed to a life of human responsibility; not being, but doing, with all the pain – and pleasure – of consciousness. For an Enlightenment thinker like Schiller, the 'Fall' represented a heroic assertion of the Self, a courageous leap out of the instinctual life into the demanding realm of reason. The story of Eden lends itself to this kind of reading because it is so recognizably an account of fundamental human impulses and their constraints.

But these kinds of evaluation of Eden are only part of its history. Again and again, commentators have returned to the central act in humanity's loss of Paradise: Eve and Adam's tasting of the forbidden fruit. In their attempts to understand the implications of 'man's first disobedience', theologians developed a definition of Eve that became the blueprint for Woman, an explanation of her character and possibilities that was applied indiscriminately to all women and embraced a wide range of ideas about female nature. The myth of Adam, Eve and the serpent was a key text for the founders of the Christian church, anxious to establish a link between the redemptive powers of Christ and the origins of human bad behaviour, and this apparently unsophisticated story, flawed by the contradictions and ambiguities that mark it as a transitional myth, has remained the essential source for Christian definitions of sexuality for nearly two thousand years. A reading of the myth in which Eve features as sexually culpable has been operative since before the Early Church Fathers uncompromisingly established the links between sexuality, sin and death – Jewish writers were the first to blame Eve for a specifically sexual 'Fall' – but what is astonishing is the potency and longevity of the Fathers' contribution. Even today, ideas about male and female sexuality and the balance of power between the sexes derive from, one might say have been contaminated by, the prescriptions for human behaviour formulated in the first centuries after Christ's death. To this day, Eve is synonymous with Woman, and her characteristics are assumed to be paradigmatic for her daughters. Eve/Woman stands accused of vanity, moral weakness and sexual frailty, while Adam/Man's role in the transaction can be summarized by the familiar defence: 'She led him on.'

The Story of Eve explores the many different stories and beliefs that have made up the composite picture of Eve as history's first bad girl, who carelessly threw away the chance of Paradise. Part 1, The Making of a Bad Reputation, traces the development of Eve's character through early Jewish and Christian tradition and the steps by which she evolved from a comparatively backstage role as Adam's wife and the mother of all living to become the sinful temptress responsible for all human suffering and mortality, and eventually even for the sacrifice of God's son, Jesus Christ. Eve's early history embraces a multitude of narratives: Jewish law codes and Greek medical theories, the stories of Pandora and Psyche and the tragic passions of Medea and Dido, accounts of the Watcher angels and legendary lives of Adam and Eve, as well as the true-life records of martyred and saintly women during the ascetic movement that revolutionized early Christianity and so fundamentally influenced Western ideas about male and female sexual behaviour. The second part of the book, Fantasies of Eve, looks at some of the ways in which aspects of Eve – as sexual temptress, helpmate and sinner – have inspired writers and artists from the Middle Ages to the present day. When the scholarly debate was finally settled, when dissenting voices had been suppressed and Augustine's baleful linkage of sexuality with sin, death and damnation had become established as the central tenet of Christian life, the human imagination took over and rewrote the story of Adam and Eve in poetry and popular drama and art: in illuminated Bibles and psalters, in stained-glass windows and sculpture that adorned churches and cathedrals and presented the history of humanity in glorious visual form, in paintings that reflected the changing status and interpretations of the Christian story, as the links between Adam and Christ, Eve and the Virgin Mary were ever more intricately developed. The Virgin Mary and Mary Magdalene became the Second Eve in a complex of interlocking narratives that embraced the Song of Songs and the garden of the Resurrection; while Eve and the serpent spawned a multitude of snaky temptresses; and poets and novelists battled over the definition of Adam's 'meet help'. In the final chapter, Eve presents her own version of the story and, not surprisingly, reveals a very different perspective on Eden and its aftermath than that of her male critics.

EVE'S HISTORY IS as diverse and ingenious as the imaginations that have so colourfully embellished her story, but however the original narrative may have become dispersed and confused in the process of commentary and retelling, it did have a single starting point in the momentous 'once upon a time' of human history, when, in the beginning, 'God created the heaven and the earth', and it is there that *The Story of Eve* begins.

PART ONE

———◆———

THE MAKING OF A BAD REPUTATION

CHAPTER 1

THE GARDEN OF EDEN

Vßtribung Ade Eue.

'I taste of death and knowledge when, as story-teller,
I adventure into the past'
THOMAS MANN, *Joseph and His Brothers*

In the beginning

UNIQUELY FOR THE Israelites, in the beginning there was God. The first chapter of Genesis describes a supreme artist-magician, a pioneering deity with the imagination to dream up the universe, the adroitness to manufacture its separate parts, and the self-confidence to approve the work when completed. Day after day, God speaks each new component of the heavens and earth into existence and sees that it is 'good'. What are the origins of God? Unlike the gods of the Egyptian and Babylonian pantheons, He does not emerge from a coupling of the sky and earth, or from primordial waters. He simply is, one and alone; and His authority to be and to do, and the authenticity of His works, are unequivocal. His creation is orderly and all-encompassing, moving from the dark waters of the formless deep to a universe teeming with plant and animal life, and culminating, on the sixth day, with the invention of the first human couple:

> So God created man in his own image, in the image of God
> created he him; male and female created he them.
>
> (Gen. 1:27)

In Hebrew, the 'man' whom He creates is *'adam*, meaning 'humankind' or 'people', a generic term which is then differentiated into the two genders, the man and the woman, who are given joint authority over the living world.

And God blessed them, and God said unto them, Be fruitful,
and multiply, and replenish the earth, and subdue it: and have
dominion over the fish of the sea, and over the fowl of the air,
and over every living thing that moveth upon the earth.

(Gen. 1:28)

After the cosmic grandeur of its opening, the second chapter
of Genesis dwindles to a reassuringly small-scale narrative, an
admonitory tale of disappointed hopes, domestic discord and divine
retribution. As this second story begins, it tells of a time during the
Creation when the heavens and earth are already in place, but all
plant life is in stasis, waiting for rain and for 'a man to till the
ground'. A versatile craftsman, God shapes a man out of dust and
breathes the breath of life into his nostrils, 'and man became a living
soul'. Having created His labourer, God plants a garden 'eastward
in Eden', which the man is told to tend. It is not a difficult
assignment, for the trees are fruitful, and the garden itself well
irrigated by four rivers that flow out of Eden into the surrounding
lands – the River Pison, which skirts Havilah, land of gold and
bdellium and other precious stones, the Gihon and Hiddekel, which
wind respectively into Ethiopia and Assyria, and the great river
Euphrates. And now we enter the familiar world of fairy tale, with
its promises and threats, its simple heroes and beguiling villains. For,
like Psyche's magic palace or Cinderella's fairy gown and pumpkin
coach, God's gifts come with a penalty clause which, if violated,
will spell disaster. God instructs the man that he may eat freely of
every tree in the garden, except of the tree of the knowledge of
good and evil, 'for in the day that thou eatest thereof thou shalt
surely die' (Gen. 2:17).

Recognizing that the man will become lonely, God sets about
making 'an help meet for him', but although He originates every
variety of bird and beast and brings them to His gardener to name,
no suitable companion is found. During this process of naming,
the man himself acquires a name, Adam, the Hebrew word for
humankind used in Genesis 1, but perhaps also a reference to
the clayey substance, the *'adamah*, from which he was formed.
Finally, God puts Adam into a deep sleep, and removes one of his
ribs from which He makes a woman and brings her to Adam. This

time, all is well – Adam immediately recognizes her, 'bone of my bones, and flesh of my flesh', and names her 'Woman, because she was taken out of Man'. Here together, in the garden, 'they were both naked, the man and his wife, and were not ashamed' (Gen. 2:25).

Enter – that same day? many days later? the narrator does not tell us – the villain, the wily serpent, 'more subtil than any beast of the field which the Lord God had made'. This is the familiar talking animal of folk tale, and he reveals his cunning by his first, seemingly innocent comment to the woman. 'Well, is it true?' is his opening gambit; 'Has God said you are not to eat of every tree in the garden?' The Hebrew text uses a rhetorical device known as aposiopesis, which leaves it to the listener (or the reader) to complete the speaker's thought: 'Even though God said: You are not to eat from any of the trees in the garden . . .!' Invited to gossip, the woman explains the prohibition, adding an embellishment of her own, 'Ye shall not eat of it, neither shall ye touch it, lest ye die.' 'Die!' exclaims the serpent, 'You will not die!' And he points out that God is well aware that if she and Adam eat the fruit, far from dying, they will become themselves like gods, 'knowing good and evil'. This is the reason for His taboo. The woman does not argue: she shrewdly assesses the fruit's attractions and eats and, good provider that she is, gives some to her husband, who also eats. Just as the serpent had foretold, they do not die, but immediately acquire wisdom, of a sort: they perceive that they are naked and stitch themselves fig-leaf aprons or, in the more ambitious manufacture of the Geneva Bible of 1560, 'They sewed figge leaues together, and made themselues breeches.' History begins with needlework.

Like any wealthy landowner, God comes to walk in His garden in the cool of the day, while Adam and the woman cower among the trees. It is the hour for relaxation, for easy wandering and pleasant conversation, and God calls out to Adam, 'Where are you?'

I heard thy voice in the garden, and I was afraid, because I was naked; and I hid myself.

Who told thee that thou wast naked? Hast thou eaten of the tree, whereof I commanded thee that thou shouldest not eat?

(Gen. 3:10–11)

Adam is quick to blame the woman – God's gift to him – and in turn she accuses the serpent, who says nothing in his own defence. As if He had always known that this would happen, God does not hesitate to pronounce sentence. The serpent is cursed above every beast, doomed to crawl on his belly, licking the dust, and to perpetual enmity with the woman and her descendants. The woman too is cursed – to the pains of frequent childbirth and subjection to her husband. For Adam, there will be no more easy days among fruit-bearing trees: thorns and thistles are to be his lot, the daily struggle to wrest a living from hostile soil, and his final doom will be to return to the dust from which he was made. Death has entered Eden – marked by God's replacing the homely fig leaves with coats made of animal skins. The woman's future role is confirmed by the name that Adam now gives her – Eve, Hawwah, 'the mother of all living'. But this is not all – man has indeed become as God, knowing good and evil, and the Lord is anxious that he should not now eat the fruit of the tree of life and live for ever. He drives him out of the garden and sets cherubim and a flaming sword east of Eden to guard the tree of life.

There are a number of puzzles in this apparently simple narrative, but what is most immediately striking is the reduced stature of God. Omnipotent and transcendent in the opening section of Genesis, He whirls in impenetrable darkness across the face of the deep, speaks and there is light, commands oceans and planets, and at a breath fructifies the earth with an abundance of life. No mention here of the creation of Adam from all-too-earthly clay, or Eve as the fallible rib made flesh; in this first account, man is created in God's own image, man and woman together, and they are jointly given dominion over the living world. How then to account for God's ungodlike behaviour in the Garden of Eden? Anthropomorphically described, He dwindles to just another character in the drama, still a potentate, but local rather than cosmic, and His actions are mystifying. Why did He invent a plausible talking serpent and set him loose in Eden, and why were Adam and Eve unable to resist temptation? After all, God had the power to make them perfect. Did He want them to eat the forbidden fruit, and if so, why? And He comes across as paranoid and deceitful in His behaviour over the two trees, lying to Adam about the fatal effects of eating the fruit of knowledge, and jealously banning Adam (and by implication Eve) from Eden 'lest he put forth his hand, and take also of the tree of life, and eat, and live for ever' (Gen. 3:22). There are other difficulties. What was the serpent's motivation? Why did Adam take the fruit from Eve and how did she persuade him to eat it? This portentous negotiation is passed over in a sentence. And, most importantly, what did 'the knowledge of good and evil' imply? These are just a few of the questions that have taxed the ingenuity of theologians and commentators for thousands of years.

The Hebrew narratives of the creation of the world and the loss of the Garden of Eden evolved over a considerable period, and the events described in Genesis 1–3 are believed to belong to originally separate accounts that were amalgamated and edited into the form that has survived as the canonical text. The story of the Garden of Eden, told in Genesis 2:4 to Genesis 3, is thought by biblical scholars to have been written by an author or compiler known as Y, because he uses the name Yahweh when referring to God, and to have been recorded around 1000–900 BC, although it probably existed in oral form many years before that date. The account of the creation in Genesis 1–2:3 is regarded as the work of the P, or priestly, author or authors, writing several hundred years later in the period after the Babylonian exile, probably around 400 BC, at a time when there was a much stronger emphasis on monotheism among the cult leaders. This would account for the contrast between the folkloric elements in the Eden narrative and the sublimity of the omnipotent creator in the seven-days account. Critics have often been puzzled as to why both these contradictory stories should have been preserved and brought together, but the anomalies between the two accounts of the creation of man and woman can perhaps be understood as exemplifying the chasm between the potential and actuality. The first chapter of Genesis provides a broad framework of beginnings, sets the grand scene of creation and establishes the transcendence and possibilities of God, before homing in on the realities of the human story. What was on offer to Adam and Eve was noble dominion over the animal and vegetable world; the reality was disobedience, recrimination and punishment, a squalid grubbing among thistles in an inhospitable wilderness. Both accounts would have struck a chord with their audiences.

The first Eves

A BEAUTIFUL WOMAN with the milky skin and rippling golden hair of a Pre-Raphaelite 'stunner' stands beside an apple tree and hands a glossy red fruit to a young man who is scratching his head as if perplexed. Both are naked except for the springing leaves of a vine that conveniently cover their genitals. At their feet, animals and birds feed peacefully together, the lion and the wild boar with the doe and the lamb, in a rural landscape which suggests tranquil abundance. Above the woman's head a snake coils half-hidden in the tree, which is heavy with foliage and inviting fruit. The woman's elegant self-possession offers an amusing contrast to her partner's lack of ease. She could be Venus whiling away a lazy summer's day by seducing a shepherd, or Aphrodite dallying with Anchises. But this nubile nymph is no classical deity; she is Eve with the gardener Adam at the pivotal moment before time began.

Lucas Cranach the Elder's version of Eve's offer of the apple was painted many centuries after the event was first recorded by the early Israelites, but it represents a view of what came to be known as 'the Fall' that has persisted from the time of early Christianity to the present day. There is no mistaking the erotic subtext of this painting: the antlers of the stag resting at Adam's feet bristle up his thigh and out of his genital area with unmistakably phallic meaning, thrusting towards the delicate girl with her worldly-wise smile. But there is no heat to the couple's encounter: both seem to brood, gazing abstractedly, as if contemplating the momentous effect of the fruit that they clasp together, she offering, he taking. Even the serpent seems to hold his breath; the only movement is the distant flurry of a white horse, briskly trotting from the doom about to fall not just on the central trio, but on the whole of the natural world.

There is nothing in Cranach's rendering of the scene that would be unfamiliar to a viewer schooled in the Christian tradition, but its suggestive representation of the Temptation of Adam might have surprised the ancient tribes among whom the Eden story evolved.

Like the Hebrew God, Eve is unique in the mythologies of the Ancient Near East, which typically describe the births of deities and their battles for supremacy. She belongs as much to folklore as to myth and, as is the case with so many heroines of folk tales, her origins are probably to be sought in the harsh realities of everyday life. The Garden of Eden is generally thought to be an aetiological myth, a story that justifies how things are. As an oral tradition, the narrative probably evolved during the formative period of settlement in Canaan, when, for better protection against attack, the Israelites typically would have been living in hilltop villages, probably in what became known as Judea, Samaria and Galilee. As Carol Meyers points out in *Discovering Eve*, her study of the everyday lives of women in ancient Israel, far from being 'a land flowing with milk and honey', this was a territory characterized by poor soil in the mountains, a sparse water supply and a difficult topography of random hills and valleys. In order for communities to settle and develop, woodlands had to be cleared, terraces hacked out for crops and deep cisterns cut in the bedrock below the surface of the hilltops to meet the year-round water requirements of people and animals. Households would have been largely self-contained, and the women in this frontier period would have been responsible for feeding and clothing their families and manufacturing necessary household goods, as well as looking after livestock, and working in the fields, gardens, orchards and terraces – the day-in, day-out routines that were essential to food production in that unwelcoming terrain. At the same time, the need for labour, for more hands to help out, would have meant pressure on women to be fertile, to bear sons to defend their territory and farm the land, daughters to tend the animals and crops, to draw water, to spin and weave and bake and brew for the growing household. Psalm 127, recommended for centuries in the Prayer Book of the Church of England for use in the churching of women after childbirth, emphasizes the importance of children (and, by implication, sons) in a warrior culture:

Lo, children are an heritage of the LORD: and the fruit of the womb is his reward.

As arrows are in the hand of a mighty man; so are children of the youth.

Happy is the man that hath his quiver full of them: they shall not be ashamed, but they shall speak with the enemies in the gate.

(Ps. 127:3–5)

The father of a large family of boys secured a committed labour force and on-site protection, social prestige as leader of a substantial household and the reassurance that the family name would be perpetuated. Girl children were valued as future wives and mothers, essential to the continuation of the community, but for their parents they were a mixed blessing. The mother had the work of training up her daughters to be useful, only to see them sold off as wives to benefit neighbouring households, whilst mates for one's own sons had to be bought in, although the bridal price received for a daughter could be useful in purchasing a daughter-in-law. Daughters who failed to marry were even more of a liability. For an Israelite mother, a large family meant more mouths to feed, more bodies to clothe and the recurrent cycle of pregnancy, childbirth and lactation to be slotted in to the woman's daily routine.

Population loss through pestilential disease, warfare and infant mortality would also have put pressure on women to produce large families. Investigations of ancient Palestinian burial sites suggest a high mortality rate for children and adolescents, while childbirth itself was risky both for mother and baby, and its pains, its fears, are a persistent theme in the Bible, as is the anxiety of infertility. Writing in times of threat and social disturbance, the prophets compare the plight of troubled Israel to the agony of a woman in labour in texts that evoke real suffering: 'Like as a woman with child, that draweth near the time of her delivery, is in pain, and crieth out in her pangs; so we have been in thy sight, O LORD', cries Isaiah (Isa. 26:17), and Jeremiah is similarly expressive, 'I have heard a voice as of a woman in travail, and the anguish as of her that bringeth forth her first child' (Jer. 4:31). Failure to produce children was regarded as a lapse of duty and a mark of God's displeasure. When Sarah is unable to conceive children by her husband Abraham, she tells him 'the LORD hath restrained me from bearing' (Gen. 16:2) and offers him her handmaid, the Egyptian woman Hagar, to bear children on her behalf. She is rewarded when she herself miraculously conceives and gives birth to Isaac although long past the age of childbearing. Rachel, Jacob's wife, also finds herself childless, and when she complains to Jacob, he makes it clear that it is God's doing: 'Am I in God's stead, who hath withheld from thee the fruit of the womb?' Again she gives him her maid as a surrogate mother, so 'she shall bear upon my knees, that I may also have children by her'. When she eventually becomes pregnant with Joseph, she says simply, 'God hath taken away my reproach' (Gen. 30:2, 3, 23). Hannah, the mother of the prophet Samuel, is barren for many years and only finally conceives when she promises God that if he gives her a male child, she will dedicate her son to God's service 'all the days of his life' (I Sam. 1:11). One can only guess at the female anxiety, humiliation and grief that underlie these simply narrated stories, but significantly it is God who imposes and lifts the curse of infertility; as in the first chapter of Genesis, nature is subject to His control.

For these early Israelites, the story of Adam and Eve's disobedience in the Garden of Eden would have offered an explanation of the facts of life – the need to labour in the field, 'cursed is the ground for thy sake; in sorrow shalt thou eat of it all the days of thy life ... In the sweat of thy face shalt thou eat bread'; and in childbed, 'I will greatly multiply thy sorrow and thy conception; in sorrow thou shalt bring forth children' (Gen. 3:17, 19, 16). The narrative also comments on the social and psychological relationship beween men and women, and again these observations should perhaps be seen as explanatory: this is why things are as they are. Later critics found plenty of ammunition for a negative evaluation of Eve in her creation from Adam's rib, her (subordinate) status as 'helpmate' to Adam, and the terms of God's curse, 'thy desire shall be to thy husband, and he shall rule over thee' (Gen. 3:16), but the story suggests a more complicated response to male/female negotiations, again perhaps pointing out the discrepancy between an ideal state of affairs and everyday reality.

The idea of a person fashioned out of a rib does have an element of the ridiculous, and lends itself to interpretations of inferiority which commentators have been quick to exploit. The Rabbis used it as an excuse for all sorts of misogynous jokes, and the Yahwist writer may himself have intended a punning reference to the rib when Adam later names the woman Eve, 'mother of all living'. In Sumerian, the words for 'life' (*til*) and 'rib' (*ti*) were depicted by the same cuneiform symbols, so that the name of the goddess NIN.TI could be interpreted as either 'lady of life' or 'lady of the rib', while the Hebrew word for 'rib', *tsela*, also means 'stumbling'. But in the context of the story itself, it is a logical next step for God. As He did with man, God forms the animals and birds out of dust, and brings them to Adam to be named. Naming can imply many things – possibly even that Adam had intercourse with the animals – but in the Jewish Bible it usually means lordship or possession. Here, it reinforces the important theological point that the Hebrew God operates alone: unlike in the neighbouring Canaanite and Egyptian religions, animals are to be dominated, not venerated. Adam asserts his authority over the animals, but feels no special bond with them. A later Jewish midrash or commentary on the text sympathetically records how Adam made the animals pass in pairs before him, but this only emphasized his feelings of loneliness and yearning: 'Every one has a partner, yet I have none'. The decision to make woman out of man's substance is a brainwave on God's part, and Adam's response is unequivocal: in Everett Fox's vivid translation, 'This-time, she-is-it!/Bone from my bones,/flesh from my flesh!' Having waited so long, Adam at last recognizes a fellow creature and he bonds joyfully with the woman. Centuries later, St Augustine interpreted the rib story as indicative of the loving union that should exist between man and wife.

As for being a 'help meet' for the man, which in English suggests that Eve is some kind of junior assistant, there is an argument for Eve to be seen, in the words of Milton's Adam, as 'Heaven's last best gift': she is God's final creation and is formed not of dust but of the raw material of humanity, and Adam had been the crown of God's activity up to this point. In any event, a better translation of the Hebrew phrase, '*ēzer kᵉnegdô*, would be 'a companion corresponding to' Adam, in other words a being of the same status, and the rib story confirms that Eve is part of Adam and therefore cannot be inferior to him. What the narrator seems to have been suggesting was the symbiotic relationship between man and woman which would justify a man leaving his parents and siblings in order to cleave to someone outside the immediate family circle (Gen. 2:24). This is appropriate because woman is part of man. The rib story establishes the 'ideal' relationship between man and woman; the narrative then goes on to explain a social reality in which the women of Israel found themselves subordinate to their husbands.

Eve nibbled the fruit and tempted Adam, and is cursed by God with repeated and painful childbearing and subjection to her husband. The precise meaning of the text of Genesis 3:16 has been especially troublesome to feminist commentators, particularly the words translated in the King James Bible, 'and thy desire shall be to thy husband, and he shall rule over thee', but however translated or interpreted, the implication seems to be that women will sexually desire their husbands and, because of or despite this, will be subject to their husband's authority. Either scenario probably more or less accurately reflected the establishment position on male/female relations in the early biblical period. Female subordination was regarded as essential to the status quo and men were repeatedly warned against the dangers of being sexually manipulated by women. Proverbs adjures them, 'Give not thy strength unto women' (Prov. 31:3), and the frequent complaints in the Old Testament about the wiles and deceits of harlots suggest that the men of ancient Israel were feared to be as susceptible to the clichés of feminine glamour, to vivid make-up and provocative clothes, as the stereotypical 'red-blooded' modern Western male. Proverbs tells the cautionary tale of the foolish young man who is ensnared by a wicked woman: typically she waylays him on the street corner, 'In the twilight, in the evening, in the black and dark night', a place and a time which a good woman would shun. But this wanton is 'loud and stubborn', 'with the attire of an harlot, and subtil of heart . . . So she caught him, and kissed him, and with an impudent face said unto him . . . I have decked my bed with coverings of tapestry, with carved works, with fine linen of Egypt./I have perfumed my bed with myrrh, aloes, and cinnamon./Come, let us take our fill of love unto the morning . . . For the goodman is not at home'. Not surprisingly, the poor fool is unable to resist such erotic enticements, and 'He goeth after her straightway, as an ox goeth to the slaughter'. It can only end in the dark chambers of Sheol, the afterworld, for this Amazon 'hath cast down many wounded: yea, many strong men have been slain by her' (Prov. 7:7–27).

Whatever this alluring tale may suggest about latent woman-power, the picture the Old Testament gives of Israelite society is of a male-dominated culture. However Genesis 3:16 is interpreted, men as warriors, householders, priests and lawmakers clearly held the executive roles, although there are hints that more equitable arrangements might have been negotiated at the household level. The story of Sarah suggests one such accommodation: her handmaid Hagar is offered as a surrogate wife to Abraham and conceives a child by him, but, perhaps inevitably, she then gets uppity and is rude to her mistress. When Sarah complains to Abraham, he wisely washes his hands of the affair, leaving her to manage it as she will. Sarah 'deals hardly' with Hagar, who runs away to the wilderness, where she is advised by an angel to return, suitably contrite (Gen. 16:1–9). Sarah is permitted to deal with an unruly servant, but important decisions at a social or domestic level – the institution of ritual circumcision, the slaughter of a beloved son – are taken by Abraham.

The subtil serpent

IN A COMMUNITY where women were expected to defer to masculine authority, it is probably significant that Eve appears to have been on her own when she encountered the serpent. Women who are left to wander alone will get into trouble is very much the theme of this section of the story. But why would they behave badly with snakes? Talking animals feature in many primitive stories, and the snake's wily nature was a commonplace of Ancient Near East mythology, so he was the obvious choice as persuasive tempter. The story of the Garden of Eden may be read as a folk tale that, among other things, explains why serpents crawl on their bellies and are generally disliked by human beings, but its survival in the Jewish Holy Books may suggest that this unsophisticated story had other resonances for nascent Israel. Lurking behind the woman's encounter with the plausible serpent may have been priestly anxiety to warn women off the tempting Canaanite goddesses who were typically accompanied by snake avatars: a fifteenth-century-BC image of the goddess Astarte, the Hebrew Ashtoreth, found in north Canaan, shows her girdled with serpents.

As the two states of northern Israel and southern Judah came under increasing pressure from the Assyrians during the eighth century BC, tribal cohesion became imperative to survival and with it developed the ideal of monotheism. Yahweh was to be worshipped as the one and only God of the Israelite people, and the priests made strenuous efforts to suppress the worship of rival deities. There are many complaints in the Old Testament against the groves where Asherah, the great Canaanite mother goddess associated with female fertility and childbearing, was typically worshipped in the form of carved wooden images or *asherim*:

> And they set them up images and groves in every high hill, and under every green tree:
>
> For they served idols, whereof the LORD had said unto them, Ye shall not do this thing.
>
> (2 Kgs. 17:10, 12)

The Old Testament confirms that Ashtoreth and the older goddess Asherah continued to be worshipped well into the Temple period, often with the encouragement of the Hebrew kings, whose foreign wives wanted the support of their domestic goddesses. As well as the daughter of the Pharaoh, and politically important Hittite, Moabite, Ammonite and Edomite women, Solomon (reigned c. 961–922 BC) married a Sidonian princess, thereby cementing friendly relations with the Phoenicians at a time when he was inaugurating his ambitious building projects. To satisfy this wife, Solomon introduced the cult of Asherah into royal worship and his son Rehoboam even brought her statue into the Temple, where it lodged on and off for more than three centuries. Although foreign wives for commoners were regarded with suspicion both because of their religious practices and the inevitable weakening of Israelite tribal identity, the many warnings against them in the Old Testament suggest that marriage outside the immediate community was an ongoing problem. The exotic foreign woman is seen as a wicked seductress, whose lips 'drop as an honeycomb, and her mouth is smoother than oil' (Prov. 5:3), while intermarriage inevitably leads to religious backsliding:

And the children of Israel dwelt among the Canaanites, Hittites, and Amorites, and Perizzites, and Hivites, and Jebusites:

And they took their daughters to be their wives, and gave their daughters to their sons, and served their gods.

And the children of Israel did evil in the sight of the LORD, and forgat the LORD their God, and served Baalim [Asherah's son] and the groves.

(Judg. 3:5–7)

What is striking about the cult of Yahweh is the lack of imaginative space it offered women. On the one hand, the family unit and frequent childbearing were heavily promoted, but, at the same time, the benign goddesses who cared for the female reproductive cycle and for children were suppressed as inimical to the one-God ideal of the priesthood. The effect was to deny women the comfort which these goddesses offered, but which had no parallels in Yahwist ritual. In practice, women did manage to sidestep the rules, probably on a fairly large scale: although the wooden images have not survived, numerous small clay figurines related to Asherah have been found in excavations all over Palestine, suggesting that her cult was energetically pursued by Israelite women. Given the persistent references in the Old Testament to barren women and painful childbirth, it is not surprising if a helpful pagan goddess or two were slipped into a household's worship routines.

The Garden of Eden story is not the only reference to suppressed snaky deities in the early pages of Genesis. The creation myth in chapter 1 seems to contain reminiscences of a more ancient and violent story in which the mother of all living things is slaughtered by a male god, who creates the sky out of her massive fallen carcass. The Babylonian creation epic, the *Enuma Elish*, celebrates the heroic deeds of Marduk, patron deity of the city of Babylon. The poem pre-dates Genesis and records the struggle for supremacy between rival gods, with humanity created only as an afterthought. The primal scene described in the *Enuma Elish* consists of water: before the heavens, before the earth, before the gods were created, there existed the salt sea-waters, personified as Mummu-Tiamat, a female creatrix, and 'primordial Apsu', the sweet, salt-free waters of springs and rivers. These two commingle 'as a single body' and the generations of the gods are born. However, as is the way with young people, their hilarity disturbs the first parents, and Apsu plots to destroy his descendants. The powerful Ea uses magic to put Apsu into a deep sleep and then kills him. Soon after, Ea's son Marduk is born; with massive limbs, four eyes, four ears and lips that blaze fire when he speaks, he is an imposing figure.

Tiamat has not forgiven the slaying of Apsu, and she determines to take revenge. Initially a personification of the oceans, she now reveals her reptilian nature, giving birth to a brood of monster-serpents and similar prodigies – eleven demons with names like the Viper, the Dragon, Mad-Dog and Scorpion-Man – and at their head she places Kingu, her son and new husband. The gods approach Marduk to defend them and, amidst general rejoicing, he prepares for battle, mounting the storm-chariot and wrapping himself in the armour of terror. He challenges the furious Tiamat to single combat and as they struggle, locked together, entangles her in a net. She opens her mouth to consume him, but he drives in the Evil Wind so that she cannot close her mouth. As Tiamat's belly balloons with the force of the gust, Marduk lets loose an arrow to split her heart and then stands in triumph on her fallen carcass. He imprisons all her supporters, and tramples the eleven demons under-foot. When all is secure, he turns back to Tiamat and splits her body into two parts as if it were a mollusc: the top half he sets into place as the sky and posts guards to ensure that her waters do not escape back to earth. There is no mention of what he does with the bottom half, but the inference may be that he uses it to form the lower part of the universe. After this first definitive act, Marduk can continue the work of creating and ordering the universe. Only now does he turn to the creation of man, whose function will be to serve the gods and relieve them of labour, and, after some discussion, Kingu is killed and man is fashioned from his blood.

This saga of warring gods links the *Enuma Elish* with Greek and other Ancient Near East theogonies rather than the Genesis account of origins, but some scholars have seen in these bellicose creation epics a mythologized account of the struggle by increasingly warlike 'masculine' societies to overcome the hitherto dominant female principle embodied by the procreative mother goddesses, who were believed to control the crucial cycle of birth, death and regeneration that maintains the survival of human and plant life. The solo God of the early Israelites who speaks His universe into being is, of course, a logical conclusion to such a struggle, with Eve's final name, Hawwah, the mother of all living, as a ghostly reminder of woman's grander role in earlier civilizations. The very substance out of which Yahweh shaped His male-created world hints at the generative female body from which at least part of the universe was constituted in popular Babylonian myth. In the beginning, Genesis tells us, the world was 'without form, and void', '*tohu-wa-bohu*'; *tohu* relates to the Hebrew loan-word *tehōm*, the primordial waters that God separated by creating the firmament of Heaven, which in turn connect with Tiamat, the name of the mother goddess in the *Enuma Elish*. Perhaps, as Eve's modern apologist, John Phillips, suggests, 'Somewhere in the back of the minds of the writers of Genesis is the Tiamat world of dark and storm, and the story of the masculine warrior-god who creates the cosmos from out of chaos, splitting the dragon-mother's corpse as the initial act of creation.'

The fruit of the knowledge of good and evil

THE BREAKING OF a taboo and the hero or heroine's subsequent adventures are a familiar theme of folk and fairy tale, while Eve's initiative in eating the banned fruit recalls other admonitory stories of female curiosity. Lot's wife is turned into a pillar of salt when she looks back to see the destruction of Sodom; Pandora and Psyche cannot resist peeking despite being warned of terrible consequences; given free access to any number of sumptuous rooms,

Bluebeard's wife hastens to unlock the one tiny chamber that her husband has forbidden her to enter. In such stories, the reason for the prohibition usually becomes clear as soon as it is broken, but the significance of the tree of the knowledge of good and evil is more baffling. The first effect of eating the fruit was an awareness of nakedness, which may simply have recognized the curious anomaly that while animals have pelts, birds feathers, and reptiles scaly coats to withstand the effects of sun and rain, humankind alone of all living creatures is not born weather-resistant. The story may attempt to answer the basic question: why do people need to wear clothes? Because they ate forbidden fruit and, stripped of God's good will, became sensitive to the elements and their own physical vulnerability.

But there is obviously more to the fruit than this. That it was Eve rather than Adam who first took the fateful bite may not have been significant. After all, someone had to move the plot along. But it seems unlikely that gender was unimportant in a culture where 'Lock up your daughters' would become a given of everyday life, and there is something undeniably phallic about the slippery, upright serpent. Adam and Eve's response to their sudden apprehension of nudity was to cover their genitals with fig-leaf aprons or loincloths, which for a modern reader and indeed for many earlier generations of critics implies sexual awareness, but, while it may seem inconceivable to post-Freudians accustomed to rooting out sexual innuendo in the least promising scenarios, and Eden is hardly that, an interpretation of sharing the fruit as Eve's sexual initiation of the 'innocent' Adam is problematic. When the woman is formed from Adam's rib, the text explains, 'Therefore shall a man leave his father and his mother, and shall cleave unto his wife: and they shall be one flesh' (Gen. 2:24), which the Rabbis understandably interpreted as the act of intercourse. The next verse remarks that they were both naked and not ashamed, and the serpent is introduced immediately afterwards. Puzzling over this order of events, one Rabbi suggested that it implied that the serpent had seen Adam and Eve making love and had conceived a passion for Eve, which is why he tried to bring about Adam's downfall. Another Rabbi thought that Eve was able to talk alone with the serpent because Adam had fallen asleep after enjoying (legitimate) sex with his wife. In Genesis 1, God commands the first man and woman to be fruitful and multiply, which suggests that sexual intercourse was part of the divine game plan from the beginning.

What, then, is implied by the nakedness of Adam and Eve prior to their eating the forbidden fruit? For the Israelites of the Yahwist period, nakedness, including the uncovering of the genitalia, had strong connotations of public humiliation. The exposure of normally hidden parts of the body was often included in the punishment of criminals and, while it is especially difficult where women's bodies are concerned to discriminate between nuances of disrepute, passages in the Old Testament suggest that the revealing of a woman's 'secret parts' had as much to do with social shaming as with sexuality. Rebuking the pride of the women of Babylon, the prophet Isaiah tells them to 'uncover thy locks, make bare the leg, uncover the thigh, pass over the rivers./Thy nakedness shall be uncovered, yea, thy shame shall be seen' (Isa. 47:2–3). Rather than ignorance of sexual modesty, the cheerful undress of Adam and the woman may suggest their childlike innocence of the taboo on public nudity.

It has been suggested that the knowledge God wished to keep from Adam and the woman was the scientific information required for developing the arts of civilization, the understanding of physical 'weal' and 'woe' that was necessary before they could emerge from the protected environment of the garden into the wilderness of real life; but it seems equally to have implied moral knowledge, the capacity for making ethical choices. Since they were given no explanation for the taboo, obedience to God's command implied blind acquiescence rather than the informed choice on which morality depends. Once they had eaten the fruit, they developed a sense of themselves as part of a wider social order with its implications for ethical responsibility, a change symbolized by the donning of clothes and, with the movement away from the animal world and nature, the early books of Genesis become preoccupied with establishing rules for how people should live socially viable lives, in harmony with one another and with God. What is evident throughout the Hebrew Bible is that the distinction between 'good' and 'bad' behaviour ratified in Hebrew Law refers both to moral and to social 'good', to what is involved in maintaining a beneficial relationship with God and the tribal community, and it is also apparent that 'evil' is more seductive than good. Just as Henry Jekyll in Robert Louis Stevenson's novella, *The Strange Case of Dr Jekyll and Mr Hyde* (1886), finds that the vicious side of his nature is the more powerful and comes to dominate the good, so the Hebrew Bible records the constant battle of the Hebrew prophets and religious leaders against the tendency of their people to misbehave. The struggle to keep humanity on the straight and narrow path of moral order remained a major preoccupation of Judaism and was transmitted to its Christian offshoot. The fault of Adam and Eve lay in their disobedience to God, the assertion of their will against His command; by eating the fruit of the knowledge of good and evil and inviting Adam to follow her example, Eve set in train a new phase of history, where humanity exchanged the simplicity and ease of unthinking obedience for the complexity and challenge of the freedom to choose.

'I chose the tree of death'

THE TREE OF KNOWLEDGE is not the only important tree in the Garden of Eden. The tree of life is 'in the midst of the garden' (Gen. 2:9), and Eve later tells the serpent that the tree of knowledge is 'in the midst of the garden' (Gen. 3:3), which suggests that the two trees were side by side. God's prohibition relates only to the tree of knowledge and no more is made of the tree of life until the end of the story when Adam and Eve are expelled from the garden. Once they have acquired the knowledge of good and evil, the guilty pair are driven out of Eden, and God posts a cherubim guard at the gate, with a flaming sword, lest they 'take also of the tree of life, and eat, and live for ever' (Gen. 3:22). The tree of life occurs elsewhere in the Bible, where it is used as a metaphor for the vital energy of life itself: wisdom and understanding are as 'a tree of life to them that lay hold upon her' (Prov. 3:18), and 'Hope deferred maketh the heart sick: but when the desire cometh, it is a tree of life' (Prov. 13:12), but these references do not appear to be connected with the Garden of Eden, where the tree of life is clearly associated with immortality.

Christina Rossetti's 'Eve', written nearly three thousand years later, in 1865, follows a long-established convention that Adam and Eve understood the tree's magical powers, and she plays on Eve's by-now-mandatory sense of guilt:

> 'How have Eden bowers grown
> Without Adam to bend them!
> How have Eden flowers blown
> Squandering their sweet breath
> Without me to tend them!
> The Tree of Life was ours,
> Tree twelvefold-fruited,
> Most lofty tree that flowers,
> Most deeply rooted:
> I chose the tree of death.'

But was it a question of choice? Did Eve know the options? And why was the tree of life not included in the taboo? It seems that it was the combination of forbidden knowledge with immortality, two powerful attributes of deity, that God found particularly threatening.

In his commentary on Genesis, Umberto Cassuto points out that the trees in the garden of the goddess Siduri in the Mesopotamian *Epic of Gilgamesh* are, like the trees in the Garden of Eden, 'pleasant to the sight' (Gen. 2:9, and see Gen. 3:6), which may suggest a connection between the two texts, and this magnificent epic ends with the search of Gilgamesh, the great king of Uruk, for the miraculous plant of youth. After many difficulties, he finds and plucks it, but a serpent snatches it from him and immediately sloughs its skin, proof of the marvellous powers of self-renewal bestowed by the magic herb. It is tempting to see a connection between Gilgamesh's plant of youth and the tree of life, and it has also been suggested that the Eden story derives from earlier tales about the serpent's theft of the fruit of immortality, but there is no firm evidence for either view.

The tree of knowledge condemns them to death – if not immediately, then certainly at some future point: 'dust thou art, and unto dust shalt thou return' (Gen. 3:19). For the early Hebrews death would probably have implied the loss of contact with God. The canonical texts evolved during a period when Hebrew ideas about death and the afterlife were subject to considerable change and modification, but the Israelites of the early settlement period would probably have followed the Semitic idea of a three-tiered cosmos, where earth and the living were poised between the upper world of the sky gods and the lower world of the infernal deities, presided over by the gloomy Mot. This underworld was known as Sheol, a place of darkness and silence, where the dead endured a shadowy existence, enlivened from time to time by the rituals of their still-living descendants, who offered food and veneration in return for blessings. As monotheism became increasingly important, ancestor worship declined. The dead themselves were cut off from God: 'For in death there is no remembrance of thee: in the grave [Sheol] who shall give thee thanks?' (Ps. 6:5). It is only the living who can celebrate God, a reciprocal arrangement in which both can take pleasure:

> For the grave [Sheol] cannot praise thee, death can not celebrate thee: they that go down into the pit cannot hope for thy truth.
>
> The living, the living, he shall praise thee . . .

(Isa. 38:18–19)

It seems to have been the life without end of divinity that God was anxious to deny Adam and Eve; the death to which he ultimately condemns them, the crumbling into dust, may have been interpreted by the early Hebrews as the nothingness of complete dissolution, or it was perhaps a descent into the shadow kingdom of Sheol. In either case, it was a far cry from the eternity of godhead, or the timeless bliss of Eden.

Hard work, struggle, pain, death: Eve's disobedience was a bitter curse on her descendants, but if they resented her for it, the Jewish Bible does not record their complaints. As we shall see, Eve does not feature in the Holy Books after the first few chapters of Genesis, and it is not until *The Wisdom of Ben Sira*, an apocryphal work that dates to around 190–175 BC, that woman is specifically named as the cause of death:

Sin began with a woman,
  and thanks to her we all must die.

The rainbow covenant

I HAVE BEEN suggesting that the story of Adam and Eve in the Garden of Eden can be read as offering a rationale for the realities of life, for physical labour and for the relations between the sexes. It explains how humanity moved from its initial special relationship with God, created in His image and with dominion over all earthly creatures, to the position in which many Israelites would have found themselves during their early history: dependent for their bread on their own hard labour in often difficult or hostile environments; tied into a social structure where men were dominant; where pregnancy was inescapable, painful and often fatal; where children were essential to their parents' future safety and support; where tribal purity and monotheism were crucial to the survival of the group; and where death (again possibly for tribal, political reasons) was envisaged not as release into some better world of comfort and leisure, but as a transition to the dark, silent realm of Sheol. The Eden story, with its well-irrigated garden, its fruit-bearing trees and obedient animals, its suggestion of ease and harmony and, above all, immortality, records a nation's dream, its passionate nostalgia for an existence at the vanishing point of memory, a paradisiacal state before history began.

The story of Adam and Eve does not stop at the cherubim-guarded gate of Eden, and should not be read in isolation. It is part of a chain of events that culminates in Noah's ark and God's rainbow covenant with humanity, and the narratives that follow the two creation stories pick up and elaborate on the themes that they introduce, emphasizing the links and pointing out the meanings through persistent verbal echoes. The story of Eve's eldest sons, Cain and Abel, which is told immediately after the expulsion from Eden, confirms humanity's freedom to make moral choices. When God accepts the shepherd Abel's gift of the firstborn from his flock, but rejects the farmer Cain's offering of crops, Cain is angry 'and his countenance fell' (Gen. 4:5). God tells him that he is free to improve matters:

> And the Lord said unto Cain, Why art thou wroth? and why is
> thy countenance fallen?
>
> If thou doest well, shalt thou not be accepted? and if thou doest not
> well, sin lieth at the door. And unto thee shall be his desire . . .
>
> (Gen. 4:6–7)

The desire to behave badly is externalized and personified as a greedy animal lying in wait at Cain's door, but, as God points out, 'thou shalt rule over him'. Cain can choose to control his evil impulses, but he disregards God's advice:

> and it came to pass, when they were in the field, that Cain rose
> up against Abel his brother, and slew him.
>
> (Gen. 4:8)

It is Cain's hostility towards his brother and its outcome, not the disobedience in the garden, that introduces the concept of sin into human life.

Of Eve's three named sons, Seth is the most important, for from him will spring the generations that lead to the one good man, the ark-builder Noah, and finally to Abraham, the true father of Judaism, whose inspiration to leave his family home in Haran inaugurates the nomad years of the Israelites. With the story of Noah the circle begins to be rounded; it is the first stage in the lifting of the curse of physical labour and death declared in the Garden of Eden, which was finally to be revoked, according to Christian belief, through the sacrifice and resurrection of Christ. Noah's role in the narrative is hinted at his birth, when his father Lamech recalls God's curse in Eden:

> And he called his name Noah, saying, This same shall comfort us
> concerning our work and toil of our hands, because of the
> ground which the Lord hath cursed.
>
> (Gen. 5:29)

Noah is born in turbulent times: as the generations who stem from Adam and Eve begin to multiply, humanity grows wicked and thinks only of evil. Where once God had looked at His creation with admiration, 'And God saw every thing that he had made, and, behold, it was very good' (Gen. 1:31), now He feels only a bitter disappointment: 'And God looked upon the earth, and, behold, it was corrupt' (Gen. 6:12), and He resolves to destroy all the living creatures that He has made, 'for it repenteth me that I have made them' (Gen. 6:7). But Noah finds grace in God's eyes: he is 'a just man and perfect in his generations' (Gen. 6:9) and he walks with God. At the Lord's instigation, Noah makes an ark of gopher wood, probably a box or chest rather than the seaworthy vessel with which he is usually credited, which he paints inside and out with black pitch to make it watertight, and he and his family, and male and female pairs of all living things, take refuge in the ark. Again, in the description of the paired animals entering and leaving the ark there are parallels with the earlier creation of all living things:

> And of every living thing of all flesh, two of every sort shalt thou bring into the ark, to keep them alive with thee; they shall be male and female.

> Of fowls after their kind, and of cattle after their kind, of every creeping thing of the earth after his kind, two of every sort shall come unto thee, to keep them alive.

(Gen. 6:19–20)

Before the Creation, all that existed was water, 'and darkness was upon the face of the deep' (Gen. 1:2); now the tamed waters are unleashed once more, 'all the fountains of the great deep [were] broken up, and the windows of heaven were opened' (Gen. 7:11). As once God breathed life into Adam's nostrils, now 'All in whose nostrils was the breath of life, of all that was in the dry land, died' (Gen. 7:22). Finally, God remembers Noah and his family, tossing on the waves in their fragile container and uncomfortably closeted with representatives from the entire animal kingdom, and He relents. Just as His 'rushing-spirit' had hovered over the face of the waters and set the new creation in motion, now He stops the flood with a wind, 'and the waters asswaged [*sic*]' (Gen. 8:1). The horrific scenes that would have greeted Noah and his family as they first set foot on the scarred wilderness were to delight the imagination of medieval artists. A magnificent illustration in the Bedford Book of Hours shows a watery mire of drowned bodies with crows still feeding on half-submerged corpses, while a casual camel, freed from the confinement of the ark, saunters across a desert littered with bones. Undaunted by all the clearing up he will have to do, Noah makes a burnt offering to God, which emits a savour so delicious that it softens God's heart. Resignedly, God accepts humankind's inclination towards sin, 'for the imagination of man's heart is evil from his youth' (Gen. 8:21), and He decides never again to curse the ground as He had done in Eden, nor to threaten the human race or any living creature with extinction. Instead, in a reprise of His command in the first chapter of Genesis, He tells Noah and his sons, 'Be fruitful, and multiply, and replenish the earth' (Gen. 9:1). Each is the new Adam, and must fulfil a similar role. As a reminder of this new and everlasting covenant, God sets his 'bow in the cloud' and He tells Noah:

> And it shall come to pass, when I bring a cloud over the earth,
> that the bow shall be seen in the cloud:
>
> And I will remember my covenant, which is between me and
> you and every living creature of all flesh . . .
>
> (Gen. 9:14–15)

We are back to where the first man and woman stood on the sixth day of creation, but with a new assurance of God's protection and His promise never again to interfere quite so drastically with the workings of nature.

And so the story of Adam and Eve and their children is rounded off: Seth's descendant Noah and his family are the only survivors of those early generations of toil and blood, of labour in the field and pain in childbed. As with the Creation in Genesis 1, the Flood narrative concludes with a new and hopeful beginning for the human race, God's instruction to Noah and his sons to 'replenish the earth' with their children; but although Noah's (unnamed) wife and daughters-in-law are mentioned at other significant points in the story, they are not referred to when God is briefing the Noah males on the re-population project, and their cooperation is taken for granted. The curse on the soil may have been lifted, but Eve/woman's destiny as subject to her husband has not been revoked. Even so, of the three sons of Noah 'was the whole earth overspread' (Gen. 9:19), and with the all-important truce between God and His creation, the real history of the Jews could begin – the many colourful tales of rivalry, inheritance and marriage, of travel and hard work and the careful forging of social laws that culminate in Moses' pioneering escape with the children of Israel from the cul-de-sac of slavery in Egypt into the wilderness of Sinai, and the start of another, crucial cycle of history, the Tablets of the Law and the bloody march into Canaan.

Many factors influenced the development of the final written form of this record. The narratives drew on a multiplicity of traditions: on stories passed by word of mouth; on earlier, now lost, Hebrew sacred texts; on the religious customs and mythologies of the rival cultures that the Israelites confronted in their long struggle towards nationhood; on priestly ideas about morality, about appropriate social behaviour and, in particular, about correct religious belief. And the narratives were not static: texts were edited, expanded and revised to affirm different emphases during their long gestation. That early story about magic trees, a serpent, a man and a woman behaving badly in a garden, was probably too persistent, too persuasive, too popular to be rejected by the priestly redactors because it was naive, contradictory, or defamatory of God, and clearly, in the context of Jewish history, the history of Adam and Eve is of the utmost importance. Not only did all future generations emerge from the joining of their two bodies – Eve's name, Hawwah, the mother of all living, reminds us of this – but Adam and Eve and their descendants had to reap the consequences of the primary disobedience and come to terms with creating order in the real world; the first chapters of Genesis record a series of experiments in living in which God is seen to participate and which culminate in God's covenant with His Chosen People, the truce that sets the stage for the history of Israel.

Into the future

THE GARDEN OF EDEN and the events that took place there continued to haunt the human imagination long after the Yahwist and the early tribes of Israel had atrophied to primordial dust, and the original meanings of the story had become so obscure as to be entirely forgotten. New explanations had to be invented and justified. Christian and Jewish theologians have persistently explored new theories about Eden; and artists, poets and musicians in Western Christendom have made influential contributions to the common stock of ideas that are now available. Part of the reason for the persistence of the myth is the crucial role that the story played in the development of Christian belief – 'For as in Adam all die, even so in Christ shall all be made alive' (1 Cor. 15:22) – and the Christian annexation of this ancient Hebrew folk tale prevented it from sinking into obscurity. But the story's appeal is wider than this; it speaks to something fundamental in human nature, tells of something universal to human experience. Perhaps, most simply, it looks back nostalgically to the irrecoverable world of childhood while justifying the necessity for change. The literary trope of the Golden Age, developed from classical times and still current in the twentieth century (Tolkien's *The Lord of the Rings*, for instance, draws heavily on its imagery and emotional resonances), celebrates a largely imaginary past enhanced by the distortions and magical embellishments of memory: the Garden of Eden is the archetypal embodiment of this fantasy. Almost every person, unless born into very dreadful circumstances, retains some memory of joyous, irresponsible childhood, perhaps fragmentary, lasting only seconds, but these recollections of uncomplicated happiness, of uncompromised response to natural beauty, to people and animals, and of the zest of being alive, are what illuminate adult life and make it more bearable. Adam and Eve's brief idyll in the Garden of Eden embodies this consciousness of a lost and happy past, but it also points to the need for change. If Eve had not eaten the fruit of knowledge, human history could not have begun. Indeed, it can be argued that Eve's decision to taste the forbidden fruit was the decisive act that kickstarted humanity out of the stasis of Eden into the harsh realities of the human condition. A reading that suggests that the events in the Garden of Eden validate human self-assertion in the face of God is anachronistic; for the early Hebrew scribes and priests who put the Holy Books together such an idea would have been unthinkable. But the story may attempt to account for the fact that change is inevitable, even if it is a change for the worse. It is impossible to stop time. That state of wellbeing rehearsed in the Eden story – a time of pleasure and fulfilment perhaps associated for the early Israelites with the idealized first years of adulthood and marriage, with good harvests, a full stomach, plentiful rainfall and fulfilled sexuality – cannot last. Seasons change; children are born; people grow old and die; and nations are riven by political change, warfare, even exile.

The Garden of Eden has continued to stimulate commentary and reworkings: it poses challenging questions about the relationship between men and women, and between humanity and God; about the power of language, and of food and sex; about memory and imagination; and the workaday world of childbearing and toil; and about suffering and happiness and death. It provides, too, a set of references that are still commonly understood, a form of cultural shorthand, and there are numerous examples in Western literature of how this immediately interpretable code can enrich or modify narrative. The chapters that follow trace the history of some of the ways in which the Eden narrative has facilitated social control or stimulated creativity. Inevitably much of the speculation and controversy has centred around the prime mover in the story – Eve – and it is with her history and changing image, and their effect on her female descendants, that this book is principally concerned. The ingredients of her story have retained their capacity to titillate the mental palate even after three millennia of stews and brews, of sipping and chewing and spitting out, and the questions persist, as flavoursome as ever. What is the status of woman as rib, as flesh, as helpmate, as mother? Just how sensible is it to listen to a woman? Is there really any special relationship between women and reptiles, between women and gardens? And what *is* the appropriate response to a naked woman offering forbidden fruit and promising secret knowledge?

CHAPTER 2

THE VIEW THROUGH ONE PAINTED EYE

The woman, says the Law, is in all things inferior to the man. Let her accordingly be submissive, not for her humiliation, but that she may be directed; for the authority has been given by God to the man.

JOSEPHUS, *Apion*, II:201

———•◆•———

AT THE CATHEDRAL OF Saint-Lazare in Autun, France, a melancholy stone Eve once reclined on the lintel of the north portal, awkwardly supporting her chin on her right hand, her gaze resting in vacuity, even as her left hand reached irresistibly behind her to pluck the prohibited fruit. Immobilized by her sculptor at the breakpoint between remorse and desire, transgression and its mirror-image, repentance, this brooding Eve movingly embodies the tension between opposing compulsions, the agonizing choice between God and the devil so ingeniously exploited by the medieval church. In the tympanum once above her head, the Raising of Lazarus would have symbolized humanity's release through Christ from the curse of sin and death imposed in Eden to a life of spiritual renewal, but Eve, now a relic in the adjacent museum, continues to creep along the ground, frozen in an endlessly repeated cycle of sin and remorse, her stooping posture a harsh reminder of humanity's inability to stand alone once it had turned away from God. This simple image stunningly communicates everything the viewer needs to understand about fallible Eve. The Adam who probably partnered her on the opposite side of the lintel has not survived; the depradations of time ironically emphasizing what had come to be seen as Eve's sole responsibility for the catastrophic Fall.

The Eve of Autun was created in the twelfth century, at a period when the flawed nature of Everywoman Eve had become a commonplace persistently reaffirmed in vernacular storytelling, in poetry and legend, in sermons and religious teaching, and, in particular, through that great educator of popular opinion, the visual imagery of church decoration. But this hostile view of Eve had developed long before the Middle Ages. By the second century after the birth of Christ, Eve had been named by the Christian theologian Tertullian as 'the devil's gateway', responsible for corrupting the pristine Adam and causing the death of God's Son. The story of how Eve acquired her disreputable character draws on many different kinds of evidence, both Jewish and Christian, dating from different periods and contexts, but it is crucially absent from the Jewish Bible. After the first few chapters of Genesis, Eve sinks from view. She is never directly mentioned in any of the many statements about women, either in the quasi-historical narratives where women feature as mothers, wives, daughters and sisters, as midwives, witches, queens and prophetesses, or in the books dealing with law and social custom, or in the Wisdom literature. Surprisingly, given her later reputation, criticisms of harlotry and female seductiveness fail to cite her as an example to be avoided, and she is not once invoked in the many warnings to men against entanglements with women. Equally astonishingly, she is never again associated in the Jewish Bible with death or the gloomy path to Sheol. Yet, by the time of the Early Church Fathers, for many commentators Eve/Everywoman had become archetypically wicked. The origins of the new ideas about Eve, and the diachotomy between good and bad women that became symbolized by the Mary/Eve polarization, have to be looked for in early Jewish attitudes to women which passed into and were mediated by the needs and pressures of developing Christianity.

Crucially, what is missing from the account, as so often with women's history, is any witness from women themselves. The documents that survive are almost certainly exclusively by male writers, although it is possible to acquire some perspective on women's experience by reading between the lines and looking for hidden evidence of how people lived. The most fruitful sources of information concern those aspects of women's behaviour that became particularly associated with Eve – the arts of seduction, practised through clothes, cosmetics and 'feminine wiles', and her roles as wife, mother and helpmate, aspects predominantly related

to the female biological function, although 'helpmate' has been a
widely interpreted role for women since the time of Eden, embrac-
ing the economic functioning of the family and the husband's
wellbeing in its broadest sense. The sources invite consideration
from two perspectives – masculine beliefs about women as revealed
in the surviving texts, and how a woman's life might have looked
from her own point of view. We have no testimony from early
Jewish women, no memoirs of a patriarch's wife, no slender volume
of poems by an educated concubine, not even a household manual
or a midwife's handbook to set alongside the Pentateuch and the
Prophets, or the copious volumes of midrash and Talmud. But from
what can be gleaned of women's experience from these volumes, it
may be possible to guess how the world might have appeared from
a woman's perspective, how it might have felt to marry at twelve,
to give birth to too many daughters and too few sons, to cook and
weave and spin and run a household according to the strict standards
required by the Torah, the essential teaching and practice of the
Law whose domestic rules were passed down from mother to
daughter.

The texts that constitute the Hebrew Holy Books, the Pentateuch, Histories, Wisdom and Prophets, offer multiple images of
women, which are further illuminated by the *Midrash Rabbah*, a
series of commentaries on Scripture, probably first edited around
the fourth to fifth centuries AD, although the material they contain
dates back centuries. For details of the social and legal position of
women, one can turn to the Mishnah, the Law code, based on the
rabbinic formulation of Oral Law, the most authoritative compila-
tion of which was finally written down soon after AD 200, and the
Talmud, an extensive commentary on parts of the Mishnah, which
gathers together the teachings of the major Jewish scholars from AD
200 to 500 in two great compilations, the Babylonian and Palestinian
Talmuds. Luckily for the inquisitive reader, these are no dry-as-dust
documents, to be heaved with groans from the library shelf in
reluctant anticipation of an hour or so of necessary boredom. The
Rabbis delighted in discussion, in argument, in pinning down the
exact meanings of theology and the Law, and the minutiae of
correct behaviour; but they were also gossips and storytellers,
revelling in anecdote, parable and legend, and curious to trace the

workings of history. The surviving texts of the Scriptures and the books of theological and legal commentary reflect their origins in an oral tradition that was upheld for centuries as the primary mode of dissemination because of its fluidity, its potential for ramification, exploration and redefinition. As the historians David Goldberg and John Rayner point out, it 'was only when the material became too massive to be memorized, and when political insecurity threatened the continuity of the oral transmission, that the principle was finally abandoned, but this was not until about 200 CE'. Because of this, 'the *contents* of Rabbinic Literature are often generations, and even centuries, older than the documents'.

These rabbinic writings evolved in a variety of historical contexts, which embraced periods of polytheism, loose tribal confederation, monarchy, conquest and exile for the Hebrew people. By the time the Mishnah was formally encoded, the Babylonians, Persians, Seleucids and Romans had in turn hung their banners on the walls of Jerusalem; Solomon's Temple with its elaborate bronze pillars, its decorated cedar panels, and the two magnificent fifteen-foot cheru- bim, the winged figures who guarded the Ark of the Covenant, had been razed and rebuilt and razed again; and the Jews themselves had become dispersed through a wide area of the Ancient Near East, with settlements in the Mediterranean, Mesopotamia and Egypt, and a correspondingly wide variety of languages and dialects, local cultures and traditions. Given the diversity of place, time and people, it would be impossible and ridiculous to claim that ideas from Jewish religious texts, however carefully extrapolated, are absolutely representative of the experience of women at any particu- lar time in the history of Israel, and scholars are now looking at a broader spectrum of archaeological and inscriptional sources to tease out a fuller picture of women's lives in the Graeco-Roman period. However, what the Mishnah and the Talmud do offer is a consensus of opinion about religious belief and practice that had been debated for centuries before it was finally written down, and was the cement that kept the Jewish faith intact. Given their precarious history, the Jews had learnt the inadvisability of a religion dependent on place or building or ceremonial figure. The key to the survival of Judaism was its flexibility and portability – a person could be a good Jew as long as he (and in a more restricted sense, she) fulfilled the Torah, the teaching or Law which embodied the essentials of Jewish faith, and this could be passed on in a synagogue in Alexandria, or practised in a private home as effectively as in the Temple in Jerusalem. The ideas about women discussed in this chapter represent normative Judaic attitudes and reflect the formal parameters of Jewish women's lives, although there are hints that the practice was somewhat more varied and flexible. These definitions fed into the imaginative literature of Judaism in which Eve came to play such a prominent role.

Eve and the matriarchs

EVE'S EARLY FEMALE descendants in Genesis were nomadic matriarchs who travelled on the first long journey from Ur of the Chaldees in ancient Babylonia north to Haran, and then down to Shechem in the land of Canaan, to Bethel and into Egypt, and back again to Canaan, wandering in search of food and precious water for their flocks of sheep and goats, living in tents and renting pastureland from local magnates, princes and warlords. Typically, they were women who followed their men: Sarah and her handmaid Hagar swept along on the torrent of Abraham's sense of destiny; Rebekah step-by-step with the more cautious Isaac; Rachel, the beloved wife, faithfully tracking the angel-wrestler Jacob; pausing to set their tents sometimes for decades before setting off again, crisscrossing the terrain that stretches north of the Euphrates and south as far as Egypt, from the Mediterranean to the Salt Sea. Sarah, Rebekah and Rachel played important roles in the evolution of Israel, and their histories illuminate early Jewish ideas about Eve, their foremother, whose character and destiny they were bound, by the terms of God's decree in the garden, to fulfil.

The first matriarch who is mentioned after Eve, the redoubtable Mrs Noah, barely features in the Flood crisis, but even her shadowy figure discloses the approved model for wifely behaviour: obedience to her husband's wishes and the ability to give birth to viable sons. She seems not to have protested at Noah's ark proposals, abandoning herself without recorded complaint to God's will and the ocean, and to being cooped up for a possibly interminable period with a representative cross-section of the animal kingdom and three daughters-in-law, who, with her sons, Ham, Shem and Japheth, are permitted to survive the Flood and give birth to the nations of the world. Medieval English dramatists, however, refused to be persuaded by this voiceless paragon and presented instead the disobedient termagant of the York and Towneley biblical cycles, and some early European religious dramas followed an Eastern legend in which Mrs Noah is tempted by the devil to hinder Noah's salvation. In the Newcastle *Noah* play, the devil urges her to make Noah drunk so that she can find out and foil his plans. In these lively retellings of her story, Mrs Noah becomes a second Eve, succumbing to the devil's blandishments and attempting to subvert her husband's good fortune. Her tart, sharp-tongued representation, the familiar contemporary model of the shrew, suggests that her creators were reading between the lines of the biblical story to capitalize on their own culture's favourite version of 'the nature of woman'. Similarly, her most recent apotheosis has been as a sympathetic heroine in Michèle Roberts' versatile *The Book of Mrs Noah*, where she displays a late-twentieth-century enthusiasm for personal growth, vegetarianism and female bonding. Roberts also identifies Mrs Noah as a potentially subversive presence, but now she has become the irrepressible voice of woman, 'the ghost in the library, cackling, unseen, from between the pages of the sacred texts'.

The significant women who succeed Mrs Noah and her daughters-in-law are psychologically distinct characters who at times appear to exert a powerful influence over the course of events. Genesis relates the birth narratives of the three principal wives, Sarah, Rebekah and Rachel, and the histories of their sons, Isaac, Jacob, and Joseph. All three women are infertile, for which God is assumed to be responsible; all three finally become pregnant and give birth to sons who are of the utmost importance in carrying through God's ultimate purposes for Israel. We have already seen how Sarah, Abraham's wife, deals with her barrenness, offering her maid Hagar to bear in her place and giving short shrift to Hagar's subsequent cheekiness. Many years later, Sarah herself is mysteriously permitted to give birth to a child, the beloved Isaac, son of her and Abraham's extreme old age. Following a familiar folkloric tradition in which divine strangers bring astounding news to an old couple, angels in the guise of desert wanderers visit Abraham's bivouac to predict the conception of Isaac. Sarah eavesdrops at the flap of the tent on the travellers' conversation with Abraham, and laughs at the idea of such a dry husk, a woman already in her ninety-first year, enjoying sexual pleasure with her antiquated husband. Challenged to explain her laughter, she is afraid and denies it, but God defends His audacious scheme with simple logic, 'Is any thing too hard for the Lord?' (Gen. 18:14). When she does conceive and bears a son, Sarah joyfully concedes: 'God hath made me to laugh, so that all that hear will laugh with me' (Gen. 21:6), and the child is named Isaac, 'He Laughs'. God's intervention in Sarah's biological destiny – withholding and then giving a child – demonstrates His authority over nature, already proven again and again in Genesis, in the creation of the universe from that first rapt scene of dark, primal waters, in the punishment of Adam, 'cursed is the ground for thy sake', and in the world's partial destruction through the Flood. Sarah's status in Hebrew history is affirmed not only by the miraculous birth, but also by God's renaming of her before Isaac's birth, from Sarai to Sarah, 'Princess', the only woman in the Jewish Bible who is renamed, in a culture where names were deeply significant as indicators both of character and destiny.

We are not told how Sarah felt when Abraham took her boy, barely an adolescent, away to a distant hilltop to slaughter him at Yahweh's request – or even whether her husband prepared her for the brutal sacrifice. Perhaps they lay awake together during the long night before Abraham's dreadful journey, arguing about what they should do, how to find other ways of appeasing Yahweh's horrific desire. Or did Abraham hold his tongue, old companions, old lovers, as they both were? When the procession returned with her child intact, did Sarah's heart bound with joy, or was she tranquil, composed, a woman whose long experience of disappointment and reversal had taught her to face even the death of her child with dignity and resignation? Whatever their private feelings, the man and the woman obey God's impenetrable will – and are rewarded by the gift of their son's life. When Sarah eventually dies, Abraham honours her memory by buying a burial-place for her, a field with a cave in Machpelah, near Hebron (Gen. 23:3–20), the first territory owned by an Israelite in Canaan and, as a burial-ground, a significant first stake in the Promised Land. In a moving coda to Sarah's death, her now very aged husband seeks out a wife for their son Isaac among Abraham's kindred in Nahor, Mesopotamia – no Canaanite woman for him! Abraham sends his trusted servant to woo the bride, Rebekah, and negotiate her marriage-dower, and to bring her back for Isaac:

> And Isaac went out to meditate in the field at the eventide:
> and he lifted up his eyes, and saw, and, behold, the camels were
> coming . . .
>
> And Isaac brought her into his mother Sarah's tent, and took
> Rebekah, and she became his wife; and he loved her: and Isaac
> was comforted after his mother's death.
>
> (Gen. 24:63, 67)

It is a glimpse of the human tenderness that is characteristic of the stories of these early Israelite families, in which the reciprocal feelings between parents and children, between a son and his mother, a husband and wife, are sympathetically evoked, and the centuries drop away, so that we muse with the grieving Isaac in the darkening field, and glance up to see the looming camel-train, and the veiled and promising figure of Rebekah approaching through the twilight.

Genesis presents Sarah as a strong-minded woman who successfully fulfilled her destiny as Abraham's principal wife and the mother of Isaac. Later, the Rabbis were to tell stories connecting her with Eve, tales that reflect the high status within Judaism of both the women. They were to say that 'four matriarchs' were buried together in Hebron: Eve, Sarah, Rebekah and Rachel's fruitful sister, Leah, with the 'four righteous men', Adam, Abraham, Isaac and Jacob, the important ancestors of the Jewish faith entombed together. Another rabbinic story linking Sarah with Eve dwells on the superior beauty and hence marital value of both these women: during a period of famine, and long before the birth of Isaac, Abraham took Sarah to live for a while in Egypt (Gen. 12:10–20), the familiar recourse of the nomadic Israelites when food was scarce, and which led to their eventual enslavement under the hostile

Pharaoh. On this occasion, according to the legend, Abraham locks Sarah up in a box to protect her from the gaze of strangers. When he comes to the customs-house at the border, the official suspects that the box contains dutiable items and demands to see the contents. Abraham at first refuses, promising to pay extravagant dues on whatever the official thinks is in the box – garments, silks, precious stones. Finally he is forced to open the box, and the land of Egypt is irradiated with Sarah's beauty. The Rabbis commented that: 'Eve's image was transmitted to the reigning beauties of each generation', and even went so far as to say that Sarah was even more beautiful than Eve. As the first woman, created by God for Adam's delight, Eve was thought to be endowed with every attraction, corresponding to the perfectionist tradition of Adam's great physical beauty and God-like intellect. Sarah and the line of matriarchal women who feature in Genesis partook of Eve's primal good looks.

The account of Sarah's sojourn in Egypt has a further significance, in which Sarah continues her foremother Eve's important destiny as childbearer. As they are entering Egypt, Abraham persuades Sarah to say that she is his sister. Because she is so beautiful, he is afraid that if the Egyptians find out that she is his wife, they will kill him and take possession of her. In the guise of Sarah's brother, Abraham will be less vulnerable, and can play an important role as her protector and negotiator with any potential suitor. As he had anticipated, the Egyptians do admire Sarah and she is removed to the Pharaoh's household of wives and concubines, in return for payment to Abraham of sheep, oxen, asses, camels and servants. But things do not go well for the Pharaoh: the Lord brings down a great plague on his household, and when he understands that this is because of Sarah, he summons Abraham to take her away. Immediately before Isaac's birth, a similar situation occurs, this time with Abimelech, king of Gerar (Gen. 20:1–18), and on this occasion, God threatens the king with death, and Abimelech hastens to restore Sarah to her husband. Once again, Sarah's chastity is not violated by her new owner, and Abraham emerges from the adventure considerably enriched. The encounter with Abimelech makes it clear that what is at stake in these stories is Sarah's sexuality: as long as she stays in his house, potentially at risk of violation by the king, all the women in his household become barren: 'For the Lord had fast closed up all the wombs of the house of Abimelech, because of Sarah Abraham's wife' (Gen. 20:18).

Throughout Sarah's history, her sexual vulnerability is counterbalanced by God's interventions on her behalf. When she is barren, she says, 'Behold now, the Lord hath restrained me from bearing' (Gen. 16:2); God, not nature, is in control of her reproductive capacity. When she finally does conceive, she is long past the menopause, and once again it is God who makes her fertile, just as God intervenes to protect her from ravishment by the stranger kings. Whilst Sarah's human authenticity cannot be discounted and is what makes her so sympathetic a character, God's wishes are ultimately what matter. Fertility and barrenness are in His gift, and are dispensed in accordance with His plans for the future of Israel. The obligation acknowledged by Eve when she bears Cain, the first human child, 'I have gotten a man from the LORD' (Gen. 4:1), is repeated by all the matriarchs. Vibrant and strong-minded as these women often appear, in the end they are God's stooges. Isaac's wife Rebekah conceives only after a spell of barrenness and her husband's special intervention with God on her behalf (Gen. 25:21). Troubled by the turbulence in her womb, she seeks God's advice and He makes clear her special destiny: 'Two nations are in thy womb, and two manner of people shall be separated from thy bowels; and the one people shall be stronger than the other people; and the elder shall serve the younger' (Gen. 25:23). Sure enough, she gives birth to twins, the hairy red-man Esau, and tricky Jacob, the Heel-Holder, so called because he plunges from the birth canal clinging to his brother's heels. The story of Rachel, Jacob's best-beloved wife, makes for particularly painful reading: she has repeatedly to endure the robust motherhood of her sister Leah and the two handmaids before she finally gives birth to Joseph, 'God hath taken away my reproach' (Gen. 30:23), and she eventually dies in childbed leaving a second son, Benjamin. With each of these women, God, not nature, has His hand on the reins.

The narratives of the matriarchs testify that none of Eve's early descendants exemplify her later character as wicked sexual temptress. Their inheritance from her and their significance is as bearers of children and loyal wives, following God's words to Eve: 'in sorrow

thou shalt bring forth children; and thy desire shall be to thy
husband, and he shall rule over thee'. The source of seductress Eve
is to be sought elsewhere, and its seeds perhaps lie in the Jewish law
codes with their dual concern to protect women and to uphold the
masculinist status quo.

The virtuous wife

He who has no wife dwells without good, without help, without
joy, without blessing, and without atonement.
   Midrash Rabbah, Genesis I, XVII:2

THIS EULOGY ON the benefits of marriage to the male partner
introduces the rabbinic commentary on God's words in the Garden
of Eden, 'It is not good that the man should be alone' (Gen. 2:18),
but the sages' benign summary is almost immediately undermined
by discussion of God's subsequent words about the 'helpmate',
which the Rabbis gloss rather sourly, 'if he is fortunate, she is a
help; if not, she is against him', and they follow this up with gloomy
stories about a Rabbi who made an unfortunate marriage. An
ambivalence about women is characteristic of the *Midrash Rabbah*,
which may in general be said to promote the view that, like the
little girl with the kitschy curl, when a woman is good, she is
(arguably) very good indeed, but when she is bad, she is horrid, and
her influence is all-pervasive. In the Rabbis' view, 'all depends on
the woman', and they tell the tale of the pious man who married a
pious woman, but, being childless, the couple felt they were of no
use to God, 'whereupon they arose and divorced each other. The
former went and married a wicked woman, and she made him
wicked, while the latter went and married a wicked man, and made
him righteous.'

At the heart of any discussion about marriage in early Judaism is
the question of what constituted a good marital arrangement. The
many statements on marriage that survive from the biblical and
rabbinic periods tend to revolve around ideas of male comfort and
economic security, and an indisputable line of inheritance. Where a
women's needs or rights are taken into consideration, it is often

with a view to the long-term convenience of her husband or other
male relatives who have some financial stake in the woman's future,
although there is also a strong sense in the marriage and property
legislation in the Mishnah and Talmud that a contented wife will
be a 'good' wife in terms of male requirements from marriage. A
woman's interests were considered, up to a point. What is lacking
is any framework for women outside marriage: almost all women
were expected to marry, and were often married when very young.
The prospects for an unmarried woman without property or family
to support her were at best unpromising, and the necessity of
community care for portionless widows is a persistent theme in both
the Jewish Bible and the New Testament. The appealing story of
the Moabite Ruth exemplifies the concern to protect widows and
dependants, while securing the dead husband's legacy. When Ruth's
young husband Mahlon dies, she makes the courageous decision to
leave her home and friends and to accompany his mother Naomi
back to her own family in Bethlehem, a surprising choice that Ruth
affirms with the conviction of divine revelation:

> Intreat me not to leave thee, or to return from following after
> thee: for whither thou goest, I will go; and where thou lodgest, I
> will lodge: thy people shall be my people, and thy God my God:

> Where thou diest, will I die, and there will I be buried: the Lord
> do so to me, and more also, if ought but death part thee and me.

(Ruth 1:16–17)

The arrival of the two women in Bethlehem poses a problem
for Naomi's rich kinsman Boaz: both women are widowed, apparently without proper means of support, and there is also the
requirement to protect the family inheritance, which is under threat
because Ruth is childless and Naomi is proposing to raise money by
selling her husband's land, which would in happier times have been
passed down to sons and grandsons. By sending Ruth alone to Boaz
at night when he is sleeping on the threshing-floor, a situation in
which a young woman's reputation would be particularly vulnerable, Naomi awakens Boaz to his responsibility to protect his
kinswomen and honour Mahlon's memory, and he neatly resolves

the difficulty by marrying Ruth, which secures a future for her and
Naomi, and buying the family land. With the birth of Ruth's son
Obed, her late husband's patrimony is doubly secured, and Boaz's
deference to familial obligation is richly rewarded: Obed will father
Jesse, whose son will be the minstrel-shepherd David, giant-killer
and beloved of Jonathan, and one of the first great kings of Israel.
The story of Ruth is a rare redemption of the customarily poor
repute of foreign women, and a cautionary tale about the protection
of widows.

The blueprint for a good wife is established in the beautiful
poem that concludes Proverbs, where, in Hebrew, each verse begins
with a consecutive letter of the alphabet: 'Who can find a virtuous
woman? for her price is far above rubies' (Prov. 31:10ff). The
poem praises the woman's skill in practical matters rather than her
beauty or talent for amorous love. She works hard at her spinning
and weaving, and her household is amply and even richly dressed,
but this is a mark of the family's social status, and credits the wife's
powers of management rather than her sense of fashion. There are
hints of her sexual integrity: her husband can trust her to look
after his interests in every way, she will always bring him good
rather than evil, but in any case she is too busy to get into mischief.
She rises before all her household, and 'her candle goeth not
out by night'. She is a thrifty provider, shopping around for bargains
so that she can feed her family and servants, and she finds time to
care for the poor. She has excellent business judgement, buying
land and planting a vineyard, and trading in fine linens which
she herself has made. Thanks to her remarkable activity, her husband is respected in the community and can take his place among
the 'elders of the land'. When she speaks it is to utter words
of wisdom and kindness, and she is blessed by all her family. This
is an idealized portrait of wifehood, and the woman seems to have
had an unusual freedom to come and go, and to act as a principal
in financial dealings. She may perhaps have been a personification
of the allegorical figure of Wisdom rather than any flesh-and-blood
woman, but the poem does offer insights into the hardworking
life that would have been expected of early Jewish wives and
mothers, and reflects some of the realities of women's lives that
persisted in medieval Europe and into the modern period. What it

also indicates is that the focus of the woman's attention, her devotion and care, is on the well-being of her husband and children and the promotion of her family's interests. A woman's job was to enable her husband to fulfil his primary functions, the spiritual struggle for dialogue with God, and the devoted study of the Torah, the Law, with its implications for personal religiosity and community welfare. While the virtuous wife occupies herself from cockcrow until well past candle-hour with domestic and even business concerns, her husband can bask in the good repute of his family.

The social and economic significance of the marital relationship in early Judaism is confirmed by the precisely detailed legal rules concerning marriage and divorce recorded in the Mishnah. As the scholar Judith Romney Wegner points out in her study of the status of women in this document, wives and daughters were regarded as being as much part of a man's property as were his slaves, his cattle, or any other potentially marketable possession, and a woman's sexuality was of huge economic importance. 'The procedure for acquiring a wife . . . treats marriage as the formal sale and purchase of a woman's sexual function', a transaction in which virginity was highly desirable and had an appropriate premium attached. The customary *ketubah* or wife's jointure was twice as high for virgins as for non-virgins, and the Mishnah provided legal redress for a bridegroom who claimed that the bride's father had deceived him in this matter. In the early biblical period, Deuteronomy had recognized the possibility that a man might take an instant dislike to a new bride, who, according to the practice of arranged marriages and the social seclusion of women, was perhaps a young girl whom he barely knew or had never met face to face, and might try to get rid of her by accusing her of coming unchaste to the marital bed (Deut. 22:13–14). But although apparently sympathetic to the plight of an unfairly rejected woman, the method recommended to test the woman's virginity was degrading to the woman concerned, and not guaranteed to reveal the true state of affairs. In such a case, the girl's parents were advised to bring proofs of their daughter's virginity, presumably bloodstained bedding or undergarments, to the city elders, who would force the husband to pay a fine to the girl's father and to reinstate his wife, whom he was not able subsequently to divorce: 'he may not put her away all his days'. If the proofs were not available, then the girl was stoned to death by the men of the city at her father's door, because she had dared to 'play the whore in her father's house' (Deut. 22:15–21), that is, had illicit sex while still under his protection. Such a scenario presumes an intact hymen, which in the case of some girls would already have been broken through natural causes by the time they reached early adolescence, or a hymen that bleeds sufficiently on rupture to cause staining; it also forces a girl, if acquitted of the charge of unchastity, to live permanently with a husband who has attempted publicly to disgrace her. It might also encourage the girl (or her family) to fake the evidence.

By mishnaic times, proof of virginity was based on cultural assumptions about a woman's previous behaviour rather than on physical examination, but the hymen nevertheless assumed enormous significance in rabbinic marital law. The legislation suggests a high level of abuse of certain classes of young girls. In the case of female slaves or captives who were freed or otherwise redeemed before the age of three years and one day, it was assumed that they would inevitably have been subject to sexual violation, but they could still fetch the full bridal price as it was believed that the hymen would have regrown. After the age of three years and a day, any manumitted slave girl was treated as a non-virgin, even if there was no evidence that she had been subjected to rape or other form of sexual intercourse. Similarly, it was assumed that unmarried girls, including those who had been widowed or divorced after betrothal (that is, before assumed consummation of the marriage) were virgins, while women divorced after the formal marriage had taken place (that is, after presumed consummation) were non-virgins and would fetch a lower remarriage jointure. The assumption of virginity, and the specification of conditions in which virginity was assumed to exist, were more important than the actuality. Virginity was again a crucial factor in the penalties imposed for rape or seduction. In Mosaic Law, if a man was convicted of violating a virgin, he had to pay a girl's father either her bride-price (and marry her), or an equivalent fine. In the case of women who were presumed not to be virgins, according to rabbinic criteria, no sum was payable. In each case, virginity as a marketable asset is the

essential factor. This economic emphasis is further illustrated by the
proviso that no fine was applicable for violated virgins under the
age of twelve, because the father had the right to sell such a girl as a
slave and could thus recoup the financial loss of the bride-price that
would have been paid for her virginity, although by the mishnaic
period the bride-price would have been assigned to the married
woman rather than her father, as a sum payable on divorce or
widowhood.

Once a woman was married, her husband had the use for her
lifetime of any money or property she might possess, but he was
liable for her maintenance and her burial, which was to be con-
ducted with due ceremony: 'Even the poorest in Israel should hire
not less than two flutes and one wailing woman.' The minimum
requirement for a wife's maintenance was set at 'two *kabs* of wheat
or four *kabs* of barley' every week (a *kab* being approximately half a
litre), with 'half a *kab* of pulse and half a *log* [one quarter of a *kab*]
of oil and a *kab* of dried figs or a *mina* [equal to 560 grammes] of
fig-cake'. Bedding and clothing were also to be provided: 'He must
also give her a bed and a bed-cover and if he has no bed-cover he
must give her a rush mat. He must also give her a cap for her head
and a girdle for her loins, and shoes at each of the [three] Feasts
[Passover, Pentecost, and Tabernacles], and clothing to the value of
50 *zuz* every year', and there was to be no skimping in the quality
and thickness of the cloth used for the garments. The clothes should
be bought new for the winter, and the wife could use the worn
clothes in summer when the weather was more clement. There
were strict rules for the husband to provide regular sexual intercourse, which was allocated according to the man's job and
presumed availability: 'The *duty of marriage* enjoined in the Law is:
every day for them that are unoccupied; twice a week for labourers;
once a week for ass-drivers; once every thirty days for camel-drivers;
and once every six months for sailors.' Students of the Law were
permitted to absent themselves from the marital bed for thirty days
to pursue their research, even if their wives objected, and the
Talmud extends this to two to three years, and gives examples of
husbands who left their wives for the full twelve years that was the
norm for Torah study in the academy. Labourers were only allowed
a week's abstention. Although by this period religious teaching

tended to regard the proper purpose of sex as procreation rather than personal pleasure or the expression of affection, these precise guidelines suggest that the wife was as much entitled to marital intercourse as was the husband, with the proviso that a man's religious studies took priority even over his duty to procreate.

A woman's marital duties were similarly carefully specified. Her refusal of sexual intercourse was fined by a reduction of the *ketubah*, calculated according to the number of days the husband was forced to abstain, and the wife was expected to perform routine duties for her husband: 'grinding flour and baking bread and washing clothes and cooking food and giving suck to her child and making ready his bed and working in wool.' If she brought servants with her, she was allowed to reassign her tasks; four servants entitled her to sit in her chair all day taking her ease. However, this was frowned on by some of the Rabbis, partly on the grounds of depression, 'idleness leads to lowness of spirit', and also because it offered an opportunity for lewdity. Rabbi Eliezer, one of the more hard-line mishnaic sages, advised, 'Even if she brought him in a hundred bondwomen he should compel her to work in wool, for idleness leads to unchastity', a hint of woman's tendency to sexual misbehaviour that became a commonplace of medieval Christian thinking. The proceeds of a wife's work belonged to her husband, although he was required to give her money for her own needs. Failure to do this meant that the woman could keep anything she earned. The weight of spun thread expected of a wife was specified, but this was reduced when a woman was suckling a child, or according to a husband's perception of his own honour and status.

The careful discussion of the marital responsibilities of both partners set out in the Mishnah confirms rabbinic concern for the social weal – a contented wife would perform her duties faithfully, releasing her husband for his more important duties outside the domestic environment – and reflects a patriarchal society where care for dependants was part of a virtuous life. As the Mishnah makes clear, except in the case of widows, divorced women, and unmarried daughters who had reached their majority, a woman 'continues within the control of the father until she enters into the control of the husband at marriage'.

★

THE MODEL WIFE of Proverbs, whose domestic and social care is so essential to the wellbeing of the community, is strangely reminiscent of the idealized women of Victorian fiction, of Marmee in Louisa May Alcott's *Little Women*, who cheerfully defies poverty and an absentee husband to fill her days with charitable works and bring up her daughters to be busy and useful, and even such real-life provident women as the indefatigable Mrs Gaskell or Fanny Trollope. In Charlotte Brontë's *Shirley*, the financially dependent Caroline Helstone reflects with envy on the virtuous woman of Proverbs, comparing the latter's profitable occupations with her own unfruitful existence, without work or income or prospects of a family of her own: '"*That* woman was a manager: she was what the matrons hereabouts call 'a clever woman' . . . 'Strength and honour were her clothing: the heart of her husband safely trusted in her. She opened her mouth with wisdom; in her tongue was the law of kindness' . . . But,"' Caroline muses, '"are we, in these days, brought up to be like her?"' and she challenges the men of England to do something about their fading, wasted girls, to save them from sickness and decline, from

> 'degenerating to sour old maids, – envious, backbiting, wretched,
> because life is a desert to them; or, what is worst of all, reduced
> to strive, by scarce modest coquetry and debasing artifice, to
> gain that position and consideration by marriage, which to
> celibacy is denied. Fathers! [she cries,] . . . [y]ou would wish
> to be proud of your daughters . . . then seek for them an interest
> and an occupation which shall raise them above the flirt, the
> manœuvrer, the mischief-making tale-bearer. Keep your girls'
> minds narrow and fettered – they will still be a plague and a care,
> sometimes a disgrace to you: cultivate them – give them scope
> and work – they will be your gayest companions in health; your
> tenderest nurses in sickness; your most faithful prop in age.'

Despite the masculinist bias of her ambitions for 'the daughters of England' – as companions, nurses, props to men – Caroline Helstone's envy of the productive woman was not ill-judged, given the miserable prospects for dowerless and unskilled girls at almost any period of history, not least in the mid-nineteenth century when

Charlotte Brontë was writing *Shirley* and remembering her own and her sisters' struggles to earn their bread; and Caroline's plea to the 'men of England' casts a more benign light on early Jewish attitudes to women's work and wellbeing. The provision for women in the Mishnah and Talmud suggests that as long as a wife fulfilled her domestic and childbearing functions, her material and emotional weal would be catered for within the limits of her husband's income and capabilities, and the religious community's power to monitor and enforce its own social regulations. Caroline's modest ambition for women is to play a supportive role to their male relatives; the virtuous wife, too, strives always for others, for the benefit of her family and the reputation of her husband, and is content to be rewarded with praise, but she also has the not-to-be-lightly despised satisfactions of constant occupation, a roof over her head, food to eat and clothes on her back, probably of her own making, and a position of authority over her household. As always, when assessing the pros and cons of women's lives at any period of history, one has to consider the alternatives. In the case of early Jewish women, marriage was almost certainly a better option than prostitution, slavery, or a subordinate role as penniless dependant in some other woman's household.

'If she will not do as you tell her, get rid of her'

> It may be written with anything – ink, caustic, red dye, gum,
> copperas, or with whatsoever is lasting; but it may not be written
> with liquids or fruit-juice or with whatsoever is not lasting. It
> may be written on anything – on an olive-leaf or on a cow's
> horn (and he must give her the cow) or on the hand of a slave
> (and he must give her the slave).
> *Mishnah, Gittin* 2:3

THE CHARM FOR the modern reader of this quaint ruling on divorce should not disguise its ominous implications. A man's right to divorce an unsatisfactory wife by handing her a bill of divorcement was enshrined in both biblical and mishnaic law. The principle is established in Deuteronomy: 'When a man hath taken a wife, and married her, and it come to pass that she find no favour in his eyes, because he hath found some uncleanness in her: then let him write her a bill of divorcement, and give it in her hand, and send her out of his house' (Deut. 24:1). Mishnaic commentary is concerned with the legally acceptable methods of preparing and delivering the bill, and the conditions under which divorce was permitted, but its discussion assumes that it is the husband's right to initiate divorce, and the 'essential formula' in the bill of divorce is directed at the woman, 'Lo, thou art free to marry any man'. The woman's lack of power in the making and breaking of the marriage bond is confirmed by the introductory statement in the betrothal legislation: 'By three means is the woman acquired and by two means she acquires her freedom. She is acquired by money or by writ or by intercourse . . . And she acquires her freedom by a bill of divorce or by the death of her husband'.

Deuteronomy is vague on the grounds for divorce, 'because he hath found some uncleanness in her', and the Rabbis were divided over how to interpret this passage, with the patrician Shammaite group taking a more conservative stance than the more liberal, plebeian Hillelites:

> The School of Shammai say: A man may not divorce his wife unless he has found unchastity in her, for it is written, *Because he hath found in her* indecency *in anything*. And the School of Hillel say: [He may divorce her] even if she spoiled a dish for him, for it is written, *Because he hath found in her indecency in* anything.

Rabbi Akiba goes even further, saying that a man may divorce his wife 'Even if he found another fairer than she, for it is written, *And it shall be if she find no favour in his eyes* . . . '. The one constraint on a man's divorcing his wife for the sake of a badly cooked meal or the fleeting glimpse of a more shapely ankle was the requirement to pay her the money legally pledged to her on marriage by the *ketubah*. Originating with the scriptural idea of the bride-price, this written agreement promised the wife a specified sum of money in the event of her husband's death or in some instances of divorce, one of the ways in which society tried to protect widows and other husbandless women. Payment of the *ketubah* might act as a powerful deterrent to whimsical behaviour, particularly if a considerable sum had been promised. However, even here, the Mishnah gives examples of behaviour that disqualify the divorced wife from receiving the *ketubah*, if, for instance, she was constrained by a vow that she had failed to reveal to her husband when he married her, or possessed bodily defects of which he was unaware.

Although a woman was not able to divorce her husband, she could ask the Jewish court to support her claim to be given a divorce in certain circumstances, but again, the act of divorce was seen as the man's prerogative. Physical repulsion was one reason that could be attested as justification for such a request, but there is evidence of a double standard at work in the rabbinic discussion over which defects in the husband were serious enough to warrant supporting the wife's claim:

> And these are they that are compelled to put away their wives:
> he that is afflicted with boils, or that has a polypus, or that
> collects [dog's excrements], or that is a coppersmith or a tanner
> . . . And of all these Rabbi Meir said: Although the husband
> made it a condition with her [to marry him despite his defects],
> she may say, 'I thought that I could endure it, but now I cannot
> endure it'. But the Sages say: She must endure him in spite of
> herself, save only him that is afflicted with boils, because she will
> enervate him [i.e. through sexual intercourse].

At a later period, childlessness was included as a ground to support a woman's claim to be divorced, if it could be proved that the husband might be to blame, and if the woman wanted children to look after her in old age, but in this case the sages were anxious to establish that the woman was not allowing personal preference or monetary considerations to weigh in her demand, and, as always, it was the husband not the wife who was responsible for issuing the bill of divorcement. While a man's tastes and personal responses to his wife were important considerations, a woman's negative feelings about her husband might be used as a reason to refuse her request to be divorced.

In all the rabbinic discussions about divorce, the emphasis is on the wife's behaviour, not the husband's, which suggests that women were subject to close scrutiny and constraint at all stages of their lives, particularly by power-hungry husbands and interfering religious leaders. Apart from the more serious charge of adultery, which could be proved by witnesses, a woman's own admission, or the barbaric trial by ordeal, a wife could be divorced for behaviour as trivial as eating or drinking greedily in the street, or suckling her baby in public, or even, according to Rabbi Akiba, 'as soon as gossips who spin in the moon light begin to talk about her', although another Rabbi felt that this was too extreme. 'If you go so far, you will not leave our father Abraham a single daughter who can stay with her husband.' The evidence from the rabbinic writings suggests that women did not hold a monopoly on scurrilous gossip; many a woman must have shuddered at a sideways glance from one of the community 'wise men', or flinched from an accusatory rabbinic finger. Concern for a man's social position and authority in the community are at the heart of these kinds of criticism, which seek to constrain frivolous or unseemly behaviour on the part of wives who were frequently barely teenagers when they first married, while other prescriptions stress the husband's emotional wellbeing. The sage and teacher, Ben Sira, considered it a moral duty to divorce a 'bad' wife, and although the misery of living with a sour, contentious companion should not be discounted, there is no disguising the rancour of his attack on women, which contains, too, the reference to Eve's responsibility for human mortality mentioned earlier:

> I would sooner keep house with a lion or a dragon
>> than keep house with a spiteful wife.
>
> A woman's spite changes her appearance
>> and makes her face as grim as any bear's . . .
>
> Sin began with a woman
>> and thanks to her we all must die.
> Do not let water find a leak,
>> do not allow a spiteful woman free rein for her tongue.
> If she will not do as you tell her,
>> get rid of her.

By contrast, 'A perfect wife is the joy of her husband,/he will live out the years of his life in peace', but Ben Sira's definition of the perfect wife runs true to form:

> The grace of a wife will charm her husband,
>> her accomplishments will make him the stronger.
> A silent wife is a gift from the Lord,
>> no price can be put on a well-trained character.
> A modest wife is a boon twice over,
>> a chaste character cannot be weighed on scales.
> Like the sun rising over the mountains of the Lord
>> is the beauty of a good wife in a well-kept house.

Grace, accomplishments that enhance her husband's reputation, silence, modesty and chastity, and good housekeeping – so far, so respectable, but carried away by eloquence and his own erotic imagination, Ben Sira suddenly loses his grip, and a satyr leers from behind the venerable eye-glasses:

> Like the lamp shining on the sacred lamp-stand
>> is a beautiful face on a well-proportioned body.
> Like golden pillars on a silver base
>> are shapely legs on firm-set heels.

'Be fruitful, and multiply'

EVE'S DESTINY AS childbearer was her most important legacy to her daughters, painfully if triumphantly fulfilled in the lives of the three 'matriarchs', Sarah, Rebekah and Rachel, who played such crucial roles in the early history of Israel. But, as the exclusion of Noah's daughters-in-law from the command to 'Be fruitful, and multiply' implies, procreation was regarded as a male rather than a female responsibility. The Rabbis were troubled that God's command to the first couple in Genesis 1:28, 'Be fruitful, and multiply, and replenish the earth, and subdue it', might be interpreted as giving power to the woman as well as the man. This was obviously ridiculous: 'it is the nature of a man to *subdue* but it is not the nature of a woman to subdue. On the contrary!' To get round this difficulty, they argued that since the verb 'subdue' is written in the singular form, the whole command is addressed solely to Adam, hence: 'A man is commanded concerning procreation, but not a woman'. Rabbi Eliezer regarded a man's failure to produce children as equivalent to committing murder, a capital crime: 'He who does not engage in propagation of the race is as though he sheds blood', and childlessness was considered grounds for a man to divorce his wife, 'If a man took a wife and lived with her for ten years and she bore no child, he shall divorce her'. However, the man should also return the wife's *ketubah*, since the responsibility for barrenness was not regarded by the Rabbis as unequivocally the woman's. The *Babylonian Talmud* discusses the case of the childless woman who marries for a third time: the Rabbis take care of the infertility issue by specifying that she must only marry a man who already has children, or else incur serious financial and social penalties. The question then arises as to whether, if she continues to be childless, her first two husbands can reclaim the jointure paid, in accordance with the *ketubah*, when they divorced her. Must the wife forfeit these payments, or is she allowed to claim that 'It is only now that I have deteriorated'? The Rabbis, perhaps surprisingly, decide that it is perfectly reasonable for her to make the latter plea. Futhermore, if a husband and wife dispute the responsibility for infertility, each blaming the other, the wife's testimony is valued over the husband's: 'In private matrimonial affairs the wife is believed. And what is the reason? – She is in a position to know whether emission is forceful [lit. 'shoots like an arrow', which was believed to be essential to fertilization], but he is not in a position to know it.'

At the root of biblical and rabbinic legislation about procreation was the ideal of inheritance as an indisputable line from father to son to grandson, with the rights of a dead man protected through the levirate laws whereby brothers or other close family members married the widow, as Boaz protected Mahlon's inheritance by marrying Ruth. Accordingly, boy children were valued above girls: at the birth of a boy, 'all rejoice', but at the birth of a girl, 'everybody is upset'. Even more damning, 'As soon as a male comes into the world peace comes into the world', but a female 'has nothing with her'. Ensuring legal paternity, the passing of the immaculate baton of inheritance from father to son, lay behind one of the most savage rituals that women were exposed to, the trial by ordeal, described in the book of Numbers, but possibly still applied seven centuries later, as discussions in the Mishnah imply. As described in Numbers, a husband can subject his wife to trial by ordeal if he as much as suspects her of infidelity, so that a wife can be arraigned simply on the grounds of her husband's jealousy, the argument being that innocence will carry her through unscathed – presumably until the next time the jealous fit falls. The suspicious man brings his wife to the priest with an offering of barley meal, 'an offering of jealousy, an offering of memorial, bringing iniquity to remembrance' (Numb. 5:15). The priest then takes holy water in an earthenware pot, mixes it with dust from the Temple floor and pronounces a solemn curse, to which the woman must say, 'Amen', and she is made to drink:

> then it shall come to pass, that, if she be defiled, and have done trespass against her husband, that the water that causeth the curse shall enter into her, and become bitter, and her belly shall swell, and her thigh shall rot: and the woman shall be a curse among her people.
>
> And if the woman be not defiled, but be clean; then she shall be free, and shall conceive seed.
>
> (Num. 5:27–8)

If the woman passes the test, she will bear a child whose legitimacy has been attested by sacred ritual. If she fails, she is rushed out of the Temple Court so as not to defile it; while her symptoms – the swollen belly and rotten thigh – may imply that, if she is pregnant at the time of the ordeal, she will suffer an aborted foetus and even permanent sterility, since, according to the test, the child she carries is probably illegitimate. Whatever the outcome, the husband emerges unscathed and is not penalized, even if his suspicions are proved to have been unfounded.

The biblical account of the trial is unpleasant enough, but mishnaic elaborations confirm that one of the purposes of the trial was the public humiliation of the woman – a warning to other women of what to expect if they behaved in such a way as to invite suspicion:

> A priest lays hold on her garments – if they are torn they are torn, if they are utterly rent they are utterly rent – so that he lays bare her bosom. Moreover he loosens her hair.

Here, Rabbi Judah prudently interpolates: 'If her bosom was comely he did not lay it bare; if her hair was comely he did not loosen it.'

> If she was clothed in white garments he clothed her in black. If she bore ornaments of gold and chains and nose-rings and finger-rings, they were taken from her to shame her. He then brought an Egyptian rope [a rope made of rushes] and tied it above her breasts. Any that wished to behold came and beheld, excepting her bondmen and bondwomen, since with them she feels no shame. And all women are allowed to behold her, for it is written, *That all women may be taught not to do after your lewdness.*

Whether the ordeal ritual was still practised in exactly this form by the time the Mishnah came to be written down is uncertain – the Jerusalem Temple, with the special patch of ground where the priest scraped up the dirt to make the bitter water, had been in ruins for well over a century – but it did give rise to a discussion between the Rabbis about whether merit might temporarily preserve a woman from the ordeal. What emerges from the discussion is the sages' sense of woman as a sexual volcano always on the brink of eruption and in need of careful containment if the social, that is male, status quo is to be maintained. The discussion proposes that certain unspecified merits may suspend punishment for up to three years, and Ben Azzai recommends that a man should instruct his daughter in the Torah, the Law, so that she will be aware of this fact. Rabbi Eliezer, he of the gimlet eye where female misbehaviour is concerned, disagrees: 'If any man gives his daughter a knowledge of the Law it is as though he taught her lechery', a view supported by Rabbi Joshua: 'A woman has more pleasure in one *kab* with lechery than in nine *kabs* with modesty', that is, a woman prefers a poorer husband who has plenty of time for sex to a man who concentrates his energies on earning a good living. Rather more reasonably, Rabbi Simeon denies that merit will nullify the effects of the bitter water, because this would make the water generally ineffective, and call in doubt the honesty of innocent women who had drunk it without ill effects – people would assume that they were guilty but saved by previous merit. Rabbi Judah closes the discussion by saying that merit does hold the punishment in suspense, but a guilty woman who comes unscathed through the ordeal will be unable to bear children and will lose her good looks, 'she will waste away by degrees and in the end will die the selfsame death.' The twin punishments – infertility and loss of beauty – indicate the Rabbis' reading of female priorities.

'Praised be God that he has not created me a woman!'

THE RABBINIC DEBATE about whether a father should teach his daughter to study the Law may have applied only to those sections in the Mishnah relating to the trial by ordeal, or it may have implied a general liberality on the part of Ben Azzai regarding the education of daughters. Elsewhere the Mishnah does suggest that both boys and girls should be given access to the Law: in a discussion on what can and cannot be done on behalf of a man who is forbidden by vow to benefit from others' actions on his behalf, allowance is made to 'teach Scripture to his sons and to his daughters', but the editor's footnote ominously warns, 'Some texts omit "and to his daughters"', and the dominant impulse of the Mishnah was towards the exclusion of women from formal involvement in public religious practice, including communal study of the Torah. The rabbinic attitude to women is perhaps seen most clearly in their discussion about religious responsibilities, which, though strictly regulated for men, in the case of women were disposed according to a contradictory code apparently cobbled together with an eye to the interests of the male members of the family, and with the effect of downgrading female participation in the core activity of Judaic life, the pursuit of religious excellence. Essential to rabbinic Judaism was observation of Mosaic Law, the obligations that God had dictated to Moses on Mount Sinai, and which were recorded in the Scriptures and formally elaborated in the Mishnah and Talmud. These rules were binding on all free adult males, but there were various categories of exemption for women, children and slaves. All the negative injunctions, the 'Thou shalt nots', had to be observed by men and women equally; the positive commandments were divided into activities that had to be carried out at a particular time, such as hearing the *shofar*, the ram's-horn, which was sounded on prescribed occasions in the Temple and in the synagogue service, or wearing *tefillin*, phylacteries that had to be worn during prayer at particular times of the day, and activities that were not time-specific, such as giving charity, or affixing the *mezuzah*, the scroll containing God's words from Deuteronomy 6:4–9 and 11:13–21, to the door of the house. In theory, women were exempted from all time-specific practices, presumably because these might interfere with their domestic duties – a woman could not easily abandon a crying baby or preparation of a meal in order to attend communal prayers; but exceptions to the rules obliged women to carry out certain time-related activities, such as eating unleavened bread at Passover, and exempted them from others not limited to time, such as study of the Torah, with the effect that women were expediently confined to the domestic sphere. As Judith Romney Wegner explains, this stems from Eve's God-given role in Eden as Adam's '*ēzer*, or helpmate:

> [Woman's] value as enabler (the '*fitting helper*' of Gen. 2:18) in
> freeing her man from domestic chores that might impede his
> own performance of Scripture's precepts overrides any personal
> desire she may have for more active involvement in the cult.
> Woman's duty – first, last, and always – is to take care of the
> physical needs of husband, home, and children so that men
> may pursue unhampered the more intellectually and spiritually
> rewarding cultic and religious duties of the Israelite.

According to the Mishnah, there are only three precepts incumbent on women, and the Rabbis ruthlessly exploited what must have been a universal female fear of death through childbirth to reinforce the carrying-out of these requirements: 'For three transgressions do women die in childbirth: for heedlessness of the laws of the menstruant, the Dough-offering [Hallah], and the lighting of the [Sabbath] lamp.' These injunctions concerned the requirement to observe *Niddah*, the strict laws of menstrual purity; the ritual separation and burning of a small piece of dough, the Hallah, in memory of the Temple tithes, when making the unleavened bread traditionally eaten on certain festivals; and responsibility for lighting candles or a lamp before sundown on the

eve of the Sabbath, so that when the men returned from communal worship later in the evening when Sabbath restrictions were
already in place, they would not be tempted to break the Sabbath
by lighting the lamp themselves, or else have to sit in the dark.
The justification for these three commands was linked in a number
of rabbinic sources to the claim that Eve was responsible for
causing Adam's death:

> Concerning menstruation: The first man was the blood and life
> of the world . . . and Eve was the cause of his death [*Genesis
> Rabbah*: she shed the blood of Adam]; therefore has she been
> given the menstruation precept. The same is true concerning
> Hallah (leaven); Adam was the pure Hallah for the world . . .
> And Eve was the cause of his death [*Genesis Rabbah*: she
> corrupted Adam]; therefore has she been given the Hallah
> precept. And concerning the lighting of the (Sabbath) lamp.
> Adam was the light of the world . . . And Eve was the cause of
> his death [*Genesis Rabbah:* she extinguished the soul of Adam,
> i.e. made him mortal]; therefore has she been given the precept
> about lighting the (Sabbath) lamp.

By the second century AD, Eve's responsibility for Adam's death
had become a commonplace of Jewish pseudepigraphic narratives,
the popular fiction of early Judaism, in which religious belief was
explored and developed through imaginative storytelling which
drew on a wide variety of legends and beliefs, many of which had
their roots in the broader history and culture of the Ancient Near
East; and these narratives in turn fed into and influenced early
Christian ideology. The Church Father Tertullian's criticisms of
Eve as 'the devil's gateway' reminded women that they participated
in their foremother's guilt: 'And do you not know that you are
[each] an Eve?' What is of particular interest here is that the three
tasks for which women are given specific responsibility in the
Mishnah appear to have been linked in the rabbinic mind with
penance rather than entrusted to women as an endorsement of
female value and abilities, and were in any case tasks which, whilst
incumbent on men, could not easily be carried out by them,
without great inconvenience and possibly even breaking other

religious injunctions. Women were conventionally responsible for baking the Hallah, and were more than likely to be at home on the evening of the Sabbath as they were exempt by gender from attending communal worship at this time; similarly, only a woman knew the details of her menstrual cycle, and was best qualified to protect her husband and family from infringing the strict menstrual taboos.

The Mishnah devotes an entire section, *Niddah*, to regulations concerning the menstruant, many of which rely on a woman's intimate knowledge of her bodily emissions, and a husband had to rely on his wife to understand and follow *Niddah* rules in order to protect his ability to participate in cultic or religious practice, which extended to taking meals at home, where rituals of blessing and ablution reflected the sacrificial customs of the lost Temple, and meant the meticulous avoidance of contact with unclean objects. Although the mechanisms of reproduction and female biology were barely understood at this time, and influenced by Greek notions of women as 'imperfect' or 'undeveloped' men, the purity laws should not necessarily be seen as particularly discriminatory against women; other forms of bodily emission, including ejaculation, were also subject to control. What the menstrual laws do indicate is that protection of the man from pollution is the priority, and it is the woman's duty to maintain the menstrual rules for her husband's sake rather than to preserve her own cultic purity.

It is impossible to browse through the rabbinic writings without a growing conviction that a woman's contribution to religious life was given substantially less weight than a man's. The *Tosephta*, a supplement to the Mishnah probably compiled at about the same period, records the threefold daily prayer in which the free Jewish male gives thanks for his birthright: 'Praised be God that he has not created me a gentile! Praised be God that he has not created me a woman! Praised be God that he has not created me an ignoramus!' This is not quite so dismissive of women as it appears at face value; the prayer goes on to say that a man would not want to be a woman, 'because the woman is not obliged to fulfill the commandments', but as Rabbi Ḥahina pointed out: 'He who is commanded and does, stands higher than he [or she] who is not commanded and does.' Even if a woman fulfils the Torah, the performance of a commandment that is not obligatory has less merit than if it is a positive requirement. It is worth recalling that the commandments were recorded, debated and elaborated by men.

Lock up your daughters

The Sages spoke in a parable about woman: [She is like] an unripe fig, or a ripening fig, or a fully ripe fig: 'an unripe fig' – while she is yet a child; and 'a ripening fig' – these are the days of her girlhood (and during both times her father is entitled to aught that she finds and to the work of her hands, and he can annul her vows); and 'a fully ripe fig' – after she is past her girlhood, when her father no more has any rights over her.
   Mishnah, Niddah 5:7

THE PERIOD OF 'girlhood' was restricted to a six-month period between the ages of twelve and twelve and a half, a crucial time for both father and daughter in the marriage stakes, because after this a daughter attained her majority and could become autonomous, with significant legal powers that included the right 'to own and dispose of property, to conduct business, to engage in litigation, and most important to choose her own husband from among her suitors'. The norm seems to have been for a daughter to be married off before achieving independence, possibly because a young, malleable wife was preferable to an older, more self-assured woman, although there was an attempt in both Scripture and Mishnah to encourage and regulate marriage with widows. The extreme youth of many first-time brides combined with the heavy burden of household responsibilities expected of them perhaps explain the careful provision to ensure that a wife was properly looked after and her behaviour monitored. Although a daughter passed to the control of her husband once she was married, her conduct within marriage continued to be of concern to her father. The *Midrash Rabbah* argues that daughters are a blessing, and tells a charming story to illustrate a father's good will towards his daughter:

Rabbi Gamaliel gave his daughter in marriage. 'Father,' she requested, 'pray for me.' 'May you never return hither,' said he to her. When she gave birth to a son she again begged him, 'Father, give me your blessing.' 'May "woe" never leave your mouth,' replied he. 'Father,' she exclaimed, 'on both occasions of my rejoicing you have cursed me!' 'Both were blessings,' he replied. 'Living at peace in your home, you will not return here, and as long as your son lives, "woe" will not leave your mouth; "woe that my son has not eaten," "woe that he has not drunk," "woe that he has not gone to school."'

Predictably, Ben Sira paints a gloomier picture of a father's responsibilities, which he interprets as close guardianship of a daughter's naturally rapacious sexuality:

> Over thy daughter keep a strict watch,
> Lest she make thee a name of evil odour –
> A byword in the city and accursed of the people –
> And shame thee in the assembly of the gate.
> In the place where she lodgeth let there be no lattice,
> Or spot overlooking the entrance round about.
> Let her not show her beauty to any male,
> And among wives let her not converse.
> For from the garment issueth the moth,
> And from a woman a woman's wickedness.
> Better is the wickedness of a man than the goodness of a woman;
> And a disgraceful daughter poureth forth disgrace.

Ben Sira's concern is with the father's reputation, threatened by woman's tendency towards promiscuous behaviour, a Juliet continually peeping through her window in hope of a chat with Romeo. The only value that a daughter offers her father is negative, she is to her father 'a treasure of sleeplessness' as he tosses and turns in bed all night, worrying about her prospects:

> In her youth, lest she pass the flower of her age,
> And when she is married, lest she be hated;

In her virginity, lest she be seduced,
    And in the house of her husband, lest she prove unfaithful;
In her father's house, lest she become pregnant,
    And in her husband's house, lest she be barren.

Ben Sira's alarming scenario, where marriage brings no relief to
the desperate father, can be seen as the mirror image of Rabbi
Gamaliel's more optimistic and benign dealings with his daughter,
and epitomizes a strand of misogyny that is interwoven with even
the most apparently reasonable rabbinic writings on women. The
idea that women are best kept secluded at home, away from the
marketplace and the company of other wives, is a commonplace of
rabbinic thinking: 'the man must master his wife, that she go not
out into the market place, for every woman who goes out into the
market place will eventually come to grief.' The Rabbis cite as an
example Jacob and Leah's unfortunate daughter Dinah, who 'went
out to see the daughters of the land' (Gen. 34:1), and was taken and
ravished by Shechem, the son of Hamor the Hivite. Although he
promptly fell in love with Dinah and offered to marry her, her
brothers seized the opportunity to play a terrible trick on Shechem
and his father. They agreed to the marriage if all the men of his city
would be circumcised, and on the third day, when the male
population were still recovering from the surgery, the brothers
overran the city, slaughtered the men, and took possession of their
wives and goods (Gen. 34:2–29). The rabbinic suggestion that
women left to their own devices are bound to cause trouble echoes
the story of Eve's misbehaviour in the Garden of Eden when found
on her own by the serpent, and Dinah's history in medieval
Christian commentary parallels Eve's later reputation as a mischief-
causing seductress. The author of the thirteenth-century *Ancren
Riwle*, a book of devotional advice written for nuns, blames Dinah
for the massacre and burning of the city: 'this evil . . . came of
Dinah . . . not from her seeing Sichem [*sic*] . . . with whom she
sinned, but . . . from her letting him set his eyes upon her.' Not
only is woman a threat to masculine self-control, but she must take
the blame if matters do get out of hand.

In Thomas Mann's sensitive retelling of the story in *Joseph and
His Brothers*, Dinah is the childish and pathetic victim of her

brothers' greed and power-mongering rather than of Shechem's lechery or any provocative self-flaunting on her part, and her fate is tragic. As the young girl leaves the devastated city with her father and brothers, 'that place of horror, over which the vultures were circling', she lets down the shade over her camel-basket and rides on in prescient darkness: 'She was with child. When her time came, the infant she brought into the world was exposed, by the stern command of her menfolk. She herself pined and withered long before her time. When she was fifteen her poor little face looked like an old woman's.' Early Jewish legend, ever anxious to tie up loose ends and provide explanations for what was puzzling in the Scriptures, envisaged a kinder fate for Dinah's baby daughter, suggesting that she was carried by an eagle to Egypt and cradled on the altar of the priest Potiphar, who took her home and reared her in great splendour and chastity, until eventually the girl, Aseneth, was given by the Pharaoh in marriage to Dinah's brother Joseph, son of Jacob and Rachel, he of the many-coloured coat and the spectacular rise to power as the Pharaoh's favourite. This account of Aseneth's racially respectable origins no doubt evolved to satisfy critics who queried how the Jewish hero Joseph could have married the heathen daughter of an Egyptian priest (Gen. 41:45).

In the centuries around the birth of Christ, Jewish women led strictly confined lives, particularly wealthier women in the larger towns and cities. Country women were allowed relatively more freedom, because of the nature of their work, drawing water, working in the fields, selling olives and other produce, but the wives and daughters of the rich were kept carefully indoors. Writing about Jewish women in Egypt, the philosopher Philo describes a positively harem-like existence: 'Their women are kept in seclusion, never even approaching the outer doors, and their maidens are confined to the inner chambers, who for modesty's sake avoided the sight of men, even of their closest relations.' Women were permitted to go out only for religious purposes, to visit the temple, and even then they were to avoid the busy market hours when the streets were teeming with shoppers and traders. Women in Palestinian Judaism were almost as closely confined: 'These are they that are put away without their *Ketubah*: a wife that transgresses the Law of Moses and Jewish custom . . . And what [conduct is such that transgresses] Jewish custom? If she goes out with her hair unbound, or spins in the street, or speaks with any man.' The worry was that a woman spinning in the street would have to bare her arms, thus inciting male lust, an anxiety again reinforced by reference to the Dinah story, which seemed to exercise some kind of morbid fascination over the rabbinic mind. Quoting the text, 'And Dinah the daughter of Leah went out',

> Rabbi Berekiah said . . .: This may be compared to one who was holding a pound of meat in his hand, and as soon as he exposed it a bird swooped down and snatched it away. Similarly, AND DINAH THE DAUGHTER OF LEAH WENT OUT, and forthwith, AND SHECHEM THE SON OF HAMOR SAW HER. Rabbi Samuel b. Naḥman said: Her arm became exposed.

It is tempting to reverse the meanings of rabbinic and other Jewish religious writings about women in order to propose an alternative reading of Jewish women as feistily rebellious, slipping out from their inner courtyards for communal gossip sessions with other women in the street, busily working their spindles, casually dressed for housework, with their hair bundled all anyhow on top of their heads and slipping from its pins. Ben Sira's anxiety about daughters could reflect a state of affairs where girls took every opportunity to exploit their sexuality, and bastard children and adultery were commonplace. However, the detailed framework of laws monitoring sexual relations, marriage and childbirth, including the death penalty for women convicted of adultery and even the victims of rape in certain conditions, militates against any such anachronistic reading. The Jewish legal codes encapsulate a view of society that favoured stable, faithful, fruitful marriage as the best possible environment in which a man might pursue his religious duties, and a woman be kept content and out of mischief, preoccupied with the management of her household and the correct rearing of her children.

Tinkling feet

IN BEN SIRA'S worries regarding daughters, in the story of Dinah, and in the rabbinic anxieties that studying the Torah will encourage woman's natural bent towards lasciviousness, we see the seeds of later Christian hostility to female adornment. Cosmetics and clothes loom large in the evolution of Eve's bad character, as she becomes linked in Jewish religious literature with the exotic Watcher angels who taught women the seductive arts of make-up and jewellery, and with admonitory accounts of feminine wiles and lust. In these narratives, female adornment is a metaphor for (wicked) female desire: women are categorized according to how they dress, and an alluring presentation is read as an invitation to sexual dalliance that will rob the male of his self-control and leave him powerless to resist, just as Adam was hijacked by Eve's tempting offer of the forbidden fruit. In the second-century-BC Jewish *Testament of Reuben*, the dying patriarch warns his sons:

> 'women are evil, my children, and by reason of their lacking
> authority or power over man, they scheme treacherously how
> they might entice him to themselves by means of their looks.'

An attractive appearance can offer women a way of exerting power in situations where they are otherwise without resource, and the sheer weight of commentary by early Jewish and Christian writers on female dress and cosmetics suggests male susceptibility to a well-presented woman. But there is something disquieting about the terms in which this male anxiety is expressed, a vehemence that verges on the manic, and it is difficult to understand quite what these men were so alarmed about. The energy they expend in trying to control sexual behaviour and to negate desire seems to backfire, creating an equally powerful urge towards the forbidden fruit. Despite a social system that regarded marriage and children as the desirable norm, the Rabbis apparently suffered from repressed sexuality as acutely as the ascetic Christian Fathers. This obsession with sexuality was taken to ridiculous lengths: witness the sages' weighty discussion of the implications of such everyday occurrences as a man falling from a raised bench or even a roof with an erect penis and thereby 'accidentally' penetrating his sister-in-law who just happened to be beneath him when he fell. In such a sexually charged climate, the equivalent of 'a glimpse of stocking' would have been likely to cause a stampede, and the Rabbis guarded against this and similar eventualities with meticulous warnings against walking behind a woman, crossing a river with a woman (because she would naturally lift her skirt and 'A woman's leg is a sexual incitement'), against talking with women, looking closely at a beautiful woman, even gazing at a woman's 'gaudy garments'. All these would lead to unclean sexual desires. Worst of all was for a man to gaze at a woman's little finger, for 'it is as if he gazed at her secret place'. At the same time, even when menstruating and therefore sexually taboo, a woman should make herself as attractive as possible for her husband: 'the early Sages ruled: . . . [a menstruous woman] must not rouge nor paint nor adorn herself in dyed garments; until Rabbi Akiba came and taught: If so, you make her repulsive to her husband, with the result that he will divorce her!'

Given that female sexuality was so carefully protected and controlled, the near apoplexy with which most religious leaders regarded make-up and brightly coloured clothes is perhaps unsurprising. Among the many Sabbath restrictions discussed by the Rabbis was the carrying of even very tiny quantities of stibium, a metallic element widely used to enhance the appearance of the eyes. It was forbidden to pick up even enough stibium to paint one eye. 'One eye?' queries a Rabbi, and Rabbi Huna replies that modest women only paint one eye. Jewish women were expected to cover their heads and faces when they appeared in public with an elaborate arrangement of plaits and kerchiefs, a decorated hairnet, and a band across the forehead with ribbons that dangled down to the chin. One eye would presumably have been left uncovered in order to be able to see where they were going. This passing reference, of interest to the Rabbis solely in the context of Sabbath regulations, casts an unexpected beam of light on the women of early Judaism, freezing a snapshot image of women in homes throughout the Jewish diaspora, from Palestine to the Elephantine colony far up the Nile near Aswan, resolutely decorating the one part of their bodies which they were permitted to expose to public view, the unveiled eye. What did they see as they gazed through that restricted aperture? And how different was the self looking out from what the viewer saw, the modestly concealed form of a woman, with the boldly painted eyelid signposting the bright consciousness within?

The reference to gaudy clothes already quoted from the rabbinic writings indicates another way in which women might have flouted the restrictions, as does the use of showy jewellery – jangling bangles on wrists and ankles, and flashes of bright gems in nose and ear – although other Jewish stories suggest that expensive clothes and adornments would have been proofs of wealth and distinction, indicating a man's ability to dress and maintain a beautiful wife. One of the most vicious attacks on women's adornments in the Scriptures is the diatribe in Isaiah against the haughty daughters of Zion, who 'walk with stretched forth necks and wanton eyes, walking and mincing as they go, and making a tinkling with their feet' (Isa. 3:16). However alluring these supercilious creatures, God will smite their jaunty heads and take away their extensive armoury of brave ornaments, described in the King James Version with an endearing disregard for changing fashion as:

> The chains, and the bracelets, and the mufflers,
>
> The bonnets, and the ornaments of the legs . . . the earrings,
>
> The rings, and nose jewels,
>
> The changeable suits of apparel, and the mantles, and the wimples, and the crisping pins,
>
> The glasses, and the fine linen . . .
>
> (Isa. 3:19–23)

The Jerusalem Bible uses brutal language to describe their fate:

> Instead of scent, a stink;
> instead of belt, a rope;
> instead of hair elaborately done, a shaven scalp,
> and instead of gorgeous dress, a sack;
> and brand marks instead of beauty.
>
> (Isa. 3:24)

This aversion to female 'stink', the stripping down of seductiveness to a foetid materiality, continued into the early Christian period and well into the Middle Ages, and finds distasteful echoes in twentieth-century misogyny. St John Chrysostom, John 'Golden Mouth', writing in the fourth century AD for the benefit of his Christian congregation at Antioch, responds with shuddering fervour to the lure of women, averting his eyes and holding his nose in a paroxysm of desiring distaste:

> if you consider what is stored up inside those beautiful eyes, and
> that straight nose, and the mouth and the cheeks, you will affirm
> the well-shaped body to be nothing else than a whited sepulchre;
> the parts within are full of so much uncleanness. Moreover when
> you see a rag with any of these things on it, such as phlegm, or
> spittle[,] you cannot bear to touch it with even the tips of your
> fingers, nay you cannot even endure looking at it; and yet are
> you in a flutter of excitement about the storehouses and
> depositories of these things?

He sees the skull beneath the skin, and for him it reeks of corruption, but St John's comments, like those of the Jewish sages, seem to be the product of anxious male fantasy rather than a balanced response to real women.

Eve and the Rabbis

THE RABBINIC WRITINGS about women imply a patriarchal society in which the protection of its female members was perceived as essential to the wellbeing of the community. A wife's happiness and dignity were important in so far as they promoted her husband's comfort, protected his social position and ensured the perpetuation of his family name, but the Jewish law codes enshrine a patriarchal belief in female inferiority and need for protection from their own weak natures. The *Letter of Aristeas*, written by an Alexandrine Jew possibly around 170 BC, tells the story of the Egyptian King Ptolemy II entertaining learned guests at a banquet and taking the opportunity to question them on various matters that interest him. ' "How can one reach agreement with a woman?"' he asks one of the scholars, an ancient variant of Freud's famous poser, 'What does a woman want?' The guest does not hesitate: '"By recognizing . . . that the female sex is bold, positively active for something which it desires, easily liable to change its mind because of poor reasoning powers, and of naturally weak constitution. It is necessary to have dealings with them in a sound way, avoiding provocation which may lead to a quarrel."' Woman's power rests in her unreasonable ability to be a nuisance, and a man demonstrates his superiority by allowing for her weakness and exerting firm control.

Female fallibility and the need for masculine guidance and control is apparent in the stories about Eve that appear in the *Midrash Rabbah*. According to one Jewish legend, before presenting the newly created Eve to Adam, God took the precaution of dressing her seductively as a bride, arranging her hair and adorning her with the twenty-four articles of finery that Isaiah had scorned when denouncing the mincing daughters of Israel. Like any wealthy father anxious to demonstrate his care for a beloved daughter, God provides Eve with the extravagant trappings of bridehood: an ample veil with an array of ribbons and headbands to cover her exquisitely plaited hair, an embroidered overdress and immaculate linen, scores of tinkling bracelets to encircle wrist and ankle, with jewelled rings for ear and nostril and to decorate each perfectly formed finger, and an abundance of floating scarves and wafting scent bottles to entice her waiting husband. In dreaming up this opulent scenario, which confirmed the bride's high economic value, the Rabbis drew on a mysterious text in Ezekiel, 'Thou hast been in Eden the garden of God; every precious stone was thy covering, the sardius, topaz, and the diamond, the beryl, the onyx, and the jasper, the sapphire, the emerald, and the carbuncle, and gold' (Ezek. 28:13). Not content with disguising Eve's gory origin in Adam's ribcage, God celebrates the marriage with elaborate ceremony, scurrying to set up the ten jewelled wedding canopies, and inviting the angels to cluster around the marriage tent while He pronounces the blessing, and then the heavenly guests dance and play musical instruments, flutes and tambourines and maybe even harps, to entertain the newlyweds. In telling this attractive tale, the Rabbis fail to mention an important detail: God performs the ritual adornment because Eve has no mother, nor any other female relative, to attend to her, not even a bosom friend or an ancient nurse. Like so many heroines of folklore, she is quite alone in the world. But this lack of attention to the mother–daughter relationship does not only apply to motherless Eve in Eden. The index to the English edition of the Mishnah lists 'Daughters, control over' and 'maintenance of', but these refer to fatherly and husbandly functions; the complex emotional and social interaction between a mother and her daughter does not appear to have been recognized in the Law codes. The most important affiliation in early Judaism was that between God and the male population, who acted as God's conduit for passing on information and exerting control over female behaviour.

This masculine pre-eminence was occasionally queried by the Rabbis, but only playfully. They were puzzled by a reference in Exodus that suggests that, when Moses and the Israelites were in the Sinai desert, God told Moses to relay His instructions to the female members of the group before briefing the men. The sages begin their discussion of God's curious request with explanations that validate women: 'Because they are prompt in the fulfilment of the commandments', or maybe, and this is even more of a compliment, 'So that they should introduce their children to the study of the Torah', but they cannot resist the opportunity for a joke at women's expense, and they conclude that the real reason for God's unusual instruction to Moses must have been woman's propensity for bad behaviour.

> ... God said: 'When I created the world, I only commanded
> Adam first, and then Eve, too, was commanded, with the result
> that she transgressed and upset the world; if I do not now call
> unto the women *first*, they will nullify the Torah'.

If women had not been given priority, they would have created havoc.

Far from endorsing a female context for women that embraces a network of family members and friends, Jewish religious literature promotes the idea that contact between women will inevitably lead to time-wasting gossip or the pursuit of lechery, and must be suppressed, and at its most extreme suggests that women are an alien and inferior species, to be approached with caution, although they may be freely discussed and should be ridiculed whenever an opportunity can be found. Their power to make trouble is canvassed in tones that veer from the humorously rueful to the undisguisedly misogynistic. In trying to explain why God gave Eve her peculiarly female characteristics, the Rabbis reveal their prejudices about the nature of woman, whom they see almost exclusively in relation to man. They describe God's careful ponderings before He decides to use Adam's rib to create Eve:

> Said He: 'I will not create her from [Adam's] head, lest she be swelled-headed; nor from the eye, lest she be a coquette; nor from the ear, lest she be an eavesdropper; nor from the mouth, lest she be a gossip; nor from the heart, lest she be prone to jealousy; nor from the hand, lest she be light-fingered; nor from the foot, lest she be a gadabout; but from the modest part of man, for even when he stands naked, that part is covered.'

Despite His forethought, God's plan goes horribly wrong:

> I did not create her from the head, yet she is swelled-headed . . .; nor from the eye, yet she is a coquette . . .; nor from the ear, yet she is an eavesdropper . . .; nor from the heart, yet she is prone to jealousy . . .; nor from the hand, yet she is light-fingered . . .; nor from the foot, yet she is a gadabout . . .

Adam's reception of his bride is at best equivocal: 'this is she who is destined to strike the bell and to speak [in strife] against me . . . it is she who troubled me all night.' The Rabbis are playing on the similarity between *pa'amon*, a golden bell, and *pa'am*, to trouble: Eve's voice, complaining and entreating, will toll in her husband's ear night and day.

As the first, prototype woman, Eve invites speculation about why God made her so different from man, and again the Rabbis cannot resist having fun with the rib:

> 'And why must a woman use perfume, while a man does not need perfume?' 'Man was created from earth,' [Rabbi Joshua] answered, 'and earth never putrefies, but Eve was created from a

bone. For example: if you leave meat three days unsalted, it immediately goes putrid.' 'And why has a woman a penetrating [shrill] voice, but not a man?' 'I will give you an illustration,' replied he. 'If you fill a pot with meat it does not make any sound, but when you put a bone into it, the sound [of sizzling] spreads immediately.' 'And why is a man easily appeased, but not a woman?' 'Man was created from the earth,' he answered, 'and when you pour a drop of water on it, it immediately absorbs it; but Eve was created from a bone, which even if you soak many days in water does not become saturated.'

These unpleasant accusations – of offensive personal odour, a piercing voice (again), and the inability to forgive and forget – are followed by the more serious charges that women are by nature guilty and were responsible for bringing death into the world:

'Why does a man go out bareheaded while a woman goes out with her head covered?' 'She is like one who has done wrong and is ashamed of people; therefore she goes out with her head covered.' 'Why do they [the women] walk in front of the corpse [at a funeral]?' 'Because they brought death into the world, they therefore walk in front of the corpse . . .'.

The point that these rules for female behaviour were man–made seems to have escaped the Rabbis. What is unmistakable is a moral atmosphere that puts women in the wrong, and this passage goes on to remind its readers of the three precepts already mentioned, the ritual observances enjoined on women because Eve shed Adam's blood by bringing the curse of death upon him, Eve corrupted his integrity and extinguished his immortal soul.

THE FULL HISTORY of Eve's entanglement with the seductive serpent is not to be found in the cautious gossip of the *Midrash Rabbah*. The Eve of the Rabbis is typically domestic, and her evolution as the first sexual temptress belongs to a parallel tradition that developed during the troubled centuries around the life of Christ: a cluster of stories that tell of the angels' lust for the daughters of men and Eve's dangerous encounter with a satanic adversary.

CHAPTER 3

ANGELIC LUST, DEVILISH ENVY

'I have sinned, LORD, I have sinned much; I have sinned before
you, and all sin in creation has come about through me.'
      Apocalypse of Moses, 32:2

————◆◆◆————

IN HIS LYRICAL 'EVE', first published in 1917, the poet Ralph
Hodgson imagines Eve as an innocent girl, a supple 'orchard
sprite' cynically seduced and then abandoned by the vengeful
serpent, who is intent on getting even with heaven for unspecified
wrongs. The only witnesses to the serpent's tricks are the birds in
Eden, who clatter angrily as the deceiver triumphantly takes his
leave, scolding him and pitying 'poor motherless Eve'. Robbed
of her dish of sweet berries and plums, Eve is left to wander the
lanes outside the orchard, haunting the garden gates that she will
never enter again, while in a tavern nearby, the serpent and his
cronies lewdly drink her health. Hodgson's sympathetic retelling of
Eve's history highlights her vulnerability and isolation, her sole
supporters the Titmouse and Jenny Wren, who can only nag after
the event and pity her gullibility. But the poem recalls a perplexing
aspect of the first Eden story: what was the serpent's motive for
tempting Eve? The answer to that question, and the origins of
Hodgson's persuasive narrative of seduction and revenge, may be
found in apocalyptic religious literature, the popular fiction of early
Judaism.

It is not surprising that the encounter between a naked girl and
her clever persuader, the most sinuously phallic of all the beasts,
should have come to be read as a seduction scene. The erotic
implications of the temptation of Eve were finally spelt out in a
narrative known as the *Apocalypse of Moses*, which probably dates to
the first century AD, but the foundations were laid much earlier in
works that sought to discover God's purposes in creating the
universe. Breathtakingly imaginative and ingenious, the writers of

these often extravagant narratives invented a whole new set of stories that explored the Scriptures and gave free rein to a story-teller's delight in fantasy. In the course of these reworkings, Eve became identified with dangerous sexuality, and the humble serpent took on the stature of an angel who dared to challenge God – the great dragon of Revelation, 'that old serpent, called the Devil, and Satan, which deceiveth the whole world' (Rev. 12:9). At the heart of their encounter was lust.

Angelic lust

EVE'S BEHAVIOUR and character came into new prominence around the second century BC, as rival Jewish sects increasingly speculated about the source of evil and the origins of human suffering. The difficulty they faced was that monotheism, the commitment to belief in an omnipotent God, left a questionmark over who was responsible for evil in the world. When disaster struck, famine or plague or a swarm of marauding locusts, when a man coveted his neighbour's wife or raised a murderous fist, who was to blame? Was human or divine agency at fault and, if the latter, what attitude were religious leaders to take towards sin? How far could humans be held accountable for their own bad actions? In their attempt to find a solution to these difficulties, commentators focused on two events described in the early chapters of Genesis – the curious episode of the 'sons of God' (the *benē 'elōhīm*), and human misbehaviour in the Garden of Eden – and fleshed out these simple stories into marvellous tales of titanic battles, cataclysmic ambition and, perhaps inevitably, the wicked wiles of seductive women. Through an intricate narrative chain, Eve's disobedience to God in the Garden of Eden became linked with a story of angelic revolt, and her reptilian tempter metamorphosed into God's cosmic opponent, the overreaching angel Satan.

The story of the rebellious angels had its origins in a curious interlude described in Genesis. In the centuries after Adam and Eve, 'men began to multiply on the face of the earth, and daughters were born unto them' (Gen. 6:1). Captivated by the beauty of these fair women, beings mysteriously known as the 'sons of God' came to earth and 'they took them wives of all which they chose' (Gen. 6:2). The narrator comments that this was a time when giants walked the earth, and the women bore children who 'became mighty men which were of old, men of renown' (Gen. 6:4). Immediately after this intriguing story, God observes that humanity has become irredeemably wicked, repents that He ever populated the earth and calls down the flood which only Noah and his family survive (Gen. 6:5ff). Probably the result of successive modifications by a series of editors, the disjointed narrative that survived as Genesis 6:1–5, and in particular the juxtaposition of the birth of the 'mighty men' (verse 4) with God's wrath at the wickedness of humanity (verse 5), raised a number of puzzling questions for religious scholars, who dreamed up ingenious solutions to explain the connection between the two events.

The story of the 'sons of God' was developed in a colourful work known as *1 Enoch*, which includes material dating from around the second century BC and probably even earlier. In Genesis, Enoch was a sixth-generation descendant of Adam and Eve, a man who 'walked with God' and whose fate remained enigmatic: 'and he was not; for God took him' (Gen. 5:24). This hint of a mystery set learned imaginations racing, and a tradition developed that Enoch was whisked away by God and given access to hidden knowledge: the secrets of the universe and what would happen to humanity in the course of its history. The longing to know the future has always been an important element in storytelling, and *1 Enoch* is a marvellous account of Enoch's tour of earth, Sheol and heaven, during which he is shown apocalyptic visions of the future of Israel, the judgement of sinners and the spiritual bliss of the virtuous. On his travels, Enoch visits Eden and sees the forbidden tree, which 'looked like the colours of the carob tree, its fruit like very beautiful grape clusters, and the fragrance of this tree travels and reaches afar'. But the writer of *1 Enoch* does not identify the events in Eden as the source of human wrongdoing. Instead, he turns to the story of the sons of God. In the section known as the 'Book of the Watchers', Enoch gives an expanded account of these beings, who have now become identified as angels and are known as the 'Watchers', probably a reference to their function as God's spies or agents. He begins with the birth of beautiful daughters to the 'children of men' and the Watchers' desire to marry them. Although this is a 'great sin', a company of two hundred angels swear to stick by their leader, Semyaz, and together they descend to the summit of Mount Hermon. They each select a human wife and share magic secrets with their spouses: incantations and valuable root and plant lore. In time, the women become pregnant and give birth to giants who are three hundred cubits tall, but far from being 'men of renown', as in the Genesis account, they grow up into monsters who devour the available food supply and then turn to cannibalism, consuming the human population and even one another.

At the same time, humanity has been corrupted by the knowledge the angels bring. The Watcher Pinem'e teaches the secrets of writing and, as the author drily remarks, 'on account of this matter, there are many who have erred . . . human beings are not created . . . to take up their beliefs with pen and ink'; and Azaz'el teaches the men how to make metal weapons and instructs the women in the arts of allure: the use of bracelets and jewels, of inviting eye make-up, 'and all colouring tinctures and alchemy', which leads to adultery and other sexual misdemeanours.

Meanwhile, the archangels Michael and Gabriel observe events from their vantage point in the sky and report back to God on the anarchy on earth. The Watchers are blamed for revealing the 'eternal secrets' of heaven, and for defiling themselves with human women and teaching them every kind of sin, and the women are accused of giving birth to giants 'to the degree that the whole earth was filled with blood and oppression'. In this influential development of the Watcher story, women are guilty of luring the Watchers to earth by their beauty – passive enticement was to be one of the major charges laid against women in the Christian tradition – and of succumbing to the angelic visitors, marrying them and giving birth to marauding giants. In particular, women are linked with forbidden knowledge and with sexual wrongdoing in which cosmetics and other feminine adornments play an essential role, and female sexuality is characterized as both contaminating and indiscriminate: women breed with no thought for the consequences.

Angry with the bloodshed and violence, God sends an angel to warn Noah of the coming flood, which is the direct result of the giants' activities, and His lieutenants, the four archangels, deal with the Watchers. Raphael buries Azaz'el in a hole in the desert, tossing sharp rocks down after him and leaving him to lie in darkness until the great day of judgement. The other Watchers are also confined underground until the final judgement and conflagration, and Gabriel sets the giants to fight one another to the death. Evil survives on earth, however, in the form of malignant spirits who emerge from the giants' dying bodies and remain to corrupt humanity. The fate of the 'daughters of men' is revealed during Enoch's tour of the earth, when the archangel Uriel takes him to a 'terrible place' at the rim of a deep pit, a site so desolate that even birds shun it. Lit by the flames of immeasurable pillars of fire, it is the torture chamber for stars who have angered God and is now the temporary prison house for the offending angels. Here Uriel reveals that the women who had mated with the angels ' "shall become sirens" ', an incorporation into Jewish apocalyptic of the fatal seductresses of Greek mythology which adds a new dimension of deadly allure to the story.

The story of the sirens is told in Homer's *Odyssey*. On his journey home from the Trojan War, the hero Odysseus is warned by the enchantress Circe against the sirens' bewitching song:

'There is no home-coming for the man who draws near them
unawares and hears the Sirens' voices; no welcome from his wife,
no little children brightening at their father's return.'

The sirens squat in a flowery meadow piled high with dead men's bones and sing out to passing ships, luring their victims with exquisite melody. On Circe's advice, Odysseus plugs his sailors' ears with beeswax and tells the men to bind him to the mast of his ship before he dares to encounter the sirens' 'liquid song', an irresistible music that promises him the priceless gift of foreknowledge. But as Circe makes clear, the penalty for stopping and engaging with the sirens is death. The classical scholar Jean-Pierre Vernant points out the sirens' combination of sexual allure with fatality: 'Their cries, their flowering meadow (*leimōn*, meadow, is one of the words used to designate female genitalia), their charm (*thelxis*) locates them in all their irresistibility unequivocally in the realm of sexual attraction or erotic appeal. At the same time, they are death, and death in its most brutally monstrous aspect: no funeral, no tomb, only the corpse's decomposition in the open air. Pure desire, pure death'. By his apparently casual reference, Uriel superimposes on the beautiful 'daughters of men' the malignant image of alluring (pagan) women who offer forbidden – and fatal – knowledge.

The story of the Watcher angels is elaborated in *Jubilees*, a commentary on Genesis that probably dates from around the middle to the end of the second century BC. In this account, the Watcher angels come to earth by God's decree, in order to teach humanity and to maintain law and order. In the course of time, however, the beauty of human women perverts the angels and leads to the birth of giants, who, as before, degenerate into cannibalism. The Watchers are again bound in the depths of the earth to await the final judgement and, once more, the monsters destroy one another. Somehow, however, demoniac spirits survive both this slaughter and the Flood, and begin to lead Noah's sons and grandsons into evil ways. Noah points out to God that matters are heading yet again for disaster, but Mastema, the leader of the wicked spirits, persuades God to allow him to retain one tenth of his followers to continue their work of corrupting the wicked and to ' "be subject to Satan upon the earth" '.

Jubilees does give an account of the Eden story, but, as in *1 Enoch*, the mating of the Watcher angels with human women rather than Eve's bite of the forbidden fruit explains the origin of evil on earth. *Jubilees* says that Adam and Eve are evicted from the Garden of Eden because they have been disobedient, and the animals are also punished. Until that moment 'the beasts and cattle and birds and whatever walked or moved' had been able to communicate using 'one language', but now they lose the power of speech. In a variation on the original story, Eve covers herself with a fig leaf *before* she offers the fruit to Adam, a logical response given that she has already eaten the fruit, and it emphasizes that physical shame was its immediate result.

There is still no suggestion in *Jubilees* of a link between Eve and the 'daughters of men' who mate with the Watchers, but the wickedness and lustfulness of women begin increasingly to feature in religious literature and eventually become Eve's particular attributes. A development in this process appears in the *Testament of Reuben*, a work that dates from around the second century BC and claims to be a copy of the last testament of Reuben, the firstborn son of the biblical Jacob and Leah, dictated to his sons as he lay on his deathbed. Misogynous in tone, it describes the horrors into which a man may be led by female enticements. In terms reminiscent of the fate of the young man in Proverbs, the dying patriarch reminds his sons that sexual desire '"leads the young person like a blind man into a ditch and like an animal over a cliff"'. Reuben's warnings are based on his own boyhood experiences, for, as Genesis records, he coveted his father's concubine Bilhah: 'And it came to pass, when Israel [Jacob] dwelt in that land, that Reuben went and lay with Bilhah his father's concubine: and Israel heard it' (Gen. 35:22). Nothing more is said in Genesis about the matter, although there is something ominous about the economy of that final phrase, 'and Israel heard it'. The story Reuben tells in his testament is that as a young man he had spied on Bilhah '"bathing in a sheltered place"' and became obsessed by her '"naked femininity"'. When she was drunk one night and conveniently asleep naked on her bed, Reuben seized his opportunity and, rather improbably, raped Bilhah without waking her. A '"messenger from God"' revealed what had happened to Jacob, who merely lamented over Reuben and prayed to God on his behalf, while refusing to have anything more to do with Bilhah.

This unpleasant anecdote is the basis of Reuben's accusations against women, and he complains to his sons: '"women are evil, my children, and by reason of their lacking authority or power over man, they scheme treacherously how they might entice him to themselves by means of their looks"', and if their good looks are not persuasive, they resort to deceit. Although Reuben has the insight to understand that powerlessness may force women into stratagem, he does not investigate this idea further, preferring the sexist fudge that he has been reliably informed by an angel that women are more promiscuous than men, and will use every harlot's device in their (considerable) repertoires to entice men from the path of virtue: '"by decking themselves out they lead men's minds astray, by a look they implant their poison, and finally in the act itself they take them captive"'. This '"harlot's manner"', he says, is how they charmed the Watcher angels.

Reuben gives a new twist to the Watcher story by claiming that the women initiated the seduction by their wiles, so that the angels were overcome by desire. Magically transformed into human men, the Watchers appeared to the women when they were having sex with their husbands. The women perceived the angels as magnificently tall and were filled with reciprocal lust, and as a result gave birth to giants. Reuben firmly pins the blame on the 'daughters of men': it was they who seduced the Watchers, it was their fault that the giants were born to wreak havoc among humanity, and they did it through adornment. The seductive use of cosmetics and bracelets that the angel Azaz'el had taught women in *1 Enoch* are in Reuben's version already known by the women and cleverly exploited to ensnare their angelic prey. As Reuben reminds his sons, such scheming women are '"destined for eternal punishment"'.

The *Testament of Reuben* expresses ideas about the nature of women that remained current in Western ideology throughout the medieval period and still leave traces in modern stereotypes of female behaviour: the insatiable lust of women, their promiscuity and deceitfulness in getting what they want, and their ruthless exploitation of their own sexual attractiveness. The superstitions that a husband might be replaced by a demon lover in the act of love, and that whoever or whatever a woman fantasizes about at the moment of conception will influence the child she bears, were widespread well into the early modern period, and the claim that men are incapable of resisting their own responses to female sexuality has been particularly persistent. The QC Helena Kennedy points out in *Eve Was Framed*, a disquieting study of the treatment of women in the British legal system first published in 1992, that the judiciary continues to condone the absurdity that a man is powerless to resist his own sexual drives:

> 'Victim to his libido' is the recurring theme in the mitigation
> plea for a convicted rapist. If a woman has been in any way
> familiar, we are presented with the old idea of man, the
> overheated engine, incapable of switching off. We are to treat

him as the functional equivalent of a handgun, something
intrinsically dangerous.

Reuben's final advice to his sons is to avoid the whole problem:
'"So guard yourself against sexual promiscuity, and if you want to
remain pure in your mind, protect your senses from women."'

Reuben's allocation of blame to the women rather than the
angels in the Watcher legend is paradoxically reinforced by the story
of the Jewish heroine, the widow Judith, who used her beauty to
gain access to Holofernes, the general-in-chief of the Assyrian army,
and then cut off his head and smuggled it out to the Jewish camp,
where it was hung defiantly from the battlements and led to a total
rout of the Assyrian army. Her history is elaborated in *Judith*, part of
the canonical Jewish Scriptures, although not included in the Old
Testament. Judith's elaborate preparations to meet Holofernes are
carefully described and include the customary trinkets:

> she washed all over, anointed herself with costly perfumes,
> dressed her hair, wrapped a turban round it and put on the
> dress she used to wear on joyful occasions when her husband
> Manasseh was alive. She put sandals on her feet, put on her
> necklaces, bracelets, rings, earrings and all her jewellery, and
> made herself beautiful enough to catch the eye of every man
> who saw her.

When Judith arrives at the Assyrians' camp, they are astonished at
her beauty which increases their respect for the Israelites: '"Who
could despise a people having women like this?" they keep saying.
"Better not leave one man of them alive; let any go and they would
twist the whole world round their fingers!"' Despite this, Judith is
allowed to enter Holofernes' tent and easily bamboozles him into
believing that God is planning to deliver the starving Israelites into
the hands of the Assyrians. Overwhelmed by Judith's wisdom and
beauty, Holofernes permits her to stay in his camp and invites her
to a banquet. As he says to his eunuch Bagoas, '"We shall be
disgraced if we let a woman like this go without knowing her
better. If we do not seduce her, everyone will laugh at us!"' Left
alone with the drink-sodden general, Judith quickly decapitates him

and, with his head hidden in a food bag, she and her maid leave the camp to pray. When the Assyrians discover the trick, they are so demoralized that the Israelites put them to flight and enjoy thirty days of looting.

As Judith leads the great procession of dancing women and garlanded warriors that celebrates the victory, the people sing a thanksgiving hymn in which they praise Judith's beauty, saying that it was this and not the onslaught of giants, a reference to the Watcher offspring, that has conquered Holofernes:

> 'it was not sons of Titans who struck him down,
> no proud giants made that attack,
> but Judith, the daughter of Merari,
> who disarmed him with the beauty of her face . . .
> Her sandal ravished his eye,
> her beauty took his soul prisoner . . .
> and the scimitar cut through his neck!'

As the mention of the giants suggests, there is something equivocal about this apparently commendatory story about a female saviour. Woman's beauty is celebrated, for once, for its convenient power to deceive, but its very effectiveness confirms how dangerous a weapon it is. Judith is praised because she uses her good looks on behalf of her fellow Israelites; but the story reinforces the message that 'women are evil, my children'. Even Judith's 'wisdom' is undermined because it is based on a lie: she deceives Holofernes into thinking she is behaving wisely in revealing Yahweh's plans, when she is really acting for the Israelites. Judith *is* clever: the plan is entirely her own conception, and she carries it out with great skill and daring, but the effect is to confirm woman's duplicity and the fatal consequences of her sexual allure. She even manages to become wealthier by her murder, receiving Holofernes' silver plate, his divans and tent and furniture as her share of the spoil. In a coda to the story, Judith lives to a ripe old age, but never marries again, resolutely turning down her many suitors, a mark of her devotion to the memory of her first husband, but also, maybe, a quiet authorial comment on her unsuitability as a marriage partner. Better not wed such a dangerous woman!

The legend of the Watcher angels with its increasing emphasis on the women's responsibility, the pseudo-Reuben's obsession with temptresses, and the ambiguous story of Judith reflect the trend towards misogyny in Jewish literature in the centuries just before the birth of Christ and, in their search for the causes of humanity's misfortunes, writers began to turn to the story of Eve and its alluring possibilities for female sexual guilt. They found ammunition for their charges against Eve in the gradual superimposition of the story of the rebellious Watcher angels and their human brides on to the serpent's encounter with Eve in the Garden of Eden. *The Wisdom of Ben Sira* states simply that:

> Sin began with a woman,
>   and thanks to her we all must die.

This might apply to the women in the Watcher story or to Eve, but the use of 'woman' in the singular suggests that it was Eve whom Ben Sira had in mind. In a section of *1 Enoch* that scholars date to late in the first century BC or early AD, a roll call of the fallen angels mentions Gader'el who 'misled [i.e. seduced] Eve'. Here, Eve is directly linked with the Watcher story and plays a similar role to the human women: her crime is sexual and is blamed, not on the serpent, but on a malignant angel. The lust that flows to and fro in the different accounts of the Watcher angels and their beautiful human brides has begun to contaminate the story of Eve's temptation in the garden. The scene is set for Eve to take on a more deadly adversary than the serpent: the apostate angel who challenged God.

Devilish envy

PIERO DELLA FRANCESCA'S fresco of the death of Adam in the church of San Francesco in Arezzo, painted in the mid-fifteenth century, is part of a cycle of paintings that tell the miraculous history of the wood of Christ's Cross, a narrative that links the quest of Seth, Eve's third son, for the oil of mercy into an intricate mosaic of legend that inspired storytellers well into the Middle Ages. With its white-haired Adam instructing Seth on his mission, and unique portrayal of Eve as a withered, sagging-breasted crone, Piero's death scene could have been an illustration for the *Apocalypse of Moses*, a Greek text dating to around the first century AD, in which the sexually tainted Eve first steps into the limelight. The story tells of humanity's first experience of illness and death, calamities that are unequivocally blamed on Eve. As the centuries pass, Adam falls ill and gathers his family at the door of his prayer house, but they do not understand the meaning of sickness and pain. His third son, Seth, thinks Adam may be pining for the food of Paradise, but Adam says Eve is to blame for his mortal illness. Left alone in the garden, she had taken the forbidden fruit from ' "the enemy" ' and fed it to her husband and, to punish Adam, God afflicted him with seventy plagues. Eve weeps at his distress, blaming herself for his sickness:

'My lord Adam, rise, give me half of your illness and let me bear
it . . . because of me you suffer troubles and pains.'

But Adam asks Eve to go with Seth to Paradise to try to obtain the oil of mercy, which flows from one of the trees, ' "and I will anoint myself and rest" '. Mother and son set off, but Seth is attacked by a wild beast on the way and Eve reminds it that once all animals were subject to human beings, the image of God. The beast turns on Eve with bitter words:

'O Eve, neither your grief nor your weeping are due to us, but
to you, since the rule of the beasts has happened because of you.'

Eve is silenced and it is left to the wounded Seth to quell the beast. When they arrive at the outskirts of Paradise, the archangel Michael tells Seth that the precious oil will not be available until the end of time, when all flesh shall be raised and shall experience the joys of Paradise. Now Seth must return to his father, for Adam's death is ordained within three days. Eve and Seth return emptyhanded, and in his anguish Adam turns on his wife: ' "Why have you wrought destruction among us . . . death gaining rule over all our race?" ' He tells her to call their family together and tell them the story of the transgression.

The old woman recalls that God had given Adam and herself separate portions of Paradise to guard; she took the south and west, and had the care of the female animals, while Adam watched over the males. The devil infiltrates Adam's territory and takes the serpent to one side, flattering him with praise of his wisdom and greatness, and pretending to be astonished at his servile position. He can enjoy the fruits of Paradise if he helps the devil to force Adam out of Paradise on account of his wife, just as the devil and his party had been cast out of heaven because of Adam. The serpent at first hesitates, but the devil persuades him that all he has to do is act as his mouthpiece; he himself will do the rest.

When the angels mount to heaven to worship God, the serpent dangles over the wall of Paradise in front of Eve, while Satan, cunningly disguised as a hymn-singing angel, lurks on the other side. Speaking through the serpent's mouth, he questions Eve about the prohibition and pretends concern that she is kept in a state of ignorance: ' "May God live! For I am grieved over you, that you are like animals. For I do not want you to be ignorant; but rise, come and eat, and observe the glory of the tree." ' As in Genesis, he lures her with the promise that if she eats the forbidden fruit she will become godlike, knowing good and evil. Although the fruit does look particularly inviting, Eve is still nervous, until the serpent/ devil says that he will pass her the fruit himself. She opens the gate and lets him in, but now he starts to prevaricate, saying that he has changed his mind and will only give her the fruit if she promises to give it to Adam. By this time, Eve is determined to taste the fruit and swears a solemn and blasphemous oath that she is later to regret. The serpent/devil then climbs the tree and ' "poured upon the fruit the poison of his wickedness, which is lust, the root and beginning of every sin, and he bent the branch on the earth and I took of the fruit and I ate" '. Lust is what gave the fruit its special savour, a subtle and seductive poison that will taint human sexuality for centuries to come.

The effects of Eve's disobedience are immediately felt. As the serpent slinks away, Eve sees that she has been stripped of the glory that had once been her natural garment and frantically looks for leaves to cover herself, but to her horror all the trees have shed their foliage. Only the fig, the tree from which she had taken the fruit, has retained its leaves, and from these she makes herself a skirt. She then calls to Adam and tries to persuade him to eat the forbidden fruit, the devil speaking through her and supplying her with enticing words. Finally Adam also eats and, immediately feeling the change, turns to Eve with angry reproaches: '"O evil woman! Why have you wrought destruction among us? You have estranged me from the glory of God."' Within the hour, their doom falls: they hear Michael sounding his trumpet to summon the angels and, as God enters on his chariot of cherubim, all the trees in Paradise burst once more into bloom. From here the story follows its well-worn path: Adam and Eve are summoned from their hiding place, all three culprits are cursed, and the serpent deprived of his hands and feet, and God sets the angels to drive Adam and Eve out of Paradise. God forbids Adam the tree of life, although he graciously promises it at the resurrection if Adam manages to forswear evil. As a special concession He allows him to take fragrant herbs from Paradise: crocus, nard, reed, cinnamon and other seeds of edible plants.

At the end of her story Eve turns to Adam in an agony of self-reproach: '"Why are you dying and I live?"' Falling to the ground, she blames herself for bringing sin into the world:

'I have sinned, O God; I have sinned, O Father of all; I have
sinned against you, I have sinned against your chosen angels,
I have sinned against the cherubim, I have sinned against your
steadfast throne; I have sinned, LORD, I have sinned much;
I have sinned before you, and all sin in creation has come about
through me.'

The *Apocalypse of Moses* concludes with a moving account of the death and burial of Adam and Eve, the latter penitent and humble to the last. As she dies, she makes a pathetic plea to be buried with Adam, '"do not separate me from the body of Adam; for you made me from his members . . . And just as I was with him in Paradise, and not separated even after the transgression, so also let no one separate us [now]."' It seems that her request was granted, for God seals Adam's tomb for six days, 'when his rib would return to him'.

The colourful enhancements of Genesis 2–3 in the *Apocalypse of Moses* reflect the influence of the Watcher stories of lust-driven encounters between angels and human women, and indicate the network of ideas accruing about the Eden narrative. Redactors wanted to make sense of puzzling aspects of the story, but there was also a commitment to assigning blame and accounting for the origins of evil, and an emphasis on the possibility of redemption. Eve's version of the story throws new light on the role of the serpent, who is now the accomplice of a vengeful angel, which provides a motive for the temptation. The words put into Eve's mouth by the author of the *Apocalypse* establish that her trespass was sexual; she allowed herself to be seduced by Satan, who deliberately sprayed the fruit with lust before she bit into it, and God's curse on Eve confirms this. He tells her that, fearing death in childbirth, she will cry out, '"LORD, LORD, save me and I will never again turn to the sin of the flesh."' Even so, God says, '"you shall turn again to your husband"'. Sexual desire is now built into the female psyche. Eve's responsibility for the loss of Paradise is also emphasized and, by a clever literary trick, she is her own chief accuser; again and again, she blames herself for eating the fruit and for tempting Adam, and the consequences of her disobedience are terrible: '"all sin in creation has come about through me"'. But death is Eve's ultimate legacy to her descendants, a fate which her husband is the first to experience and, in the account of Adam's final days, the author of the *Apocalypse* is careful to highlight Eve's culpability and isolation.

The new stress on Eve's delinquency and Adam's suffering on her account may have derived from the misogyny characteristic of contemporary writings on female behaviour, but it may also have been an offshoot of the perfectionist idea of Adam that had become an important theme in the Eden tradition. In *1 Enoch*, the tree of good and evil is called the tree of wisdom and, in the Wisdom literature, Adam is named as dwelling under Wisdom's protection:

The father of the world, the first being to be fashioned,
created alone, he had her for his protector
and she delivered him from his fault;
she gave him the strength to subjugate all things.

The verses in Ezekiel concerning the prince of Tyre were also
thought by some commentators to refer to Adam:

Thou sealest up the sum, full of wisdom, and perfect in beauty.

Thou hast been in Eden the garden of God; every precious stone
was thy covering . . . thou hast walked up and down in the midst
of the stones of fire.

Thou wast perfect in thy ways from the day that thou wast
created, till iniquity was found in thee.

(Ezek. 28:12–15)

Jewish tradition endowed Adam with all the physical, moral and
spiritual beauty appropriate to a being made in God's image, and he
was credited with inventing every craft known to humanity, including the art of writing, and all seventy of the known languages. The
Christian Fathers also enjoyed fantasizing about Adam's exceptional
powers. Athanasius, the Greek prelate, (*c.* 296–373), claimed that
he was endowed with 'a vision of God so far-reaching that he could
contemplate the eternity of the Divine Essence and the cosmic
operations of His Word'; the Roman churchman Ambrose (*c.*
339–397) imagined him conversing with God 'face to face', and
Augustine (354–430), bishop of Hippo in North Africa, said that
Adam's mental powers 'surpassed those of the most brilliant philosopher as much as the speed of a bird surpasses that of a tortoise'.
For Dante, he was the 'fruit that alone wast brought forth ripe'. It
was difficult to explain how such an exalted being could fall for the
serpent's tricks, and the emphasis on Eve's responsibility may have
been an attempt to accommodate Adam's legendary attributes with
his loss of Eden through naivety and childlike disobedience. Milton
resolved the problem by saying that Adam shared the fruit through

an excess of husbandly tenderness, 'not deceived,/But fondly over-come with female charm', and earlier revisions of the story similarly preferred to elide Adam's responsibility by putting the blame on Eve.

The *Vita Adae et Evae*, the Latin version of the life of Adam and Eve, may date to as late as the fourth century AD. Like the *Apocalypse of Moses*, it probably derived from an earlier Hebrew source and the *Vita* has many features in common with the Greek version, but it omits Eve's account of the temptation, telling instead an equally damning tale of Eve's shortlived repentance in the days immediately following the expulsion from Eden. It also develops the hint in the *Apocalypse of Moses* that the devil's behaviour in Paradise is the result of his envy of Adam, here expanded into a dramatic rebellion in heaven that recalls the disobedience of the Watcher angels.

The story begins in the first wretched days of wandering outside the Garden of Eden. Typically, Eve loses heart and blames herself, saying to Adam: '"My lord, would you kill me? O that I would die! Then perhaps the LORD God will bring you again into Paradise, for it is because of me that the LORD God is angry with you."' The more pragmatic Adam suggests that they should show their repen-tance by an extended fast. Eve is to go to the River Tigris, find a stone and stand up to her neck in the waters for thirty-seven days; Adam, being rather hardier, is to endure forty days of immersion in the Jordan. All goes well at first, but after eighteen days Satan, disguised as a shining angel, persuades Eve that God has accepted her repentance and she is invited to feast once more in Paradise. When the malicious devil leads her to where Adam is still patiently soaking in the Jordan, Adam is not deceived and accuses Eve of having been seduced all over again. Eve then begs the devil to explain his hostility: '"What have we done to you, that you should pursue us with deceit?"'

The devil says that it is Adam's fault that he and his followers have been cast out of heaven. When Adam was first created, the archangel Michael commanded the angels to worship him as the image of God, but the devil refused to kneel to what he regarded as a younger, inferior creation, and his supporters followed his example. Michael threatened the devil with God's anger, but he retaliated by challenging God: '"If he be wrathful with me, I will set my throne above the stars of heaven and will be like the Most

High."' But God cast the rebel angels out of heaven on to the earth, where they were gnawed with resentment at Adam's enjoyment of Paradise until, finally, Satan was able to take his revenge: ' "So with deceit I assailed your wife and made you to be expelled through her from the joys of your bliss, as I have been expelled from my glory." ' Shocked by the devil's malice, Adam begs God to free him from his opponent, at which the devil vanishes, and Adam stoically continues his penance in the waters of the Jordan.

Eve acknowledges her unworthiness:

> 'You live on, my lord. Life is granted to you, since you have
> done neither the first nor the second error, but I have been
> cheated and deceived, for I have not kept the command of God.
> And now separate me from the light of such life, and I will go to
> the sunset and stay there until I die.'

In great sorrow, she walks towards the west, away from her lost garden and, finding herself three months pregnant, builds a solitary shelter in which to await the birth of her first child. Gripped by labour pains, she calls out to God for mercy, but He does not hear, and she begs the stars to give Adam her news when they return east. By some psychic miracle, Adam hears her call and rushes to her, thinking that she has yet again been tempted by the serpent. Seeing her plight, he prays to God on her behalf and the angels rally round to act as midwives to Cain, her 'lustrous' son, by implication the fruit of Eve's second dalliance with the devil.

The *Apocalypse of Moses* and the *Vita Adae et Evae* link Eve with the figure of a demoniac tempter, an association, with its implications of female gullibility, moral frailty and sexual rapacity, that has persisted throughout the history of women in Western Christendom, and has had a major impact on how women have been treated by the church and the law. Its effects were felt during the European witchcraft scares of the sixteenth and seventeenth centuries, when it was believed that female sexual desire and credulity made women particularly susceptible to the devil's persuasions. Women talked to the devil and in their insatiable lust even had sex with him, deriving powerful magic which they could use for evil purposes. But the consequences were death and the terrible tortures of hell. Hans

Baldung Grien's *Eve, the Serpent and Death*, painted in the early sixteenth century, is a typical example of the ideas that clustered around Eve and the devil's henchmen. Eve is shamelessly naked, the apple half-hidden behind her back, an expression of sly complacency on her face. Lurking behind the tree trunk around which the snake coils is the hideous figure of death, his flesh stripping away from his face and limbs to reveal the skeleton beneath. His left hand clutches Eve's forearm as she clasps the serpent's tail; at the same time, the serpent's jaws are clamped on to death's wrist, shackling the three figures together. Death brandishes a second apple in a gesture of triumph, but Eve's sidelong simper suggests sexual complicity rather than fear.

Just as Eve's malign character evolved in early Jewish and Christian literature by a process of association and accretion, so too did the personality of Satan, but where Eve ends up as the scapegoat for human bad behaviour, Satan, or the devil, metamorphoses into a cosmic adversary of enormous power and authority, whose origins lie in the Ancient Eastern mythologies that predate Judaism, in stories of the battles of gods and fabulous beasts, Baal's defeat of the water-god Yamm, and Marduk's cleaving in two of the great mother goddess Tiamat. Behind the angel who refuses to honour Adam may be traced the shadowy figures of the Canaanite monsters who opposed Yahweh at the beginning of history, the great dragon Leviathan, the snakes and sky-dragons and the primeval deep itself. He preserves, too, traces of the earthly kings whose rebellion was seen by their Israelite critics in cosmic terms:

> How art thou fallen from heaven, O Lucifer, son of the morning! how art thou cut down to the ground, which didst weaken the nations!
>
> For thou hast said in thine heart, I will ascend into heaven, I will exalt my throne above the stars of God: I will sit also upon the mount of the congregation, in the sides of the north:
>
> I will ascend above the heights of the clouds; I will be like the most High.

> (Isa. 14:12–14)

This is not the story of Adam's jealous opponent nor yet of the Watcher angels, but is thought to have predicted the downfall of the King of Babylon and his crestfallen entry into Sheol, where his collapse is mocked by the shades of dead kings. Through the later association of this passage with the fallen angel story, Lucifer became current in patristic times as an alternative name for the devil. The Greek anti-heroes, Prometheus and Phaethon, may also have influenced the development of the devil's story. Prometheus was another overreacher, who outwitted Zeus by a clever trick and stole the precious gift of fire, again a form of forbidden or occult knowledge, which he transmitted to humanity, introducing the domestic comforts of warmth and cooking, and the ability to fire clay pots and forge weapons. But he was terribly punished: Zeus had him chained naked to a pillar in the Caucasian mountains, where day after day a vulture tore out his liver, which re-grew again during the night. In Ovid's account of Phaethon, the ambitious youth borrowed the chariot of the sun with the reluctant consent of his father, the sungod Phoebus, but was unable to control the horses, who ran their own eccentric path across the heavens, dashing against the stars and laying waste the earth with fire. Finally, Zeus was persuaded to intervene and unleashed his thunderbolts, quenching the fires and striking Phaethon from the chariot. The dying boy, his streaming hair aflame, hurtled down through the aether trailing smoke and plunged into the river Eridanus.

The devil did have a named antecedent in the Old Testament, an angel known as 'the Satan', who plays a prominent role in the story of Job. The term refers to a function rather than any specific character – the root *śtn* means 'one who opposes, obstructs, or acts as adversary' – and the Satan appears initially to have been a member of the heavenly court, sent out by Yahweh to act as a necessary check or obstruction on human activity. In the story of Balaam and his ass, Balaam's path was blocked by an angel, who 'stood in the way for an adversary against him (*le-śāṭān-lō*)' (Num. 22:22). In Greek, the term used for the adversary was a cognate of *diabolos*, which would later be translated as 'devil', but at this stage, like the term 'Satan', it lacked negative connotations and meant simply 'one who puts something in one's way, or across one's path'. Balaam's journey with the princes of Moab had been forbidden by God, who sent the obstructing angel to make sure that Balaam obeyed instructions. In the book of Job, the Satan's role is more aggressive and he is already showing signs of independent thought: he questions God's faith in Job, and more or less challenges God to let him prove that His trust is misplaced. The book of Job is difficult and ambiguous, but what emerges from Job's conflicts is that God has a darker side with which Job has to come to terms; this shadow aspect of God is dramatically realized by splitting it off into the Satan figure who is made responsible for Job's trials. In this context, the Satan acts as a convenient method of indicating that difficulties might be part of the divine plan rather than attributing misfortune to human sin, and allows God to express and resolve His doubts about the worth of faith that has not been tried. The Satan's role becomes increasingly adversarial in the Old Testament, eventually outgrowing Yahweh's jurisdiction and ultimately blending with the multiple traditions that combined to make up the personality of the Christian devil, the horrific force for evil to whom Eve, 'the devil's gateway', had exposed humankind.

The identification of Satan with the serpent in the Garden of Eden is further suggested in an enigmatic reference in The Revelation of St John the Divine. The merest glance at these astonishing chapters, placed at the very end of the New Testament, as if they offer the Bible's final comment on itself and propose its legacy to its readers, reveals the richness and strangeness of the writer's imagination, and its potential for equally extravagant interpretation. Christian exegetes scoured the holy texts for clues to contemporary theological problems, and in the 'old serpent' of Revelation 12, they saw the familiar, now composite figure of the fallen angel and the Tempter in the Garden of Eden. The serpent-dragon, a great red monster with ten horns and seven heads each bearing a crown, with his tail 'drew the third part of the stars of heaven, and did cast them to the earth' (Rev. 12:4), a possible reference to the rebellious angels in the Watcher legend as well as the cohorts who followed the devil in the *Vita Adae et Evae*. He appears in response to 'a great wonder in heaven; a woman clothed with the sun, and the moon under her feet' (Rev. 12:1), who cries out with her birth pangs. The dragon waits to devour the baby as it emerges from the womb, but the woman, interpreted as a figure of Christ's mother Mary, flees with her child to the wilderness:

> And there was war in heaven: Michael and his angels fought against the dragon; and the dragon fought and his angels,
>
> And prevailed not; neither was their place found any more in heaven.
>
> And the great dragon was cast out, that old serpent, called the Devil, and Satan, which deceiveth the whole world: he was cast out into the earth, and his angels were cast out with him.
>
> (Rev. 12:7–9)

In deceiving Eve, mother of all living, Satan had led astray the whole of humanity, and in a passage reminiscent of God's curse on the serpent in Eden, 'her seed . . . shall bruise thy head, and thou shalt bruise his heel', the incident concludes with the dragon's hostility to the woman, 'And the dragon was wroth with the woman, and went to make war with the remnant of her seed' (Rev. 12:17). Later, like Azaz'el and the other Watcher angels in *1 Enoch*, the 'old serpent' is bound underground by God's lieutenant:

> And I saw an angel come down from heaven, having the key of the bottomless pit and a great chain in his hand.
>
> And he laid hold on the dragon, that old serpent, which is the Devil, and Satan, and bound him a thousand years,
>
> And cast him into the bottomless pit, and shut him up, and set a seal upon him . . .
>
> (Rev. 20:1–3)

Writing in the early 1900s, Edmund Gosse recalled the compelling effect of these 'wild Oriental visions' on his parents, who accepted the words of the seer as a commentary on their own lives in Victorian England, and showed remarkable resourcefulness in trying to pin down what events the texts predicted. Edmund's father, Philip Gosse, (1810–88), was a brilliant naturalist, whose dedication to the literal truth of the Bible, and in particular God's instantaneous creation of the universe, won him a humiliating notoriety with the publication of *Omphalos* in 1857. Anxious to refute theories about the mutability of species which contradicted Genesis by implying the long slow development of organic forms, Gosse came up with the ingenious idea that when God created the earth, he cleverly faked matters so that 'the world presented, instantly, the structural appearance of a planet on which life had long existed'. The title of his book refers to Adam's navel, which had been the subject of speculation among theologists: if Adam was made by God rather than born of woman, would he have had a navel? Sir Thomas Browne thought not; reflecting on original sin in *Religio Medici* (1642), he admitted that 'the man without a Navel yet lives in me'. James Joyce was later to agree with Browne's opinion on the first couple's lack of umbilici. 'Heva, naked Eve,' he comments in chapter 1 of *Ulysses*; 'She had no navel.' In Gosse's rationale, however, Adam 'would certainly possess hair and teeth and bones in a condition which it must have taken many years to accomplish, yet he was created full-grown', and would equally certainly 'display an *omphalos*, yet no umbilical cord had ever attached him to a mother'. To Gosse's astonishment and lasting mortification, his theory exposed him to almost universal ridicule, the press interpreting it as suggesting 'that God hid the fossils in the rocks in order to tempt geologists into infidelity', and Charles Kingsley writing woundingly that he could not 'give up the painful and slow conclusion of five and twenty years' study of geology, and believe that God has written on the rocks one enormous and superfluous lie'. Gosse's literalism in explaining Genesis was a late echo reverberating along the centuries of early rabbinical and Christian obsessions with the why and what of God's purposes.

By the time the Greek theologian Justin (*c.* 100 – *c.* 165), one of the early Christian Fathers, wrote in his *First Apology*: 'Among us the chief of the evil demons is called the serpent and Satan and the devil, as you can learn from examining our writings', the wily talking serpent had become inseparable from the arch-villain of Christian theomachy, the devil himself, whose baleful presence in the Garden of Eden focused a relentless spotlight on Eve's activities, and who ultimately became the fully fledged devil of medieval theology, a figure irrevocably linked with Eve and humanity's 'Fall' from grace. The story of the angel's fall through envy was widely disseminated, but was to wait until the 1660s to receive its most substantial and inspired literary treatment in *Paradise Lost*. Despite the centuries that intervened, the tremendous anti-hero of John Milton's epic reflects his mythological antecedents. He first appears as a massive chained Leviathan, recalling the sea-dragons quelled by Yahweh, stretched out on a burning lake, tormented by flames and racked by the memory of what his ambition has sacrificed. Like the fallen angel of the *Vita Adae et Evae*, his bid for lordship over heaven has failed, and he has been hurled by God down into the chasm of bottomless perdition, where he has languished with his defeated cohorts, like Azaz'el penned in the depths of the earth, for nine terrible days and nights, gazing with baleful eyes on a scene of the utmost desolation. Just as the Watchers were held in *1 Enoch* in the burning prison-chamber of the laggard stars, Satan and his forces are similarly embraced by a fire that burns without consuming:

> A dungeon horrible, on all sides round
> As one great furnace flamed, yet from those flames
> No light, but rather darkness visible
> Served only to discover sights of woe,
> Regions of sorrow, doleful shades, where peace
> And rest can never dwell, hope never comes
> That comes to all;

Like the Satan of the *Vita*, he does not give up, but vaunts his will anew:

> Farewell happy fields
> Where joy for ever dwells: hail horrors, hail
> Infernal world, and thou profoundest hell
> Receive thy new possessor: one who brings
> A mind not to be changed by place or time.
> The mind is its own place, and in itself
> Can make a heaven of hell, a hell of heaven.

Satan's decision to take revenge on God through Adam is expanded by Milton into the great council of the fallen angels in Pandaemonium, the capital of Satan's new realm, where the defeated angels finally agree to punish God by suborning His favoured new creation. Satan volunteers to undertake the perilous venture and sets off alone on the journey to Eden, where he hears about the forbidden fruit and manages to secure an audience alone with Eve.

Was Eve tempted to have sex with Milton's persuasive, sinewy Satan, attractive even in his guise as serpent, his crested head towering upright above mazy coils, with his carbuncle eyes, and burnished golden neck 'erect/Amidst his circling spires, that on the grass/Floated redundant'? Despite the voluptuous setting in which their meeting takes place, Milton does not give this slant to the encounter, attributing Eve's disobedience to a desire for wisdom. Yet the first effect of her persuading Adam to eat the fruit is carnal desire, which the human couple express through lascivious glances, lust and, finally, sexual dalliance. The legend of Eve's copulation with the serpent still survives, however, in the popular narratives of the Limba people of Sierra Leone, who tell a tale of the first couple Adamu and Ifu that closely resembles Genesis 2–3. In their version, the serpent, a 'very long, red, and spotted fatal snake', makes love to the woman Ifu before he tempts her, a pleasurable experience for both since they 'travelled far in that love', but there is no suggestion in the Limba tale that the serpent represents any kind of demon. Like the original Genesis story, it is an aetiological myth that explains the hostility between snakes and humans and the hard conditions of life for the Limba people.

In the *Vita* and the *Apocalypse of Moses*, Eve was linked with the devil in his contest with Adam, an accomplice, however unwillingly, to Adam's loss of his birthright, and stood condemned on her own admission for introducing sin, physical hardship, sickness and death into the world. Eve's sexual guilt was reinforced in other Jewish holy writings. Although the Rabbis regarded the serpent as merely a reptile, there is the rabbinic story of the serpent's passion for Eve; and Rabbi Johanan ben Zackai went much further, claiming not only that Eve copulated with the serpent, but that the serpent injected her with 'filthy lust', an accusation that is repeated in three different sections of the *Babylonian Talmud*. In *The Fourth Book of the Maccabees*, probably written in *c.* 63 BC–AD 70, the mother of seven martyred sons boasts about her sexual integrity in terms that clearly recall Eve's seduction by the serpent:

> 'I was a chaste maiden and did not leave my father's house; but I
> kept guard over the rib built into woman's body. No seducer of
> the desert nor deceiver in the field corrupted me, nor did the
> seducing and beguiling serpent defile my maidenly purity.
> Through all the days of my prime I stayed with my husband.'

The desert was regarded in Judaism and early Christianity as the haunt of evil spirits and demons who lay in wait to lead women astray; this woman protected her chastity, symbolized by the rib, by staying quietly at home.

Despite the tradition of Adam's superiority, not all commentators blamed Eve. The author of the Syriac *Apocalypse of Baruch* charges Adam with a damning catalogue of disasters, including sexual passion and the generation of children:

> For when he transgressed, untimely death came into being,
> mourning was mentioned, affliction was prepared, illness was
> created, labour accomplished, pride began to come into
> existence, the realm of death began to ask to be renewed with
> blood, the conception of children came about, the passion of the
> parents was produced, the loftiness of men was humiliated, and
> goodness vanished. What could, therefore, have been blacker and
> darker than these things?

The Fourth Book of Ezra similarly blames Adam, '"For the first Adam, burdened with an evil heart, transgressed and was overcome, as were also all who were descended from him."' Adam's 'evil heart' refers to the doctrine of the evil imagination, the *yēçer ha-ra'*, which the Rabbis believed was implanted into every human creature at birth. The phrase is drawn from Genesis 6 where, following the birth of the giants, 'God saw that the wickedness of man was great in the earth, and that every imagination of the thoughts of his heart was only evil continually' (Gen. 6:5). The evil imagination was not always a bad thing. Commenting on Genesis 1:31, where God looks at everything He made, 'and, behold, it was very good', Rabbi Samuel ben Nachman said, 'Can then the Evil Desire be very good? That would be extraordinary! But for the Evil Desire, however, no man would build a house, take a wife and beget children'. The *yēçer ha-ra'* can act as a stimulant to the important activities in life.

WITH THE DISAPPEARANCE of Jewish millennial hopes after the destruction of Jerusalem, the doctrine of the evil impulse, or inclination, took over from the Watcher angel and Eden narratives as the standard rabbinic explanation for the problem of the existence of sin, but the Fall of Adam and Eve passed into Christian doctrine via the Epistles of Paul to become the cornerstone of the Catholic Church's teaching about human wickedness and the potential for redemption through Christ. Despite more positive interpretations, the view of Eve as an inferior and sexually fallible creation chimed with ideas about women widely current in religious, recreational and scientific literature, which was written almost exclusively by men, and was absorbed into the thinking of early Christian commentators, who interpreted Eve's character through the distorting prism of their own sexual anxieties and established it as the paradigm for Woman.

CHAPTER 4

CURIOUS WOMEN:
EVE, PANDORA AND PSYCHE

Here in close recess
With flowers, garlands, and sweet-smelling herbs
Espoused Eve decked first her nuptial bed,
And heavenly choirs the hymenean sung,
What day the genial angel to our sire
Brought her in naked beauty more adorned,
More lovely than Pandora, whom the gods
Endowed with all their gifts, and O too like
In sad event, when to the unwiser son
Of Japhet brought by Hermes, she ensnared
Mankind with her fair looks, to be avenged
On him who had stole Jove's authentic fire.

JOHN MILTON, *Paradise Lost*, IV:708–19

'Beautiful evil'

IN THE MID-SIXTEENTH century, the French artist Jean Cousin painted a beautiful nude. Small-breasted and firm-fleshed in the classical tradition, her pudenda modestly veiled by folds of drapery, and with artfully coiffured hair and haughty patrician profile, she reclines in what appears to be a wooded arbour. One languid hand rests on the lid of a decorative pot or urn, while a second urn stands on a small elevation behind her, its lid flung suggestively open. Her left arm is closely encircled by a malevolent-looking serpent, and she lounges negligently on a skull. Trees and foliage form an arch above her head from which hangs a painted tablet naming the lovely subject as 'EVA PRIMA PANDORA'. The identification is confirmed by the branch of the fateful tree that she holds in her right hand. The message of Cousin's carefully posed subject is ominously clear: female flesh spells death, but it also represents beauty and art, pleasing to the eye and intellect alike, embodying a diachotomy between evil and good that was invented by men and has been used against women since the stories of Eve and Pandora were first narrated.

Cousin's fruitful association of Eve with the legendary first woman of Greek mythology was not original: it had been made over a thousand years before by the doctrine-makers of the early Christian church, Tertullian using it as an opportunity for an orotund joke. In an address to women criticizing the fashion for wearing flowered crowns, he writes:

> If there ever was a certain Pandora, whom Hesiod cites as
> the first woman, hers was the first head to be crowned, by the
> Graces, with a diadem; for she received gifts from all and was
> hence called 'Pandora'; to us, however, Moses – a prophetic
> rather than a poetic shepherd – describes the first woman, Eve,
> as being more conveniently encircled with leaves about the
> middle than with flowers about the temples.

Tertullian's brief commentary is revealing of the difference between Greek and Christian attitudes to feminine beauty: for the outspoken advocate of penitential sackcloth and ashes as female daily wear, a woman's body should be concealed, masked in fig leaves, not brazenly celebrated by a chaplet of flowers.

The apocalyptic visions of Judaism were not the only source of ideas about Eve during the early Christian period: an equally rich and tempting literature was that of the Graeco-Roman cultural tradition in which many of the early Church Fathers, those influential shapers of ideas about female character and behaviour, were educated. The Pandora story was popular during the first and second centuries AD as an alternative creation myth, and it continued to fascinate the Church Fathers even as they refuted it in favour of the Genesis account. It was perhaps inevitable that the personality of Pandora should influence their accounts of Eve. In both cases, what was identified as a typically feminine interest in poking their noses into forbidden secrets brought all the ills known to humanity crashing down on their male partners' heads.

The 'poetic shepherd' who had first recorded Pandora's story was the Greek Hesiod, writing towards the end of the eighth century BC, some two or three hundred years after the Genesis account of Adam, Eve and the talkative serpent, but unlike the Yahwist's straightforward narrative, Hesiod's account of the 'bitch' Pandora seems to be steeped in the sour, black bile of woman-hating. He gives two versions of the story, the first a brief account in the *Theogony*, a marvellous narrative of the origin and genealogies of the Greek gods, and of the battles that led to Zeus becoming their king. Unlike the spare scenario of Genesis, the one God whose dignified creation is a unified act of will and authority, Hesiod's pantheon includes three hundred different gods and goddesses, who typically seethe with jealousy, lust and malevolence. Where Genesis concentrates on humanity's struggles to come to terms with God and its own mortal destiny, the *Theogony* is preoccupied with titanic upheaval, as generations of gods and goddesses war for supremacy, and the troubles of humankind are very low on the celestial list of priorities. Hesiod does, however, give a brief explanation of the origin of all human misfortunes: the existence of woman.

Zeus is brought into confrontation with the race of men – for this is a time before women have been invented – through the pranks of the insubordinate Prometheus, a glamorously daring troublemaker reminiscent of the rebellious angel who so fascinated Jewish writers. Prometheus' first trick is to beguile Zeus out of his due share of a slaughtered ox, whose flesh and bones are being split between the gods and mortal men as part of a peace treaty. For the gods, Prometheus lays out the choicest portions of the animal, the flesh and nutritious entrails glistening with fat, but he makes them appear unattractive by hiding them under the ox's stomach. For the race of men, he puts out the pile of fleshless bones, but covers them with a tasty-looking layer of fat. Zeus predictably objects to the stomach and demands the fat-covered portion, only to discover his mistake once he has explored his share of the booty. Zeus rather unfairly punishes human beings for the trick, refusing them the gift of fire, but again the wily Prometheus outwits him, taking it to earth concealed in the stem of a giant fennel, whose slow-burning pith is excellently suited to the task of carrying fire.

Rumbling with thundrous ire, Zeus summons Hephaestus, the great smith and skilled craftsman of the gods, and orders him to mould from earth 'the likeness of a modest maiden', to be made to

Zeus' own design. Once again, as with Eve, the first woman is a masculine production, in this case made up by the artisan god to his ruler's specification. Zeus' daughter, the 'pale-eyed' Athene, dresses the newly made girl, the first of her kind, in a dazzling white robe, and places on her head an intricate golden diadem or crown depicting the myriad creatures that inhabit land and sea, so cleverly wrought that they seem almost alive, so great is Hephaestus' skill. When the 'beautiful evil' (*kalon kakon* in Greek, the teasing contradiction emphasized by the similarity of the two words) is complete, she is shown off to the gods and to human men who are astonished at the 'precipitous trap' that Zeus has contrived. Hesiod spells out the ill effects of this affliction Zeus has made for men: from her is descended the female sex, those drones who live off the hard work of others, consumers and troublemakers, who are only fit partners for wealthy men. And to add to the burden, Zeus makes sure that the man who avoids marriage is equally punished, because then he has no one to look after him when he grows old, and no close family to inherit his goods. Even the man lucky enough to find a good wife cannot relax because of all the other evils women have brought in their wake, whilst the horrors of a bad wife mean lifelong unhappiness for the unfortunate husband: 'it is an ill without a cure.'

Hesiod's complaints about the double bind of marriage are reminiscent of the response Socrates was supposed to have made, several centuries later, to a young man who asked whether he should marry. Perhaps thinking about his own unfortunate experiences with Xanthippe, infamous as one of history's most preposterous shrews – Socrates' biographer, Diogenes Laertius, claimed that the only reason the philosopher lived with Xanthippe was because it was such excellent preparation for whatever else he might have to face in life – Socrates paints a gloomy picture of male destiny:

> On the one hand loneliness, childlessness, the dying out of your
> stock, and an outsider as your heir will be your destiny; on the
> other eternal worry, one quarrel after another, her dower cast in
> your face, the haughty disdain of her family, the garrulous tongue
> of your mother-in-law, the lurking paramour, and worry as to
> how the children will turn out.

The *Theogony* account of the famous first woman of Greek myth lacks a number of features which appear in Hesiod's second version, but the thrust of his argument is already clear. The story of the bones seductively clothed in fat reminds us of the familiar adage, 'All that glisters is not gold', and its association with the exquisitely formed and robed first woman is uncomfortably close to St John Chrysostom's disgust at the 'phlegm, blood, bile, rheum' that constitute a woman's bodily beauty, or even the Rabbis giggling about women smelling nasty because, like Eve, they were created from putrefying bone. Hesiod's narrative long predated the Rabbis and the fastidious John 'Golden Mouth', but the streams of Greek and Jewish myth flowed together in the first centuries after Christ, the Christian Eve contaminated by Hesiod's 'beautiful evil'. Both women share the common 'bane' for men, of looking good and bringing unimaginable trouble in their wake. There are other echoes of the Eden myth in the *Theogony*. Forbidden knowledge, the grasping of secrets, is central to both stories. Prometheus' theft of fire provides men with a desirable gift so far denied them by the father of the gods. The blessing of fire can be interpreted in many ways, but, like the knowledge taught by the Watcher angels, it suggests a range of possibilities beyond the useful ability to cook food, or warm one's body in cold weather, to shape tools, metal weapons or other utensils. Expressed symbolically, Prometheus' precious gift could represent scientific knowledge or physical healing, quasi-magical powers of transformation and metamorphosis that could benefit or empower humanity once they had been taught how to exploit the resources available in the natural world. It might even stand for the flame of consciousness itself. Whatever its implications, Hesiod wants his audience to understand that this precious, prohibited benefit is gained at terrible cost.

The elaborate crown made for Pandora by Hephaestus is never explained, but it may hint at some previous, now vanished or suppressed role for Hesiod's first woman. Just as Eve was named by Adam as the mother of all living, and given joint domination over all living creatures by God, so this unnamed first woman will become mother to all the race of women at least, and her elaborate animal-decorated crown links her with the teeming world of living creatures, over which she may once have ruled in some earlier manifestation as Lady of the Beasts, the Great Mother goddess whose image tantalizingly and ambiguously lingers in scraps of story and artefact from the Ancient Near East and its environs. When Hesiod retells the story in the *Works and Days*, he calls the woman Pandora, 'all gifts', because all the gods donate some special quality to her, a name which was also given to Gaia, the 'broad-breasted Earth' as Hesiod describes her in the *Theogony*, the first to emerge from the Chaos or Chasm that existed at the beginning of all things, the fertile, nourishing mother, truly 'the giver of all gifts', a shadow meaning of 'Pandora'. The connection between Pandora and Gaia is illustrated by the design on a red-figured amphora or wine-jar now in the Ashmolean Museum in Oxford. Emerging from the earth with outstretched arms in a gesture that combines welcome and self-applause – 'Here I am' – is a woman wearing an elaborate crown. To her right stand Zeus and wing-footed Hermes with his magician's staff, and receiving the woman is Epimetheus, the brother of Prometheus, carrying a hammer. A tiny Eros hovers overhead, holding a slender ribbon with which to adorn the new bride. As the classical scholar, Jane Harrison, points out, this could be 'the familiar scene of the rising of . . . Ge [Gaia]', but the female figure is carefully labelled 'Pandora': 'Pandora rises from the earth; she *is* the Earth, giver of all gifts.' Hephaestus used a hammer both in the making of Pandora and in breaking open Zeus' head so that Athene could spring forth; in the Ashmolean amphora, the hammer has been passed to Epimetheus.

The first woman's hidden legacy to her daughters may be subliminally whispered by her golden crown, but Hesiod does not dwell on it and may not even have known the implications of its decorations. He was probably repeating details from a story long passed down in oral tradition. What he does spell out is the baleful character that the race of women inherit from their foremother, that maddening combination of sexual allure and troublemaking that Zeus ill-wished on the race of men, a legacy that they share with Eve's female descendants in the parallel Jewish tradition.

Hesiod gives a more elaborate version of Zeus' revenge on men at the beginning of the *Works and Days*, an otherwise charming ragbag of advice on the importance of work, with tips on successful farming and seagoing, and what one of Hesiod's translators calls 'the grandmotherly deposits in Hesiod's mind', a miscellany of folklore and superstition. The story comes very early in the poem and, like the Eden narrative, it is an aetiological myth, an attempt to justify the hard facts of life, why man has to work and struggle against all kinds of difficulties instead of leading the paradisiacal existence one would expect under such a benign ruler as Zeus. Once again, the father of the gods commissions the creation of woman as revenge for Prometheus' theft of fire, and Hephaestus mixes her from earth and water, and models her on the exquisite forms of the goddesses. Clever Athene makes sure she is skilled in crafts, the weaving that is the defining symbol of femininity; Aphrodite, goddess of love, lavishes charm on her, the seductive sexual allure that creates obsessive yearning in men; but Hermes, the fleet-footed, winged-heeled divinity associated with cunning, theft and general rascality, is told to give her 'a bitch's mind and a knavish [thieving] nature'. The woman is made according to Zeus' instructions, the Graces deck her in gold jewellery and the Seasons add spring flowers, while Hermes makes sure she is every bit as lying and deceitful as the father of the gods requires. She is named Pandora, 'All gifts', because all the Olympians have donated something to her, and is then sent to Prometheus' brother Epimetheus (meaning 'Afterthought', while his brother is 'Forethought'). True to his name, Epimetheus forgets all about his brother's warning never to accept anything from Zeus for fear of the consequences, and happily receives the glamorously packaged time bomb. What happens next is told in the briefest of narratives by Hesiod. The poet simply says that 'the woman unstopped the jar and let it all out, and brought grim cares upon mankind'. Once again, what Hesiod is making clear is that human affliction – deadly sickness, hard work and all other nasty happenings – were unknown to man before woman came on the scene. What does remain nestling in the jar is Hope, whom Pandora traps by rapidly replacing the lid, an act which Hesiod attributes to Zeus' prompt and beneficent intervention.

The bare facts of the story as told by Hesiod are muddling: we know nothing about the jar, whether Pandora brought it with her, whether it was provided by Zeus, or had been already sitting around in Epimetheus' house waiting for someone to open it, nor are we told what prompted Pandora to open the jar, or at what stage of her life with Epimetheus this happened. The logic of trapping Hope in the jar suggests that it was denied to humanity, although Hesiod obviously means us to understand that, thanks to Zeus' good will, it was the one positive good left to man after Pandora's meddling. As for Pandora's famous magic box, that neat little jewel-casket so alarmingly depicted in Dante Gabriel Rossetti's lurid, fire-tinged painting of Pandora, with the threatening column of yellow smoke seeping out through its barely closed lid, it turns out to have been a jar, possibly one of those tall, curved earthenware containers still in use today in the Mediterranean to store wine, or oil, or olives, or maybe even honey.

The later confusion over the jar (*pithos*) was probably introduced by Erasmus of Rotterdam, along with other more familiar features of the story as it became known in the Renaissance tradition. Erasmus retold the story in his widely read *Adagiorum chiliades tres* (1508), where he says that the exquisite Pandora was sent to Prometheus with a beautiful box (*pyxis*) that concealed every kind of disaster. Prometheus, sensibly, refuses to have anything to do with her, so she visits his brother, seduces him by her great charm and beauty, and the box is opened there and then, whether by Epimetheus or Pandora is not entirely clear. This would appear to be the source of the popular version of 'Pandora's box' still retold in modern mythologies, a rather different story from Hesiod's, although the message is the same: woman is to blame for all the ills of a harsh, inhospitable world.

Like Adam and Eve, Pandora is fashioned by a male creator rather than nurtured in a mother's womb. The earth from which she is so dextrously shaped by Hephaestus is, of course, 'broad-breasted' Gaia, but, once Earth had given birth in an act of spontaneous generation to her partner Heaven, the pattern was for more conventional couplings between the deities, although Pandora's sponsoring goddess, Athene, sprang fully formed from her father Zeus' head and Aphrodite, also named as one of Pandora's principal donors, was the product of the frothy semen that flowed out of Heaven's severed genitals after he had been castrated by the scheming Kronos, another son with dynastic ambitions.

Pandora's shaping from earth links her with Adam rather than Eve, although the creations of all three express the idea of being crafted rather than born. The forming of humanity out of clay was not unique to Hesiod: there are many references in the long tradition of Babylonian myth that considerably predated his accounts of origins. One narrative, the *Theodicy*, describes how:

> Narru, king of the gods, who created mankind,
> and majestic Zulummar, who dug out their clay,
> and mistress Mami, the queen who fashioned them,
> gave perverse speech to the human race.

Mami is better known as Aruru, the mother goddess, who, in the ancient *Epic of Gilgamesh*, is asked by her fellow gods to create a boon companion, a 'second self', to deflect the boisterous king Gilgamesh from despoiling his kingdom. 'So the goddess conceived an image in her mind ... She dipped her hands in water and pinched off clay, she let it fall in the wilderness' and the 'noble Enkidu' was created, the innocent savage who lives freely and fearlessly with the animals, eating grass with the gazelles and drinking from the waterholes with the wild creatures. Similar references are found in the Sumerian *Myth of Enki and Ninmah*, where the wise Enki (Sumerian Ea, and Zulummar in the *Theodicy*) uses his own blood mixed with clay as the raw material from which humanity is shaped in order to provide agricultural labour for the gods. In the Babylonian *Epic of Atrahasis* a god is slaughtered to provide flesh and blood to be mingled with clay; Enki treads the mixture like a potter, Mami the mother goddess pinches off fourteen pieces of clay, and the birth goddesses make seven pairs of humans, who emerge after a nine-month gestation period. In the *Enuma Elish*, the female deities have disappeared, and Ea presides over the slaughter of a rebel god whose blood is now the sole shaping ingredient, although humanity is again created to serve the gods. What all these stories have in common is the notion of the manufacture of human beings, sometimes from earth, sometimes from their own flesh and blood, initiated by a male god or gods, with female deities, when they are involved, playing enabling roles, which typically require the use of hands not wombs, a pattern that is repeated in the making of Pandora, although here the divine blood has been dispensed with in favour of earth. In Genesis, God similarly resorts to *'adamah*, the primal clay, for the making of the first man, Adam, but, uniquely among the crowded pantheons of ancient religions, He operates alone. The question of the creation of human men is entirely ignored in the *Theogony*; they pre-exist Pandora and mysteriously seem to have been able to reproduce themselves, but their origins and generative powers are not explained.

Hesiod's account of the origin of woman is a bleaker scenario than the Yahwist's story of Eve's creation. The shaping of Eve from Adam's rib, however much the story lent itself to subsequent belittling of women as subordinate, dependent creatures, does at least imply intimacy, a link between man and woman that operates at the most basic level: 'bone of my bones, and flesh of my flesh' was Adam's possessive but joyous welcome to his partner. There is no such sense of profound physical connection between Pandora and Epimetheus. Pandora is truly 'other', an alien being whose beauty and attainments arouse wonder in men and gods, but whose 'bitch's mind' in the *Theogony* and culpable curiosity in *Works and Days* make her a creature to be shunned. In Eden, the price of forbidden knowledge is hard work, suffering and death, but the punishment is shared between the man and the woman: Adam and Eve exit under the angel's fiery sword to a mutually burdened fate. But as far as Hesiod is concerned, the penalty and the pain fall on men alone, while women wallow in their cosy waxen cells, growing fat on their husbands' labours. The sense of Pandora's physical isolation is augmented by Hesiod's silence about her sexual relationship with Epimetheus and her role as first mother. In the *Theogony* she is named as the mother of the race of women; in the *Works and Days* all she seems to produce are disasters, released when she lifts the lid of the jar. The critic Froma I. Zeitlin has suggested that Pandora's opening of the jar implies the breaching of her virginity, with Elpis, or Hope, as the potential child left within the jar/womb, a plausible analogy between two curved-bellied containers. But Pandora gets no joy out of her reproductive abilities in Hesiod's slanted narrative; as a number of commentators have noted, 'box' is modern slang for the female genitals, and the poet would probably have applauded the negative sexual symbolism of Pandora's jar as illustrated by Paul Klee in his drawing, *Die Büchse der Pandora als*

Stilleben (1920), in which the 'box' is represented by a two-handled vase, whose decorative flowers are tainted by a puff of noxious-looking smoke that bellows out of a vagina-like opening in its bowl.

Eve's punishment for eating the apple is the pain of repeated childbirth, and the Rabbis added menstruation, Eve's 'curse', as an additional penalty, but however burdened and constrained, Eve does have a future. She will be the mother of all living in a shared life with Adam, and Genesis records the successful outcome of their labours. Despite the false start with Cain and Abel, they initiate generations of descendants and are ensured genetic survival through Noah's progeny. No such luck for Pandora. Hope may mean a child, a promise for the future left lurking in the sheltering maternal jar, but Pandora does not receive any credit for it. Instead she is blamed for humanity's troubles and is not mentioned again by Hesiod, although she is named elsewhere as the mother of Pyrrha, who marries her cousin, Prometheus' son Deucalion. Like Noah and his children, these two are the sole survivors of a disastrous flood, this time sent by Jupiter, to wipe out mankind, and Pandora's daughter becomes a new 'mother of all living'.

The story of Pyrrha and Deucalion is told in Ovid's *Metamorphoses*. Human life begins with the Golden Age, a period of natural justice and harmony, when the earth blossoms Eden-like in a perpetual spring. With the passing of Saturn, the world moves into the age of silver, when the seasons are introduced, and people for the first time seek shelter from the cold and use animals to till the soil. After this comes the bronze age, when men are more prone to war, but still free from wickedness, and finally 'the age of hard iron', a terrible time of treachery, crime and lawlessness, of warfare and greedy exploitation of the world's resources. One by one the immortals slink away and giants even attempt to assail heaven, piling up mountains to the stars. Jupiter is so enraged by their exploits that he hurls his thunderbolt down through Olympus and crushes the usurpers under their own tumbling ramparts. The earth, drenched in streams of her sons' blood, reinvigorates it and shapes it into the form of men, but the new races are no better than the giants. Now the horrified gods agree to the total destruction of humanity and Jupiter sends a great storm to flood the world. As in the flood sent by God to punish humanity's wickedness, almost every living thing is destroyed. Luckily, two virtuous and devout people, Deucalion and Pyrrha, run aground in their little boat on the top of Mount Parnassus. Their first act is to offer prayers to the local deities, and Jupiter, recognizing their essential goodness, calls off the floods and storm clouds and restores order. Appalled by the emptiness of the world, the survivors consult the goddess Themis, who instructs them to loosen their girdles and throw behind them the bones of their great mother. At first they are puzzled, but finally understand that the oracle is referring to the earth herself. They follow Themis' instructions and throw stones behind them as they walk. The stones gradually begin to soften and acquire a recognizable human shape, those thrown by Deucalion forming males, while Pyrrha's stones recreate the race of women, and the human facility for hard labour derives from these 'stoney' beginnings.

Ovid's tale of the flood follows on from his myth of ages, and preludes a new beginning for humanity in an attractive story in which Pandora's daughter Pyrrha plays a positive role, and indeed her fabled tomb at Cynus, near Opus, became a popular tourist attraction. Hesiod gives a typically gloomier version of the myth of ages in *Works and Days*: he tells it immediately after the Pandora story, making it clear that humanity is still enduring the miserable age of iron, and it is impossible to escape the inference that all its horrors are a direct result of Pandora's opening the jar.

Like so many of the nasty charges levelled by Greek men against women, or the misogynous jokes of the Rabbis, Hesiod's gibes at extravagant female drones and his hostile view of women as deceitful troublemakers imply a collusive male audience undermined by their susceptibility to female authority, either through the power of sex, the constraints of family life, or the financial demands women were entitled to make in a male-dominated society, and eager to take revenge. The idea of Pandora as 'other', a manufactured creature who is physically distinct from the pre-existent race of men, and whose difference makes her potentially disruptive, may have gained substance from contemporary Greek ideas about the physical structure of women. According to the Hippocratic Corpus, a collection of medical theories written down in the fifth and fourth centuries AD, but probably reflecting beliefs that considerably predated this period, a woman's flesh was differently constituted from that of the male: softer and more porous, less able to process the blood derived from nourishment and therefore prone to physical malfunction. The female body's inferior substance was believed to be reflected in erratic mental behaviour.

The idea of woman's separateness and unpredictability is exploited by the poet-philosopher Semonides of Amorgos, writing in the seventh century BC, in a sourly misogynous poem 'On Women'. He begins by saying that, from the beginning, a woman's mind was created as a 'thing apart', and he goes on to qualify this 'apartness' by identifying different 'types' of woman with species of animal. The indolent sow-woman lives in shit, her home and her person filthy, while she guzzles food. The bitch-woman is a nosey gossip, the fox-woman is crafty, the donkey-woman stubborn. The weasel-woman is crazy for sex, but so hideously unattractive that her husband wants to vomit whenever he approaches her; while the mare-woman neglects the housework in order to pamper her beautiful body. Semonides even makes a covert reference to Pandora, the woman the gods fashioned from dust, who he says is a fool, unable to distinguish between good and bad: on freezing days, she even lacks the sense to pull her chair closer to the fire. The only woman he approves is the industrious bee-woman, an example among women, who is reminiscent of the virtuous wife in Proverbs:

> The man is lucky who gets her.
> She is the only one no blame can settle on.
> A man's life grows and blossoms underneath her touch.

She and her husband grow older together in loving amity, while their children prosper, and, unlike other women, she does not enjoy gossiping about sex.

Semonides concludes that all men are in the same boat, blind fools where women are concerned, and have been since the 'fight about a wife', a reference to the Trojan War, which began when Paris eloped with the peerless Helen, who, like Pandora, brought all kinds of disaster in her wake. Like Hesiod, he blames it all on Zeus:

> For women are the biggest single bad thing Zeus
> has made for us; a ball and a chain . . .

What seems to worry both Hesiod and Semonides is not so much women's sexual allure in itself, as the power of their natures to do harm. Physical beauty draws a man in, but what he has to live with are woman's mendacious, thieving, slovenly ways, and his own gullibility in the face of her sophisticated game-playing. This is a rather different emphasis from the anxieties of the Christian Fathers, who were obsessed with tempting female flesh *per se*, but justified their mania by the charge that women's beautiful bodies masked all kinds of character defects. Sexual temptation was clearly at the forefront of John Chrysostom's mind when he penned his rhetorically brilliant equivalent of Hesiod's economical 'beautiful evil': 'What else is woman but a foe to friendship, an inescapable punishment, a necessary evil, a natural temptation, a desirable calamity, a domestic danger, a delectable detriment, an evil nature, painted with fair colours?'

Jean Cousin's panel painting with which this chapter began embodies the Christian image of Pandora/Eve as 'a desirable calamity': this is Eve naked in the garden rather than white-robed, golden-crowned Pandora. But there are resonances of the classical tradition in which Pandora evolved. The two decorative urns that Cousin gives his 'delectable detriment', although rather small, are closer to Hesiod's *pithos* than Erasmus' *pyxis*, and Cousin may have intended a reference to Zeus' two jars, described by Homer in the *Iliad*, when the aged King Priam comes to beg his opponent Achilles for the body of his son Hector. Touched by the old man's grief and the reminder of his own father Peleus, alone at home while his son is caught up in the interminable Trojan wars, Achilles speaks bitterly of human fate: 'We men are wretched things, and the gods, who have no cares themselves, have woven sorrow into the very pattern of our lives.' Zeus the Thunderer, the ruler of the gods, keeps two jars in his palace, one containing evils, the other blessings. From these he doles out his gifts, sometimes a mixture of good and ill, but 'when Zeus serves a man from the jar of evil only, he makes him an outcast, who is chased by the gadfly of despair over the face of the earth and goes his way damned by gods and men alike'. Like Zeus in a bad mood, Cousin's Eve/Pandora dispenses only the gadfly of despair. As in Semonides' poem, this covert reference to the Trojan War would have reminded an educated audience of that other woman who sowed destruction in her wake, Helen of Troy, credited by both Homer and Virgil with bringing death to hundreds, maybe thousands of Greeks and Trojans, as well as disaster on many of their wives and children. The snake bracelet worn by Cousin's Eve/Pandora would also have recalled Cleopatra, the Egyptian queen famous for her dangerous sexuality and a popular subject for Renaissance artists. In a sixteenth-century Flemish engraving, she is shown beneath a tree in a clear identification with Eve. The association between Eve, Pandora and these other sexual tempt-resses, the bane that inevitably followed the first caress of promising flesh, would have been equally available to the Christian moralists of the first centuries after Christ.

The butterfly girl: Psyche

And there shall be for thee all soft delight
That shadowy thought can win,
A bright torch, and a casement ope at night,
To let the warm Love in!

JOHN KEATS, 'Ode to Psyche', ll.64–7

IT IS SURPRISING that such an apparently skilled classical scholar as Erasmus should have mistranslated Pandora's jar as a box, and the art historians Dora and Erwin Panofsky have suggested that he may have been influenced by paintings of the Magdalene with her pot of ointment, a popular subject in the fifteenth and sixteenth centuries. He may even have seen the version by the Flemish painter Rogier van der Weyden, now in the Louvre, in which a gravely beautiful Magdalene, discreetly weeping over her past sins, sits on what appears to be a small knoll or outcrop, holding the lid of her precious alabaster pot, with a rocky landscape across a sweep of fields behind her. Quietly brooding, her thoughts apparently far away, she could indeed be Pandora, meditating on the consequences if she lifts that tightly sealed lid, even a little. Alternatively, and possibly more likely, given the classical context, Erasmus may have been sidetracked by the tale of Psyche, who brings back from the underworld the merest whiff of Proserpine's beauty trapped in an ornamental box to give to her lover's vengeful mother. The story of Psyche and Eros, another admonitory account of forbidden knowledge and female curiosity, has interesting parallels with the story of inquisitive Eve and offers insights into its interpretation. For once, it is a story with a happy ending, but true to the classical romance genre from which it derives and which typically reunited youth and maiden after terrible misadventures, the heroine, poor Psyche, undergoes severe trials before she is reunited with her lover Eros, or Cupid as he was known in the Roman tradition.

Psyche's sufferings are recorded in Lucius Apuleius' *The Golden Ass*, probably written in around AD 158, a picaresque account of the adventures of a young man also named Lucius, who by error is magically transformed into an ass and only finally redeemed, after pages of more or less bawdy adventures, by a spectacular initiation into the cult of the great goddess Isis. Psyche's history is a tale within a tale, a consolatory bedtime story narrated by an old woman to distract a young girl, Charite, who has been kidnapped by robbers on her wedding night and is being held to ransom in their den. It begins in the classic style of fairy tale with a king and queen who have three lovely daughters. The youngest, Psyche, has the misfortune to be so beautiful that not only does she alienate the Goddess of Love, Venus herself, by attracting her worshippers, but her good looks seem also to intimidate any would-be suitors. While her sisters make respectable marriages, Psyche remains on the shelf, and finally her father is so worried that he consults the venerable oracle of Apollo at Miletus, only to be told that Psyche must be decked out as a bride and left on a mountaintop to be claimed by 'a dire mischief', a 'winged pest'. Her brokenhearted parents and indeed the entire city accompany the wretched victim on her gloomy bridal journey, and she is left alone on top of a hill to face her doom. But the West Wind sweeps her gently down into the steep valley below, using her clothes as a kind of sail or parachute, and lays her to rest on a bed of flowered turf. After a refreshing sleep, Psyche feels able to pursue her adventure and, following a limpid stream through woodlands, comes at last to a magnificent palace. Once there she is tended by unseen spirits, disembodied voices that offer her food, a bath and rest, and entertain her with music and song. Finally, when she goes to bed, Psyche is visited in darkness by her unknown husband and is a maiden no more. Even this rite of passage is tenderly negotiated, for as her lover rushes away before the light of dawn, gentle voices breathe consolation for her lost virginity. Surrounded by every kind of comfort, Psyche soon settles into a happy routine, the only limitation on her enjoyment being her husband's injunction that she is to meet him in darkness and must never attempt to see his face.

Once again in the best fairy-tale tradition, enter the wicked sisters to disrupt the heroine's idyllic life. Despite her husband's warnings, Psyche entertains her sisters in her magic palace and sends them home showered with gifts. Alas for Psyche – her generous treatment merely increases their resentment at her good fortune. Like the envious angel of the *Vita Adae et Evae*, they plot against her, tempting her to break the one taboo imposed in her Paradise; in this case, warning her that she is mated to a horrific serpent who is planning to consume her and the child she carries in her womb. They persuade her that she must cut off the monster's head by the light of a lamp which she should hide behind the tapestry. Greatly troubled, Psyche agrees to their suggestion and that night, when her husband falls asleep, she uncovers her lamp and holds it close to his head so that she can do the desperate deed. To her astonishment, she finds that it is Love himself, the beautiful boy Cupid, who is gracing her pillow. First she tries to kill herself for shame, but the knife twists out of her hands; then she grows braver and examines her husband more closely, admiring his golden curls, the gently flushed skin, and quivering white wings. She even touches his arrows, but, disastrously, pricks her finger and falls desperately in love with him. As she flings herself on to her husband in an abandonment of passion, the lamp, perhaps spurting in sympathy, lets fall a drop of burning oil on the god's shoulder. He awakens and, as he flees away, reproaches her for lack of faith. Commanded by his mother Venus to punish Psyche for her beauty by making her fall in love with some hopeless character, he had married her himself; by listening to false friends, she has forfeited their happiness and will be punished by the loss of her husband.

Even this far in Psyche's story, there are similarities with Eve's. Both women find themselves in paradisiacal surroundings, both are warned not to pry into forbidden secrets, both succumb to siren voices and find themselves miserable and in exile. Childbearing is a feature of both their narratives: for Eve, pain in childbirth is part of her punishment; for Psyche, pregnancy an additional burden that she has to bear in the long search to recover her husband. But there is another link between their two stories, a component that often, sadly, seems to get lost in accounts of Eve. Both are narratives of adolescent love, of the first perilous, blissful encounter with adult sexuality, with all its attendant fret and misunderstandings, the prevalence of emotion over reason, of sex over common sense. The Rabbis argued that Adam and Eve were created fully developed and in their prime, which they thought of as the age of twenty, and Adam's behaviour in the *Vita Adae et Evae* suggests the self-conscious caution of a young man suddenly all too aware of his adult responsibilities. But in the many representations of Adam and Eve that burgeoned in European art during the Renaissance, Eve is typically depicted as a young girl, often barely past puberty, and, unlike the precocious Cupid whose amorous tricks and lubricious pranks had long scandalized the Olympians, Adam was sexually a novice, a point well understood by the artist Lucas Cranach the Elder. His twin portraits of Adam and Eve, now in the Uffizzi Gallery in Florence, brilliantly capture Adam's naivety and inexperi-ence as he wistfully contemplates the nymphet, surely no more than fifteen, who so enigmatically confronts him with her apple. In Gérard's sumptuous *Psyche Receiving the First Kiss of Love* (1798), Psyche, a supremely tender portrayal of female innocence and vulnerability, is on the point of being embraced by her beautiful golden boy, whose hands hover over her naked flesh as if reluctant, yet, to touch her. What these representations affirm is the anxiety of youthful sexuality, along with its promise of physical pleasure, a tension that is at the heart of both stories, but they also suggest the innocence of the first sexual encounter, something touching, radiant and tremulous that can never be recovered. Looking at the fresh, unmarked bodies of these teenage lovers, one can see why Adam and Eve's story acquired such resonance for the learned sages, the stuffy savants who pored over its meanings through the centuries. For those respectable theologians, weighed down by scholarship and doctrinal responsibility, the Paradise of youthful sexuality had indeed been lost for ever.

But it cannot, in any case, endure in real life. Eve's bite of the forbidden fruit opens her eyes to the realities of life; she sees that she is naked; she becomes aware of the penalties of female sexuality, that desire is linked to the pain of repeated childbearing; she discovers that her husband must cease to be a carefree companion and lover, and take on the responsibility of providing for their growing family. In Erich Neumann's Jungian reading of the myth of Cupid/Eros and Psyche, he sees Psyche's act of exposing her lover's face to the light as the courageous first step towards adult awareness and individuation, a movement from the relinquishment of self in sexual passion to the higher consciousness necessary if she and Cupid are to experience reciprocal adult love. By her act, she exposes herself and Cupid to 'suffering, guilt, and loneliness', but it is necessary to work through this desolation if they are to fulfil their masculine and feminine natures. In this interpretation, the persuasive sisters represent aspects of Psyche herself: the voices of her subconscious need to progress out of the darkness of sexual subjection. In the same way, Eve's 'heeding of the serpent leads to expulsion from paradise and to a higher consciousness'.

In an essay on Ulysses' stay-at-home wife Penelope, who guards her husband's estates while he enjoys twenty years of travel and escapade, the critic Carolyn Heilbrun points out that 'through all recorded history, women have lived by a script they did not write. Their destiny was to be married, circulated; to be given by one man, the father, to another, the husband; to become the mothers of men. Theirs has been the marriage plot, the erotic plot, the courtship plot, but never, as for men, the quest plot.' Genesis tells us that Eve, like Psyche, did make an attempt to initiate a quest plot of her own; as Schiller almost put it,

> As soon as her reason realized its initial powers, she spurned
> nature and her protective arms – or, better said: at the behest
> of an instinct which she herself did not even recognize, and
> unconscious of the greatness of the act she performed at that
> moment, she tore herself free from the benevolent ties which
> bound her, and with an as-yet-weak reason, accompanied only
> from afar by the instincts, flung herself into the wild play of life
> and set forth on the treacherous path to moral freedom.

But Schiller was writing about Adam and, apart from the reference to nature, always conveniently female when opposed to 'masculine' reason and intellect, the female pronouns in the quotation were written by him as male. Even though Eve was the first to eat the apple, the quest plot was unthinkingly handed by Schiller to Adam. Eve's only adventure begins and ends with her encounter with the serpent; from then on, she is caught up in the female plot of marriage and motherhood, and although the Jewish storytellers embellished her subsequent history, her actions are of interest because of her responsibilities as Adam's wife and the potential mother of sons. After Eve's transient break for freedom, a zero in the aeons of human time, the door to adventure was closed, and her daughters submitted to centuries of a predetermined narrative in which biology was rationalized as fate. When women did have adventures, it was usually as part of some other, male plot; after her first heroic initiative, Psyche is given the opportunity to test her resilience, but even she is constrained by the plot of 'woman in search of her lover', whose inevitable outcome, if successful, will be the end of exploration.

Even so, there are many possible readings of Psyche's quest and her contest with Venus, and Apuleius' narrative presents a more interesting image of woman than the stories of Eve and Pandora. In the struggles that follow, Psyche again reveals a resolution and a capacity for ruthlessness that lift her out of the category of passive victim and establish her as a fully fledged heroine. Her first act after Cupid's abrupt departure is to take a terrible revenge on each of her sisters and she then sets out on the toilsome journey to find her husband. Her quest is hindered when Venus puts out a search warrant for her daughter-in-law as a runaway slave, and Psyche is unable to find refuge with the fertility goddess Ceres, or even with Juno, goddess of marriage and childbirth, whose special remit was helping pregnant women, because they are reluctant to upset their furious relative. In despair, she makes the bold decision to give herself up to Venus, who treats her brutally, beating her and setting her a series of horrific tasks intended to finish her off. First Psyche must sort a great heap of mixed seeds into separate piles, which she does with the help of a team of sympathetic ants; then she gathers handfuls of golden wool from a flock of dangerous sheep, this time advised by a musical reed how to avoid the animals' sharp horns and poisonous teeth; finally, the greatest danger of all, she is sent to collect water from a precipitous cascade guarded by sleepless dragons. Once more, just as she is about to despair, she finds unexpected aid. Jupiter's royal eagle, remembering a debt he owes Cupid, flies down and fills the crystal flask to the brim for her. Venus is all the more infuriated when she finds that Psyche has somehow escaped the deathly traps set for her. She now gives her a box which the girl must take to the underworld so that Proserpine, Pluto's queen, can give her some of her beauty to recompense Venus for her faded looks due to worrying about Cupid. All this while, her son has been lying desperately sick in Venus' house, suffering from the burn where the lamp oil splashed on his shoulder.

At this commission, Psyche understands that she is literally being sent to her death and decides to take a short cut by jumping off a high tower. But the tower takes pity on her and gives her advice on how to get in and out of the underworld unscathed. Its final warning is not to open the box once Proserpine has filled it with her divine beauty. Psyche follows the tower's instructions, bypassing every pitfall and avoiding all temptations until she has been safely ferried back across the river of the dead by the boatman Charon. Now, at her highpoint of achievement, Psyche 'allowed her curiosity to get the better of her'. Thinking that she will borrow a little of Proserpine's beauty for herself, she opens the box, only to be overcome by a deadly, Stygian sleep. Luckily Cupid has by now recovered and, as much in love with Psyche as ever, rushes to her rescue, wakes her, puts the sleep cloud back in the box and sends her on her way to Venus. He then flies off to Jupiter to put his case before the great father of the gods. Jupiter calls a heavenly council and ordains that Cupid must be united with Psyche if only to stop the flow of complaints about his unseemly behaviour. To satisfy Venus' worries about Cupid marrying beneath him, he gives Psyche a cup of precious ambrosia to drink so that she becomes one of the immortals. Cupid and Psyche are ceremonially married in Heaven, and eventually she bears him a daughter whom they name Pleasure. But of Psyche's grieving parents, who have now lost all three beautiful daughters, and of Psyche's subsequent adventures, the story has no more to say.

Unlike the brief accounts of Eve and Pandora, Apuleius' sophisticated narrative allows Psyche to demonstrate a complex range of responses to experience. On the one hand, she is culpably inquisitive, incapable of learning even through bitter experience to heed the strongest taboos (although even this has its positive side, as Neumann points out); she listens to gossip and tends to take a gloomy view of events, on several occasions ready to commit suicide if she had not been prevented by some external agent: characteristics that are reminiscent of Eve in the *Vita Adae et Evae* and the *Apocalypse of Moses*. On the other hand, she is courageous and resourceful, resolutely facing up to Venus and her challenges, and even venturing down to the underworld in the hope of winning back her husband, a tenacity that became recognized in allegorical interpretations of the story, which saw it as representing the journey of the soul through the dangers and difficulties of human life. In Gérard's painting, Psyche is shown with an open-winged butterfly hovering above her head, itself a symbol of magical transformation, from the dark constraint of the pupa to the light, airy creature able to flutter at will in the bright aether, no doubt a common sight throughout the countries that bordered the Mediterranean. But as a quest narrative, her story suffers from being imposed on her by others; her most dangerous adventures are forced on her by Venus, and her ultimate destiny is silence. Once safely married and a mother, there is nothing more to be said about her, any more than Genesis says anything about Eve after the birth of Seth.

This kind of closure is not essential to narrative. When Odysseus left Troy, it took a bookful of adventures to get him home and, even then, he did not linger with Penelope, but embarked on a new quest to placate Poseidon. In Dante's version, Odysseus does not return home, but, after leaving Circe, sets off anew with just one ship and a tiny crew, driven by the insatiable desire to experience whatever is to be known in life. ' "O brothers," ' he urges his sailors, ' "who through a hundred thousand perils have reached the west, to this so brief vigil of the senses that remains to us choose not to deny experience, in the sun's track, of the unpeopled world." ' Sailing through the Pillars of Hercules and heading south, the company travel furiously on with winged oars, until finally on the fifth day they sight land, only to be overwhelmed by a giant wave that is thrown up from the shore and spins the boat round in a maelstrom that plunges them to their deaths deep beneath the seas. This hunger for action was understood by Tennyson, most uxorious, most restless of men, whose ageing Ulysses (the Roman name for Odysseus) similarly sails off on a last voyage into the unknown, driven by his defining vision of experience as

> an arch wherethrough
> Gleams that untravelled world, whose margin fades
> For ever and for ever when I move.

In Virgil's great epic of the founding of Rome, Aeneas tears himself away from the wrack of Troy to pursue a life of adventure and derring-do before he finally reaches his destination. In Homer and Virgil, men travel, fight, suffer hunger and shipwreck and have adventures. They encounter and survive sirens and witches, Cyclopes and sea-dragons, and every ill that god or man can invent. Above all, they have such fun that their stories have endured for thousands of years and are still being circulated, retranslated, analysed anew. In every case, as the heroes forge on, the women, whether good or evil, are left behind, like Penelope and Clytemnestra, to plot new ways in which their marital or erotic narratives can begin anew.

THESE POPULAR TALES that lingered on in the Graeco-Roman cultural tradition were important reminders of what it meant to be human: 'This is how a woman behaves, this is what a man does.' The stories of Pandora and Psyche, inquisitive women who brought misery by prying into forbidden secrets, endorsed Judaism's defining myth about the nature of woman and, like the adventures of Ulysses and Aeneas, have continued to speak to subsequent generations in very different cultural environments. But there were other popular narratives about women which explored the sensitive balance between a woman's body, mind and the status quo, and looked at what could go wrong when the orderly structure of courtship, marriage and childbirth was disrupted. Despite their often sym-pathetic treatment, the tragic passions of women played a part in developing the negative attitudes to female sexuality that were so enthusiastically taken up by the Christian Fathers.

CHAPTER 5

THE TRAGIC PASSIONS
OF WOMANHOOD

I am alone; I have no city; now my husband
Insults me. I was taken as plunder from a land
At the earth's edge. I have no mother, brother, nor any
Of my own blood to turn to in this extremity.

EURIPIDES, *Medea*

———◦—◦—◦———

I N HIS *CONFESSIONS*, written at the end of the fourth century
AD, the Christian theologian Augustine recalled his enthusiasm
as a boy for the adventures of Aeneas, the hero of Virgil's epic
narrative of the fall of Troy and the survivors' search for a new
homeland. Even as he deplored the sins of his thoughtless boyhood,
Augustine could still recall the excitement of his response to Virgil's
great romance: 'the wooden horse and its crew of soldiers, the
burning of Troy and even the ghost of Creusa made a most
enchanting dream, futile though it was'. What he remembered best
from his readings of the *Aeneid* were his tears for Queen Dido, 'who
killed herself for love'. Augustine's autobiography is almost unique
among the texts that have survived from late antiquity: carefully
polished, it yet speaks with the accents of lived experience out of
that shadowy past. By a strange chance, only a few years before
Augustine undertook his difficult work of self-analysis and expia-
tion, a second Christian bishop, Gregory of Nyssa, was writing the
biography of his sister Macrina, another invaluable eye-witness
account of the unfolding of a religious life. Gregory tells us that
Macrina was taught at home by her mother Emmelia, but, unlike
the educated boys of her social class, was not encouraged to read
the classical Greek and Latin authors, Emmelia considering it
unsuitable 'that a tender and plastic nature should be taught either
those tragic passions of womanhood which afforded poets their
suggestions and plots, or the indecencies of comedy'. For both these
children, one growing up in Thagaste, now Souk Ahras in Algeria,

the other on family estates in Pontus and Cappadocia in Asia Minor, the 'tragic passions of womanhood' were defining texts, wooing the passionate boy to tears of sympathy, and explicitly forbidden to the privileged little girl, marked out from birth for sainthood.

The early Church Fathers left behind an avalanche of material – letters, sermons, commentaries – that reveals their familiarity with the Graeco-Roman cultural tradition as well as the Jewish Holy Books which were Christianity's founding texts. It was not only Rachel, Leah and the obstreperous Queen Jezebel who shaped ideas about women in late antiquity; Penelope, Clytemnestra and the adulterous Helen played prominent roles, along with the more prosaic commentaries of doctors, philosophers, scientists and historians. As in the works of the sages and Rabbis of early Judaism, the message is often contradictory and the evidence badly flawed, being limited almost exclusively to what the male stilo felt authorized to enscribe. Over the thousand or so years in which social ideas were formulated in the Greek and Roman empires, conditions changed, rules were amended, fashions came and went. Relationships between men and women then as now depended on a complex network of social, economic and political factors that were in themselves fluid and susceptible to adjustment, but their favourite myths suggest that, as in Genesis, the orderly organization of society was an important theme for the classical authors, and that this assumed a typical female plot of courtship, marriage and childbirth.

In discussing Graeco-Roman ideas about women and the use made of them by Christian doctrine-makers, the term 'misogyny' is too blunt a tool to be useful. Women's rights were simply not an issue, at least not in the terms in which they are understood today. Just as with Jewish women, the *raison d'être* of the well-born woman throughout the classical period was the exploitation of her fertility within a carefully structured family unit, a destiny that Macrina was able to avoid only through unusual determination. For most women of her class in late antiquity, even among Christian converts, marriage and childbirth were the accepted norm. During the prosperous and well-regulated era of the Antonine emperors in the second century AD, the emphasis on public discipline had a profound effect on attitudes towards the married couple, whose ordered lives were a daily reminder of the state's aspirations for itself. For well-heeled notables of the Roman Empire, regard for personal status and the maintenance of the Empire were primary considerations, and suitable marriages were a priority. At a period of high infant and maternal mortality, girls typically married early and were expected immediately to embark on bearing legitimate children to stock the Empire's body bank. What is surprising is that, despite the importance attached to childbirth with its emphasis on producing sons, woman's ability to procreate was not regarded as a matter for congratulation or respect, but was identified with physical weakness and inferiority, following the negative evaluation of the female body established in Greek medicine and philosophy.

Unstable bodies, febrile minds

THE PRINCIPAL MEDICAL texts in use in late antiquity were written in Greek by male doctors, and although the authors drew on women's observation of their own experience, this was interpreted in the light of prevailing theories about woman's nature and social role, providing 'scientific' justification for the widespread notion of female inferiority. A major source used well into the Christian era was the Hippocratic Corpus, a collection of medical writings by several anonymous doctors from different parts of the Greek empire, largely dating from the fifth and fourth centuries BC. In a society where the well-toned, athletic body was most admired, doctors explained woman's fleshier physique as evidence of physical inferiority. Men and women were differently constituted at the most basic level: a woman's flesh was softer and more porous than a man's and therefore more prone to absorbing moisture, becoming loose and flabby where a man's body was firm and hard. Moisture derived from food and drink was converted into blood and stored in the body; in excess in a woman's case, since her spongelike flesh greedily drank up fluid. Menstruation was necessary to evacuate the superfluity, which during pregnancy was used to nourish the foetus, and converted into milk during the lactation period. A woman's larger, fleshier breasts were particularly prone to an excess of blood, which could lead to madness; while failure to menstruate could similarly lead to manic behaviour. The womb, too, might wander round the body causing fainting fits, suffocation and a variety of other unpleasant physical symptoms, and one way of coaxing the womb back to its proper site was by applying foul or sweet-smelling odours to the nostrils or vagina, which were thought to be linked by one long channel. The Greek doctor Soranus, who lived in Rome at the beginning of the second century AD, while censuring the practice of womb-enticement, lists in his *Gynecology* the sorts of substance used to create a stink: 'burnt hair, extinguished lamp wicks, charred deer's horn, burnt wool, burnt flock, skins and rags, castoreum with which they anoint the nose and ears, pitch, cedar resin, bitumen, squashed bed bugs', which were offset by fragrant suppositories of spikenard and storax. The implication of these ideas about female physiology was that women's bodies were by nature unbalanced, and required restraints and therapies to maintain order and health.

Equally influential were the ideas of the Greek philosopher Aristotle (384–322 BC), who deduced from his study of natural history that the male of any given species was almost always superior to the female. Like the Hippocratic writers, his theories prized the well-developed, muscular male body over flaccid female flesh, but he explained the variations between the bodies of men and women by a theory of vital heat. Man's greater heat was better able to convert nourishment into blood, and thence into the muscle and bone of a strong, athletic body. The surplus blood was concocted into the thick white-hot froth of seminal fluid. A woman's cooler body was less efficient at processing nourishment, and could only concoct the surplus blood into the menstrual flow. This was the basis for Aristotle's influential theory concerning the respective contribution of male and female in generating a child: 'the female is as it were a deformed male; and the menstrual discharge is semen, though in an impure condition; *i.e.*, it lacks one constituent, and one only, the principle of Soul'. He concludes that, in forming a child, 'The female always provides the material, the male provides that which fashions the material into shape . . . Thus the physical part, the body, comes from the female, and the Soul from the male, since the Soul is the essence of a particular body.'

As with the Hippocratics, physical inferiority is linked with

intellectual disability. Women are typically soft, mischievous, cunning and impulsive: 'The fact is [sic], the nature of man is the most
rounded off and complete . . . Hence woman is more compassionate
than man, more easily moved to tears, at the same time is more
jealous, more querulous, more apt to scold and to strike. She is,
furthermore, more prone to despondency and less hopeful than the
man, more void of shame, more false of speech, more deceptive,
and of more retentive memory.' The latter quality sounds promising, but Aristotle was probably referring to woman's famed ability
to hold grudges.

The ideas of Galen, the official doctor of the Imperial Court of
Rome from AD 169–192, like those of Aristotle, persisted well
beyond the Middle Ages. Galen extended Aristotle's heat theory to
suggest that women are literally 'half-baked'. They share the same
basic genital structure as men, but the parts remain inside the female
body because women have insufficient heat thoroughly to 'cook'
them, and Galen ingeniously described how the external male sexual
paraphernalia are situated within the female. He cited the female
lack of an external penis and facial hair as further proof of woman's
inferiority. As with several of his predecessors, Galen pointed out
the need for mutual sexual pleasure in order to achieve conception,
and attributed female hysterical symptoms to lack of sexual intercourse, specifying this as a particular problem for widows, a belief
that was taken up with gusto in the Middle Ages, where the
frustrated, feisty widow became the popular butt of male humour.

Central to the debate about women's bodies between the
Hippocratic period and the first Christian centuries was the question
as to whether a woman was physiologically essentially the same as a
man but with variations, or entirely other. The Hippocratic doctors
argued that the two sexes were distinct and should be treated
accordingly, but by late antiquity doctors had come round to the
view that men and women were similarly constituted and that the
same basic principles should be applied in their treatment, whatever
the specific variants in symptoms. There were also changes in ideas
about the generation of children. The Hippocratic physicians
thought that male and female produce identical, androgynous seeds,
but the female seeds are weaker than the male. Aristotle's idea that
the semen contributes the essential, life-giving element was modi-

fied by Galen who said that both partners produce seed which mixed together forms the embryo, in other words both introduce elements of the *pneuma*, the soul or vital spirit of a person. The woman's seed is simply inferior to that of the man, and the male seed was credited with playing the major role in initiating generation. This idea was to prove useful in Augustine's thinking on original sin, which he saw as sexually transmitted. Pondering why Paul should claim that 'by one man sin entered into the world' (Rom. 5:12) rather than following Genesis in saying that it came through Eve, he decided that it is the male seed, infected by the concupiscence or lust biologically necessary for the discharge of semen, that is primarily responsible for generation, and it thereby passes on original sin to the foetus. Where Augustine differed crucially from the pagan theorists was in condemning the pleasure in intercourse that led to the mutual release of seed.

There was also a significant change in attitude towards menstruation by the early Christian period. Whereas the Hippocratic doctors had regarded it as beneficial to women, an inbuilt mechanism for ridding the body of surplus blood, Aristotle regarded menstruation as potentially weakening, and Soranus found it positively harmful, observing that women who did not menstruate tended to be more physically robust, although he rejected the extreme point of view that menstruation was in itself abnormal, an indication of a diseased uterus. That men found something at least distasteful and even threatening about the female discharge of blood is indicated by the abnormal powers attributed to the menstruant: a passage in *On Dreams* attributed to Aristotle claims that if a menstruating woman looks into a mirror, the surface 'becomes bloody-dark, like a cloud', which is explained as the inflammation of the blood during the menses affecting the blood vessels in the eyes, which in turn influence the objects of a woman's gaze. Pliny, writing his *Historia Naturalis*, a thirty-seven-volume compendium of encyclopaedic information, completed in AD 77, goes even further, crediting the menstruant with, in Lesley Dean-Jones' summary, the 'capability of withering plants, stopping hail, killing caterpillars, removing bitumen, dimming mirrors, blunting knives, souring wine, drying up seeds, and driving dogs mad'. These superstitious ideas were still being discussed during the Renaissance, and it would be interesting to know how far the bad press increasingly attached to menstruation influenced the ascetic women of early Christianity. One of the effects of anorexia, or self-starvation, is the cessation of menstrual periods.

What is unknown is how far medical theory reflects what actually happened. When a doctor was called in to treat a sick or distressed woman, to what extent were the woman or her female relatives able to influence the course of the consultation? What role did the husband play in listening to the diagnosis and monitoring subsequent treatment? What leeway was there for a woman to manipulate both diagnosis and treatment to suit her own requirements? As Helen King points out, '[d]enying that your womb has moved to your liver gets you nowhere, but agreeing that it has moved, and adding that it is now safely back in place, stops the treatment'. But, alluring as it is to think of women in the ancient world adroitly negotiating their way through the male-formulated rules that controlled their lives, the effects of living in a society where the male body was publicly approved as the norm and the female regarded as an aberration can only have been detrimental.

It is, however, difficult to see Aristotle and his peers as engaged in some malevolent plot to subjugate women. No doubt they considered their assessments of the female were reasonable, based on careful personal observation. As the Italian scholar Giulia Sissa points out, 'Great men said terrible things about women. Great philosophies and respected sciences established false and contemptuous ideas about the feminine', but, even so, Sissa makes a plea for objectivity and contextualization. What is important is why men of the ancient world categorized women as inferior and why their ideas have been so tenacious, and it is worth bearing in mind the classicist John Winkler's view that, 'it appears that much of men's [public] talk about women *and about themselves* was a calculated bluff'. As well as reflecting a status quo that valued and empowered men, adamantine assertions of male superiority imply a deep unease in the writers, a need to conform to cultural expectations and a friability that they are not prepared to acknowledge. Even the accusations they level at women – untruthful, emotionally labile, sexually unreliable, weak, dependent, prone to disease – pinpoint the areas in which they may have felt themselves most vulnerable to women, most susceptible to damage. At the same time, their writings testify to a concern with protecting women, albeit the wives, daughters and sisters of the socially viable; slaves, prostitutes, the socially deprived or impoverished, were a different matter.

The appalling things that were written about women through-out the classical period are distressing to modern sensibilities however much they may be dismissed as a comfortable masculine pose, a prop to support male fallibility and fear of inadequacy, but how far they affected individual domestic life can only be conjec-tured. We cannot know for certain how far women accepted the message of their inferiority to men. Modern anthropological studies suggest collusive patterns of role-playing in many so-called primitive communities, in which men are permitted to assert their authority in public, while the women operate with quiet authority behind the scenes. This kind of 'face-saving' may have been common for differing social groups in many periods and communities. More evidence about women's lives in the classical period is now being uncovered in epitaphs, legal and medical records, and other non-literary texts, but for the moment one can only guess at the difficulty for women of the lack of a public voice of their own, the unpleasantness and frustration of being scrutinized, discussed and regulated by men.

The belief that women were physically inferior to men, biologi-cally undeveloped and closer to animals, inevitably affected the evaluation of women's mental capacities. Ideas that would today be termed misogynous were discussed by Greek and Roman physicians as a pragmatic response to the data they were able to observe at a time when dissection of human corpses was not acceptable, but their interpretation of this data appears to have been predetermined by a generally low evaluation of women as irrational, emotional and uncontrolled, liable to spill over with loquacity, tears and sexual exuberance, tendencies attributed to generic physical inferiority. Women were also seen as a dangerous cause of dissension between men through jealousy and competition. Like children they needed to be carefully monitored and controlled and, while men were considered capable of managing their own regimes under expert guidance, women and children, like slaves and barbarians, required restraint from an external, preferably male source.

These negative beliefs undermined a woman's authority, the power of her words, and raised the difficult question of how to deal with the emotional pain of women, a theme that was taken up by poets and dramatists, who explored the sometimes disastrous consequences if a woman was deprived of a husband's support and guidance.

The wise Penelope: female plots in Homer's *Odyssey*

THE FAVOURITE NARRATIVE in Ancient Greek literature was the Trojan War, the long and bloody struggle between Greeks and Trojans sparked off by Helen's adulterous relationship with Paris. Homer's *Odyssey*, probably written some time in the eighth century BC, but based on older oral traditions, records the wanderings and homecoming of King Odysseus, who had sailed to Troy with a great company of Greek warriors when Helen, wife of Menelaus, King of Sparta, was seduced and carried off by Paris, son of King Priam. The Greeks had spent nearly a decade encamped outside the city while the battle hung poised between the well-matched opponents and their presiding deities. When the *Odyssey* begins, it is already nine years since the fall of Troy, but Odysseus has still not returned home to his wealthy kingdom of Ithaca, an island off the west coast of Greece. Despite their lengthy absence, the fate of Odysseus and his party is unknown, and it is this uncertainty that is pivotal to the plot. As long as Odysseus stays away, his absence unexplained, his family and indeed his kingdom remain in stasis. His wife Penelope and son Telemachus cannot observe the rituals for burial and mourning, his ageing father Laertes abdicates responsibility and becomes a recluse, and Odysseus' home and property are threatened by the scores of suitors who throng to court Penelope, a still young and beautiful woman, gifted with wisdom and skilled in the household arts. The assembly of nobles and dignitaries who would customarily restrain the wild behaviour of the young men has been suspended, and when it does finally meet at Telemachus' instigation, there is no clear leadership.

1. Wild animals peacefully cohabit in Eden before Adam bites the apple.
Lucas Cranach the Elder, *Fall of Man*, 1526.

2. Adam and Eve turn away in shame after the Fall. Fourth-century sarcophagus of Junius Bassus.

3. Eve torn between desire and repentance, carved by Gislebertus, *c.* 1130, once above the north portal at St-Lazare Cathedral in Autun.

4. God performs the first wedding ceremony. Jean Corbechon,
The Marriage of Adam and Eve, c. 1415.

5. Adam digs while Eve spins; paired with Noah's Ark.
Speculum Humanae Salvationis, fifteenth century.

6. An energetic serpent with female head and torso in Michelangelo's
Fall and Expulsion, 1509–10.

7. Eve's apple clearly
shows the marks of her
teeth. Lucas Cranach the
Elder, *Eve*, 1528.

8. Cleopatra's pose links her with Eve,
another sexual temptress.
Sixteenth-century Flemish engraving.

9. The Watcher angels descend with glowing phalluses on a daughter of men. William Blake, *c.* 1824/1827.

10. Humanity's spiritual odyssey from the Fall to Christ's Redemption. Hans Holbein the Younger, *Allegory of the Old and New Testaments*.

11. The Burney Relief, *c.* 2300–2000 BC, generally thought to depict Sumerian Inanna-Ishtar, but also linked to Lilith.

12. The newly created Pandora greeted by Epimetheus as she springs out of the earth. Red-figure crater, *c.* 450 BC.

13. The mother goddess Tiamat, depicted as a serpent or sea-snake, conquered by Marduk. Cylinder seal, *c.* ninth–eighth century BC.

14. The butterfly, symbol of transformation, hovers above
Psyche's head in François Gérard's *Amor and Psyche*, 1798.

15. Mary recoils from the news that Gabriel brings. Matthias Grünewald, *Annunciation*, detail, *c.* 1512–16.

16. Mary and saints in a *hortus conclusus*, symbol of Eden and the garden in the Song of Songs. Überrheinischer Meister, *The Garden of Paradise*, *c.* 1410–20.

The *Odyssey* describes the domestic and emotional disruption that follow in the wake of war, and the difficulties for a family when the head of the household, its principal protector, disappears. As Telemachus says of his father, 'His death itself . . . would have caused me less distress. For in that case the whole Achaean nation would have joined in building him a mound, and he would have left a great name for his son to inherit. But . . . [h]e has ceased to exist for us, and to me has left nothing but sorrow and tears.' In the ordinary course of events, Telemachus would have inherited his dead father's property and status, and his mother would have returned home to her father so that arrangements could be made for her courtship and remarriage. But as matters stand, Penelope bides her time in the hope that Odysseus, now absent for nearly twenty years, almost the whole lifetime of their son, will eventually return. And because she waits, against all reasonable expectation, the suitors take advantage of the situation to batten on Odysseus' flocks and stores of wine. Day after day they feast in his halls, seduce the maidservants and abuse the dignity of the boy Telemachus, who despite his anger feels inadequate to challenging the unruly mob. When he does, finally, assert his authority, the suitors plot to murder him.

The poem begins with a vivid portrayal of Penelope's desperate holding operation, fending off her suitors by all manner of skilful tricks, seeming to favour one and then another, '"in her private messages to each making promises that she has not the slightest intention of keeping"', whilst vowing that she cannot even consider marriage until she has finished making a winding sheet for Laertes. The manipulative weaving of the shroud is emblematic of Penelope's attempt to maintain order in her unruly domain. By day she performs a task that particularly symbolizes womanly duty, patiently and expertly deploying her spindle and loom, but at night she secretly unpicks her work by candlelight. Until Odysseus returns or is known to be dead, his family mark time, trapped in a cycle of repetitive acts that can never achieve the relief of closure. But Penelope's ploy with the shroud is betrayed by one of her maids, and the suitors insist that the work should be completed. Isolated and vulnerable in a situation where even her own maids, many of whom are sleeping with the enemy, cannot be trusted, Penelope continues her delaying tactics, while weeping in solitude for her missing husband. At the heart of her efforts is the attempt to preserve Odysseus' property and goods, to ensure the maintenance of his flocks and the produce of his farms, to hold the inheritance together against the day of his return or her son's legal assumption of his father's position, and to keep intact the family unit. At the same time, she is poised on the brink of chaos, as every day the suitors' greed and misbehaviour become more outrageous.

Penelope's gifts, 'her skill in fine handicraft, her excellent brain, and that genius she has for getting her way' and above all her 'wits', her ingenuity and flexibility in managing a difficult situation, are credited to the goddess Athene, who is the presiding deity of the narrative, committed to getting Odysseus safely back home and to supporting both Telemachus and Penelope in their fight against the suitors. The intervention of Athene, a formidable deity, whose wide-ranging responsibilities included the pursuit of reason, the domestic arts and the civic status quo, confirms that the movement of the work is towards the restoration of social harmony, while Odysseus' adventures and his often reckless challenging of events suggest a counter impulse, the desire for change and disturbance that is the dominant motif of the adventure plot. ' "*Make voyages! — Attempt them!*" ' cries the ageing Byron in Tennessee Williams' *Camino Real*, before setting off on his final adventure. What Homer suggests is the allure and necessity for Odysseus of voyaging, even as he demonstrates the burden to his relatives and the threat to his family's economic stability. Again and again, Odysseus wrecks his chances of a swift return to Ithaca by pursuing a new adventure or a challenge that he finds irresistible. Having blinded Polyphemus, the one-eyed Cyclops, and escaped from his cave, Odysseus cannot resist taunting his victim as his crew feverishly row away from the Cyclops' island, and his boasting very nearly sabotages the ship as Polyphemus hurls a great rock at it. Even then, despite the sailors' pleas, he challenges the giant again and, goaded beyond endurance, Polyphemus begs his father, the sea-god Poseidon, that, if Odysseus is allowed to return home to Ithaca, ' "let him come late, in evil plight, with all his comrades dead, and when he is landed, by a foreign ship, let him find trouble in his home" '. Much is made later in the poem of Odysseus' wisdom, but at this stage of the story, egoism overcomes prudence and delays the return to his wife and son by many years. On other occasions, sensual self-indulgence seems to rule Odysseus' actions: having nullified the magic of the enchantress Circe, he lingers on her island for a year, '"feasting on meat galore and mellow wine"', and enjoying the pleasures of her bed.

Both Odysseus and Penelope show considerable mental agility and flexibility in coping with difficulty, but whereas Penelope is confined to a narrow domestic sphere, Odysseus operates in the wider world of travel and exploration, motivated as much by impulse and curiosity as by his declared aim of returning home. In this, Odysseus is an extreme type of the male adventurer. When the action of the *Odyssey* opens, all the other Greek survivors of the Trojan War have long since returned to their wives and families or died en route. In contrast to chaotic Ithaca, other kingdoms visited by Odysseus and Telemachus are models of order, ruled by courteous kings and gracious queens, living in harmony with well-bred sons and daughters: Alcinous and the wise Queen Arete listen sympathetically to Odysseus' traveller's tales; Nestor, the tamer of horses, and his family welcome Telemachus with generous hospitality; even Menelaus and Helen are living together in mutually tolerant domesticity and present a united front to their guests. The delights of marriage are repeatedly celebrated. Nestor is described by Menelaus as '"happy in his marriage"'; Menelaus indulgently recalls how Helen very nearly sabotaged the Trojan horse by imitating the voices of the wives of the men hidden inside, tempting them to leap out and embrace the women from whom they had been separated for so long; and Odysseus himself, when he meets the beautiful and virtuous princess, Nausicaa, gives an encomium of marriage that is the leitmotif of the *Odyssey*: '"may the gods grant you your heart's desire; may they give you a husband and a home, and the harmony that is so much to be desired, since there is nothing nobler or more admirable than when two people who see eye to eye keep house as man and wife, confounding their enemies and delighting their friends'".

In the course of his travels, Odysseus meets a number of women who both help and hinder his purposes, but, like Penelope, these women, even the goddesses Circe and Calypso, are part of

Odysseus' story and stay put, while he moves on to the next encounter. Only Athene appears to have real independence, assuming a variety of disguises, able to move with incredible rapidity between different locations, and flitting to and from Olympus when she wants to win Zeus' support for her schemes. The 'good' women Odysseus meets are dignified queens and princesses, the exemplary wives and daughters of substantial men living in comfort in well-appointed domestic settings, like Nausicaa, who is the daughter of Alcinous, King of the Phaeacians, and whose discreet and helpful behaviour towards Odysseus confirms her as having been formed in the same mould as Penelope – the wellbred, modest girl, trained for marriage and the sensible management of her husband's household. The distracting or dangerous women, like witchy Circe and Calypso, the deadly sirens in their field of bones, and repulsive, multiple-headed Scylla, have little to do with conventional domesticity, but conform instead to patterns of female subversion and even monstrosity which reappear throughout the history of Western society, and are often connected with negative readings of Eve as vamp, enchantress and serpent-tailed monster.

The roles played by women in the *Odyssey* mirror the range of models available for early Israelite women, suggesting the homogeneity of gender traditions across the Mediterranean and Ancient Near East. Penelope recalls the virtuous wife of Proverbs, who attends to her household, ensuring it is well run and amply provisioned, leaving her husband free to pursue his activities with his male peers, while the enchantress Circe and the alluring goddess Calypso resemble those tempting harlots whose honeyed kisses and perfumed beds can only lead to Sheol. Circe does actually send Odysseus to the underworld for a consultation with the blind seer Tieresias, and there is a hint that this encounter with the ghosts of Hades will separate him for ever from the tranquil comforts of marriage, marking him as a man in search of his own death. Like women in the Old Testament, Homeric wives and daughters and female servants play an important role in domestic ritual, which is emphasized by the use of formulaic phrases to describe their activities: the 'staid' housekeepers who liberally serve the travellers with the best their larders can offer, the hospitable queens who make up the guests' beds in the porticoes of their palaces and then retire to sleep companionably alongside their husbands, the maids who pour water for the washing of hands before meals and bathe the male guests, massaging their bodies with olive oil. Another link with Jewish tradition and a sign of the well-regulated household is the persistent spinning and weaving undertaken by the women. Even Circe is described as ' "weaving one of those delicate, graceful, and dazzling fabrics that goddesses love to make" ', a proof of her femininity that wins the confidence of the foraging party and helps to lure them into her palace.

There is no doubting Odysseus' affection for Penelope, even if he dallies on the journey back to her. When the nymph Calypso holds him captive long after his sexual enthusiasm for her has evaporated, he frankly acknowledges, ' "my wise Penelope's looks and stature are insignificant compared with yours" ', but even so, ' "I long to reach my home" '. But when Odysseus does finally reach Ithaca, he takes careful soundings of Penelope's fidelity before identifying himself. His caution is understandable in the light of his meeting in Hades with Menelaus' brother Agamemnon, who was murdered by his wife Clytemnestra's lover on his return from Troy, a warning of the fate that may await an absentee husband. Like the history of the Trojan War, Agamemnon's story goes back to distant events, to a ghastly barbecue served up to his uncle Thyestes and the curse on the house of Atreus, but his own actions as well as adverse fortune bring about his death. At the beginning of Greek hostilities against Troy, Agamemnon was appointed Commander-in-Chief of the Greek army, which mustered at Aulis, a conveniently sheltered bay on the east coast of Greece. But for months the great fleet of ships was trapped in the harbour by unpropitious winds and Agamemnon was advised by the prophet Calchas that the virgin goddess Artemis was angry and could only be appeased by the sacrifice of his daughter Iphigenia, also a virgin. Agamemnon protested, but was mocked as a coward by his fellow officers, and finally sent word to Clytemnestra pretending that Iphigenia was to be married to Achilles and must be sent at once to Aulis. As soon as the girl arrived, the sacrifice was made and the winds changed, allowing the fleet to set sail for Troy. Left alone in Argos, Clytemnestra plotted revenge for her husband's murder of their daughter and took a new lover, Thyestes' son Aegisthus, who had his own grim motive for wishing Agamemnon dead. On Agamemnon's return, he was murdered by Aegisthus, while Clytemnestra killed the pathetic prophetess Cassandra, brought back as spoil from the Trojan War. In the final act of this bloody family history, Agamemnon's son Orestes avenged his father's death by murdering his mother and her lover, an initiative which is repeatedly praised in the *Odyssey*, signifying approval for a deed which, however barbarous, restored social order.

This tale of dysfunctional family life was used by Homer as a counterpoise to the relationship between Odysseus, Penelope and their son Telemachus, highlighting Penelope's moral worth by comparison with Clytemnestra's perfidy and indicating just how disastrously things can go wrong when family loyalties are breached. Despite Homer's empathy with his female characters – so marked that Samuel Butler thought that the poem had been written by a woman – he appears to have had little sympathy for Clytemnestra. Like the maidservants who are hanged by Odysseus for consorting with the suitors, Clytemnestra is harshly judged for her disloyalty to her husband and disregard for family pieties. Ignoring his own expedient murder of his daughter, Agamemnon tells Odysseus, '"for brutality and infamy there is no one to equal a woman who can contemplate such deeds"'. What makes her crimes particularly shocking is the fact of her sex; for a woman even to think of committing such acts, she must be barbarous indeed. And, as with Eve, the effect of her actions is to burden women for ever with the same evil character: '"now, in the depth of her villainy, she has branded not herself alone but the whole of her sex and every honest woman for all time to come"'. Agamemnon warns Odysseus, '"Let this be a lesson to you also . . . Never be too gentle even with your wife, nor show her all that is in your mind."' While he acknowledges that '"wise"' Penelope could never be a murderess, he advises caution: '"Do not sail openly into port when you reach your home-country. Make a secret approach. Women, I tell you, are no longer to be trusted."'

The contrast between the two queens confirms Penelope's status as a model of decorum in the *Odyssey*. After Odysseus kills the suitors, their souls flock down to Hades where they are greeted with astonishment by Agamemnon, but when he hears their tale, he exclaims:

'Unconquerable Odysseus! . . . Ah, happy prince, blessed in Icarius' daughter with a wife in whom all virtues meet, flawless Penelope, who has proved herself so good and wise, so faithful to her wedded love! Her glory will not fade with the years, but the deathless gods themselves will make a song for mortal ears, to grace Penelope the constant queen. What a contrast with Clytaemnestra and the infamy she sank to when she killed her wedded lord! Her name will be cursed wherever she is sung. She has branded all her sex, with every honest woman in it.'

He seems indifferent to the tragic fate of so many young men, whose deaths might have been avoided had Odysseus hurried a little more, and Penelope flirted a little less. But it is Penelope, far more than her husband, son or father-in-law, who holds together the family and its inheritance, which of course includes her own substantial marriage portion, refundable should she return to her father and marry again. The final scenes of the poem record the resumption of civic and domestic order in Ithaca under the guidance of Athene, with Odysseus' reinstatement as head of his household and his kingdom, and the joyful reunion of husband and wife in the marital bed, a coming together in which sexual enjoyment is the prelude to conversation, the pleasure of intimate gossip and the sharing of two decades of news. The necessity for a further journey to placate Poseidon is not allowed to overshadow this homecoming.

The tender night of sex and gossip after nearly twenty years of separation is a reassertion of the trust Penelope and Odysseus have in one another. Their shared enterprise – his journey to Troy and her care for his home in his absence – has worked because, despite doubts, difficulties and distractions, neither partner lost faith. Their confidence in one another turns out to have been justified and they are able to come together without disappointment or compromise. Penelope's stratagems are particularly praiseworthy: she has worked within her confined situation and used her limited female role to the best possible advantage. But behind Homer's happy ending lurks the shadow plot of a woman who has clutched at her last handful of straw, and Penelope's mounting desperation breaks through in the scenes where she weeps over her vanished husband, where she hectically flaunts herself in front of the suitors, where she anxiously questions the stray travellers who turn up in Ithaca, her eyes watchful behind her veil. Homer tells an action-packed tale of Odysseus' adventures, but what the *Odyssey* seems to suggest is a bias towards well-regulated domestic life, the harmonious running of the household and estate, and the text's greatest praise is reserved for the woman who does most to protect this – Odysseus' wife Penelope. At face value at least, Homer's portrait of Penelope contradicts the negative view of women that Hesiod so maliciously exploited, and suggests that a woman is quite capable of planning and executing a series of self-protective strategems, even though she does so on the brink of a precipice: Penelope's ruses succeed because Odysseus arrives in the nick of time.

Tragic passions

CLYTEMNESTRA'S SITUATION is very different from Penelope's. Her faith in Agamemnon was destroyed by his sacrifice of their daughter, and their marital relationship was further damaged by the news that he had taken Priam's daughter Cassandra as his concubine, but both Homer and Aeschylus in his Oresteian plays imply that there is something unfeminine about Clytemnestra's behaviour. In the *Odyssey*, Agamemnon says that she set new standards of barbarity for women, while Aeschylus presents her as a Greek version of Lady Macbeth, 'in whose woman's heart/A man's will nurses hope'. In this version of the story, she herself kills Agamemnon after first binding him in a voluminous net. But where Homer condemns, Aeschylus shows understanding of Clytemnestra's pain and suggests that there can be no simple apportionment of blame.

Euripides' version of the story of Medea is another example of a woman who reacts in an extreme, 'unnatural' way to an initial breach of trust and, again, the playwright shows that there is no easy moral judgement to be made about her behaviour. The play takes place in Corinth where Jason and Medea have been living for some years with their two young sons, but now Jason has fallen in love with Glauce, the beautiful young daughter of King Creon, and has decided to marry her. His decision is motivated partly by desire, but also because of his own anomalous position in Corinth. The marriage will give him political authority and guarantee the safety and comfort of his first family. These arguments bear no weight with Medea; she sees Jason's marriage plans as a bitter betrayal of their relationship and all that she has dared and endured for his sake. Medea's background, gradually revealed during the course of the play, marks her as being both exotic and suspect. She is the granddaughter of Helios, the sun, and has a reputation for witchcraft, possibly derived from her connection with Circe whom some versions of the story claimed as Medea's aunt, but a dubious recommendation for the Greeks, who were hostile to female magicians. Despite her father's ancient claim to the throne of Corinth, Medea is regarded as a foreigner, a non-Greek, princess of Colchis in Asia, where Jason first met her when he came in his ship, the *Argo*, in search of the Golden Fleece. By means of her magic arts, Medea had helped Jason to achieve his quest in return for marrying her and taking her away with him. Before they set sail with the precious fleece, Medea took the precaution of abducting her young brother Absyrtus, and she slowed down their father's pursuit by slitting her brother's throat, dismembering the body and dropping the segments overboard, sure that King Aeetes would stop to pick up the pieces. On their arrival in Iolcus, Medea had a second chance to demonstrate her ruthlessness. When Jason delivered the fleece to King Pelias, the king failed to meet his side of the bargain, refusing to acknowledge Jason's claim to the throne, and Medea literally cooked up a plot to have Pelias' daughters murder their father. Capitalizing on the ageing king's desire for perpetual youth, she demonstrated how an old ram, cut up and boiled with a selection of magic herbs, emerged metamorphosed into a healthy lamb. The daughters followed the formula, but Pelias of course stayed dead, the hunks of his severed flesh steaming dismally and untransformed in the pot. As a result, Jason and Medea were forced to flee to Corinth, but, although Medea remains a welcomed but unassimilated exile, Jason eventually seizes the opportunity for political integration and power in Corinth.

The play begins with Medea in collapse, weeping and refusing to eat, raging at Jason for insulting her love and her honour by his proposed marriage, and regretting her father and her homeland, lost to her for ever by her support of Jason and murder of her brother. Abandoned by Jason, as she interprets the situation, Medea has no refuge, no home to turn to, no family to defend her or to take her in. Her sense of isolation and of being an outcast in Corinth is emphasized throughout the play, and she speaks bitingly of female dependence in marriage:

> If a man grows tired
> Of the company at home, he can go out, and find
> A cure for tediousness. We wives are forced to look
> To one man only. And, they tell us, we at home
> Live free from danger, they go out to battle: fools!
> I'd rather stand three times in the front line than bear
> One child.

What makes her writhe is the thought that people will laugh at her as a rejected wife, and it is this humiliation that goads her into extreme action. When she hears that Creon, frightened that she will damage his family, has banished her and her sons from Corinth, Medea plans a terrible revenge. She sends her young sons with a gift to Glauce – a golden crown and elaborate gown bequeathed by her grandfather, the sun. The princess cannot resist at once trying on the beautiful present and for a moment or two rotates in front of her mirror, admiring the effect of the shimmering coronet against her bright hair and watching how the dress falls in elegant folds to her pretty feet. But she is suddenly convulsed as the poison in crown and gown begin to work; both seem to weld themselves to her body and, when her father runs in to try to help her, he too is gripped by a burning torment which dissolves his flesh but will not allow him to release his hold. In the end, both lie welded together, horribly intermingled in an unrecognizable lump of blood and bone. This is only the prelude to Medea's defiance of Jason; in a final terrible act of retribution, she slays their sons, destroying Jason's stake in the future. As the play ends, Medea flies off in a dragon-drawn chariot, sent by Helios, to bury her dead and then take refuge in Athens.

Medea's murder of her sons has branded her as that ultimate villainess, the mother who can kill her own children, but Euripides shows that it is no easy, cold-blooded decision. Most of all it is her rejection by Jason, her wish to punish him for destroying their mutual trust, that motivates her. Jason's calm explanations of his own behaviour, his rational approach to securing his and his children's future, do not touch her. Where feelings are concerned, politics and astute financial planning can have no influence over Medea, and it is the insult to her love that she feels most. When she has abandoned all personal ties and security for the sake of Jason, and committed such terrible deeds to secure their life together, how can he renege on their reciprocal fidelity? What he dismisses as female sexual jealousy is a fundamental commitment for her: they are either together, a tightly knit unit, or broken apart. No other position is possible. But the decision to kill her children is terrible to her, and in a long, moving speech she argues whether or not she can bring herself to do it, ricocheting from one position to another, mourning in advance the waste and loss, and her own misery alone in exile, and bleakly recognizing that what drives her is her own stubbornness: 'My misery is my own heart, which will not relent.' Finally, although she knows that she will suffer far more than Jason for the death of her children, she imagines her enemies mocking her and steels herself to act.

Dido's story in the *Aeneid*, which made such an impression on the young Augustine, is also about betrayal. Dido was the widowed Queen of Carthage who had the misfortune to fall passionately in love with Aeneas as the result of sorcery commissioned by his mother Venus, the goddess of love. Just as Athene's guardianship of Penelope promised the return of order and domestic harmony, Venus' influence over Dido suggests emotional disorder and tumult, for Venus was notoriously unable to control her own immoderate passions. In her Greek manifestation as Aphrodite (eventually iden-tified with Roman Venus), she was held up to humiliation in front of all the male gods when her husband Hephaestus trapped her in a bronze net as she was clandestinely dallying with her lover Ares, and on another occasion she was lured by Zeus into a liaison with a mortal man, the young Anchises, by whom she bore Aeneas. Aphrodite/Venus' jealous protection of her reputation for beauty was the cause of the Trojan War, through her promise to Paris of Helen, and her behaviour to her son's wife Psyche similarly indicates how intolerant she was of competition. Dido's passion is magically aroused in order to safeguard Aeneas, to ensure that she will offer him a safe harbour until he is ready to continue his journey to found the new Troy; for the queen's welfare, Venus cares not a jot. When Aeneas eventually leaves Carthage, deaf to Dido's pleas to remain with her, the queen is maddened by grief and stabs herself on top of the huge funeral pyre that she has had erected in the inner court of her palace. As the fleet of Trojan ships speeds away across the waves, the sailors see the blaze, without understanding what it means.

> But what they knew of a great love profaned
> In anguish, and a desperate woman's nerve,
> Led every Trojan heart into foreboding.

What the stories of Dido, Medea and Clytemnestra confirm is the confinement of the female marriage plot, which makes women dependent on the good will and faith of men. As Medea says:

> if . . . our husband does not struggle
> Under the marriage yoke, our life is enviable.
> Otherwise, death is better.

They explore the conflict between (male) reason and (female) passion, and demonstrate the difficulty of maintaining social order when trust has broken down. Civilization is a veneer, these narratives seem to say, beneath which seethe tumultuous and un-predictable emotions, and they communicate an idea of female vulnerability and instability that can topple over into madness. All three women are provoked into violent and bloody action by the failure of their domestic lives: they are all betrayed by the men they trust, and they react intemperately. A modern interpretation might say that they were perfectly justified in their rage and in taking revenge, but, as well as bringing misfortune and even death to their men, these women's actions rebound negatively on their own lives. Clytemnestra exposes herself to the possibility of civil war in her kingdom, and becomes fatally vulnerable to her children's hatred; Medea loses Jason, her sons and the home where she has lived for many years; Dido kills herself. In their attempts to break out of their cages, they choose masochistic options and end up dead or wretched.

Behind these portrayals of women acting self-destructively *in extremis* was the long tradition of medical and philosophical ideas about female vulnerability which presupposed a lesser capacity in women for self-regulation, the *sōphrosunē*, or self-control, that was considered fundamental to rational life and good citizenship. These popular stories highlight the importance of domestic life to the financial and emotional wellbeing of a family's members, as well as to the social weal, and expose the havoc caused by breaches of trust between men and women. As in the parallel Jewish biblical narratives, marriage and motherhood are the standard boundaries of a mortal woman's life, whatever freedoms may be permitted goddesses, and these dramas make serious attempts to address male responsibilities and women's responses, offering a new perspective on the female weakness and inferiority predicated by doctors and philosophers. One can understand why Emmelia had reservations about a vulnerable young girl studying such incendiary material.

Joseph and Aseneth

ONE OF THE FEW surviving early Jewish narratives to dwell at length on a woman's experience is the Greek romance of the conversion of Aseneth. Unlike Eve, Sarah, Rebekah and Rachel, the founding women of Judaism, Joseph's Egyptian wife receives only the briefest of mentions in Genesis (41:45, 50), but the gaps in her story are imaginatively filled in *Joseph and Aseneth*, which provides a richly embroidered account of the domestic and emotional life of its turbulent heroine. Written some time between

100 BC and AD 200, possibly for the improvement and entertainment of educated well-to-do Jews and proselytes living in Egypt, the first part of the novella tells the dramatic story of Aseneth's first meeting with Joseph and her subsequent spiritual odyssey. Like Apuleius' story of Psyche and Cupid in *The Golden Ass*, this is a pacey narrative of the achievement of love through difficulty and the abasement of a beautiful, wayward heroine, who is tamed by her passion for a handsome, but ultimately passive young man. Both Aseneth and Psyche are the main actors in their stories; their lovers charmingly regret the inconvenience they cause, but remain the puppets of supernatural powers who manipulate the women's desires to suit their own ends.

The story begins when Joseph is travelling through Egypt, stockpiling grain for the Pharaoh's storehouses. The priest of the town of Heliopolis is Pentephres, one of the Pharaoh's counsellors and father of Aseneth, a beautiful eighteen-year-old virgin. Even though her many suitors include the Pharaoh's firstborn son, Aseneth scorns them all, hiding in her luxurious rooms and devoting her energies to the worship of heathen Egyptian gods. Aseneth is waited on by seven virgins, all born on the same night as she, who live in the seven antechambers that guard her apartments. None has ever so much as spoken to a man. Cloistered in virginity, Aseneth sleeps alone in a bed on which no one but she has ever sat. The courtyard surrounding her father's house is protected by a high wall and four metal-bound gates; each of the gates is further guarded by eighteen powerful armed men. Along the walls of the courtyard are fruit-bearing trees and, when the story begins, it is harvest-time and the trees are pendulous with fruit.

This highly charged atmosphere of female seclusion and touch-me-not virginity is disrupted when Pentephres tells Aseneth that she is to marry Joseph. Aseneth disdainfully refuses, but runs away to her window to watch Joseph's arrival. Alas for Aseneth – the sight of Joseph, effulgent in royal gold and purple and with a great fruit-bearing olive branch in his hand, is physically overwhelming. As he is brought into the courtyard, she trembles with fear at his magnificence and vows herself his slave. At this moment, Joseph happens to look up and observing Aseneth still leaning out, asks Pentephres to make her leave the house. Joseph's good looks have been a source of endless trouble to him; warned by his father Jacob not to have anything to do with corrupting foreign women, he has spent his years in Egypt piously resisting the advances of the wives and daughters of the nobility, who harass him with messages and gifts. Pentephres reassures him that Aseneth is a respectable virgin, but when Aseneth attempts to give Joseph a sister's kiss, he holds her off. A man who worships God cannot defile himself by kissing a heathen foreign woman. When Aseneth bursts into tears, Joseph is moved to ask God's blessing for her and then departs, promising to return in a week's time.

And now begins a dreary time of repentance for proud Aseneth. Rejecting any help from her virgin guardians, she locks herself away in her rooms and dresses in mourning, casting out her jewels and golden ornaments. She similarly destroys her Egyptian idols and throws away the ritual food. Clothed in sackcloth and ashes, she weeps for seven days; on the eighth she pauses to consider what she is to do. Her parents will reject her because she has destroyed their household gods and she is generally unpopular because of her haughty rejection of her suitors. Even Joseph's God will hate her because she has worshipped other gods, but she resolves to cast herself on His mercy. She humbly confesses her sins and begs God to give her to Joseph as his slave. As she finishes her prayer, the sun rises and a shining man emerges from the terrifying light burning at its heart. He is the commander of God's angels, and instructs Aseneth to wash and dress herself in virgin linen. He tells her that God has accepted her repentance and she will be given to Joseph as his bride. Aseneth persuades the angel to sit on her undefiled bed and brings him bread to eat from her storeroom, but the man tells her to go back and fetch the honeycomb that she will find there. He shares with her a small piece of the comb, which he tells her possesses magic properties reminiscent of the tree of life; it was made by bees from the dew of the roses of life in the 'paradise of delight', a contemporary synonym for the Garden of Eden, and all who eat of it will live for ever. From that day her flesh will flourish 'like flowers of life', her bones will grow as strong as the cedars of Eden, she will have boundless energy and her youth and beauty will never fade; and she will be like a walled mother-city to all who wish to take refuge in God. Perhaps to emphasize her regenerative powers, the angel touches the comb where he broke off the piece and makes it whole once more. Then the angel conjures a swarm of bees from the comb, an immense throng winged in purple and wearing golden crowns; some encircle Aseneth, covering her body from head to foot, while others build a replica honeycomb on her mouth and eat from the oozing cells. Finally the angel burns the comb, blesses Aseneth's virgin keepers and departs heavenwards in a chariot of fire.

It is the eighth day after Joseph's first visit to Pentephres and, true to his promise, he calls at the house again and is astonished to find Aseneth robed like a bride and radiant with supernatural beauty. She explains her penance and the events that followed, and Joseph acknowledges her as his intended wife. Their marriage is celebrated with great splendour and the narrative concludes with Aseneth's song of confession and thanksgiving.

Joseph and Aseneth is a very different work from the stories of Greek and Roman heroines considered earlier. Its aim was to extol the benefits of conversion to the Jewish faith, the partaking of God's life-giving honey, whilst pointing out the emotional and spiritual effort required to embrace the God of the Israelites. An ancillary purpose may have been to resolve the nagging dilemma of Joseph's marriage to a non-Jewish woman. Its overwhelming effect, however, is to focus on the erotic life of Aseneth. The voluptuous detailing of her virgin seclusion is matched by the emotional force of her impetuous passion and repentance, and her sensuous meeting with the angel. In a text replete with symbolic meaning, the mystery of the honeycomb is particularly intriguing, connecting Aseneth with the Garden of Eden and the tree of life, reaffirming Eve's maternal destiny and reversing her curse as death-dealer. The life-giving fecundity of the bees transfers itself to Aseneth in the replenishing honey which she eats, whose sweetness is rebuilt on her lips in a second comb that the bees feed from in a reciprocity of vital nourishment and energy. Aseneth's purity is emphasized by the unpolluted bed where the angel sits while he performs his transformations, while her fertility is implied by the fruit-bearing trees beneath her window, guarded by zealous wardens who significantly lock Joseph inside the protected garden on his first visit to the house. Aseneth's alarming encounter with the swarming bees and her quiet acceptance of bombardment by the furry battalions are perhaps symbolic of her new status, initiate into God's mysteries, and potential wife and childbearer to one of Israel's foremost sons.

By one of those strange coincidences that link experience across centuries, Aseneth's adventure with the bees is illuminated by a parallel incident in the novel *Remembering Babylon* (1993) by the Australian writer David Malouf, in which a young girl, Janet, living in a remote settlement in Queensland in the middle of the nineteenth century, takes to spending her free time with the local beekeeper. Janet's attraction to the bees is that she senses in their organized lives – and particularly in the sound they make, 'the single vibrant word resounding in their furry heads' – some guiding principle, 'not just *what* they were, in their individual bee bodies, but *why* they were'. 'If she could escape, she thought, just for a moment, out of her personal mind into their communally single one, she would know at last what it was like to be an angel.' One unusually hot and oppressive day, Janet has been working with the bees and has just removed her bonnet and protective veil when a sudden wind stirs in the grove and in an instant the swarm is upon her:

> She just had time to see her hands covered with plushy, alive fur gloves before her whole body crusted over and she was blazingly gathered into the single sound they made, the single mind.
>
> Her own mind closed in her . . .
>
> She stood still as still and did not breathe. She surrendered herself.
>
> You are our bride, her new and separate mind told her as it drummed and swayed above the earth. Ah, so that is it! They have smelled the sticky blood-flow. They think it is honey. It is.

There are striking similarities between Janet and Aseneth's experiences. Janet feels that knowledge of the bees' communal mind will put her in touch with an angel's power to understand the secrets of the universe; Aseneth meets an angel who initiates her into God's mysteries by feeding her honey made in Paradise. Both find themselves unexpectedly physically enclosed by bees like a second skin and neither flinch nor feel afraid, but give themselves over to the experience and emerge spiritually transformed. For both, the encounter with the bees symbolizes a female as well as a spiritual rite of passage, which both willingly embrace: Janet's first menstruation, which she understands is what attracts the bees to her as a source of honey, and Aseneth's joyful relinquishment of her long-cherished virginity in order to marry Joseph.

EVE'S STORY NOW moves into the early Christian world and an atmosphere of sexual reform in which asceticism unexpectedly became the norm. The chilly austerities of Christian belief were remote from the passionate outpourings of betrayed Medea or Dido, or even from Aseneth's joyous capitulation to Joseph and his faith, and at times appeared almost to abandon the ideal of family life. Christianity's new ideal of virginity cut across social hierarchies, linking Jew and pagan in a spiritual democracy whose values focused on the individual's relationship with God. Social, civic and personal duties devolved from this core commitment, which, paradoxically, held out the possibility to women of new freedom, new responsibilities and revolutionary new plots.

CHAPTER 6

THE TERRIBLE FLESH

'Our life has been a vain attempt at self-delight. But self-abnegation is the higher road. We should mortify the flesh – the terrible flesh – the curse of Adam!'

Sue Bridehead, in THOMAS HARDY, *Jude the Obscure*

I N HIS NOVEL *Northern Lights*, Philip Pullman proposes the ingenious idea that original sin is physically manifested in the form of elementary particles that are popularly known as Dust. In Pullman's imaginatively skewed version of the world, the pre-pubertal child is relatively Dust-resistant, but at the moment the personality becomes fixed, the Dust that pours down on the world via the Aurora Borealis begins to cling, and the all-powerful Church authorities attribute to it all the mental and emotional ills that dog humanity, 'the sin, the misery, the destructiveness', and ultimately death. Destroy the source of Dust, says Pullman's demonic hero, Lord Asriel, and death itself will die. This is an idea not a million miles remote from the early Church's teaching on sexuality, and Pullman's re-working of the Eden myth, his resourceful Lyra/Eve's insight that Dust may in fact be of benefit to humanity and must be preserved at any cost, would probably have been suppressed by the Christian Fathers with as much rigour as they quashed any idea that the free expression of sexuality might be a legitimate, even God-given, pleasure. The Church's repressive view of human sexuality in some ways reflects the moral strictures of early Judaism, but its similar support for orderly family life was compromised by the even greater enthusiasm for asceticism which filtered through the diverse Christian communities of late antiquity.

During the four hundred years between the crucifixion of Jesus and the death of Augustine of Hippo, the Christian Church meta-morphosed from illegal gatherings of the supporters of a suspected revolutionary to becoming, with the conversion of the Roman

Emperor Constantine in AD 313, the acknowledged spiritual mouth-piece of the Roman Empire. During this period, it developed its own complex hierarchy of officials and regulations, its public buildings and offices, its duties to the state and its own civic status and dignity, and its enormous power to regulate the citizen, body, mind and soul. Christianity did not spring fully fledged out of the life and ministry of Jesus with a whole new set of ready-made rules by which people agreed amicably to live. It evolved with remarkable speed, spreading like wildfire through the Roman Empire and beyond, but it was forced to lock horns en route with Roman social mores, and to take into account a multiplicity of local ideas and customs. It also had to deal with the diverse beliefs of the many sects that the new faith spawned. In particular, it had to confront and if possible accommodate the strict tenets of Judaism, not an easy task given that even the founder members of the Christian church did not see eye to eye on such fundamental questions as the necessity for circumcision of Gentile converts, or the observation of cleanliness rituals. In the course of this process of religious change and assimilation, there was a revolution in ideas about individual morality and a radical new approach to human sexuality, in which marriage and procreation became, for some Christians, inferior alternatives to continence and even perpetual virginity.

In investigating the evolution of early Christianity, the enquiring reader enters a melting pot of ideas and cultures, where notions about sexuality were continually being explored and modified, and where different contexts and customs threw up radically different solutions to the newly pressing question of how to live a fully Christian life. It is an environment in which it would be dangerous to accept even the simplest statement about sexuality at face value. Always one has to ask oneself, 'What is going on here? What is the subtext of this message?' The ministry and death of Jesus of Nazareth had an extraordinary effect not only on the Jewish communities in ancient Palestine, but in far-flung regions of the Roman Empire. From Gaul to the parched terrain of desert Egypt, from Syria to Augustine's home town in North Africa, beautiful, ilex-planted Thagaste, people were stirred with new faith, new enthusiasm and new messianic hopes. Out of the mêlée of opposing factions and strident, clashing beliefs from which the closely defined and tautly regulated structure of the universal Catholic Church was finally to emerge, stepped an extraordinary band of men, the great shapers and leaders of the new faith: ascetic Anthony who, after twenty years of wrestling alone in the desert to subdue his spirit to God's, stepped from his cell with the well-toned body of an athlete and the fine-honed mind of a hellenist philosopher, his will finally transparent to the light of God's grace and shedding its radiance on all who met him; urbane Jerome, opinionated, emotional, irascible, pouring out advice and exhortation in a stream of letters to his coterie of female supporters; vehement Tertullian, who lambasted women as daughters of Eve, the devil's gateway; the elusive scholar Ambrose, who made such a powerful impression on the young catechumen Augustine; and the towering figure of Augustine himself, who left his *Confessions* as a unique first-person witness to the tormenting struggle between body, mind and spirit. From the shadowy hinterland of the anonymous Jewish narrators of *Jubilees* and *1 Enoch*, we move into the glaring landscapes of early Christianity, where personalities stand in sharp focus. This is the era of the individual, and what writers these Christian Fathers were, how competitive, how alert to the nuances of human behaviour, and in particular to what had been in debate among different cultural groups in the Ancient Near East since long before the coming of Christ: the regulation of the mind and the appropriate control of the body's pressing needs – for food, for sex, for shelter. With the spotlight beamed on to personal responsibility, to probing motivation and searching out the heart's innermost secrets and most despicable desires, the Hebrew account of origins, that ancient story of Adam and Eve in the Garden of Eden, acquired new resonances and assumed a form and meanings that were to have a momentous effect on Christian men and women, and still continue to influence Western ideas about human sexuality today.

It is tempting, when dealing with the attitude of the early Church to Adam and Eve, to apply a pick-and-mix approach – to put in a thumb and pull out the ripe plums of misogyny, the damning phrase or polemical statement that seems to confirm a wholesale prejudice against women, and in particular a deep suspicion of female sexuality. But the situation was more complex than such an approach would imply. Given the revolutionary attitudes of

Christianity towards domestic and social behaviour, its emphasis on sexual relationships between men and women was perhaps inevitable. Procreation had been enormously important to Jewish racial survival, while Greek and Roman tradition also laid a heavy emphasis on family and inheritance. At the same time, there were significant differences in cultural attitudes to such practices as homosexuality, prostitution, abortion and infanticide, which were legally acceptable to some pagan communities but not to Jews, who were, however, quite happy to accommodate polygamy and divorce. Jesus' teaching challenged many of these traditional beliefs, and in particular introduced the possibility of celibacy as the goal of the truly Christian life.

Jesus made only one reference to the Genesis account of Adam and Eve. When asked by the Pharisees what constituted legitimate grounds for divorce, he referred them to Genesis 2:24:

> Have ye not read, that he which made them at the beginning
> made them male and female,

> And said, For this cause shall a man leave father and mother, and
> shall cleave to his wife: and they twain shall be one flesh?

> Wherefore they are no more twain, but one flesh. What
> therefore God hath joined together, let not man put asunder.

> (Matt. 19:4–6)

This answer displeased the Jewish community by putting a total ban on divorce, when what concerned the different religious factions were the legitimate grounds for ridding oneself of an unsatisfactory wife. What Jesus appeared to be saying was that marriage was more important than procreation: just because a wife was barren or repugnant to her husband was no reason to dissolve a solemn commitment. When his followers protested that in this case it would be better not to marry at all, Jesus proposed an even more radical idea, 'there be eunuchs, which have made themselves eunuchs, for the kingdom of heaven's sake' (Matt. 19:12). Luke records a further statement by Jesus that appeared to favour celibacy over marriage:

The children of this world marry, and are given in marriage:

But they which shall be accounted worthy to obtain that world, and the resurrection from the dead, neither marry, nor are given in marriage:

Neither can they die any more: for they are equal unto the angels; and are the children of God, being the children of the resurrection.

(Luke 20:34–6)

These revolutionary ideas, shocking as they were to traditional Jewish belief, have to be read in the context of Jesus' total message which preached that the Kingdom of God was literally at hand, and that there was no time to waste in order to prepare for its coming. The advice to relinquish wealth and property and to abandon family ties and obligations in favour of a new life of dedication to God reflects Jesus' sense of the urgent necessity to 'get in shape' for the new age that was dawning.

'Better to marry than to burn . . .'

The teachings of Jesus' disciple Paul are to be seen in a similar context of Christian belief in the impending end of the world. A Greek-speaking Jew, Paul famously converted to Christ on a journey to Damascus, a moment of revelation which left him temporarily blind (Acts 9:3–9). Whereas no primary texts survive of Jesus' words – the gospels were written after his death and reflect the writers' own interests in the way they report Christ's life and message – the New Testament includes a number of Paul's letters to the churches he helped to establish in the course of his astonishing journeys, energetically crisscrossing the Empire along the excellent roads constructed by the Romans, striding from Ephesus to Caesarea in Judea, proselytizing along the coast to Antioch, expostulating across Cappadocia and Galatia as far as Philippi in Macedonia and beyond, resolutely dealing with the problem of reconciling Christ's urgent message of salvation with the rigidities of Mosaic Law. The celibate Paul saw marriage as a necessary nuisance:

> I say therefore to the unmarried and widows, It is good for them
> if they abide even as I.
>
> But if they cannot contain, let them marry: for it is better to
> marry than to burn.
>
> (1 Cor. 7:8–9)

Some groups even read his advice as promoting celibacy within
marriage: 'they that have wives be as though they had none' (1 Cor.
7:29), although the context of this extreme situation is Paul's
concern that time is short, 'the fashion of this world passeth away'
(1 Cor. 7:31). Marriage is a distraction from the necessary con-
centration on God at this extraordinary moment of crisis when
Christians await the imminent coming of His kingdom:

> But I would have you without carefulness. He that is unmarried
> careth for the things that belong to the Lord, how he may please
> the Lord:
>
> But he that is married careth for the things that are of the world,
> how he may please his wife.
>
> (1 Cor. 7:32–3)

Paul does not neglect women in his advice to concentrate on
priorities:

> There is a difference also between a wife and a virgin. The
> unmarried woman careth for the things of the Lord, that she may
> be holy both in body and in spirit: but she that is married careth
> for the things of the world, how she may please her husband.
>
> (1 Cor. 7:34)

He concludes his recommendations by saying that while marriage is
acceptable, it is preferable to remain an unmarried virgin or celibate
widow.

Paul's advice to the Corinthians reflects the difficulties faced by
the new religion in balancing Christian ideologies and, in particular,
ideas about the coming of the new age with conservative Judaism,
and the authentic Pauline documents repeatedly record his earnest
attempts to deal with conflicts between pagan and Jewish tradition

and Christianity's revolutionary ideas about human behaviour. His ideas about the veiling of women should probably be read in the same light. Women in the Corinthian congregation had been appearing with their heads uncovered at religious gatherings and, in a complex and somewhat contradictory passage, Paul argues that although women's hair is their glory, it should be covered because in the spiritual hierarchy, 'the head of every man is Christ; and the head of the woman is the man; and the head of Christ is God' (1 Cor. 11:3). Whilst man is the 'image and glory of God', a reference to Genesis 1:27, and should therefore more appropriately go about with his head bare,

> the woman is the glory of the man.
>
> For the man is not of the woman; but the woman of the man.
>
> Neither was the man created for the woman; but the woman for the man.
>
> (1 Cor. 11:7–9)

Here Paul was clearly thinking of the creation of Eve from Adam's rib, and he goes on to stress the interdependence of man and woman, 'For as the woman is of the man, even so is the man also by the woman; but all things of God' (1 Cor. 11:12), echoing the substance of Adam's words in Genesis 2:24, after he has welcomed Eve as bone of his bones and flesh of his flesh: 'Therefore shall a man leave his father and his mother, and shall cleave unto his wife: and they shall be one flesh.' This whole passage can be seen as Paul's attempt to work out local problems in the Corinthian community connected with the relationship between men and women, and female behaviour, by reference to traditional Jewish teaching. Subsequent generations of Christians, however, read Paul's comments as lapidary pronouncements about the veiling of women and their subordination to men. Even as late as the mid-seventeenth century, Milton's famous description of Adam and Eve in the Garden of Eden draws on Paul:

> in their looks divine
> The image of their glorious maker shone,

> Truth, wisdom, sanctitude severe and pure,
> Severe but in true filial freedom placed;
> Whence true authority in men; though both
> Not equal, as their sex not equal seemed;
> For contemplation he and valour formed,
> For softness she and sweet attractive grace,
> He for God only, she for God in him:

To demonstrate this hierarchic relationship, Adam's 'hyacinthine locks' only 'manly hung' to his 'broad' shoulders, while Eve's hair falls to her waist, and Milton elaborates Eve's hairstyle into a cloying and ambiguous image of her subjection to her husband. Her 'golden tresses':

> in wanton ringlets waved
> As the vine curls her tendrils, which implied
> Subjection, but required with gentle sway,
> And by her yielded, by him best received,
> Yielded with coy submission, modest pride,
> And sweet reluctant amorous delay.

There is danger in that profusion of unveiled, 'wanton' curls, and one is reminded of Robert Graves' gleefully malicious portrait of hair-fetichist Milton, snared by Marie Powell's abundant tresses in the novel *Wife to Mr Milton*.

But there are other texts attributed to Paul that represent more extreme reactionary views: the pastoral letter to Timothy affirms the subordination of women, and links it specifically with Eve's susceptibility to error, thrusting women back into their traditional role as childbearers. The popular subject of women's dress also gets an airing, the author advising:

> that women adorn themselves in modest apparel, with shamefacedness and sobriety; not with broided hair, or gold, or pearls, or costly array;

> But (which becometh women professing godliness) with good works.

> Let the woman learn in silence with all subjection.

But I suffer not a woman to teach, nor to usurp authority over the man, but to be in silence.

For Adam was first formed, then Eve.

And Adam was not deceived, but the woman being deceived was in the transgression.

Notwithstanding she shall be saved in childbearing, if they continue in faith and charity and holiness with sobriety.

(1 Tim. 2:9–15)

Although Pauline in character, this was almost certainly not Paul's work, and probably dates to a later, increasingly conservative period of the early Church, when many Christians reacted against asceticism in favour of traditional family values. It seems an extraordinary irony that this brief text, not even written by Paul, should have become the cornerstone of later Christian teaching about women, blasting their lives with the injunction to silence and submission, and offering salvation only through repeated childbirth, ideas that were rehearsed again and again in sermons, pamphlets, and popular and learned literature throughout the early modern period, and whose traces have survived in the Christianized West well into the twentieth century.

'In Adam all die'

MICHELANGELO'S GREAT PROGRAMME for the Sistine Chapel ceiling in the Vatican at Rome was begun on 10 May 1508. '[E]l papa resta assai ben sodisfato' was the artist's laconic comment when the work was finally completed, and the pope, Julius II, might well have been delighted. In two bursts of activity, Michelangelo had created the most ambitious decorative scheme ever seen in a Christian church, a fitting showroom for the pomp and power of the papacy and a testimony to the most fundamental beliefs of Christianity in the early sixteenth century. At its mid-point is the Creation of Eve, flanked by two frescoes showing the Creation of Adam, and the Temptation, Fall and Expulsion from Eden, the trio representing the beginning of human history with Eve as Mother of All Living. Michelangelo's schema presents a densely populated narrative that was to culminate in its final scene, painted on the wall behind the altar twenty-two years later: the Last Judgement, whose vast Christ towered menacingly above the illustrious visitors to the papal presence as they made their dignified egress from the chapel. In its totality, the programme demonstrates the close connection between the Old Testament and the New, depicting the early history of humanity under Mosaic Law and then under the revised covenant symbolized by Christ's sacrifice and promise of redemption, the successive stages linked by innumerable references that move to and fro in time.

It was Paul who established the vital connection between Adam and Christ that became so fundamental to the Church's teaching on sexuality, sin and redemption. In his first letter to the Corinthians, Paul went to great pains to spell out just what Christ's resurrection meant for his followers, the triumph over death itself:

> For since by man came death, by man came also the resurrection of the dead.

> For as in Adam all die, even so in Christ shall all be made alive.

> (1 Cor. 15:21–2)

In a closely argued passage, Paul emphasized Christ's shared humanity with Adam, but he went on to answer critics who sneered at the idea of the resurrection of corruptible flesh and blood by distinguishing between the 'natural' and the spiritual body:

> The first man Adam was made a living soul; the last Adam was made a quickening spirit.

> Howbeit that was not first which is spiritual, but that which is natural; and afterward that which is spiritual.

> The first man is of the earth, earthy: the second man is the Lord from heaven.

> (1 Cor. 15:45–7)

Flesh and blood cannot inherit the kingdom of God; first there must be a transformation:

> Behold, I shew you a mystery; We shall not all sleep, but we shall all be changed,
>
> In a moment, in the twinkling of an eye, at the last trump . . .
>
> So when this corruptible shall have put on incorruption, and this mortal shall have put on immortality, then shall be brought to pass the saying that is written, Death is swallowed up in victory.
>
> O death, where is thy sting? O grave, where is thy victory?
>
> The sting of death is sin . . .
>
> (1 Cor. 15:51–2, 54–6)

What brings Paul's message home with particular acuity is his almost throwaway reminder that he himself had seen the risen Christ: 'And last of all he was seen of me also' (1 Cor. 15:8) – a reference to that moment of revelation on the road to Damascus, 'Saul, Saul, why persecutest thou me?' (Acts 9:4). One of the reasons for Paul's enormous status in the early Church was that he was a witness-bearer; he spoke with the authentic voice of a man who had personally experienced Christ through the literally blinding light of his presence. Who better to testify to Christ risen?

Paul's beautiful words about the defeat of death have continued to resonate through the Christian world. But the connection he made between Jesus Christ and Adam was to have far wider repercussions than the early Church's attempts to come to terms with the practical implications of the resurrection of the dead. Paul's reading of Genesis 3:19 was uncontroversial: Yahweh specifies death, the return to dust, as Adam's punishment for eating the forbidden fruit. But by linking Adam's disobedience with Jesus' death and resurrection, Paul implicated all humankind in Adam's fault, as well as its fatal consequences, proposing a concept of original sin that was further confirmed in his letter to the Romans:

Wherefore, as by one man sin entered into the world, and death by sin; and so death passed upon all men, for that all have sinned . . .

For as by one man's disobedience many were made sinners, so by the obedience of one shall many be made righteous.

(Rom. 5:12, 19).

He also says that Adam was 'the figure of him that was to come' (Rom. 5:14), an idea that was enthusiastically embraced by Christian theologians who loved to establish connections between the Old Testament and the New, a form of biblical exegesis known as typology, in which events in the Old Testament were interpreted in the light of Christian revelation: 'In the Old Testament the New lies hid; in the New Testament the meaning of the Old becomes clear.' Accordingly, Christ was the second Adam, born of the Virgin Mary as Adam had been born of virgin soil, and he lived out a perfected version of Adam's life. Adam's disobedience to God implied Christ's obedience; the tree of knowledge brought sin and death, just as the True Cross brought death and redemption from sin. Perhaps predictably for a converted Jew, accustomed to the idea of men as moral and social leaders, Paul named Adam rather than Eve as the bringer of sin into the world. For Paul, the point was that Adam, despite his masculine superiority, ate the forbidden fruit, a far more serious act than any lapse on woman's part, which would have accorded with conventional Jewish teaching about female frailty.

Paul does make two references to Eve, both in the context of behaviour to be avoided. Fearing that the Corinthians would be corrupted away from Christ by false testimony, a very real anxiety in the early days of Christianity when a multiplicity of rival sects jostled for power, Paul wrote magisterially:

For I am jealous over you with godly jealousy: for I have espoused you to one husband, that I may present you as a chaste virgin to Christ.

But I fear, lest by any means, as the serpent beguiled Eve through his subtilty, so your minds should be corrupted from the simplicity that is in Christ.

(2 Cor. 11:2–3)

Rather more unconventional was his warning that sleeping with a prostitute was to become 'one flesh' with her, just as Adam had become 'one flesh' with Eve:

> What? know ye not that he which is joined to an harlot is one
> body? for two, saith he, shall be one flesh.
>
> But he that is joined unto the Lord is one spirit.
>
> (1 Cor. 6:16–17)

In a city like Corinth, where consorting with prostitutes was commonplace for young men, this was astonishingly prohibitive. But the point for Paul was the antithesis between flesh and spirit, which he developed into a concept of opposing forces that was to have a radical effect on Christian attitudes to the body. He introduced the idea of the sacredness of the body, which belongs not to the individual but to God:

> What? know ye not that your body is the temple of the Holy
> Ghost which is in you, which ye have of God, and ye are not
> your own?
>
> (1 Cor. 6:19)

But the body, with its tendency to indulge sinful appetites, lust and greed and drunkenness, was only part of what Paul meant by 'the flesh', which he identified with that hardness of heart that Jewish teachers saw as the source of evil, the stubborn human resistance to God's will. As the critic Peter Brown puts it,

> A weak thing in itself, the body was presented as lying in the
> shadow of a mighty force, the power of *the flesh*: the body's
> physical frailty, its liability to death and the undeniable penchant
> of its instincts toward sin served Paul as a synecdoche for the state
> of humankind pitted against the spirit of God.

Paul's concept of labile, rebellious flesh captured the imagination of generations of Christian exegetes, partly because it was so powerful and fertile a topic for discussion and commentary, but also because of the opportunity it offered for personal interaction with

God. By subduing the flesh, by martyrdom, asceticism, multiple acts of renunciation and self-denial, the active Christian could feel, instant by instant, in his or her bodily responses the enormous gratification of fulfilling – or flaunting – God's will. At the same time, humanity's complicity in Adam's sin, the belief that men and women are fatally flawed from birth, drove Christian believers into the arms of the Church, the source of salvation through the sacrifice of Jesus Christ. 'For as by one man's obedience many were made sinners, so by the obedience of one shall many be made righteous' and 'as in Adam all die, even so in Christ shall all be made alive': thus the 'Fall' of Adam and Eve became established as the primal disaster that necessitated the Redemption. But this still left open the question of what had actually happened when Eve and Adam ate the forbidden fruit: what was the nature of their sin and what were its implications for Christian behaviour?

Sex in Eden

THE STORY OF Adam and Eve was of enormous importance to early Christians because they saw it as a statement of God's original purposes in creating mankind. Deciding how the first man and woman had lived together in Eden and what they had done to forfeit God's good will would be first steps towards defining how the followers of Christ should live. What Christians sought was a return to humanity's primal relationship of harmony with God before tasting the forbidden fruit. At first, ideas about Eden reflected the belief in the imminent new age, but as the years passed without its promised arrival, the need for urgent preparation abated and Christians began to understand that more long-term solutions were required, practical measures that could accommodate a broad spectrum of social behaviour under the umbrella of Christian salvation. There were many different solutions proposed to the problem of the loss of Eden, ideas that reflected the great variety of communities and beliefs that made up the early Church, but out of the confusion of theory and counter-theory emerged a clutch of seminal doctrines that were to influence two millennia of Christian practice. At the centre of the debate was human sexuality.

In the eastern Mediterranean during the second century after Christ, the Encratites, a group whose name derived from *enkrateia*, meaning 'continence', used the story of the 'Fall' of Adam and Eve to support a radical programme of sexual abstinence. Their leader Tatian interpreted Genesis 2:24, 'Therefore shall a man leave his father and his mother, and shall cleave unto his wife', not to denounce divorce as Christ had done, but to explain why Adam had become subject to death. By leaving his 'father' and 'mother', God and His Spirit, Adam was forced to 'cleave' to Eve through marital intercourse. In order to be reunited with God's nurturing Spirit, humanity must renounce sexuality, even in marriage. The Encratites saw Adam and Eve, when first created by God, as being separate from the animals, a distinction marked by their union with God's Spirit and their immortality. Once they had chosen to forfeit this special relationship, they became closer to the animals and subject to death. Extreme Encratites even suggested that sex was the cause of their loss of God's Spirit: the serpent took the idea of intercourse from seeing animals mating and persuaded Adam to do the same with Eve. For many Christians, this was a particularly degrading idea, as the urbane exegete Clement of Alexandria indignantly pointed out: 'For it makes human nature weaker than that of the brute beasts if in this matter those who were first created by God copied them.' But the Encratites argued that the only way to regain humanity's original distinction from the animals was to renounce the whole cycle of marriage and procreation, and thereby cheat death of its 'sustenance'. It was a message with peculiar resonance for women, endorsing their right to deny their bodies to men, and offering a spiritually rewarding alternative to traditional marriage and motherhood. The *Acts of Thomas* records the noblewoman Mygdonia's defiance of her husband Charisius, refusing to sleep with him and fleeing from their chamber, her naked body wrapped in the bed-curtain, for the sake of her new commitment to Jesus, a story which sets the idea of 'saved by childbearing' on its head. The duty of the new Christian woman was to return to the spiritual condition of prelapsarian Eve by preserving her body from the taint of sexuality and its now unwelcome fruits.

It was not a lifestyle that appealed to more moderate Christians.

The careful churchman Clement, writing for a sophisticated Alexandrian readership, criticized 'those . . . who under a pious cloak blaspheme by their continence both the creation and the holy Creator', accusing them of distorting their source material. A popular support for continence was found in the apocryphal *Gospel According to the Egyptians*:

> When Salome asked the Lord: 'How long shall death hold sway?'
> he answered: 'As long as you women bear children.'

But Clement robustly opposed any negative interpretation of this text, pointing out that Jesus was only teaching 'the ordinary course of nature. For birth is invariably followed by death.' His words are reminiscent of Gertrude's when she rebukes Hamlet for overmourning his father: 'Thou know'st 'tis common – all that lives must die,/ Passing through nature to eternity.' The difference, perhaps, for Clement's audience was that the concepts of both 'nature' and 'eternity' were still hotly bubbling in the melting-pot of early Christianity. Defy 'nature' and stop the human cycle, said the Encratites, and the lost eternity of Eden could be reclaimed, but Clement rejected such ideas, denying another popular text relating to childbirth and death:

> They say that the Saviour himself said 'I came to destroy the
> works of the female,' meaning by 'female' desire, and by 'works'
> birth and corruption.

'Has this destruction in fact been accomplished?' Clement asked. Of course not, 'for the world continues exactly as before'. What had been destroyed were 'the works of desire, love of money, contentiousness, vanity, mad lust for women, paederasty, gluttony, licentiousness, and similar vices . . . this is the incontinence referred to as "female"'.

Clement settled in Alexandria in around AD 180 and became head of a school for instructing converts. As well as teaching, he was a prolific writer, and his essay *On Marriage* suggests that he was writing for a very different community from the self-confidently abstemious Encratites. Indeed, he denounced strict adherence to continence, skilfully rereading Paul to support the argument for monogamous marriage:

> In general all the epistles of the apostle teach self-control and continence and contain numerous instructions about marriage, begetting children, and domestic life. But they nowhere rule out self-controlled marriage.

A married man, and writing for a community where family life was important, Clement wrote sympathetically of marriage as a supportive framework for Christians: 'we ought to share suffering with another and "bear one another's burdens," lest anyone who thinks he stands securely should himself fall'. He went on to reassure his readers: 'It is of second marriage that the apostle says, If you burn, marry.' Christ did not marry as he was already married to the Church, and 'he was no ordinary man that he should also be in need of some helpmeet after the flesh'; but Peter had children, and Clement even managed to persuade himself that Paul had had a wife, whom he left at home for reasons of convenience. Wives had been rather useful to these early Christian preachers, Clement pointed out, as they could pass on Christ's teaching to housewives, infiltrating the women's quarters without causing scandal.

Clement's measured arguments must have reassured many Christians anxious about how to reconcile the asceticism of Christ and Paul with more traditional domestic arrangements, but on the question of sexuality in marriage Clement sounds a more jarring note. According to his interpretation, humanity's first sin was not sexuality in itself, and he goes to great trouble to argue the case for marriage and procreation as part of the divine intention. Adam and Eve had sexual union 'by nature', but the difficulty was that they rushed into 'the favour of marriage' when they were still too young, and were punished for disobeying God's will. This view was supported by Clement's near-contemporary, Irenaeus, who says that Adam and Eve were juveniles:

> For having been created just a short time before, they had no understanding of procreation of children. It was necessary that

first they should come to adult age, and then 'multiply' from that time onwards.

Clement does not agree with the view that the 'coats of skins' God gave to Adam and Eve were physical bodies, a belief that stigmatized the human body itself as a constant reminder of the first sin. For Clement, 'birth is holy', proved by the fact that Christ himself 'came in the flesh'. Clement equates married intercourse with the 'knowledge' that Adam and Eve acquired by eating the forbidden fruit, by which he means knowledge of the right time to procreate, and he is thereby able to argue that the right use of marriage gives access to the tree of life. The responsibility was Adam's, who chose the wrong time to procreate in Eden, and was punished for it, but, and here Clement plays on the idea of 'knowledge' and the verb 'to know' meaning to have intercourse, later he gets it right: '"And Adam knew his wife Eve, and she conceived and bore a son, and they called him by the name of Seth."' Clement argues away Paul's opposition between flesh and the soul by pointing out that 'if the flesh were hostile to the soul, [the Saviour] would not have raised an obstacle to the soul by strengthening with good health the hostile flesh'. Just as the Saviour heals the soul, so He heals 'the body of its passions'. What is important is self-control, and herein lies the rub. The erudite Clement, well-versed in the classical authors, explains the pagan idea of bodily control: 'The human ideal of continence, I mean that which is set forth by Greek philosophers, teaches that one should fight desire and not be subservient to it so as to bring it to practical effect. But our ideal,' he continues, as if it were the simplest thing in the world, 'is not to experience desire at all.' It is not enough to repress desire; what is required is not to feel it in the first place. A man who marries because he wants children 'must practise continence so that it is not desire he feels for his wife, whom he ought to love, and that he may beget children with a chaste and controlled will'. Later, he makes the point even plainer: 'the law intended husbands to cohabit with their wives with self-control and only for the purpose of begetting children'. At a stroke Clement had introduced a fundamental chasm into Christian married life, whereby the sexual act itself was to be divorced from desire, a chaste and solemn ritual enacted solely for the purposes of procreation. Elsewhere, Clement went into detail about what sexual acts were allowable within marriage, excluding any that would not allow the possibility of procreation, such as oral and anal intercourse, or intercourse with a woman disabled from childbirth by reason of age, infertility, menstruation or existing pregnancy. Even the time of day was prescribed, with 'the light of reason' and the potential for procreation as the two guiding principles by which married Christians could sexually come together. It was a heavy sentence.

Clement's attempts to reconcile Pauline austerity with marriage and childrearing helped to establish ambivalent attitudes towards sexuality which have characterized Christianity ever since. What he and his contemporaries worked out was an ideal of modified chastity: if virginity or abstinence proved impractical, then a monogamous marriage denuded of sexual desire was a good second best. It was a programme that endorsed celibacy above marriage, and condemned sexual desire in any circumstances, thereby setting human beings in permanent conflict with their own biological drive to mate and procreate, and it was to lead to all manner of bizarre and contradictory practices, driving Christians to extremes of self-abnegation, to whips and scourges and fasting, to ludicrous tests of will and endurance, to agonies of guilt and repentance. Above all, it was doomed to fail, and as such it became the foundation stone of the confessional, of the elaborate Catholic rituals of atonement and remission of sins. The sheer impossibility for millions of people of not experiencing sexual desire meant that the established Church was founded on an almost superhuman ideal of behaviour. Kill desire, triumph over nature, and free oneself for the life in Christ – and if you could not achieve this, the Church was there to give you a hand.

But Clement at least left a window of hope for humankind: the possibility of choosing not to sin. Eve 'first began transgression', but not all her descendants are committed to wrongdoing. How can a newborn baby commit fornication, Clement asks, how can any child who has done nothing fall under the curse of Adam? The point for Clement is that although a baby may be conceived in sin, as Adam and Eve's children were, the child is not in itself sinful. Eve was called 'Life' (Hawwah) because she was responsible for the

generations that followed her, 'the mother of righteous and unright-
eous alike, since each one of us makes himself either righteous or
disobedient'. Later Christians were denied even this valuable freedom of choice.

The rebellious member

IN HIS *CONFESSIONS*, Augustine describes his conversion to mainstream Christianity at the age of thirty-two in terms of a struggle to
renounce sexual desire. Born in North Africa in AD 354, Augustine
was the product of a mixed marriage between a passionate Christian,
Monica, and a pagan father, but initially he rejected his mother's
faith, intellectually repelled by what he saw as the crudity and
obscurity of the Latin Bible. Instead he turned to Manicheism, a
quasi-Christian religion which saw the universe in dualistic terms of
a continuing cosmic conflict between Light and Dark, the evenly
matched forces of good and evil. Although fully fledged Manichees
were committed to absolute celibacy, Augustine never progressed
beyond being a Hearer, a role in which he was permitted sex within
careful guidelines. Augustine's susceptibility to women has already
been suggested – that boyhood sympathy for abandoned Dido –
but for a young man without independent fortune and living off
his intellect, an early marriage was impracticable, and in his late
teens Augustine settled into an unformalized relationship with a
unnamed woman with whom he lived in contented fidelity for
thirteen years. A son, Adeodatus, was born in their second year
together.

Monica's views on the position of women were conservative –
her son records her no doubt irritating habit of reminding battered
wives that marriage was a contract which bound a woman to obey
her husband – but she seems to have exercised a profound influence
over Augustine, even when he felt unable to accept her faith, and
tried to maintain close contact with him. When he left Carthage for
Rome, some years before his conversion, Monica wept bitterly at
their separation, and he remarked that her unhappiness was 'proof
that she had inherited the legacy of Eve, seeking in sorrow what
with sorrow she had brought into the world'. Eventually, Monica

found a young woman from a suitably prestigious family for her upwardly mobile son to marry, but the girl was still under age, possibly as young as twelve. With great pain Augustine separated from his long-term companion, 'a blow which crushed my heart to bleeding, because I loved her dearly', but while she returned to Africa and dedicated herself to a life of celibacy, Augustine filled the sexual gap for the two years in which he had to wait for his bride by taking another mistress. The habit of sex had become too deeply rooted for him to resist. Characterizing himself in the *Confessions* as 'a slave of lust', Augustine felt he was manacled by an iron chain forged by his own deviant will. This had first led him into lust, which then became a habit and from there a necessity. When he became fully aware of the Christian God, the new will to serve Him conflicted with the old will of desire, setting spirit and flesh in combat, 'and between them they tore my soul apart'. Trying to respond to God's summons, he could only answer with 'the drowsy words of an idler – "Soon", "Presently", "Let me wait a little longer"'. He was caught in a vicious circle of habitual sin: 'For the rule of sin is the force of habit, by which the mind is swept along and held fast even against its will, yet deservedly, because it fell into the habit of its own accord.'

At this crucial moment, Augustine was teaching in Milan where he had already been profoundly impressed by the city's Christian bishop Ambrose, when he was visited by a fellow countryman. Ponticianus was a devout Christian and, finding that Augustine had been studying St Paul's letters, he told him about the Egyptian monk Anthony and the revolutionary impression that reading about his life had made on two young men, friends of Ponticianus', who had immediately renounced their worldly lives and dedicated them-selves to God. This simple story had an equally overwhelming effect on Augustine, who found himself face to face with his own moral deformities. In bitter self-loathing, he recalled his boyish prayer, '"Give me chastity and continence, but not yet"', and grieved over the years in which day by day he had put off the renunciation of worldly pleasures in order to fulfil his own bodily lusts. In turmoil, he ran into a small garden nearby to wrestle between his two opposing wills, conscious that all he had to do to resolve the conflict was to perform a single-minded act of will – and yet he could not do it. His mind was divided against itself, weighed down by the habit of wrongdoing from exerting its full force towards the will to do good. What held him back was partly the thought of what he must give up. Anticipating the nostalgia of renunciation, that premonition of an eternity of lack that is surely one of the most powerful deterrents to giving up forbidden pleasure, he described how his former attachments 'plucked at [his] garment of flesh and whispered, "Are you going to dismiss us? From this moment we shall never be with you again, for ever and ever."' Augustine did renounce both marriage and sex, and committed himself to a life of continence in God, but he continued to brood over his experience of the repetitive trap of sensual longing and of the divided will. His conclusions helped to determine his final reading of the Fall of Adam and Eve.

Augustine's interpretation of Genesis 1–3 developed over a considerable period and was a response both to his personal struggle to understand the individual's relationship with sin, and the argument then raging in the Christian church between the rival claims of asceticism and marriage. Prompted by the teachings of Jesus and Paul, the ascetic movement had developed rapidly in Syria and Asia Minor, and in Egypt thousands of Christians had followed Anthony into the desert to live as hermits, renouncing worldy goods and social standing in order to concentrate on the difficult task of coming to terms with the self as a first step to knowledge of God. From some points of view, the influence of asceticism could be seen as socially catastrophic, undermining the ideals of family life and community service that had been fundamental to the Empire's self-image and effective management. The new focus on individual freedom to choose how to live, with the promise of personal salvation as a direct result of one's own actions, threatened the traditional hierarchy of the male as head of a household of women and slaves, while sexual abstention offered women a truly radical programme, freed from the life-threatening cycle of pregnancy, lactation and childrearing, or the heartbreaking burden of infertility, that had traditionally consumed their lives from puberty.

Asceticism did not lack its critics. For many Christians, including prominent Roman families, it was too difficult or austere a programme, demanding changes to their lifestyle and social standing that they felt reluctant to embrace, and some theologians even questioned the biblical evidence for praising celibacy over marriage. In the early 390s, Jovinian, although himself a celibate Christian monk, argued that there was no superiority in being an ascetic. All those who had been baptised as Christians, whether virgin, married or widowed, assuming that they were equally virtuous in other respects, were of equal merit, and would receive the same rewards in heaven. In support of his argument, he referred his readers to Genesis and to Christ's words about marriage in Matthew:

> First of all, [Jovinian] says, God declares that 'therefore shall a
> man leave his father and his mother, and shall cleave unto his
> wife: and they shall be one flesh.' And lest we should say that this
> is a quotation from the Old Testament, he asserts that it has been
> confirmed by the Lord in the Gospel – 'What God hath joined
> together, let not man put asunder': and he immediately adds,
> 'Be fruitful, and multiply, and replenish the earth.'

Jovinian's views aroused a storm of protest from senior churchmen, anxious to defend the position that although marriage is holy, virginity is holier still. Jerome was particularly abusive, saying in his polemic *Against Jovinianus* that the monk's words were 'the hissing of the old serpent; by counsel such as this the dragon drove man from Paradise', and claiming that Adam and Eve were virgins in Paradise:

> they who, while naked and unhampered, and as virgins
> unspotted enjoyed the fellowship of the Lord, were cast down
> into the vale of tears, and sewed skins together to clothe
> themselves withal.

The marriage of Adam and Eve came after the Fall, and would therefore by implication not have been part of God's original plan:

> And as regards Adam and Eve we must maintain that before the
> fall they were virgins in Paradise: but after they sinned, and were
> cast out of Paradise, they were immediately married.

Although he had earlier grudgingly allowed marital intercourse for the sake of procreation, carried away by his own rhetorical fervour Jerome even argued the extreme position that 'in view of the purity of the body of Christ, all sexual intercourse is unclean'. Jerome's invective, with its particularly negative view of human sexuality, did little to help the Christian cause, especially since his texts caused such a popular scandal in Rome that his friends were left with an almost impossible task of damage limitation. Although Jovinian was repudiated by the Church, the difficulty he had raised did not go away and, as Christianity moved centre stage as the approved religion of the Roman Empire, the question of establishing a position on celibacy and marriage that would be acceptable to the vast majority of its congregation became pressing. Again, the debate centred on God's intentions for humanity as expressed in the Genesis account of Adam and Eve.

Augustine worked out a careful analysis of the events in the Garden of Eden in his *City of God*, a monumental work written between AD 412 and 427, in which he attempted to assimilate pagan and Hebrew religious and philosophical traditions within the Church of Rome. As with the *Confessions*, the writing is vigorous, the approach well-mannered and the arguments crystalline, although, appropriately to the nature of the text and its intended audience, the measured accents of the sage and venerable churchman are in the ascendant. Where Augustine differed substantially from such leading churchmen as Jerome and Ambrose was in accepting that sexuality was part of Adam and Eve's prelapsarian existence in Paradise; indeed, he believed that God had intended them to procreate in Eden: 'For myself, however, I have no shadow of doubt that to increase and multiply and fill the earth in accordance with God's blessing is a gift of marriage, and that God instituted marriage from the beginning, before man's Fall, in creating male and female'. Augustine supports his argument by pointing out the clear difference in physical structure between a man and a woman: 'There is no denying the obvious evidence of bodies of different sex, which shows that it would be a manifest absurdity to deny the fact that male and female were created for the purpose of begetting children', and he concludes, 'if there had been no sin, marriage would have been worthy of the happiness of paradise, and would have given birth to children to be loved'. This innovation put marriage and the family back on the map for many Christians, reassuring them that structures that were fundamental to their idea of society were not simply the result of a necessary compromise on God's part.

What fascinated Augustine was the rather different question of what had happened to the human will as a result of the Fall. Why did people experience powerful resistance to good and attraction to wrongdoing? It was a reformulation of that old problem that had troubled Job and was to vex generations of Rabbis: if the Creator was acknowledged as benign, what was the origin of evil in the universe? In thinking through this difficulty, Augustine returned to his own experience of sexual desire, which had persisted inadvertently long after he had consciously committed himself to continence. In the *Confessions*, he had brooded over the power of dreams to awaken sexual longing and even to force him to 'commit in sleep . . . shameful, unclean acts inspired by sensual images'. Where was his will in this? In the *City of God*, he concludes that for Adam and Eve enjoying connubial relations in Paradise, such a dislocation between will and sexual activity would have been unthinkable: 'Without doubt, the marriage in paradise would not have known this opposition, this resistance, this tussle between lust and will'. What brought it about was 'that guilt of disobedience'. Even though the 'injunction forbidding the eating of one kind of food, where such an abundant supply of other foods was available, was so easy to observe, so brief to remember', Adam and Eve chose to disobey God's commandment, a 'misuse of free will' that 'started a chain of disasters'. That first disobedience led to 'a novel disturbance in their disobedient flesh', the punishment appropriately fitting the crime by the permanent rebellion of the offending sexual organs. For Augustine, the loss of primal harmony between desire and deed, the apparently random nature of the sexual impulse acting independently of the will, was a direct result of the Fall, and the effect of Adam and Eve's sin had been to bring about an irrevocable weakening of the human will: 'human nature . . . was vitiated and altered'. This explained that devastating fissure in the self's identity that Augustine had experienced in his own moment of crisis in the garden in Milan: 'it was I who willed to take this course and again it was I who willed not to take it. It was I and I alone . . . I was at odds with myself.' Even then, he had concluded: 'It was part of the punishment of a sin freely committed by Adam, my first father.'

In the *City of God* he makes it clear that this 'original perversion, a kind of corruption at the root' was passed by Adam into all humanity: 'For we were all in that one man . . . there already existed the seminal nature from which we were to be begotten. And of course, when this was vitiated through sin, and bound with death's fetters in its just condemnation, man could not be born of man in any other condition.' No one can escape: 'the whole human race was in the first man, and it was to pass from him through the woman into his progeny . . . And it was not man as first made, but what man became after his sin and punishment, that was thus begotten'. It is a sentence of doom on all humanity: 'We bring with us, at our birth, the beginning of our death'.

Augustine's theory of the Fall paradoxically removed the stigma of sexual misbehaviour from the actual event: disobedience, not sexuality in itself, was the first sin, and it was caused by Adam's pride. He was 'too pleased with himself', and chose to live by his own standards, to carry out his own will, not his creator's, a 'falling away from the work of God'. Self-regard was the original evil that cost Adam Paradise, but the physical manifestation of Adam and Eve's disobedience was that 'novel disturbance in their disobedient flesh', by which Augustine seems principally to mean the tendency of the penis to rise and fall according to its own impulse rather than under instruction, although his description of orgasm could apply to either sex: a (dangerous) pleasure so intense 'that when it reaches its climax there is an almost total extinction of mental alertness; the intellectual sentries, as it were, are overwhelmed'. It is this loss of control that makes people ashamed of their sexual feelings and impotence so particularly humiliating: 'the genital organs have become as it were the private property of lust, which has brought them so completely under its sway that they have no power of movement if this passion fails, if it has not arisen spontaneously or in response to a stimulus. It is this that arouses shame; it is this that makes us shun the eyes of beholders in embarrassment.'

Rebecca West attributed Augustine's 'exaggerated sense' of the importance of sex to a fear of appearing ridiculous, due perhaps to 'the less dignified anatomy of man, a point on which Augustine copiously complained', or to 'the disadvantageous situation of man in the sexual act, who finds that for him it ends with physical collapse and the surrender of power, whereas for his partner it ends with motherhood and an increase of power'. From a physical point of view, Augustine's near-obsession with the rebellious member suggests that impotence or inappropriately spontaneous erections may have been a personal problem; but there is no doubt that he experienced sexual desire as a powerful force that he suppressed with difficulty and anguish, as that heartbroken lament in the *Confessions* attests: ' "From this moment we shall never be with you again, for ever and ever." ' This shameful turbulence would have been avoided had there been no sin: 'the man would have sowed the seed and the woman would have conceived the child when their sexual organs had been aroused by the will, at the appropriate time and in the necessary degree, and had not been excited by lust'. Sexuality that resulted from the conscious will would have allowed the woman to retain her virginity: 'Moreover, although we cannot prove this in experience, it does not therefore follow that we should not believe that when those parts of the body were not activated by the turbulent heat of passion but brought into service by deliberate use of power when the need arose, the male seed could have been dispatched into the womb, with no loss of the wife's integrity'. This would have been accomplished by a similar mechanism to that which allowed virgins to menstruate without loss of maidenhead: 'For the seed could be injected through the same passage by which the flux [i.e. the menstrual flow] is ejected.'

This bizarre argument, drawing on medical ideas then current about female biology, confirms the extent to which technical virginity had become an obsession for the early Church, although Augustine does have the grace to acknowledge lack of practical evidence to support his theory. His solution to the death-sentence imposed on the human race was salvation though the grace of God, mediated by Christ, whom he argued had escaped the taint of original sin by being born of the Virgin Mary. But even here, his message was rather grim: a person's future prospects were something of a lottery depending on whom God in His generosity chose to elect for special privileges. What Augustine's theory of original sin confirmed was the power and authority of the Church as a means of grace through the sacraments it administered: the remission of sins through baptism and the new life in God through the Eucharist.

Augustine follows the by now conventional reading of Adam as the senior partner in crime; he refers to Eve as 'the inferior of the human pair' and accepts the ruling in Genesis 3:16 that a woman should be subject to her husband. In the *Confessions*, he had pointed out that Adam was made in God's image and likeness and ruled over the irrational animals, while 'in the physical sense, woman has been made for man'. He explained this distinction by saying that although men and women are equal in nature in respect of mind and rational intelligence, 'in sex' woman needs to be ruled by the man, just as the 'natural impulses' need to be subordinate to the 'reasoning power of the mind'. What this seems to mean is that men and women have equal mental capacities, but that woman is controlled by her emotions and needs an injection of steady masculine reason to ensure that her actions are 'inspired by the principles of good conduct'. She cannot be trusted to think clearly or act morally: a familiar reading of female incapacity. Elsewhere he points out that marriage must have existed in Eden for the simple reason that a woman, not a man, was created as Adam's helpmate. Masculine friendship was important to Augustine and he clearly felt that Adam would have been better off with a male companion, had it not been for the requirement to 'be fruitful, and multiply'.

Augustine's account of Eve's temptation by the serpent follows popular Jewish legends about the fallen angel. He, too, suffered from pride, which had made him rebel against God in the first place, jealous of His authority, and now he envies the two human beings for their unfallen state. Disguised as the serpent, 'the arrogant angel' approached Eve first, 'no doubt starting with the inferior of the human pair so as to arrive at the whole by stages, supposing that the man would not be so easily gullible, and could not be trapped by a false move on his own part, but only if he yielded to another's mistake'. As Milton was to do many years later, Augustine employs some special pleading on Adam's behalf. He softens up his readers by reminding them that the only reason that Solomon worshipped false gods was because he was 'induced . . . by feminine cajolery';

similarly Adam 'fell in with [Eve's] suggestions because they were so closely bound in partnership'. Augustine is careful to point out that even though gullible Eve believed the serpent, it is unthinkable that Adam was similarly deceived. He was simply guilty of an excess of uxoriousness: '. . . Adam refused to be separated from his only companion, even if it involved sharing her sin'. Milton put it rather more gracefully, but the sentiments are the same:

> for with thee
> Certain my resolution is to die;
> How can I live without thee, how forgo
> Thy sweet converse and love so dearly joined,
> To live again in these wild woods forlorn?
> Should God create another Eve, and I
> Another rib afford, yet loss of thee
> Would never from my heart; no no, I feel
> The link of nature draw me: flesh of flesh,
> Bone of my bone thou art, and from thy state
> Mine never shall be parted, bliss or woe.

Adam's susceptibility to Eve's persuasions was a persistent stumbling block for Jewish and Christian commentators, which they frequently resolved by eager but unconvincing arguments about feminine persuasion, whitewashing Adam's culpability in a flurry of excited protest against woman's wicked wiles.

Augustine's pessimistic view of fallen humanity seemed to many Christians to reject two fundamental tenets of the faith, the goodness of God's creation and the freedom of the human will, and he was even accused of supporting Manichaean ideas that he had rejected many years before. One of his challengers was the ascetic Pelagius whose views were current in Italy in the early 400s. Pelagius deplored the idea that people were committed willy-nilly to wrong-doing, which he saw as making a nonsense of moral action, a recipe for inertia and passive dependence on external authority. In his more liberal interpretation of human nature, the sin of the first man and woman had been limited to themselves and had not been transmitted to the rest of humanity. The universality of sin was due to social custom, following Adam's initial bad example, but people were free to choose whether they pursued good or evil lives, and God's grace was useful but not essential, a point of view that substantially limited the role of the Church as well as of God in an individual's life. Death, in Pelagius' view, was a biological necessity, not a punishment for sin.

After Pelagius had been condemned as a heretic by the Bishop of Rome in AD 418, his disciple Julian, bishop of Eclanum in southern Italy, took up the debate with Augustine. At the heart of their dispute was the question of what is 'natural'. For Augustine, human experiences such as death, pain in childbirth, congenital deformity, even sexual desire had been imposed on humanity as a result of original sin; in Julian's more optimistic, Mediterranean view of the world, they were all 'natural', part of God's good plan for His universe. While Augustine proposed that the only hope for fallen humanity lay in God's grace, mediated through Christ and the Church, Julian relied on a more psychological solution to life's ills, a programme of spiritual optimism in which the individual is capable of choosing good or ill: 'God created fully innocent natures, capable of virtue according to their will'. The controversy continued until Augustine's death in AD 430, when the Church eventually came to support his views over those of Julian, and indeed some of the issues they raised are still debated among theologians to this day. What is just as interesting from a lay point of view, looking back at Augustine's astonishing influence over the ideologies of the early Church, is why such a gloomy view of human nature and indeed of God came to prevail over the more optimistic theories proposed by other Christians. In her study of the Garden of Eden story in early Christianity, the scholar Elaine Pagels suggests that, at a time when Christianity moved from being a banned religion to the moral mouthpiece of the Empire, political and economic interests would have played a role. Once sexual desire had been linked with sin and death, Christians would almost inevitably be driven, at some point in their lives, into the arms of the Church for rebuke, advice or consolation, and the Church in turn would wield unprecedented control over its congregation's lives and coffers. By the beginning of the fifth century, 'Augustine's theory of Adam's fall, once espoused in simpler forms only by marginal groups of Christians, now moved, together with the imperially supported Catholic church that proclaimed it, into the center of western history.'

THIS BRIEF RÉSUMÉ of some early Christian ideas about the nature of the sin committed in Eden suggests that Adam and Eve were seen as a unit. They were mutually involved in the loss of Eden, and although there was a long tradition of Eve's inferiority to Adam – 'And Adam was not deceived, but the woman being deceived was in the transgression' – the focus of attention was less on apportioning blame than on hypothesizing about their behaviour and its consequences. Given the Church's obsession with sexual behaviour, theories inevitably concentrated on sex in Eden and its aftermath. Despite the differences in beliefs among early Church commentators and their critics, the concept of sexual self-control as a means to spiritual progress had become central to the Church's teaching, and Augustine's idea of a basic flaw in humanity that was transmitted from parent to child through the act of procreation chimed with the distrust of the body's random motions that had disconcerted generations of ascetics, and provided a core role for the Church, whose sacraments offered a route to redemption from the sin and death to which everyone was committed through the very act of being born. Where Eve became particularly an object of the doctrinists' attention was in her ability to distract Adam from the path of virtue and obedience. The early Church was crammed with women of all ages – wives, virgins, widows, dedicated ascetics, mothers of large families – all of whom were seen as a potential threat to the spirituality of the male congregation. The message to early Christian women was: 'Beware of your power to tempt and deceive', and in a culture which had inherited a long tradition of female psychological frailty and inferiority, the message could not be repeated too often or too vehemently. Women themselves appear to have colluded in the attempts to dampen down the effects of their sexuality: for many, the new opportunities offered by asceticism must have been too attractive and liberating to quibble about rhetoric, or fight for the often dubious privileges of marriage and childbirth. There were more important goals at stake.

CHAPTER 7

DAUGHTERS OF EVE

Blessed are the bodies of the virgins, for they shall be
well-pleasing unto God . . .
    Acts of Paul, II:6

———◆◆———

WRITING IN THE second century after the birth of
Christ, the Christian theologian Tertullian reminded
women in the church at Carthage of their tainted
legacy from their foremother Eve:

> And do you not know that you are [each] an Eve? The sentence
> of God on this sex of yours lives in this age: the guilt must
> of necessity live too. *You* are the devil's gateway: *you* are the
> unsealer of that [forbidden] tree: *you* are the first deserter of
> the divine law: *you* are she who persuaded him whom the devil
> was not valiant enough to attack. *You* destroyed so easily God's
> image, man. On account of *your* desert – that is, death – even
> the Son of God had to die.

Tertullian's words, although addressed to his 'most beloved sisters',
reflect the longstanding male anxiety in both Greek and Jewish
culture about female weakness and permeability: woman's worrying
lack of the physical firmness that was believed to be essential to
masculine codes of behaviour. Just as Eve had managed to subvert
Adam, even though he was made in the image of God and strong
enough to resist the devil, so the women of Carthage might
undermine male morale by a provocative use of ornaments and
pretty clothes. Tertullian points out that if Eve had known about
gorgeous fabrics, gold and gleaming pearls and flashing onyx-stones,
'if the mirror, too, already had licence to lie so largely', then, even
when condemned by God to death, she would still have craved all
these beautiful snares. Woman is by nature unredeemable and must

protect herself from her own moral frailty by dressing humbly, 'walking about as Eve mourning and repentant' in order to expiate her inherited sin. Stylish dress is the scarlet letter that proclaims a woman's bad intentions and confirms her character as daughter of Eve.

Modest and matronly women were also considered a threat to male members of the early Christian community, although perception of the danger varied with time and place. Tertullian could calmly advise an elderly widower to cohabit with a Christian 'sister' – or two – in order to have someone to keep house for him: '[Then] take some spiritual wife. Take to yourself from among the widows one fair in faith, dowered with poverty, sealed with age . . . A plurality of *such* wives is pleasing to God.' But John Chrysostom, bishop of Constantinople, writing in the late fourth century, was in no doubt about the danger for male ascetics of cohabiting with celibate women:

> Just as someone captures a proud and fiercely-glaring lion, then
> shears his mane, breaks his teeth, clips his claws, and renders him
> a disgraceful and ridiculous specimen . . . so these women make
> all the men they capture easy for the devil to overcome. They
> render them softer, more hot-headed, shameful, mindless,
> irascible, insolent, importunate, ignoble, crude, servile, niggardly,
> restless, nonsensical, and to sum it all up, the women take all
> their corrupting feminine customs and stamp them into the souls
> of these men.

For the fiery bishop, even these mutually supportive and, in theory at least, asexual domestic arrangements, quite common in early Christian communities, would prove disastrous to a man's self-discipline and spiritual salvation. The terrible fear of effeminacy which governed male deportment in the Roman empire had spilled over into Christian belief and mingled with hysterical anxiety about women's almost supernatural powers to seduce and suborn. Once the idea had taken hold that freedom from sexuality meant spiritual liberation, women became increasingly under scrutiny as possible inciters to male wrongdoing, and advice to women on codes of dress and sexual behaviour proliferated in the writings of the early

Church leaders. We have already seen Jewish phobia about the horrors that might result from the incautious glimpse of a seductive ankle; the ascetic Christians took this to giddy extremes, and sought to commit women to similar sexual renunciation in the process: no longer a case of 'Lock up your wives and daughters', but 'Women, be chaste!' This is Jerome, in around AD 384, warning Eustochium, one of his many female correspondents, against the dangers of sexual temptation, fluently mingling the loss of Eden with the pagan myth of the sirens to make his point:

> And yet ought I not to weep and groan when the serpent again
> invites me to take forbidden fruit, and when, after driving us
> from the Paradise of virginity, he tries to clothe us in tunics of
> skin . . . What have I to do with the short-lived pleasures of
> sense? What have I to do with the sirens' sweet and deadly
> songs?

Reminding Eustochium of the sentence passed on Eve in Genesis 3:16, he lists each judgement pronounced by God in order to argue that virginity is the preferred state for women:

> You must not be subject to the sentence whereby condemnation
> was passed upon mankind: 'In pain and in sorrow shalt thou
> bring forth children.' Say to yourself: 'That is a Law for a married
> woman, but not for me.' 'And thy desire shall be to thy
> husband.' Say to yourself: 'Let her desire be to her husband who
> has not a Husband in Christ;' and at the last 'Thou shalt surely
> die.' Say once more: 'Death is the end of marriage. But my vows
> are independent of sex. Let married women keep to their own
> place and title: for me virginity is consecrated in the persons of
> Mary and of Christ.'

Jerome affirms his belief that 'Eve in Paradise was a virgin: it was only after she put on a garment of skins that her married life began', and he encourages Eustochium that, 'Paradise is your home. Keep therefore as you were born'. As for the command to be fruitful and replenish the earth:

The command to increase and multiply is fulfilled after the
expulsion from Paradise, after the recognition of nakedness, after
the putting on of the fig leaves which augured the approach of
marital desire. Let them marry and be given in marriage who eat
their bread in the sweat of their brow, whose land brings forth
thorns and thistles, and whose crops are choked with brambles.
My seed produces fruit a hundredfold.

He sums up his position with audacious arrogance, 'I praise wedlock, I praise marriage; but it is because they produce me virgins.'

John Chrysostom also saw virginity as the natural state of Adam
and Eve:

Scarcely had they turned from obedience to God than they
became earth and ashes and, all at once, they lost the happy life,
beauty and the honour of virginity . . . Do you see where
marriage took its origin? How it had of necessity to be preceded
by the breaking of the divine commandment, by malediction and
death? For where there is death, there too is sexual coupling; and
where there is no death, there is no sexual coupling either.

This reading of the Fall sought to impose the constraint of sexual
renunciation on both men and women, and saw female sexuality in
a particularly negative light, but it would be inappropriate to
condemn Jerome, John Chrysostom, Augustine and their peers as
thoroughgoing misogynists, at least as the term is understood today.
Their warnings and admonitions overflowed from the extreme
anxiety felt by many groups in the early Church, across many
communities, about how to follow the sometimes inscrutable and
contradictory teachings of Christ and the apostles, particularly Paul,
whose words or those attributed to him make up a significant
portion of the New Testament. Far from hating or shunning
women, the evidence suggests that many of these early Church
leaders had strong and supportive relationships with female members
of their congregations, and depended on practical and financial aid
from wealthy and influential benefactresses, women used to administering estates and large households. Jerome had a coterie of loyal

followers with whom he exchanged a voluminous correspondence, although only the letters written by him have survived; Augustine's respect for his devout mother Monica is well-attested in the *Confessions*; even John Chrysostom, the 'Golden Mouth', had a close friendship with a wealthy benefactress, Olympias, who was described in the anonymous *Life of Olympias* as a model of female virtue: 'she kept watch without sleeping, she had an immaterial body, a mind without vainglory, intelligence without conceit, an untroubled heart, an artless spirit, charity without limits, unbounded generosity, contemptible clothing, immeasurable self-control'. Perhaps most significant was Olympias' indifference to her personal appearance: a sexually unthreatening confidante to the fastidious John.

Any attempt to summarize attitudes to women in early Christian communities is fraught with this kind of contradiction and difficulty. The trends that were discernible in early Judaism and in the Graeco-Roman tradition are even more apparent in the first centuries after the death of Jesus of Nazareth: the outspoken criticism of female character and behaviour in public writings and the warnings against seductive female sexuality, balanced by evidence in private life of mutually rewarding relationships between men and women, and of male care and protection of women, however much a modern reading might see this as restrictive and patronizing. The problem for the Christian doctrine-makers and their Jewish counterparts in producing prescriptive literature for or about women was dealing with the troublesome male libido, which, the more it was suppressed, the more it appeared to spring up to goad and torment its unfortunate victim. This is Jerome again, attempting to subdue his unruly sexual appetite in the desert:

> But though in my fear of hell I had condemned myself to this
> prison-house, where my only companions were scorpions and
> wild beasts, I often found myself surrounded by bands of dancing
> girls. My face was pale with fasting; but though my limbs were
> cold as ice my mind was burning with desire, and the fires of lust
> kept bubbling up before me when my flesh was as good as dead.

Hieronymus Bosch recreates the torments that besieged the desert hermits in his triptych, *The Temptation of St Anthony* (c. 1510): the right wing shows the saint meditating in a rocky landscape where revellers literally fall under the table from the effects of drink, and a naked women entices him from the mouth of an improvised tent. Perhaps inevitably, the more they fantasized about women as forbidden fruit, the more the male doctrinists longed to gobble them up and the more they blamed women for their own repressed desires. For women, paradoxically, the highly charged sexual atmosphere of early Christianity offered a revolutionary opportunity to renounce traditional roles.

The spirit-endowed woman

FOR CHRISTIAN WOMEN who could read and for others who might hear the stories discussed in church or read aloud at home, the Old Testament had much to offer wives and mothers looking for narratives to which they could relate. As well as ample prescriptive documentation – the rules of behaviour, the models of approved virtuous women and the wicked minxes who were to be avoided at all costs – the Jewish Holy Books are rich in stories that represent women in their homely everyday aspects, even if the heroines encounter out-of-the-ordinary challenges and dangers. Sarah's snort of amusement when her male guests predict that she will become pregnant, Hagar's despair when she is exiled to the desert alone with her young child, even Delilah's practised persuasion of her patsy Samson, are stories that convince because they describe recognizable human behaviour. 'Yes, I can imagine what that feels like' is one of the most satisfying responses to narrative. But the reader who turns from the densely peopled canvas of the pre-Christian Bible to the New Testament may well be tempted to echo (with one minor amendment) Jane Austen's Catherine Morland, who complained when faced with the bleak landscape of '"real solemn history"': '"the men all so good . . . and hardly any women at all"'. There *are* women in the New Testament, including Eve, but they generally appear in the context of some argument, an admonitory story or polemical point that the author is anxious to make. Far more than in the Old Testament, women in Christianity's central text are marginalized, shadowy figures, whose histories are at best fragmentary, ciphers in some other, more privileged plot. If one wants to find women in early Christian narrative, apart from rare exceptions such as Luke's tender evocations of the miraculous pregnancies of Mary and her cousin Elisabeth, and John's teasingly elliptical account of Martha and Mary of Bethany, the two sisters loved by Jesus, one must look outside the New Testament.

The idea of the sexual body as a hindrance to spirituality is closely linked with Christian readings of the story of Adam and Eve, but one possible positive role model for women was Eve herself in the alternative readings of the Genesis story proposed by the religious group now known as Gnostics. Active from the first century after the birth of Christ, Gnostics bypassed the authority of the Christian bishops and other religious leaders and sought to know God directly through a process of spiritual awareness that they called *gnosis* or 'insight', and many Gnostics read the story of Adam and Eve as an allegory of the individual's struggle towards the self-knowledge necessary for *gnosis*. In place of the perfect Adam of Jewish tradition, some writers even interpreted Adam as a lower being than Eve, representing the mind, the ordinary responses of thinking and feeling, while Eve was the higher consciousness of evolved spirituality. *The Hypostasis of the Archons* ('Reality of the Rulers') tells how the archons, tyrannous rulers, take a woman from Adam's side as he lies in the deep sleep of ignorance:

> And the spirit-endowed woman came to him and spoke with
> him, saying, 'Arise, Adam.' And when he saw her, he said, 'It is
> you who have given me life; you will be called "Mother of the
> living." – For it is she who is my mother. It is she who is the
> physician, and the woman, and she who has given birth.'

The woman awakens Adam to his spiritual potential, but when the archons see the woman talking to Adam, they are overcome with lust and seek to defile her. The woman easily evades them, leaving behind a shadow self to trick them, and then enters the snake to instruct Adam and the 'carnal woman', by implication the image of Eve she had left behind, in the benefits of eating from the tree of the knowledge of good and evil. When the couple eat, their imperfection became apparent . . . and they recognized that they were naked of the spiritual element, and took fig leaves and bound them upon their loins.

But the first couple are expelled from the garden by the wicked archons, who throw them into a life of toil so that 'mankind might be occupied by worldly affairs, and might not have the opportunity of being devoted to the holy spirit.'

The division of Eve into her higher spiritual and baser material components is developed in *On the Origin of the World*, where Eve is identified as Zoe or Life, the daughter of Sophia or Wisdom. Once again, her role is to enlighten Adam:

> After the day of rest Sophia sent her daughter Zoe, being called Eve, as an instructor in order that she might make Adam, who had no soul, arise so that those whom he should engender might become containers of light. When Eve saw her male counterpart prostrate she had pity upon him, and she said, 'Adam! Become alive! Arise upon the earth!' Immediately her word became accomplished fact. For Adam, having arisen, suddenly opened his eyes. When he saw her he said, 'You shall be called "Mother of the Living". For it is you who have given me life.'

Another Gnostic text, *The Gospel of Philip*, blames human suffering on the differentiation of the sexes that took place when Eve was taken from Adam's body:

> When Eve was still in Adam death did not exist. When she was separated from him death came into being.

Christ's function is to remedy the division, a sacred reunion that will take place in the spiritual bridal chamber and will restore humanity's original androgyny:

> . . . Christ came to repair the separation which was from the beginning and again unite the two, and to give life to those who died as a result of the separation and unite them. But the woman

is united to her husband in the bridal chamber. Indeed those
who have united in the bridal chamber will no longer be
separated.

Promising as these ideas are, Gnosticism and its strange, ambiguous texts, with their imaginative symbolism of the journey through self-knowledge to God, were suppressed as heresy and had no lasting place in the development of mainstream Christianity. The often contradictory attitudes towards women expressed in the writings that have survived reflect the sexual and social anxieties of the first centuries after Christ, when abstinence from the pleasures of the flesh was increasingly seen as the path to spiritual life. One has to look elsewhere for role models for women, only to find that the familiar female plot has undergone a startling metamorphosis. Gone are the heroic wives and mothers of early Judaism; procreation is no longer on the agenda. The new 'muscular' woman of the early Christian era is at best a virgin, or at least a committed widow, and in any case a woman who has renounced her sexuality in order to concentrate on spiritual marriage with God. A new breed of tales developed during the early Christian period, tough accounts of suffering and overcoming, which celebrated the spiritual struggles and achievements of individuals whose narratives had unfolded within living memory of the tellers and their audiences, although others were probably apocryphal, exemplary tales that evolved to explore new models for human behaviour and were circulated as markers of what men and women, inspired by the example of Christ and his disciples, could achieve. Women were allowed to participate in the new opportunities for choice and self-expression that these stories revealed, emerging as doughty heroines, martyrs and saints, outstanding for their courage, self-discipline and unquestioning faith. But what these stories most notably did for women was reposition their sexual identity, and dispute the norm that biology is fate. The new heroine typically overrode her destiny as wife and mother and pledged herself as the bride of Christ.

St Thecla and St Paul:
feisty heroine meets man of God

PAUL'S ADVOCACY OF celibacy, however moderate, was enthusiastically adopted by some Christian communities, and its continuing
influence is reflected in the story of the virgin Thecla, whose
miraculous life secured her cult status as a saint with a particular
following among women. Her history is told in the *Acts of Paul*, an
apocryphal work probably dating to around AD 160, nearly one
hundred years after the death of Paul, and it satisfyingly combines
female heroism and beauty with magical interventions and successful
flouting of the authorities. Female bonding, cross-dressing and a
hefty dollop of nudity and sado-masochism ensure that the narrative
goes with a swing. The story begins in Iconium, a city in Asia
Minor, with the virgin Thecla craning out of her window, refusing
to eat or sleep, while she listens to Paul preaching chastity to an
assembly of Christians at a nearby house:

> Blessed are the bodies of the virgins, for they shall be well-
> pleasing unto God and shall not lose the reward of their
> continence, for the word of the Father shall be unto them a
> work of salvation in the day of his Son . . .

Thecla's mother, Theocleia, is so disturbed by her daughter's
eccentric behaviour that she sends for the girl's wealthy fiancé
Thamyris. Unable to reason with Thecla, Thamyris hauls Paul
before the governor, Castelius, accusing him of having corrupted all
the women in the city. When Castelius imprisons Paul overnight,
Thecla bribes the jailers so that she can sit with Paul and humbly
kiss his chains, and her family finally find her 'bound with him, in
affection'. A throng of protesters demand that Paul be put away as a
sorcerer, but the moderate Castelius invites Thecla to explain why
she now refuses to marry Thamyris. When Thecla does not reply,
her mother cries out, 'Burn the lawless one, burn her that is no
bride in the midst of the theatre'. Thecla's punishment will be a
lesson to other disobedient women. A huge crowd swarms to the
theatre, but Thecla is sustained by an image of the Lord who appears

to her in Paul's likeness. Thecla mounts the pyre, provocatively naked, and a great fire immediately blazes up, but God saves her by a torrential downpour which threatens the lives of many of the spectators.

Some days later, Paul, who has been banished from Iconium, is praying by the roadside when Thecla arrives and, amid general rejoicing, proposes cutting her hair short like a man's and following Paul. He refuses to baptize her, but takes her with him to Antioch, where Thecla gets into trouble once more. The wealthy notable, Alexander, is captivated by Thecla and tries to bribe Paul to hand her over, apparently thinking she is some kind of slave or prostitute. Paul disowns his acolyte, leaving Alexander to make a crude grab for her in the middle of the highway. Thecla fights back, tearing Alexander's clothes and plucking the wreath or crown, symbol of his high status, from his brow. She is dragged off yet again, to account for her behaviour to the governor of Antioch, who condemns her to be thrown to wild beasts. This time, the women of the city are vociferous in Thecla's defence and she is given into the care of a local noblewoman known as queen Tryphaena.

The next day, Tryphaena personally escorts Thecla to the games and, amidst tremendous tumult, Thecla is stripped naked and thrust into the stadium with ferocious lions and bears. A lioness unexpectedly champions her and, when the animal is eventually killed, Thecla resourcefully flings herself into a tank of man-eating seals, baptizing herself in Jesus' name. Clothed in divine fire, she emerges unscathed and the women in the audience fling down narcotic herbs to paralyse the ravening beasts. Thecla is now bound by cords to Alexander's savage bulls, only to escape once more with the help of the divine flames. Overcome by nervous anxiety, Tryphaena collapses and the governor stops the games. Thecla declares her credentials as 'the handmaid of the living God' and is released to the accompaniment of triumphant cries from her female supporters. Tryphaena offers to make Thecla her heir, but the girl yearns after Paul and, dressing herself in a man's robes, she goes to Myra where Paul is preaching, before returning with his blessing to Iconium where she finds Thamyris providentially dead. Several Greek versions of the tale add that Thecla lived until she was ninety, ending up on Mount Calamon where some rude youths tried to molest her. But, as she prayed, a rock opened up to receive her, from whence she may have found her way to Rome where her body was believed to reside.

This is an extraordinary narrative and it is difficult at this distance of time accurately to gauge its writer's intentions, just as it is impossible to know for sure whether Thecla was entirely fictitious. Her story was taken up by Christian women who saw in her a worthy role model, but in the context of the period and of other apocryphal Acts that were popular reading at this time, it would probably be wrong to claim it as a proto-feminist text, and it was almost certainly written by a male author. A number of critics have seen its roots in the classical romance genre, in which hero and heroine suffer terrible vicissitudes before being finally happily married, the acceptable outcome for a potent male and fertile female. If so, this is a romance with a peculiarly Christian twist in its tail. Its trajectory may be to unite Thecla (briefly) with the (untypically reluctant) beloved, Paul, but its thrust is anti-marriage and in particular anti-procreation. Thecla's subversive demand to live a virgin life is punished far more severely than Paul's call to continence – while he is merely beaten and sent out of Iconium, she is threatened with fire and then wild beasts – but she survives undamaged, fulfilling her ambition to become a baptized member of God's church, even if she has to perform the ceremony on her own behalf, and to live as a virgin preacher, an outcome that was particularly appealing to women smarting under the young Church's increasingly rigorous application of Paul's recommendation in his first letter to Corinthian Christians:

> Let your women keep silence in the churches: for it is not permitted unto them to speak; but they are commanded to be under obedience, as also saith the law.

> And if they will learn any thing, let them ask their husbands at home: for it is a shame for women to speak in the church.

> (1 Cor. 14:34–5)

Paul's advice need not imply any particular animosity towards women. He was simply restating conservative Judaism's approach to women as preachers or disputants in matters relating to doctrine, but his words became useful ammunition in a religious culture that wished to suppress female leaders.

Some scholars suggest that the pseudo-Pauline commentary in Timothy – 'I suffer not a woman to teach, nor to usurp authority over the man' – may have been intended to counteract popular tales, such as the Thecla romance, of women preaching and baptizing. But, for the author of the *Acts of Paul*, the right of women to teach or baptize was possibly not the issue. The scholar Kate Cooper sees this as a text where male values are at stake and argues that central to Thecla's story is the question of civic duty, which is daringly subsumed to 'a patently antisocial vision of religious heroism'. She points out that

> it is essentially a conflict *between men*. The challenge posed here
> by Christianity is not really about women, or even about sexual
> continence, but about authority and the social order. In this
> way, tales of continence uses [*sic*] the narrative momentum of
> romance, and the enticement of the romantic heroine, to mask
> a contest for authority, encoded in the contest between two
> pretenders to the heroine's allegiance.

Paul's challenge to the masculine status quo, the wealthy householder who wants to marry Thecla, and to her mother's socially respectable ambitions for her, ultimately wins out over all that Thamyris or the governors can do to win her back to her woman's destiny. But if Paul's battle with civic norms was intended to be the main thrust of the story, the writer, as so often in religious narrative, subverts his own intentions by producing a rollicking tale in which the reader's attention is persistently distracted from the 'message' by the colourful events that roll in rapid, vivid sequence before the mind's eye, and in particular by the resourcefulness of its appealing heroine. Thecla rather than Paul becomes the focus for rebellion, both by her 'unwomanly' activities and by the support she wins from other women, including her wealthy and influential patroness, queen Tryphaena. At a time when the image of the devoted couple working together in harmony was publicly celebrated by the emperor Marcus Aurelius, who had his wife Faustina the Younger depicted on coins with the significant motto *concordia*, Thecla breaks all the rules of acceptable behaviour for women of her class.

One of the most intriguing aspects of the story is the hold Paul exerts over Thecla. We know from the beginning that this is no conventional romance by the description of Paul with which the story commences: 'a man little of stature, thin-haired upon the head, crooked in the legs, of good state of body, with eyebrows joining, and nose somewhat hooked'. Hardly the stuff of female erotic fantasy, even allowing for differences of period and culture, but the author goes on to say that Paul was 'full of grace: for sometimes he appeared like a man, and sometimes he had the face of an angel', suggesting the attraction of the charismatic and inspired preacher. But Thecla becomes committed to Paul before she even sees his face and throughout the story there is an intriguing hint that Paul holds her in thrall by witchcraft. Theocleia tells Thamyris that her daughter, 'like a spider at the window, bound by his words, is held by a new desire and a fearful passion: for she hangeth upon the things that he speaketh, and the maiden is captured'. Later Paul is accused by the populace of being a wizard, who has corrupted their wives, and a sorcerer. He is a spellbinder whose charm is language: seductive words which seem in particular to influence women, the respectable wives and daughters of the city's ruling classes. Although he is nowhere explicitly compared to the serpent, whose honeyed tongue deceived Eve in the garden, the idea of a woman beguiled to disobey the status quo by the insinuating power of language haunts the text. Thecla herself seems to be equally capable of witchcraft in her astonishing ability to survive fire and the tearing teeth of wild beasts, while in true romance tradition retaining her beauty and resisting attempts to violate her chastity. She keeps herself intact – for God. What is also intriguing is the less than chivalrous behaviour of the anti-hero Paul, who comes across as grumpy and unpredictable, abandoning Thecla to burn in Iconium while he retreats to a safe distance, refusing to baptize her, disowning her in Antioch and quick to suspect her of sexual deviance because of her cross-dressing activities. Perhaps the apostle's reluctance was intended to warn women that emulating the more extravagant aspects of Thecla's behaviour would be unlikely to meet with approval from the Church authorities. But what the story communicates most vividly to today's audience and, apparently, to the women of early Christianity, starved for role models, is the cheering image of the feisty heroine, defying social convention and finally setting off on her own to pursue a typically masculine life of preaching and virgin dedication to God.

It is unsurprising that the latter part of Thecla's life is not explored. The story would have been less glamorous and may have made for painful reading: even when she was an old woman, there was a rumour that she was pestered by youths and, according to one reading, these were not boys, but local doctors who were angry at her reputation as a faith healer, and wanted to put an end to the virginity which they identified as the source of her power, an indication of the kind of suspicion and jealousy that an unmarried woman trying to run a public career might have encountered. Even if Thecla had lived at home with her mother rather than pursuing an independent or itinerant life, her attempts at public preaching must have led to verbal and possibly physical abuse by non-converts, to sexual harassment, mockery and straightforward attempts to suppress her work. This is no happily-ever-after scenario, although Thecla is such a tough, resilient character that she would no doubt have made short work of her opponents, perhaps with the aid of a little more divine intervention, as in the final 'miracle', her disappearance into the rock.

The mother of Saint Macrina dreamt before her daughter's birth that Thecla was her baby's secret name, and it is understandable that women adopted her as a favourite saint. As her legend grew, she was credited with miracles, ascetics flocked to her shrine outside Seleucia (modern Silifke) in Isauria, and the nun Egeria considered her visit to Thecla's sanctuary to be one of the great moments of her pilgrimage to the holy sites of the east. Egeria, a Roman citizen who hailed from some western province bordering the Atlantic coast, visited the east between AD 381 and 384, and wrote an account of her travels for her sisters back home. Her description of her visit to Thecla's martyrium, although it is sadly sparse on details of the site itself, confirms its popularity and also the extent to which asceticism had become an acceptable mode of life for women. Egeria's rapturous encounter with her dear friend Marthana also hints at a network of female pilgrims linked by the religious sites of the east: a circle of women travellers enjoying the pleasures of gossip and sociability while they paid reverence to the icons of their faith.

> Holy Thecla's is on a small hill about a mile and a half from the city . . . Round the holy church there is a tremendous number of cells for men and women. And that was where I found one of my dearest friends, a holy deaconess called Marthana. I had come to know her in Jerusalem when she was up there on pilgrimage. She was the superior of some cells of apotactites [early Christians who had renounced worldly possessions] or virgins, and I simply cannot tell you how pleased we were to see each other again. But I must get back to the point.
>
> There are a great many cells on that hill, and in the middle a great wall round the martyrium itself, which is very beautiful . . . In God's name I arrived at the martyrium, and we had a prayer there, and read the whole Acts of holy Thecla; and I gave heartfelt thanks to God for his mercy in letting me fulfil all my desires so completely, despite all my unworthiness.

There is something charming in this image of energetic, devout Egeria solemnly re-reading Thecla's raffish history in the cave where the saint was believed to have spent the final years of her ministry before vanishing into the surrounding rock, but Thecla's following among such seriously pious women as Macrina's mother and the deaconess Marthana indicates that her story was read by the early Church as an exemplary woman's life, although its spicier features no doubt made it more digestible. Even the Church Fathers approved of Thecla, at least once her story had been disentangled from the debate over women preachers. In his work *On Virginity*, Ambrose recommended her as a model for virgins along with Mary, the mother of Jesus Christ: 'Let . . . Thecla teach you how to be offered [i.e. sacrificed]'.

Thinking back to those Greek and Hebrew narratives which stressed the ill effects of social disorder and sought to secure women in protected wife- and motherhood, Thecla's story seems astonishingly subversive and even daunting, and its popularity with Christian women suggests that it fed a need for exemplars of female behaviour for the new social conditions in which marriage and motherhood were no longer priorities.

The apocryphal story of Thecla indicates one way in which women could assert themselves outside conventional family life; other narratives relate how women sidestepped their negative image as daughters of Eve to become deaconesses, financial sponsors and leaders of religious communities, and there were moving and often lurid tales in circulation about reformed prostitutes or other 'fallen' women who embraced Christian asceticism: many legends began to accrue around the ambiguous figure of Mary Magdalene, the first witness to Christ risen, a second Eve who helped to reverse the bane of the first by a momentous dawn encounter in a garden. But many of these narratives suggest the heavy cost to women of the renunciation of conventional behaviour, and the paths they took sometimes led to fatal extremes. Jerome in Rome became spiritual adviser to a circle of aristocratic women which included the wealthy widow Paula. It was her daughter Eustochium to whom he wrote to extol the virtues of virginity. Another daughter, Blaesilla, was widowed when still only twenty and in her distress turned to extremes of religious asceticism, refusing to eat, sleeping on the bare floor despite being ill with a fever, and spending hours in prayer. She died within three months of subjecting her body to this regime, causing a terrible scandal and eventually forcing Jerome, as her spiritual mentor, to relocate to Bethlehem. Blaesilla's anorexia and compulsively self-punitive behaviour recall the thousands of girls who responded to new demands on the female body in the mid-twentieth century by similar acts of self-abuse, although, as Caroline Bynum points out in her study of medieval anorectics, it would be a mistake to draw easy analogies between very differing historical situations. Even so, Paula's bewildered grief is all too recognizable. Writing to her after Blaesilla's death, Jerome rather sharply urges her to control her sorrow, but his irritable accusations reveal a woman torn between grief over her prematurely dead daughter and guilt over what Jerome suggests is a lack of submission to God's will: 'You call to mind Blaesilla's companionship, her conversation, and her endearing ways; and you cannot endure the thought that you have lost them all. I pardon you the tears of a mother, but I ask you to restrain your grief.' Reminding her of Job's terrible trials,

Jerome suggests that Paula is 'over-delicate', and he concludes waspishly, 'Well, choose which alternative you please. Either you are holy, in which case God is putting your holiness to the proof; or else you are a sinner, in which case you have no right to complain . . . you endure far less than your deserts.' Despite this bullying, both Paula and Eustochium remained loyal to Jerome, accompanying him to the Holy Land, where Paula embraced Christian renunciation so wholeheartedly that, when she died, she left Eustochium overwhelmed with debts that she could never hope to repay.

The narratives that follow are two radically different accounts of the cost of female renunciation, each representative of different stages of the Christian movement. Both are histories of real-life women and have the peculiar advantage of being in the first case written by the woman herself and in the second by a close male relative. Both open unexpected windows on female experience of Christianity almost two thousand years ago.

God's athlete

IN THUBURBO in North Africa, in around AD 203, Vibia Perpetua, a young matron from a good family, cast off her family obligations and submitted to public martyrdom for the sake of her faith. Her story has particular resonance as it is one of the rare instances of first-person female witness in antiquity. It is told in *The Martyrdom of Saints Perpetua and Felicitas*, which begins with an introduction by an anonymous author, who explains that Perpetua and one of her brothers were Christian catechumens, receiving instruction as a prelude to baptism. There is no mention of her husband, although Perpetua is described as newly married and nursing a young son. She and a number of other young catechumens, including the female slave Felicitas, whose martyrdom is described later in the same document, had been accused of refusing to perform a pagan act of worship to the Emperor.

The story that follows is told entirely as Perpetua herself wrote it down and begins with Perpetua under legal surveillance, but not yet in prison. Her father is trying to persuade her to renounce her faith and Perpetua's response is typical of her straightforward approach to opposition throughout the narrative. Pointing to a water-container, she asks her father whether it can be called by anything other than its proper name; when he agrees that it cannot, she says that she too cannot be called anything except a Christian. Her angry father leaves, to Perpetua's great relief. Her expectations of the ordeal that lies ahead are realistic and his pressure is only adding to the strain. A few days later she and the rest of her group are thrown into prison, a horrific experience of noise and crowds and heat, exacerbated by the soldiers' attempts at extortion. Above all, Perpetua is tortured by anxiety for her baby son, but she eventually gets permission for the child to stay with her.

Her brother suggests that she should ask God about the outcome of their trial and Perpetua has the first of four extraordinary visions. She dreams that she sees an immensely long bronze ladder reaching up to heaven, so narrow that people can only mount it one at a time. At the sides of the ladder are all kinds of weapons which have to be avoided by climbing carefully, keeping one's eyes fixed on the way ahead. At the bottom there is a huge serpent who lies in wait for anyone who wants to climb the ladder. Saturus, one of Perpetua's companions, is the first to mount the ladder and he encourages Perpetua to follow, warning her to avoid the serpent's bite. When the serpent cautiously peeps out, she uses its head as the first rung. At the top, she finds an extensive garden where a white-haired man dressed as a shepherd is milking sheep among a great throng of people clothed in glimmering white. He offers Perpetua what he has been milking, a kind of curds or cheese, which she takes in both hands and eats, while the crowd says, 'Amen.' The sound awakens her and she finds herself 'still chewing something indefinable and sweet'. She hurries to tell her brother about her dream and 'we understood that it would be mortal suffering; and we began to have no more hope in the world'.

Some days later there is a rumour that their case is about to be heard, and Perpetua's father pleads with her that if she does not turn back, her son will die and her family will always be watched. Perpetua says that the outcome of the tribunal is in God's hands, and the group is finally taken to the forum. When it is Perpetua's turn to confess, her father arrives with her baby and drags her off the platform, begging her to perform the submission that she and the other Christians have refused. Even the governor asks her to reconsider, but she says staunchly, '"I am a Christian."' The old man is flung out of the tribunal and beaten, and the Christians are condemned to the wild beasts and return to prison in joyful mood. Perpetua's father now refuses to let her have her child, but to her relief she finds that the baby no longer needs her milk and she has ceased to lactate.

Perpetua now has two more visions, both of which concern her brother Dinocrates, who had died from facial cancer when he was only seven years old. In her dream, she sees him coming out of a dark, crowded place, hot and thirsty, with dirty clothes and the repulsive wound still vivid on his face. He attempts to drink from a pool of water, but the rim is too high for him, and Perpetua wakes up, resolved to pray for help in his struggle. Her prayers are rewarded by a further dream. She sees Dinocrates restored to health and wellbeing, his clothes fresh and his terrible wound healed to a scar. The pool is now on a level with the boy's navel, and he drinks freely both from the pool and from a golden bowl above the rim, splashing the water with childish glee. Now Perpetua understands that her brother has been freed from his suffering.

In the meantime, she and her fellow Christians are moved to a military prison so that they can fight in the games to celebrate the Emperor's birthday. Her narrative ends the day before the battle in the arena, which we know she did not survive, with a final, extraordinary vision. In this dream, the deacon Pomponius knocks at the prison gate, which Perpetua opens for him. He is dressed in glistening white and tells Perpetua that they are waiting for her, she must come. They scramble together along winding pathways and he takes her into the middle of the arena, where he disappears. 'And I saw the immense, astonished crowd.' Instead of wild beasts, Perpetua is to fight an ugly Egyptian, but, stripped naked, she finds she has been transformed into a man and her supporters rub her with oil as if for a wrestling match. And now a hugely tall man appears, dressed in formal purple, and carrying a stick or baton, as if he were training athletes, and a leafy branch laden with golden apples. He says that if the Egyptian wins, he can kill Perpetua, but if she wins, she will earn the green bough. The two combatants

fight and Perpetua finds herself miraculously able to fly through the
air, striking her opponent with her heels. Finally she fells the
Egyptian and places her foot on his head. She has earned the right
to walk out of the arena through the Gate of the Living. When she
wakes up from this benign vision, she writes simply: 'And I knew I
should have to fight not against wild beasts but against the Fiend;
but I knew the victory would be mine.' Here her narrative ends.

This account of the last days of a young Christian martyr is so
open, so transparent that it is generally accepted as being an
authentic testimony. Apart from the human interest of the story and
its firsthand description of the arrest and imprisonment of a group
of Christians, it offers a rare insight into a woman's life and feelings,
'a priceless document' as the historian Henry Chadwick calls it. Like
Thecla, but rather more convincingly, Perpetua breaks through the
conventional framework of female life to pursue the demands of her
Christian conscience. Unlike Thecla's robust adventures, her odyssey is accompanied by considerable anxiety and distress, and what
magic there is in her story is a function of her own subconscious
mind and what it is able to teach her through dreams. In waking
life, she agonizes over her baby, and the tension about whether she
should look after him in prison or leave him with her family is not
resolved until late in the narrative, when by some kind of sympathetic rupture of the mother/child bond, the baby no longer needs
her milk and the flow – and her anxiety – spontaneously cease. It is
hugely upsetting to Perpetua to flout the respect due to her father,
both as his favoured daughter and because of his age; she feels the
blows when he is beaten by the guards as if they had been aimed at
her own body. Her mother's and brother's distress similarly exacer-
bate her own unhappiness. Prison itself is a terrible experience, and
her horror reveals itself in the dream about her dead brother, who,
like her, emerges dirty, hot and thirsty from a dark and crowded
place, only to find relief tantalizingly out of reach. Her brother's
name had flashed into her mind after a long period of not thinking
about him, and it may be that she suddenly remembers the pitiful
young boy with his repulsive sore because his situation so nearly
mirrors her own. Both are innocent of the wish to do harm, but
both appear obnoxious to others; Perpetua through the unacceptable

behaviour that is analogous to a hideous wound, alienating her father and condemning her, like Dinocrates, to a humiliating and painful death and permanent separation from her family. Prayer is her only resource in this nightmare and it does, movingly, reward her with the hopeful vision of her brother happy and restored, a foretaste of her own joyous healing and restoration after a bloody death.

Perpetua's ladder dream suggests the one-way path of martyrdom that she must travel, beset by sharp weapons in case she should stray or, like Lot's nostalgic wife, look back, and the good shepherd is perhaps Christ or at least a reassuringly benign father-figure, waiting at the end of the perilous climb to offer the sustaining curds in a garden that hints at Paradise. The reptile at the bottom of the ladder may be a reminder of God's threat to the serpent in Genesis: 'I will put enmity between thee and the woman, and between thy seed and her seed; it shall bruise thy head, and thou shalt bruise his heel' (Gen. 3:15). The serpent seems to cower at her approach, but, on her journey up the ladder, it does not bruise her heel. Perpetua may also have known of the great dragon from Revelation, one of Satan's most impressive manifestations, who was cast out by the mighty archangel Michael. In the final dream, having forced the Egyptian to the ground in a classic posture of submission, she treads on his head, and on waking is immediately able to identify her opponent as 'the Fiend'.

Like Thecla, Perpetua is well aware of the advantages of masculinity. Her ability to communicate directly with God in asking for her visions recalls Adam, who conversed with his Creator in Eden in the cool of the day and, in her final vision, she miraculously metamorphoses into a man for her battle with the Fiend. For a woman who had so recently given birth and whose breasts had only just ceased to ache with unexpressed milk, the transformation to the well-oiled body of the wrestler, God's athlete with metaphoric wings on his/her heels, must have been extraordinarily seductive, particularly given the message of female physical inferiority that is likely to have been part of Perpetua's mental make-up. Her enjoyment of her flexibility and power sings through the text and, when she wins the wrestling bout, she is rewarded with the bough of golden apples, perhaps the legendary apples, symbols of the unattainable or even of immortality, that were tirelessly guarded in the Garden of the Hesperides by the unwinking dragon.

What we learn from Perpetua's story is that in late antiquity some women did dare to dream beyond the confines of the family, and were prepared to stand up for their beliefs, whatever the personal cost. Perpetua's narrative reveals a remarkable self-confidence and poise in the face of terrible difficulties, and demonstrates an educated mind and sophisticated imagination, making one wonder how many other Perpetuas there were whose personal histories were never recorded or have failed to survive. For Perpetua and the slave Felicity who died in the same persecution, Christianity seems to have offered an unprecedented opportunity to oppose conventional mores, a liberation from domestic confinement and the suffocating folds of history, but one which sadly and paradoxically condemned both of them to a horrifying death.

Macrina: immaculate sainthood

MARTYRDOM OR THE ISOLATED LIFE of a woman preacher were not the only options open to women as Christianity became more generally accepted. Macrina, like Perpetua, was a real-life Christian heroine, from an even more privileged background. She left no record of her own, but was memorialized by her brother, Gregory of Nyssa, who made of her history an exemplary saint's life, a tract for Christian men and women that remained inspirational long after it was written in the late fourth century AD. Macrina was the eldest daughter in a family of ten children, of which nine survived infancy. The family was wealthy, with substantial estates in Cappadocia and Pontus, and had remained steadfast to Christianity through the persecution. Of the five daughters, only Macrina achieved public distinction; not even the names of the others have survived, although it is recorded that they made 'satisfactory marriages'. More is known about Macrina's brothers. Basil the Great, bishop of Caesarea, was the most outstanding, but Gregory of Nyssa, the brother who recorded Macrina's story, the ascetic Naucratius who died young in a tragic accident, and Peter were all committed

Christians. Macrina's fame is that of a lifelong virgin devoted to good works and, in her case, possessed of considerable organizational skills. Her life was written by Gregory between AD 380 and 383, after Macrina's death in AD 379 at the religious house in Annesi which she had founded, and took the form of a letter to the monk Olympius. Gregory's reason for writing the life was 'to prevent such a life being unknown to our time, and the record of a woman who raised herself by "philosophy" [i.e. Christian asceticism] to the greatest height of human virtue passing into the shades of useless oblivion'. It is a woman's life, but Gregory says that 'woman' is perhaps an inappropriate term for Macrina, 'for I do not know whether it is fitting to designate her by her sex, who so surpassed her sex', a proviso that is depressingly familiar in accounts of successful women, whose achievements are typically hijacked as peculiarly masculine. But Gregory was not on the whole an unsympathetic narrator, although it is pleasant here and there to detect a leavening of irony, the hint of a grimace in his hagiographical account of his exemplary – and formidable – sister.

Gregory tells Macrina's story from her birth, probably around AD 327, and places an interesting emphasis on her female forebears, an important ancestry for a woman whose life was carefully moulded towards sainthood, beginning with her illustrious grandmother for whom she had been named: 'a famous Macrina . . . who had confessed Christ like a good athlete in the time of the persecutions'. But Macrina also had a secret name, donated in a vision before she was born. Macrina's mother, the pious Emmelia, had particularly desired to remain unmarried, but for her own protection, fearing her good looks might lead to abduction, she had decided to marry the sober landowner Basil. At the moment of Macrina's birth, Emmelia fell asleep and seemed to hold the new baby in her hands; 'some one in form and raiment more splendid than a human being appeared and addressed the child' as 'Thecla', the name of the resourceful Christian virgin. As in Hebrew custom, the giving of names was believed in late antiquity to be significant for a person's character and fate, and Gregory sees this vision as a forecast of the young child's future life.

Emmelia attended to Macrina's education herself, which was perhaps unusual at a period when girls as well as boys would typically have had tutors. As we have seen, she taught her daughter to avoid pagan poetry and drama with its unsuitable models for female behaviour, preferring 'inspired Scripture', particularly the Wisdom of Solomon, and Macrina could recite the Psalter by heart. However, this exemplary little girl was not allowed to escape one accomplishment thought essential to seemly womanhood: she attained 'considerable proficiency in wool-work', a link across the centuries with that other angelic child, Lucy Deane in *The Mill on the Floss*, who developed the useful ability to make 'worsted flowers' grow under her fingers. Perhaps Macrina was taught to stitch something rather more useful than knickknacks to be sold at a charity bazaar.

By the age of twelve, she was a radiant beauty – like the classic fairy-tale princess, she excelled in all the virtues and looked good into the bargain. Suitors crowded round her, but her cautious father selected a steady young man more than twice her age as her betrothed, an eloquent speaker, who used his powers 'on behalf of the wronged'. All Basil's care was voided by the young man's premature death, but Macrina, to her family's astonishment, declared that her father's intention was as binding as any real marriage could have been and she therefore was entitled to remain single, as if she were indeed an honourable widow. She justified her decision by reminding her parents of the resurrection to come, which meant that her intended husband was 'absent only, not dead; it was wrong not to keep faith with the bridegroom who was away'. Centuries later, Emily Tennyson was similarly troubled by the second marriages of her friends and relatives: 'two spirits bound on earth by union so close and holy can know no severance, even in that world where there is neither marrying nor giving in marriage'. In Macrina's case, extraordinary as her decision was – she was still only twelve at the time – she did manage to persuade her family to accept it, refused all other suitors, and from then on, in order to protect her decision, she clung to her mother's side, possibly a mixed blessing as far as Emmelia was concerned. Gregory drily records that their mother 'would often say that she had carried the rest of her children in her womb for a definite time, but that Macrina she bore always, since in a sense she ever carried her about'. But Gregory, often subversive in his comments on his siblings – he refers to Basil as 'the great Basil', and talks about him returning from university as a young man 'puffed up beyond measure with the pride of oratory' – hastens to point out what a help Macrina was to her mother. With typical eldest-daughter bossiness, she set about reorganizing the household, preparing her mother's meals herself and, as the senior Basil had by now died, assisting with her complicated financial affairs, which included paying taxes to the governors of three separate districts.

Macrina's earnest efforts to reform her mother's domestic life may be seen as an anxious attempt to justify her decision to remain unmarried by indicating how useful she could be at home. But there was more to Macrina's reforms than that. Gregory says that her bent was always towards 'philosophy', by which he means the ascetic life, and she certainly influenced her brothers in this direction and demonstrated it in her own behaviour, which was radically democratic by the standards of the time. By now, the family had probably moved to their country estate, which would typically have been ornately decorated and staffed by numerous servants and slaves. Even so, Macrina encourages Emmelia to give up social hierarchies within her household, first by the simple but unusual act of baking her mother's bread herself, and then by persuading her to live on equal terms with her servants as if they were her sisters, and to eschew the showy way of life that would have been usual for so rich and well-established a family. When Emmelia's unworldly son Naucratius is killed in an accident while on a fishing expedition, Macrina supports Emmelia, who collapses with grief, and exerts considerable self-control in order to react sensibly and rationally to the tragedy.

Naucratius' history is told as a kind of aside, a tale within a tale intended to demonstrate Macrina's 'lofty character', but it offers an interesting insight into the dynamic of this unusual family. Naucratius was the second son, a beautiful and gifted boy who might have been expected to do great things. Instead, at the age of around twenty-one, he renounced worldly success and went off by himself to pursue a life of solitude and poverty. His slave refused to leave him and they lived together on the banks of the River Iris, taking care of some poor old men who lived close by. As in the case of Macrina, there is no hint of any family dissension over his decision, suggesting that his mother was prepared to tolerate unusual and even anti-social behaviour in her children, perhaps because so many of them had survived to young adulthood – four sons and five daughters, four of whom made advantageous marriages, would calm any anxieties about inheritance. Naucratius' unexpected death when still a young man is blamed on the 'Adversary', that is Satan, and nearly destroys his mother, who is literally felled by the evil news, 'thrown to the ground ... like some noble athlete hit by an unexpected blow'. (Christian women were often compared to athletes, suggesting the self-discipline and abstemiousness their role required.) Through Macrina's support and powerful moral qualities, Emmelia is comforted and led gently to count her blessings and, as Macrina gradually weans her mother from luxury, they pursue harmonious, continent lives in mutual poverty with their servants. Gregory remarks without apparent irony that they were so good as to be almost angels.

The story now moves to Macrina's inspirational death. By this time, Macrina and her youngest brother Peter have established a double monastery at Annesi, where Macrina is in charge of the women and Peter the men. When he makes his final visit in AD 379, Gregory has had several troubled years as bishop of Nyssa, and both his mother Emmelia and his brother Basil are dead, but despite these family losses, Macrina has remained firm, 'like an invincible athlete [that image again] in no wise broken by the assault of troubles'. Even her own death finds her able and prepared. As with her birth, it is presaged by a vision, this time granted to Gregory, who dreams as he is travelling to visit Macrina that he is carrying 'martyrs' relics' that glow with blinding light. Three times the vision comes and goes. When he arrives at Macrina's retreat, he discovers her lying on a sack which covers a board on the floor, her head propped 'comfortably' against another board. She tries to raise herself, but is too weak; finally 'by putting her hands on the floor and leaning over from the pallet as far as she could, she showed the respect due to my rank'. Despite her laboured breathing and evident physical distress, Macrina engages Gregory in lofty discourse, listening to his troubles, but encouraging him to be thankful for his lot, and reminding him of the divine source of all human blessings. Fittingly

– and romantically – Macrina dies with the fading of daylight. Her bed has been turned to face the east and as the end comes, she withdraws her attention from her human companions and addresses herself exclusively to God: 'as if she discerned the beauty of the Bridegroom more clearly, she hastened towards the Beloved with the greater eagerness'. In her dying words, she recalls Christ's sacrifice, his reversal of God's sentence of death in the Garden of Eden, and brings together powerful images from Genesis and Revelation, '"Thou hast saved us from the curse and from sin . . . Thou hast broken the heads of the dragon who had seized us with his jaws, in the yawning gulf of disobedience. Thou hast shown us the way of resurrection, having broken the gates of hell, and brought to nought him who had the power of death – the devil."' By breaking the flaming sword that had barred the gates of Eden since first Adam and Eve were thrust out by God's cherubim, Christ opened up the possibility of a return to Paradise. As the evening lamp is brought in, Macrina can barely speak and as she finishes mouthing the thanksgiving for the Lighting of the Lamps, 'she drew a great deep breath and closed her life and her prayer together'.

Gregory wants us to feel that this is a fitting end for a great Christian saint, but the story does not finish here. Testimony to his sister's holiness and a hint of miraculous doings are needed to complete her sanctification. Both are willingly supplied by women in her community. Vestiana and Lampadia advise him on Macrina's burial robes, demonstrating that, contrary to custom, she had no valuable clothes hidden away in a secret chest or cupboard for this important moment. As Lampadia indignantly exclaims: '"She knew of one store-house alone for her wealth, the treasure in heaven."' Nevertheless they come to an agreement about suitable attire and Macrina is dressed in the pristine white of the virgin bride which they mask from public view with her mother's dark robes. The women show Gregory a small scar above his sister's breast, where she had once had a dangerous tumour. Despite Emmelia's pleas, she had refused to see a doctor as she thought it immodest to uncover her body in front of a man: such was her exemplary delicacy. After a night of weeping and prayer to the '"God of healing"', Macrina had covered her wound with the mud formed when her tears fell on the ground. When next her mother enquired, Emmelia was persuaded to make the sign of the cross over the wound and the tumour disappeared.

This was not the only miraculous happening connected with Macrina. After she has been buried in the family grave next to her mother in token of their unbroken comradeship, Gregory meets a distinguished soldier who tells him how Macrina had cured his little daughter's eye disease with the powerful drug of prayer. There are other things Gregory might mention – a harvest of unlimited corn in time of famine, '[h]ealings of diseases, and castings out of demons, and true predictions of the future' – but he keeps these details to himself as he thinks that most people will be incredulous and suspicious. Like any good rhetorician, Gregory knows the benefit of the fertile fact, quietly planted to do its work in his readers' imaginations.

Gregory's biography of his sister has its touching moments, but, unlike Perpetua's apparently spontaneous narrative, it is a formal document, carefully written by a polished orator to highlight the saintly aspects of his sister's life. Perhaps because of this, Macrina does not seem sympathetic: her enthusiasm for organizing others, along with her highminded piety and rigorous self-control, seem rather uncomfortable characteristics. The hint of Emmelia's impatience with her daughter's persistent attentions, the sense that giving up the good life did not come easily to the mother, the whisper that Basil was conceited and bumptious – all these, combined with Naucratius' resolute turning his back on communal family life and going off to squat on the riverbank, suggest that the strong personalities of the eldest sister and brother were not easy for any of the family to live with. But the Life is conscious hagiography and, reading between the lines of Gregory's careful construction of a saint's life from birth to death, Macrina's character emerges as extraordinary even if not entirely amiable. Her pledging of herself to virginity at so young an age and in such a culture was both courageous and intriguing: maybe she felt that she had a vocation, or that her ambitions for social reform and to manage her own life would have a better chance of being realized in her parents' home. Marriage would inevitably have committed her to childbearing and to a lifestyle which reflected the standards of other wealthy families in the region, and a husband might not have been as amenable to her ambitions as her parents proved to be. She does seem to have held the family together in important ways, apparently making no objections to her sisters' advantageous marriages. There is no suggestion that she tried to persuade them to share her own commitment to virginity, perhaps because she wanted to avoid sororal competition, perhaps because she understood too well the difficulties and tensions of being an unmarried daughter. She encourages her brothers to work towards more ascetic, Christian behaviour, not a bad thing given their commitment to the religious life, and makes the effort even when seriously ill to exhort Gregory to brace up under difficult professional circumstances. She supports her mother in practical as well as emotional ways and, an enormously wealthy woman, gives away her worldly goods to benefit others, looks after their servants as if they were family, and founds a celibate order that provides a secure home for widows as well as young virgins. If all this required a certain amount of managerial enthusiasm, it seems excusable in terms of what she was able to achieve.

Gregory's attitude towards her appears to have combined respect with a degree of caution; as the third son, he seems to have been vulnerable to the family pecking order and was bullied by his more forceful brother Basil into accepting the difficult bishopric in Nyssa. Macrina's 'count your blessings' approach to life's vexations may have been trying, even by the standards of those godly times. But Gregory pays her the compliment of recording her words and indeed of taking the trouble to write her life, and that perhaps says more than anything about his feelings for her – he wanted her and her achievements to be remembered.

The second Eve

THESE STORIES SUGGEST other possibilities for women besides the traditional and partly discredited roles of wife and mother, and allowed them to bypass the tarnished inheritance of foremother Eve. But they are drastic models, describing extremes of behaviour that many women would not have wished to emulate, and which it would not have been possible to embrace without drastic dislocation of their domestic situations. Women could not all be martyrs or virgins or even picaresque heroines like Thecla, able to rely on divine intervention for their safety and wellbeing. It was simply not practical. Other, less extreme roles did become available to women during early Christianity, offering new responsibilities and social authority, and records indicate a wide variety of female practices and behaviour, but, by some curious sleight of hand, the lasting doctrines that influenced Christian teaching centred on a hypothetical and polarized view of woman as immaculate bride of Christ or naughty daughter of Eve. As the centuries passed the most persistent role model for Christian women was the paradoxical figure of Christ's mother Mary, the second Eve, who managed to remain at one and the same time perfect mother and *virgo intacta*. This irresolvable fissure in female biological destiny meant that women were pledged to an ideal of behaviour that they could never realize, whether they devoted themselves to the hurly burly of domestic family life or the cloistered austerities of virginity. It seems a curious, malignant and ridiculous sentence.

PART TWO

FANTASIES OF EVE

CHAPTER 8

THE SECOND EVE

I sing of a maiden that is matchless:
King of all kings to her son she chose.
ANONYMOUS

Ave Maria

LONG AGO, IN THE distant histories of the twelve tribes of
Israel, there was a rich man named Joachim, who gave
bounteously of his goods to God and to His people, but was
without reward, for he and his wife Anna had no children. So
grieved was Joachim that he retired to the wilderness to fast and
pray, leaving Anna to mourn the double loss of her husband and
the children she was now too old to bear. Remembering God's late
gift of the child Isaac to Abraham and Sarah, she dressed herself in
her bridal robes and sat in her garden beneath a laurel tree. There
she shed the bitter tears of the outcast, for even the sparrows in the
branches above her head reminded her that she alone was barren in
a fruitful universe. But as she wept, an angel came to Anna and told
her that she would conceive and bear a child who would become
renowned throughout the world, and in tremulous gratitude Anna
promised to dedicate the baby to God. Joachim, too, was brought
the good news by an angel, and rushed home for an ecstatic reunion
with his wife, who was waiting to greet him at the garden gate.
And so was conceived the child who would grow up to be the
mother of Jesus Christ. There is a painting by the Master of
Moulins, now in the National Gallery in London, that shows the
middle-aged Anna and Joachim, dressed in the richly coloured but
serviceable robes of burghers of the artist's period, around 1500, at
their first glad greeting after Anna's visitation by the angel, their
arms stretched out to embrace one another as they lean forward for
a healing kiss. By now, tradition had placed their meeting at the

Golden Gate outside the walls of Jerusalem, and claimed that it was at this moment that the Blessed Virgin was conceived.

The early history of the Virgin Mary does not appear in the Gospels, but in the apocryphal *Book of James*. By the second century after the birth of Christ, his mother, an almost invisible figure in the scriptural accounts of the life of Christ, had already become the subject of speculation and veneration, and this hagiographical narrative was an early chapter in a rapidly proliferating literature recording her marvellous properties and powers, a corpus that is still being augmented as new sightings of the Virgin, of her image weeping blood, miraculous healings and so on, continue to be reported. The *Book of James* goes on to describe how Anna kept her promise, dedicating Mary at the age of three to the Temple, where she passed a typically blameless and blessed childhood 'as a dove that is nurtured: and she received food from the hand of an angel'. But as the young girl developed towards puberty the priests became concerned about the problem of defilement – a menstruant could not be accommodated within the Temple – and the aged Joseph was eventually singled out as her husband through divine intervention in the form of a dove. Reluctant but resigned – the *James* narrator is sympathetic to the embarrassment of a respectable elderly widower betrothed to a very young girl – Joseph took Mary into his house prior to their formal marriage and then went on a journey to attend to his business. While he was away, the angel Gabriel visited Mary with extraordinary tidings, and Joseph returned to find his espoused wife six months pregnant. He was aghast, comparing himself to Adam whose wife Eve had been deceived by the serpent while he, too, was about his lawful business. The priests came and accused Joseph and Mary of unlawfully preempting their marriage rites, and made them drink the waters of bitterness, the horrific trial by ordeal of their chastity, but the couple survived unscathed and could not be condemned. Through all these trials and mortifications, Mary protested her innocence, and the cumulative effect of the narrative is to reinforce what distinguished the mother of Christ from all other mothers in Jewish tradition: her virginity. 'As the Lord my God liveth I am pure before him and I know not a man.' As further proof, the *Book of James* goes on to tell the story of doubting Salome, a midwife and healer who is determined to test for herself whether the young woman who has just given birth in a cave in Bethlehem can possibly be a virgin. She boldly inserts her arm into the newly parturient Mary's vagina, only for it to emerge withered and useless, and the shamefaced Salome has to have the limb miraculously restored by the newborn baby.

It is the great irony of Christianity that, on the one hand, it laid enormous emphasis on female salvation through motherhood while, at the same time, venerating a virgin mother as its supreme image of maternity. The concept of the Virgin Birth, in tandem with the pseudo-Pauline dictum that women could be saved from Eve's sin 'in childbearing', was perhaps the biggest tease that could have been devised to perplex and confound Christian women, and led to centuries of muddled thinking about female sexuality. But the biblical authority for Mary's virginity is equivocal. It is not mentioned by Mark or John, and the evidence in Luke is contradictory. Matthew does say that Mary conceived through the agency of the Holy Ghost (Matt. 1:18–20), but then goes on to claim this as fulfilment of the prophecy in Isaiah 7:14, 'Behold, a virgin shall be with child, and shall bring forth a son, and they shall call his name Emmanuel, which being interpreted is, God with us' (Matt. 1:23). Matthew's interest was in establishing the links between Christ's ministry and Jewish prophetic traditions about the coming of the Messiah rather than in making any particular point about Mary's virginity. To add to the potential confusion, the text of Isaiah used by Matthew would have been the Greek Septuagint translation, in which the Hebrew word 'almah, meaning a young woman eligible for marriage, was rendered by the Greek parthenos, a term with much stronger implications of physical virginity. On such a fragile foundation was constructed the monolith of the Virgin Birth.

The increasing emphasis on Mary's virginity in Christian teaching from the fourth century AD was influenced by Augustine's theory of original sin. Just as Christ was the Second Adam, in Paul's striking image, so Mary became the Second Eve, by her virginity freeing humanity from the fatal taint of sexuality passed from generation to generation since the Fall. Jerome makes the point with his customary verve: 'In the old days . . . Eve continually bore children in travail. But now that a virgin has conceived in the womb a child, upon whose shoulders is government, a mighty God,

Father of the age to come, the fetters of the old curse are broken. Death came through Eve: life has come through Mary.' Just as Christ was freed from the contamination of original sin through Mary's unbroken virginity, so it became important that Mary herself should be seen to be the product of a miraculous birth. Although the dogma of the Immaculate Conception, the belief that Mary's mother Anna conceived without human intervention, was not proclaimed until 1854, its seeds had been sewn as early as the *Book of James* with the visit of an angel to a weeping woman and a joyous embrace at a garden gate. The effect of these powerful ideas about sex-free maternity was to separate Mary from the common lot of womankind and from normative processes of sexual intercourse, childbirth and even death. While Eve was condemned to give birth in travail, it was reported that Mary's labour was painless and even that she had retained her virginity after the birth of Christ, an idea that was strenuously argued by the early Church. In 451, however, at the Council of Chalcedon, she was officially designated *Aeiparthenos*, 'Ever-virgin', confirming her virginity at every stage from conception, childbirth to *post partum*, a ruling that became dogma at the First Lateran Council, in 649. Finally, through the dogma of the Assumption of the Virgin, declared as late as 1950, the centuries-old tradition of Mary's ascension into heaven in the full radiance of uncorrupted flesh received papal warranty, confirming her power to overthrow God's curse of death on Adam and Eve, 'for dust thou art, and unto dust shalt thou return'.

But their relationship to human sexuality and death was not the only way in which Mary and Eve came to represent opposite poles of what a woman should or should not be. In Giovanni di Paolo's beautiful *Annunciation*, painted around 1445, the eye is invited to focus on the tableau enacted under an elaborate canopy: the angel Gabriel is giving Mary the momentous news that she is God's chosen vehicle for the birth of His Son, a task that the young girl acknowledges with the utmost humility in Luke's account of the Annunciation, 'Behold the handmaid of the Lord; be it unto me according to thy word' (Luke 1:38). To the right of the imperious angel and the assenting girl, God is directing operations from a gilded cloud while an angel literally shoves Adam and Eve through the outskirts of a flowery Paradise where some cheerful rabbits still frolic. The implications of this contrast between Mary's obedience and Eve's rebellion were pointed out in the second century AD by Irenaeus, bishop of Lyons:

> And just as it was through a virgin who disobeyed [namely,
> Eve] that mankind was stricken and fell and died, so too it was
> through the Virgin [Mary], who obeyed the word of God, that
> mankind, resuscitated by life, received life.

As the human Adam was restored by the divine Christ, so 'Eve [had necessarily to be restored] in Mary, that a virgin, by becoming the advocate of a virgin, should undo and destroy virginal disobedience by virginal obedience'. In this case, both participants on the seesaw of Fall and Redemption are human and, as the historian Jaroslav Pelikan points out, 'It was absolutely essential to the integrity of the two narratives that both the disobedience of Eve and the obedience of Mary be seen as actions of a free will, not as the consequences of coercion, whether by the devil in the case of Eve or by God in the case of Mary.' This was a crucial factor in Mariolatry, the stepping-off place for her exemplary devotion as mother and her powers as intercessor between sinful humanity and the divine Judge: she had freely accepted God's will, with all the inconvenience, humiliation and suffering that it involved.

The French conduct book known as *The Goodman of Paris* confirms that Mary's unquestioning obedience continued to be a model for female behaviour well into the Middle Ages. Written between 1392 and 1394 by an elderly husband for his teenage bride as a guide to wifely behaviour and good household management, the book includes a lengthy section on being 'humble and obedient to your husband', in which the Goodman tells the popular story of patient Griselda whose husband subjected her to daunting pain and humiliation to test her loyalty. She emerges with flying colours, and the Goodman goes on to point out Mary's willingness to accept public shame in her humble obedience to God's will. When Gabriel brought her news of the conception:

> She did not answer, 'It is not reasonable, I am maid and virgin,
> I will not suffer it, I shall be defamed'; but obediently she

answered, '*Fiat mihi secundum verbum tuum,*' as who should say,
Be it unto me according to thy word. Thus was she truly humble
and obedient, and of her humility and obedience great good hath
come to us . . .

and he contrasts Mary's selfless submissiveness with Eve's pride and
wilfulness:

by disobedience and pride cometh great ill and a foul end . . .
as ye may read in the Bible of Eve, by whose disobedience and
pride she and all women that were and shall be after her, were
and have been accursed by the word of God.

The Goodman explains that Eve was twice cursed because she
sinned twice. She was proud and set herself up to be like God, and
was accordingly cast down into a position of subjection to her
husband:

before she sinned, she was somewhat in subjection to man, for
that she had been made of man his rib, but that subjection was
full gentle and mild, and born of right obedience and true will,
but after this curse she was subject in all things of necessity,
whether she would or no, and all other women that sprang and
shall spring from her, have had and shall have to suffer and obey
all that their husbands would . . .

Eve's second punishment – presumably for her disobedience – was
the terrible pain of childbearing.

By the time the Goodman was preparing his child-bride for her
duties as wife and chatelaine – duties that he sensibly assumed would
survive his own death and follow her into a subsequent marriage –
the contrasting images of Eve and Mary had long been established
as touchstones for female behaviour, and woman's responsibility for
human good and ill had become a commonplace. Eve through
wilful curiosity threw away humanity's right to Eden; Mary through
selfless acceptance regained its hope of Paradise. Even Eve's name
was interpreted as confirming her direct link with Mary, the Latin
Eva reversing to become *Ave*, the greeting with which Gabriel

announced his presence to the Virgin in the Vulgate version of
the Bible. Peter Damian, the eleventh-century reformer, neatly
expressed the idea in a Latin verse which translates:

> That angel who greets you with 'Ave'
> Reverses sinful Eva's name.
> Lead us back, O holy Virgin,
> Whence the falling sinner came.

Just as Mary was Eve spelt backwards, so Mary represented the
obverse of all those negative characteristics that had become attached
to the idea of woman, a chaste, selfless, benignly maternal influence
in place of Eve's self-seeking greed and sexuality, her irrationality
and lack of self control.

Schooled by centuries of Christian tradition about appropriately
passive female behaviour, or indeed by classical myths about the
depradations of gods, Zeus falling into Danae's lap as a shower of
gold or ravishing Leda in the guise of a swan, it is perhaps all too
easy to take for granted Mary's quiet acceptance of God's decision
to take possession of her virgin body, although the German artist,
Matthias Grünewald, was alert to the likely shock and panic of the
young girl. In his harshly sexual *Annunciation*, one of nine great
paintings with which he decorated the Isenheim altarpiece in around
1510–15, Mary's book tumbles to the floor and her head seems to
reel away from the aggressive angel, who towers over her in a whirl
of threateningly red and ochre robes, two fingers extended over her
head in a gesture that is less blessing than stern direction, while with
the other hand he menaces a long narrow golden rod with a
suspiciously bulbous tip. In her poem 'First Coming' (1994), Susan
Wicks describes the Annunciation as a terrifying rape in which the
victim, perhaps tranquilly baking bread or pounding linen, is unexpectedly seized and her body penetrated by a liquid that burns like
acid. At the same time, bite, fight as she may, there is no physical
body there for her to resist. The poem ends with the sombre reality
of morning sickness:

> Now she can sing
> her magnificat – sing it each morning

as she bends over the cool basins,
her hair sticking to her cheeks, her new body

shaking, as if it did not belong to her.

But for the majority of women in the Christian tradition, Wicks'
painfully clear-sighted reading of the Virgin's impregnation would
have been unthinkable, and they were left with an ideal of womanhood that denied the physical realities of sexuality and maternity.
John Phillips, in his study of the idea of Eve, cogently summed up
the dilemma: coitus had become 'the means by which the sins of
the fathers and mothers are visited on the sons and daughters. Sin,
sexuality, and death were thus woven into the tapestry depicting
Eve; obedience, virginity, and eternal life became the shining
attributes of Mary.'

The cult of Mary reached its height between the eleventh and
fifteenth centuries. At its simplest, it indicated the difficulty for men
and women of the negative interpretations of the Fall, which left
each of the sexes desperate for the model of a good woman. If
women were, as the Church insisted, essentially vicious, corrupt and
unreliable, what hope of tranquillity was there for man or self-
respect for woman? In developing the counter-image of the Virgin
Mary, the Church and the folk traditions that reworked the ideas of
the theologians for a popular audience provided an outlet for the
recognition and admiration of the feminine that was denied sinful
Eve. Sadly for women in a culture where marriage was the norm,
unbroached virginity was fundamental to Mary's goodness. The
Church's let-out that Eve's sin could be redeemed by the pains of
repeated childbearing only added to the pressure. Mary's unattainable virtue could comfort and assuage when the burden of the
feminine became unbearable, but for the women who knelt on the
stone flags of the churches and cathedrals that burgeoned throughout the Christian world, their human destiny was tragically
conditioned by Eve's fault and graphically illustrated in the stone
and tinted glass above their heads, where not only could they see
Eve driven out of Eden, sometimes dragged and kicked by a
resentful Adam, but also Luxuria with her sceptre and mirror,
emblems of woman's sensuous rule over man, her coquetry and

powers of seduction. The Vice of Luxuria or Lust was typically represented as female and her association with nudity and snakes links her visually with Eve. In a twelfth-century sculpture at Autun, she appears with flaming locks, the sign of Satan, and robustly naked to tempt her smitten admirer whom the devil already has by the hair, while at the Church of Sainte-Croix at Bordeaux, she talks intimately with the devil while serpents feed on her naked breasts. What these often obscene images recalled to their audiences were the dangers of female sexuality and Eve's responsibility for plunging humanity into the terrors of hell-fire and death. In the beautiful and poignant words of an Old Irish lament:

> I am Eve, the wife of noble Adam; it was I who violated Jesus in the past; it was I who robbed my children of heaven; it is I by right who should have been crucified.

> I had heaven at my command; evil the bad choice that shamed me; evil the punishment for my crime that has aged me; alas, my hand is not pure.

> It was I who plucked the apple; it went past the narrow of my gullet; as long as they live in daylight women will not cease from folly on account of that.

> There would be no ice in any place; there would be no bright windy winter; there would be no hell, there would be no grief, there would be no terror but for me.

The polarization between Mary and Eve bit deep into the Christian consciousness and was a favourite theme in religious art, where the two images were often closely juxtaposed. As the art historian J. B. Trapp wrote in his brief study of the iconography of the Fall, 'The door closed by Adam and Eve is opened by Christ and the Virgin', and this interdependent relationship in the Christian drama of Fall and Redemption is apparent in Francesco Marmitta's *Virgin and Child* now in the Louvre. Probably painted towards the end of the fifteenth century, the wooden panel shows the Virgin sitting, with the naked child on her lap, on a throne-like structure, flanked by Saints Benedict and Quentin and two musical angels. The throne is elevated on a podium, and just beneath the Virgin's bare toes, which peep out from under her robe, there is a small lozenge bearing a relief image of the Fall with its typical grouping of Adam and Eve on each side of the tree, symbolically represented by a pole around which the serpent coils. This almost formulaic painting, with its grandly enthroned Madonna and tiny Fall, like a subliminal message flashed during a TV advertisement, is paralleled in other paintings of the same period. Mantegna's *Madonna of Victory* (1495) is a more decorative and imposing version, while eleven years later Mariotto Albertinelli placed the Virgin standing at full height on the podium, her figure dominating a hilly landscape that embraces both town and country. Again she is flanked by adoring saints, this time Jerome and Zenobius, and once again Adam and Eve enact their tragedy below her feet.

These paintings show Mary in queenly mode as *Theotokos*, mother of God, with Eve reduced to a cipher; but other representations suggest a more intimate relationship. In an extraordinary painting by an artist now known as the Master of the Straus Madonna, dating to around 1410, the Virgin and Child are enthroned, flanked by angels and intensely brooding saints. At the foot of the throne lies Eve, her otherwise naked body loosely draped in a diaphanous robe, and holding a miniature tree of knowledge in her hand. Like the worshipping saints and angels, she too gazes intently at the Holy Mother and Baby. Berthold Furtmeyer's miniature of the *Tree of Life and Death*, painted in around 1481 for the *Salzburger Missale*, an important instrument for transmitting Church doctrine, neatly encapsulates the contrasts between the two women, who stand on each side of the tree and are physically mirror images of one another. The crucial difference is that Mary's body is swathed in robe and voluminous mantle, and her head adorned with halo and crown to mark her holy, regal status, while Eve's long hair frames her naked body, outlining the voluptuous hips and prominent buttocks. While Mary takes from the tree the host, 'the bread of angels, the food of pilgrims' and the antidote to mortal sin, to feed to a queue of suppliants, Eve deals death, plucking the forbidden fruit from the serpent's jaws with a dark and skeletal devil grimacing in the background. In the tree above Eve's head is a monitory skull, while behind Mary hangs the crucified Christ. Half-lying on the ground at their feet, one hand clutching his brow as if in bewilderment or to soothe a terrible post-coital hangover, is the naked Adam. The choice between the two opposing ways of life is quite clear and yet, as was increasingly the case with depictions of Eve, there is something very seductive about the beautiful naked girl, who is placed more prominently than Mary in the foreground of the painting, an example of how art is particularly well equipped to mime life's temptations as well as encode its moral warnings. The visual contrast between the two women follows pictorial conventions: while Mary is generally a fully clothed, dignified figure, her sexuality nullified by her significant attributes of purity, maternity and queenship, Eve is typically portrayed naked or minimally clothed in fig leaf or animal skin, and generally modelled according to contemporary criteria of female beauty. From the charming Temptation, Fall and Expulsion of the *Très riches heures du duc de Berry* to Rubens' tantalizingly fleshy Eve of 1598, the equation of Eve with female eroticism is unmistakable.

Representations of Eve focus on the pivotal moments in the Garden of Eden, increasingly concentrating on the Temptation of Adam with its potential for depicting the naked human body in its most pristine and highly idealized state, sometimes collating the Temptation, Fall and Expulsion into a cartoon-strip narrative and occasionally following the fallen couple into the wilderness, where Eve spins, or suckles her baby, while Adam delves in the sweat of his brow. In contrast to this rather sparse visual lexicon, the Virgin inspired a rich, multi-stranded iconography that in turn expanded and enhanced her image. Her attributes multiplied as her reputation grew and the legends associated with her mushroomed, offering a range of images of the feminine reverenced and emulated by women in the furthest outposts of the Catholic congregation. From scant details gleaned from the Gospels, a substantial biography was constructed for the simple girl chosen by God. The Annunciation, Jesus' humble birth, the mysterious visits by wise men from the East and marvelling shepherds, Joseph's dream and the flight into Egypt, and Mary's brief appearances at significant moments in Christ's life, and later, pitifully, her presence at her son's crucifixion and the last,

17. The story of Adam and Eve in strip-cartoon form. Book of Genesis,
Moutier-Grandval Bible, Tours, ninth century.

18. God presents Eve to Adam in an enigmatic landscape.
Hieronymus Bosch's *The Earthly Paradise*, *c.* 1500.

19. God draws Eve fully formed out of the sleeping Adam's side.
Bartolo di Fredi's *Creation of Eve*, 1356.

20. and 21. Masolino's classically beautiful couple, poised on the brink of
catastrophe, are in striking contrast to Masaccio's agonized exiles, 1420s.

22. Eve as a wrinkled, ancient woman with drooping breasts. Piero della Francesca, *Death of Adam, c.* 1452–7.

23. Eve identified with the 'beautiful evil', Pandora, who released all human ills from her jar. Jean Cousin the Elder, *Eva Prima Pandora*, 1550.

24. The serpent links Eve with the hideous figure of death, his
flesh peeling away to reveal the skeleton as he flourishes an apple.
Hans Baldung Grien, *Eve, the Serpent and Death, c.* 1510–15.

25. In Pol de Limbourg's MS illustration, the Garden of Eden is represented as a circle, an image of wholeness broken by the couple's ejection through the gate, *c.* 1410.

26. An angel pushes Adam and Eve out of Eden, while Mary, the Second Eve, listens quietly to Gabriel's news. Giovanni di Paolo di Grazia, *The Annunciation*, detail, *c.* 1445.

27. Eve, clad in a diaphanous shawl and holding a miniature tree of knowledge, at the feet of the enthroned Virgin and Child. Master of the Straus Madonna, *Virgin and Child Enthroned with Angels and Saints, c.* 1410.

28. The haggard face and straggling hair of the watching serpent are a grim warning of Eve's fate; the iris foreshadows Mary's grief at the Crucifixion of Christ. Hugo van der Goes, *Adam, Eve and the Serpent, c.* 1470-75.

sad, dawn visit to the tomb, these momentary glimpses of a mother's pride and pain provided the promising raw materials of what became an elaborate hagiography, a densely textured narrative of a literally wonderful woman, the model for all her sex. In sculpture, glass and paint, in the gold and jewel-bright illustrations of private missals and Books of Hours, men and women from every estate of life were bombarded with images not only of what a woman had been in the person of sinful Eve, but also of what a woman could be – obedient, compassionate, long-suffering and, above all, chaste. A favourite subject was the Annunciation, where the Virgin was generally the passive recipient of the angel's tidings, as in Andrea della Robbia's terracotta glazed panel in La Verna in Italy, in which an acquiescent and scholarly Mary sits with her book on her knee, her hand to her throat in patient acceptance of Gabriel's news, her purity underlined by lilies and a hovering dove. There are quantities of tender, medit-ational images of the Virgin holding or suckling her child which provide an ironic counterpoint to disturbing scenes of the crucifix-ion, as in Rogier van der Weyden's *The Descent From the Cross*, where Mary faints with anguish as her son's body is lifted down from the crucifix; images that recall Mary's possible iconographic links with Egyptian Isis, the mother nursing her child Horus and the grieving consort mourning the torn limbs of her beloved Osiris. Sometimes a visibly pregnant Mary visits her cousin Elisabeth to share news of their coming births, as in the richly gilded Visitation in Marshal Jean de Boucicaut's Book of Hours.

In the 1860s, centuries after the heyday of portraits of the Virgin, Julia Margaret Cameron daringly created a series of photographic studies of the Madonna and Child which offered a new departure in Marian iconography, not simply because of the innovative medium, but also because Cameron's studies emphasized the mother's physical presence and sexuality, reincorporating the spirit-ual Mother of God into the lived reality of vulnerable flesh and blood. Even more recently, the French psychoanalyst and critic, Julia Kristeva, in her essay 'Stabat Mater', parallels a discussion of the cult of Mary and its implications for the understanding of motherhood with an impressionistic account of her own experience of maternity. As with Cameron's disturbingly earthy Madonnas, there is no escaping the body. Kristeva's two texts – the learned and the personal – are loosely juxtaposed on the page, with the personal narrative, set in bold typeface, breaking into the formal discourse at irregular intervals. The effect is not so much subversion – the body's experience does not necessarily contradict the mind's careful analysis – as illumination. The physical reality of motherhood, as far as the written word can recreate its sensuous experiences, forces itself on to the reader's attention, closing the gap between theory and practice. Kristeva's point is that room has to be made in modern society to accommodate motherhood in all its plenitude: the desire for children, the act of childbearing, the experience of mothering. Her disruptive text reinforces the message: the body's testimony cannot be ignored or denied.

But Mary's role was not solely maternal and self-suppressing and, as her cult developed, she assumed ever grander titles reflecting her increasingly queen-like status and quasi-divine powers. Her multiple roles as Woman of Valour, Mediatrix, Woman Clothed with the Sun, Queen of Heaven and so on, drew freely on religious and secular metaphor and provided fresh incentive to the artistic imagination, while at the same time separating her even further from fallen Eve. Yet Eve was always a shadowy presence in Mary's triumphant elevation. Without her there would have been no need for Mary, and her mythology influenced and enriched Mary's cult. Two themes linking the Mother of All Living with the Mother of God proved particularly fruitful and tenacious: the concept of the *hortus conclusus*, the enclosed garden, and the *felix culpa*, the happy fault.

A garden enclosed

IN THE BEAUTIFUL lyric, 'Come into the garden, Maud', the erotic climax of Tennyson's monodrama *Maud* and prelude to a terrible, unpremeditated murder, the unnamed hero waits impatiently in a garden for his beloved. Maud is young, beautiful, richer than her lover, and has been dancing the night away at a ball to which he has not been invited, but she has promised to steal away from the revels to meet him among the roses. Tennyson's sensuous poem of sexual yearning is suffused with imagery that links it with the Song of Solomon, the great biblical love song which the early Church, with its facility for transmuting eroticism into self-repressive spirituality, had eagerly appropriated to develop its rhetoric of the Virgin Mary. Like *Maud*, the Song of Solomon, also known as the Canticles or the Song of Songs, is a celebration of erotic desire, but the biblical poem takes the form of a dialogue between a woman and her lover, and evokes not only the longing for the beloved, but also the supreme happiness of consummated love. There are, however, a number of parallels with 'Come into the garden, Maud'. The enclosed garden where the lover impatiently lingers recalls the description of the beloved in the Song of Songs, 'A garden inclosed is my sister, my spouse' (4:12), an image of fruitful interiority read by the Church Fathers as a metaphor for Mary's unbroached virginity, but in both poems used to symbolize the sexual promise of the young woman's body, and the voluptuous potential of the metaphor is fully exploited. Both gardens are fertile and spicily perfumed: the garden in the Song of Songs has 'Spikenard and saffron; calamus and cinnamon, with all trees of frankincense; myrrh and aloes, with all the chief spices' (4:14), and the woman begs the winds to 'blow upon my garden, that the spices thereof may flow out' (4:16), while in the dawn garden in *Maud*, 'the woodbine spices are wafted abroad,/And the musk of the rose is blown'. Both women are compared with the same exuberantly fragrant flowers: Maud is 'Queen rose of the rosebud garden of girls', 'Queen lily and rose in one', while the beloved in the Song of Songs is 'the rose of Sharon, and the lily of the valleys' (2:1), later used to designate the Virgin. The cumulative effect of flowers and scents in *Maud* is to goad the lover to a state of extreme sexual arousal, while in the Canticles the lover is fortunate enough to go down into his garden, 'to the beds of spices, to feed in the gardens, and to gather lilies' (6:2). As the Bride triumphantly declares, 'I am my beloved's, and my beloved is mine: he feedeth among the lilies' (6:3). Water, a symbol of erotic love and fertility, gushes through the gardens: the Bride's garden is 'A fountain of gardens, a well of living waters, and streams from Lebanon' (4:15), and Maud's lover recalls that during his night vigil:

> . . . long by the garden lake I stood,
>> For I heard your rivulet fall
> From the lake to the meadow and on to the wood,
>> Our wood, that is dearer than all;

It does not require much imagination to work out the implications of the lake and the rivulet, and that especially valued woodland.

Both poems are suffused with erotic longing. 'Stay me with flagons, comfort me with apples: for I am sick of love' says the Bride (Song of Solomon 2:5), and her lover knocks impatiently at her door crying, 'Open to me, my sister, my love, my dove' (5:2). Maud's lover assures her,

> . . . the rose was awake all night for your sake,
>> Knowing your promise to me;
> The lilies and roses were all awake,
>> They sighed for the dawn and thee.

The beloved is eagerly awaited: 'The voice of my beloved! behold, he cometh leaping upon the mountains, skipping upon the hills', cries the Bride in the Song of Songs (2:8), while the closing lines of Tennyson's lyric mimic the rhythmic energy of sexual climax as the lover anticipates Maud's imminent arrival:

> There has fallen a splendid tear
>> From the passion-flower at the gate.
> She is coming, my dove, my dear;
>> She is coming, my life, my fate;
> The red rose cries, 'She is near, she is near;'
>> And the white rose weeps, 'She is late;'
> The larkspur listens, 'I hear, I hear;'
>> And the lily whispers, 'I wait.'

> She is coming, my own, my sweet;
>> Were it ever so airy a tread,
> My heart would hear her and beat,
>> Were it earth in an earthy bed;
> My dust would hear her and beat,

Had I lain for a century dead;
Would start and tremble under her feet,
And blossom in purple and red.

The Song of Songs was fabled to have been an epithalamion
sung at the wedding of King Solomon to the Pharaoh's daughter,
although others believed it was Solomon's love song to the Queen
of Sheba, whose visit to the king attracted its own cluster of legends
and sometimes prurient speculation. For the pious exegete Origen,
however, writing in the third century after the birth of Christ, it
was an allegory celebrating the love of Jesus for his spouse, the
Church, and for the individual soul, a spiritual rather than secular
passion, and this sober interpretation of the sumptuous language and
imagery of what probably originated as a collection of secular folk
songs suited the ascetic mood of later patristic writers. Both Jerome
and Ambrose, leading exponents of asceticism within the Latin
West, drew substantially on the Song of Songs to support programmes of sexual abstention. In a letter written to his young female
friend, Eustochium, in AD 384, Jerome compares the dedicated
virgin to the Bride in the Song of Songs, and writes sympathetically
about the advantages of spiritual over human passion: 'It is hard for
the human soul not to love something, and our mind of necessity
must be drawn to some sort of affection. Carnal love is overcome
by spiritual love: desire is quenched by desire: what is taken from
the one is added to the other.' As Eustochium lies on her couch at
night, he advises her to repeat 'continually' the phrase from the
Song of Songs: ' "By night have I sought Him whom my soul
loveth." ' Later he describes the virgin's chaste bedchamber as the
scene of ecstatic spiritual congress with the Bridegroom, Christ,
again drawing freely on the Song of Songs to enhance the sensuous
impact of the meeting between human bride and heavenly lover:

Let the seclusion of your own chamber ever guard you; ever
let the Bridegroom sport with you within. If you pray, you are
speaking to your Spouse: if you read, He is speaking to you.
When sleep falls on you, He will come behind the wall and will
put His hand through the hole in the door and will touch your
flesh. And you will awake and rise up and cry: 'I am sick with

love.' And you will hear Him answer: 'A garden inclosed is my
sister, my spouse; a spring shut up, a fountain sealed.'

Here Jerome uses the metaphor of the enclosed garden to
recommend that Eustochium shut herself away in ascetic seclusion,
and he reminds her how the Bride in the Song of Songs scoured
the streets looking for the Bridegroom, but in vain: ' "I sought him
but I could not find him: I called him but he gave me no answer." '
In a letter to his sister Marcellina, Jerome's contemporary, Ambrose,
bishop of Milan during Augustine's apprenticeship as Christian
catechumen, elaborates on the relationship between virginity and
the enclosed garden of the Canticles, reminding Marcellina of the
story of Susanna who staunchly defended her chastity when she was
spied on while bathing by lubricious elders, and developing the
symbolic resonance of the associated images of the sealed fountain
and highly perfumed flowers:

> It [i.e. virginity] loves to grow in gardens, in which Susanna,
> while walking, found it, and was ready to die rather than it
> should be violated. But what is meant by the gardens He Himself
> points out, saying: 'A garden enclosed is My sister, My spouse,
> a garden enclosed, a fountain sealed;' because in gardens of this
> kind the water of the pure fountain shines, reflecting the features
> of the image of God . . . For this reason, too, that modesty of
> virgins fenced in by the wall of the Spirit is enclosed lest it should
> lie open to be plundered . . . a garden inaccessible from without
> smells of the violet[,] is scented with the olive, and is resplendent
> with the rose, that religion may increase in the vine, peace in the
> olive, and the modesty of consecrated virginity in the rose.

With the dramatic increase in Mariolatry during the late fourth
century, the Song of Songs, now established as a paean to virginity,
was increasingly applied to the exemplary Virgin of the early
Church, and the 'garden inclosed' and 'fountain sealed' were cited
to support the case for Mary's virginity *in partu*, that is, at the
moment of giving birth. Ambrose, for example, argued that Jesus
passed through Mary without 'opening' her, so that she remained 'a
garden inclosed'. The association between Mary's intact virginity

and the enclosed garden continued to bear fruit in Christian exegesis and religious poetry and art well into the seventeenth century, proposing an impossible model for women of sexually uncontaminated fertility whose persistence confirms its appeal to the male imagination, reflected in the Church's sustained squeamishness about female sexuality. The twelfth-century *religieux* Adam of St Victor typically described Mary as:

> that sealed fount, ne'er drying,
> That walled garden, fructifying
> By the good seed in it sown:
> She is that close-fastened portal,
> Shut by God 'gainst every mortal
> For some secret unknown.

In 1633, the *Partheneia Sacra*, an emblem book dedicated to the Virgin and attributed to the Jesuit Henry Hawkins, is still pondering the pleasing enigma of the impenetrable wall of Mary's garden:

> *The* Virgin *was a* Garden *round beset*
> *With* Rose, *and* Lillie, *and sweet* Violet.
> *Where fragrant Sents, without distast of Sinne,*
> *Invited* GOD *the* Sonne *to enter in.*
> *But it was clos'd:* Alma's shut up, *we know,*
> *What Gard'ner then might enter in to sow?*
> *Or plant within this* Eden? *Or, what birth*
> *Might be expected from a virgin-earth?*
> *The* Holie-Spirit, *like a subtile wind,*
> *Peercing through al, only a way could find.*
> *As th' Earth brought forth at first, how't is not knowne:*
> *So did this* Garden, *which was never sowne.*

Just as the earth mysteriously fructified in Genesis, so does Mary's garden; and in both cases the 'subtile wind' of the Holy Spirit is the vitalizing force. Hawkins describes how it alone can pierce its way into Mary's intact womb and, by his reference to the Creation, links the birth of Christ, the New Creation, with the origins of life. In the beginning, there was darkness until the Spirit of God moved across the face of the waters, 'And God said, Let there be light'. The birth of Mary's baby re-enacts that first great illumination of primordial darkness by the light of creation, a new beginning that Christ acknowledged when he said, 'I am the light of the world' (John 8:12).

In his preparatory section to the *Partheneia Sacra*, Hawkins was careful to distinguish between the garden of the Canticles, 'the Paragon of Gardens', and other possible gardens, including the Garden of Eden, but as the short extract above indicates, Hawkins does rhetorically conflate the two: '*What Gard'ner then might enter in to sow?/Or plant within this* Eden?', and it was perhaps inevitable that Mary's 'Mysticall GARDEN' should be identified with the Garden of Eden before the Fall and the closely related Earthly Paradise. The origins of the Paradise garden, a pleasure ground with carefully tended trees and flowers and refreshed by running waters, date back to the ninth to fourth centuries BC when the Medes and Achaemenians settled in Persia and developed the enclosed gardens known as *pairidaeza*, a word that meant 'enclosure' or 'park'. This became Hebrew *pardes*, which the Greek Septuagint rendered as *paradeisos*. Planted with shade-bearing trees and orchards, colourful with many different species of flowers which were eventually collected and cultivated, and watered by sophisticated irrigation systems, these Persian 'paradise' gardens offered pleasant oases of shelter and refreshment from baking heat, and could also provide parkland for roaming animals or pets, protected from external predators. The features of these gardens were eventually incorporated into carpet designs and the famed Spring Carpet of the sixth-century-AD potentate Chosroes showed a garden irrigated by four main canals which crossed at the centre, a scene, with its fertile fruit trees emblematic of spring and of life itself, that recalls the garden built by God east of Eden, where he walked in the cool of the day to talk with his gardener Adam.

Medieval literature is replete with gardens, the site of both amorous and spiritual experience, that incorporate the essential features of the Paradise garden, with its echoes of prelapsarian Eden, a place of bliss where the trees simultaneously bear fruit and flower, the sign of perpetual spring. In Giovanni Boccaccio's *Decameron* (1349–51), a group of wealthy young Florentines take refuge from the plague in the Fiesole hills, in a beautiful and ornate palace with a wonderful walled garden, which Boccaccio describes in detail:

> The garden was surrounded and criss-crossed by paths of unusual width, all as straight as arrows and overhung by pergolas of vines, which showed every sign of yielding an abundant crop of grapes later in the year. The vines were all in flower, drenching the garden with their aroma, which, mingled with that of many other fragrant plants and herbs, gave them the feeling that they were in the midst of all the spices ever grown in the East. The paths along the edges of the garden were almost entirely hemmed in by white and red roses and jasmine, so that not only in the morning but even when the sun was at its apex one could walk in pleasant, sweet-smelling shade . . . In the central part of the garden . . . there was a lawn of exceedingly fine grass, of so deep a green as to almost seem black, dotted all over with possibly a thousand different kinds of gaily-coloured flowers, and surrounded by a line of flourishing, bright green orange- and lemon-trees, which, with their mature and unripe fruit and lingering shreds of blossom, offered agreeable shade to the eyes and a delightful aroma to the nostrils. In the middle of this lawn there stood a fountain of pure white marble, covered with marvellous bas-reliefs.

All the essential features are in place: the carefully planted trees, the fragrant, shady paths, the blossom- and fruit-bearing trees, the flowery mead and the plashing fountain, source of the garden's well-constructed irrigation system, and it is no wonder that the young aristocrats 'all began to maintain that if Paradise were constructed on earth, it was inconceivable that it could take any other form'. To add to their pleasure and to enhance the garden's resemblance to Eden, they find that it is 'liberally stocked with as many as a hundred different varieties of perfectly charming animals', all harmless and wandering about the grounds as if they were tame.

The Garden of Pleasure in Guillaume de Lorris' section of *The Romance of the Rose*, written between 1225 and 1230, is similarly described as 'the earthly paradise'. The young narrator of the

Romance falls asleep and dreams that it is the month of May, widely celebrated in Europe as the beginning of spring and dedicated to the Virgin. In his dream, he finds himself outside a beautiful walled garden which he is eventually permitted to enter. Once inside the tiny wicker gate, he discovers that the garden has been designed as a perfect square and, like Boccaccio's garden, is a feast for the senses, with melodious songbirds, fruit-bearing trees, an abundance of flowers and fragrant spices, playful rabbits, and the refreshment of huge shady trees and pleasant running water. This garden, however, like Eden, has its forbidden pleasures; gazing into Narcissus' spring, the narrator sees reflected a profusion of roses with one particularly beautiful bud that he craves beyond all others. As he yearns towards the exquisite flower, he is wounded by Love's five arrows and forced to embark on his trouble-strewn quest of the rose.

The garden in Chaucer's *Franklin's Tale* proves equally problematic. Once again it is May in a garden that resembles Paradise in its matchless beauty:

> And this was on the sixte morwe of May,
> Which May hadde peynted with his softe shoures
> This gardyn ful of leves and of floures;
> And craft of mannes hand so curiously
> Arrayed hadde this gardyn, trewely,
> That nevere was ther gardyn of swich prys,
> But if it were the verray paradys.

But there is already a hint of trouble in this Eden, the seemingly casual reminder that even a spring garden cannot relieve the body's sickness or a heart oppressed:

> The odour of floures and the fresshe sighte
> Wolde han maked any herte lighte
> That evere was born, but if to greet siknesse,
> Or to greet sorwe, helde it in distresse;
> So ful it was of beautee with plesaunce.

Tempted perhaps by the flowers, the fresh green of the leaves, the excitement of dancing and the promise of light and air after the dark winter, the young squire Aurelius does confess his heart-sickness, the passion he feels for the virtuous wife Dorigen, and manages to extract from her a promise that she will accept his suit if he performs the apparently impossible task of clearing the Breton shoreline of the rocks that threaten shipwreck to her beloved husband. Needless to say, with the help of a magus, Aurelius achieves his task, and Dorigen is required to fulfil her rash promise . . .

The enclosed Paradise garden with its powerful reminders of Eden's more ambiguous pleasures became enmeshed with the spicy, fruitful, bounteously irrigated garden of the Canticles, the mysterious *hortus conclusus* of the Virgin's inviolate body, an interplay of images and associations that immeasurably enriched poetry and painting in the medieval period and beyond. The *Garden of Paradise* by an unknown Rhenish artist, dating to around 1410–20, brings together many of these extraordinarily evocative images and illustrates the opportunity they offered for imaginative interpretation. The painting shows an enclosed garden that appears to be attached to a castle. Most of the garden has been allowed to flourish freely as a flowery mead – an expanse of verdant grass with a luxuriant growth of flowers, including lily-of-the-valley, peonies, periwinkles and a strawberry that is simultaneously in flower and fruit. Towards the rear of the garden there is a raised flower bed constructed of wooden planks and containing the more stately flowers: flag irises and hollyhocks. Brightly coloured birds perch on the walls and trees and flutter in the air, and the garden is full of people. Towards the rear of the painting is the nevertheless dominant figure of the Virgin, reading a book while comfortably propped against a huge red cushion, and wearing a delicate gold filagree crown and her traditional deep blue and white robes. Her long golden hair is tucked behind a dainty porcelain ear and flows demurely over her shoulders. White, taper fingers hold the heavy book and fastidiously turn the pages. To her right, St Dorothy picks cherries from the tree of life, seeming to commune with the bird that perches on the topmost branch, while St Martha scoops water from a small well. In the centre foreground, the infant Jesus plays at Mary's feet, strumming a psaltery which St Cecilia holds out for him. To the right of the picture and again in the foreground are three male figures, closely grouped under the fruit-less tree of death and, despite their decorative clothes, making a sombre contrast to the carefree, innocent activities of the women. The winged St Michael lounges on the grass, his demon at his feet in the form of a small, dark, ugly ape. In front of him sits St George, a diminutive dragon on its back beside him, legs splayed in the air to indicate that it is well and truly dead. St George is apparently telling St Michael the story of the infancy of Jesus, while a melancholy young man, probably the knight whose prema-ture death the painting memorializes, leans on the tree of death to listen all the more attentively. The plants add an additional level of allegorical significance: roses for God's love, lilies for the Virgin's purity, the strawberry for righteousness, its tripartite leaf symbolic of the Trinity, the iris recalling Jesus' descent from the royal house of David. The painting confirms that the devout Christian who follows the life of Christ will conquer the devil and taste the joys of heaven, symbolized by Dorothy's juicy cherries. Eve is not physically present in this painting, but is, nevertheless, a shadowy participant; the *hortus conclusus*, with its trees of life and death, and pleasant birds and blossoms, a clear reminder of the Garden of Eden, where the naked temptress Eve paved the way for the demure Virgin Mary:

> That angel who greets you with 'Ave'
> Reverses sinful Eva's name.
> Lead us back, O holy Virgin,
> Whence the falling sinner came.

The *Garden of Paradise* indicates the enormous potential for fantasy and artistry offered by Christian symbolism of the garden, but there was another collection of stories that extended the imaginative possibilities even further. The *hortus conclusus* of Mary's intact virginity and the Garden of Eden where Eve fell were joined in popular tradition by memories of a third significant garden, the garden of the sepulchre where the crucified Jesus had been laid, a garden which was again haunted by the ambiguous figure of a woman, the medieval church's favourite penitent, Mary Magdalene.

As is the case with the Virgin Mary, the four Gospels say very little about Mary Magdalene. Luke identifies her as one of a number of women, all healed of various infirmities and evil spirits, who accompanied Christ and the twelve disciples on his preaching tour of the cities and villages of Galilee: 'Mary called Magdalene, out of whom went seven devils' (Luke 8:2). Three Gospels name her as one of the women who witnessed the crucifixion (Matt. 27:56, Mark 15:40, John 19:25) and, while Luke does not name her specifically, later evidence in his account suggests that she would have been among the grieving watchers (Luke 23:49, 24:10). Again with some of these women, she observes the wealthy Christian Joseph of Arimathæa wrap Jesus' body in clean linen and place it in his own freshly hewn tomb (Matt. 27:59–61, Mark 15:46–7, Luke 23:53, 55), and on the third day, Easter morning, she and the other women bring ointments and spices to embalm the body (Mark 16:1, Luke 23:56, 24:1). She is among the women who first discover that the tomb is empty and are instructed by the angel who guards the tomb to carry the good news to the disciples that Christ is risen (Matt. 28:1–8, Mark 16:1–8); while Luke gives the slightly varying account that the women find two angels, who say to them 'Why seek ye the living among the dead?', perhaps the most welcome words that could be said to any mourners returning, still numb with grief, to the tomb of their beloved (Luke 24:1–10). Matthew adds the important detail that Jesus himself appears to the women as they run to tell the disciples, but John's account differs significantly from the other three Gospels, identifying Mary Magdalene as the only woman who returns to the tomb and the sole witness to Christ risen. As John tells the story, Mary comes early on the Sunday morning and sees that the stone covering the entrance to the sepulchre has been removed. She runs back to tell Peter and John what has happened, and the two men race to the tomb and find the linen clothes and the napkin that had covered Christ's head. They return home without investigating further, but Mary remains outside the tomb to weep, and after a while she looks in and sees two angels sitting, one at the head, the other at the feet of where Christ's body had lain.

'Woman, why weepest thou?'
'Because they have taken away my Lord, and I know not
where they have laid him.'

She turns away from the tomb after this brief exchange, to see Jesus
standing behind her, but fails to recognize him, thinking he is the
gardener. Then Jesus calls her by her name, 'Mary', and she knows
him at once, 'Rabboni', 'Master', but Jesus warns her not to touch
him. She is to tell the disciples that he is ascending to his father
(John 20:1–18).

The simplicity of John's account enhances its emotional depth.
Mary's persistence in staying by the tomb, her dazzled eyes as she
turns away from the bright angels in the gloom so that she mistakes
the man she sees outside, her hand spontaneously stretching out to
touch the living Christ, are hinted rather than spelled out, but the
power and poignancy of this momentous meeting were recognized
by Hippolytus (c. 170 – c. 235), a bishop of Rome, whose commentary on the Song of Songs identified the Bride or Shulamite seeking
her lover, as Mary Magdalene, whom Hippolytus calls Mary and
Martha, who went to the garden with her spices and ointments to seek
the body of Christ: ' "By night, I sought him whom my soul loveth":
See how this is fulfilled in Martha and Mary.' Once Mary/Martha has
found Christ, she becomes the New Eve. As once the first Eve wil-
fully forfeited her right to the tree of life in the Garden of Eden, now
Mary/Martha clings to the tree of life, Christ, in the resurrection
garden. Adam was betrayed to everlasting death by Satan who persuaded Eve; Christ, the Second Adam, stands firm against Satan in his
new guise as Judas. Eve failed to recognize the serpent as Satan; Mary
eventually does recognize Christ, neatly reversing Eve's mistake.
Once again, obedience is an important attribute of the New Eve:

> [And] so that the apostles [the women] did not doubt the angels,
> Christ himself appeared to them, so that the women are Christ's
> apostles, and compensate through their obedience for the sin of
> the first Eve . . . Eve has become apostle . . .

Mary Magdalene's association with the Song of Songs survives
in the liturgy for her feast day on 22 July, which incorporates verses

from the Canticles, symbolizing the love of Mary Magdalene and through her, of the Church, for Christ:

> Set me as a seal upon thine heart, as a seal upon thine arm: for love is strong as death; jealousy is cruel as the grave: the coals thereof are coals of fire, which hath a most vehement flame.
>
> Many waters cannot quench love, neither can the floods drown it: if a man would give all the substance of his house for love, it would utterly be contemned.
>
> (Song of Solomon 8:6–7)

The typological association between Mary Magdalene and the Bride is celebrated in a mid-fifteenth-century *Biblia Pauperum*, now in Corpus Christi College in Cambridge, in an illustration which shows Mary Magdalene, identified by her pot of ointment, kneeling at Christ's feet in a fenced-in garden; to the left is a second panel in which King Darius finds Daniel alive in the lions' den, while, to the right, the Bride finds the Bridegroom in the Song of Songs, both Old Testament events believed to prefigure the New Testament incident. It was unfortunate for women – and for Mary Magdalene's subsequent reputation – that the association which proved most popular and persistent was not, however, the idea of Mary as the spiritual Bride of Christ, but of Mary as the New Eve, increasingly seen as a symbol of sexual penitence.

Mary Magdalene was set apart by the brief encounter in the garden as the first disciple to see and talk with the risen Christ, suggesting a special relationship between Mary and Christ that was elaborated by Gnostic writers in the early centuries after Christ's death into outright rivalry between Mary and the male disciples. The *Gospel of Philip* describes how Jesus loved Mary more than all the other disciples and angered them by showing his affection, often kissing her intimately in front of them all. Peter is particularly hostile to Mary, and the *Gospel of Mary* and *Pistis Sophia* indicate that his anger is due partly to jealousy but also to misogyny. In *Pistis Sophia*, Mary tells Jesus of her reluctance to speak freely to him given Peter's animosity: 'I am afraid of him, because he hates the female race.' Jesus reassures her by saying that anyone inspired by the Spirit can speak, whether man or woman. The Gnostics were prepared to countenance the idea of a specially privileged female disciple, and to support the right of women to speak, but, true to form, the institutionalized early Church was reluctant to allow Mary the status of trusted disciple and witness without dragging in a colourful past that would make her a particularly suitable object for Christ's compassion, and would support the Church's preference for categorizing women according to their sexual rather than intellectual functions. The idea that Christ himself might have had a sexual relationship with Mary Magdalene was buried along with the suppressed Gnostic texts, although it has recently been revived in Michèle Roberts' sensuous fantasy, *The Wild Girl* (first published in 1984), a marvellous picaresque novel in which Roberts draws imaginatively on Gnostic texts to create an endearing 'life' of the feisty, beautiful girl beloved by Christ.

The Church's more conventional attempt to provide Mary Magdalene with a biography led exegetes back to the Bible and to the simple expedient of collating the identities of several women mentioned in the Gospels. In his homily on Luke's Gospel, probably written in AD 591, Gregory the Great assimilated Mary Magdalene with Luke's repentant sinner, the woman who anointed Jesus with precious unguent and bathed his feet with her tears (Luke 7:36–50):

> She whom Luke calls the sinful woman, whom John calls Mary,
> we believe to be the Mary from whom seven devils were ejected
> according to Mark. And what did these seven devils signify,
> if not all the vices? . . . It is clear, brothers, that the woman
> previously used the unguent to perfume her flesh in forbidden
> acts. What she therefore displayed more scandalously, she was
> now offering to God in a more praiseworthy manner. She had
> coveted with earthly eyes, but now through penitence these are
> consumed with tears.

Mary Magdalene was thus equated with the woman guilty of fornication – and with what delight Gregory fantasizes about her sexual use of precious ointments – and committed to a penitential role suited to her parallel identity as Second Eve. She had also become a powerful weapon in the Church's drive to discredit and suppress female sexuality.

There were further identifications. John names the woman with the pot of ointment as Mary of Bethany, sister of Martha and the man Lazarus whom Christ had raised from the dead (John 11:2, 12:1–3), and Luke tells of two sisters, Mary who sat at the Lord's feet, and Martha who busied herself with waiting on the company (Luke 10:38–42). Based on these tenuous clues, Mary Magdalene became equated with Mary of Bethany, regarded during the Middle Ages as the representative of the contemplative life, while Martha stood for active Christianity. More damagingly, Mary Magdalene was also identified with the woman taken in adultery (John 8:1–11) and the much-married woman of Samaria (John 4:7–30). By the Middle Ages, the ecstatic Mary who was greeted by the risen Christ in a dawn garden had acquired a substantial and shocking past as an adulterous whore. Jacobus de Voragine's *The Golden Legend*, a collection of legends of the saints composed around 1260, gives a well-spiced account of Mary's biblical and legendary life, which reveals that she was nobly born, much travelled and reputed to have been espoused to John the Evangelist, who was called away just before the wedding to follow Christ, thus causing an indignant Mary Magdalene to give herself up 'to every sort of voluptuousness', but de Voragine dismisses this tale, at least, as 'false and frivolous'.

The association of Mary Magdalene with the Bride passionately seeking the Bridegroom in the aromatic garden of the Song of Songs continued during the Middle Ages. The medievalist, David C. Fowler, draws attention to a number of these parallels, found in particular in the late-fifteenth-century Digby play of *Mary Magdalene* and in the beautiful lyric 'Maiden in the moor lay'. The Digby play, a spectacular example of medieval religious theatre, draws freely on the Bible and *The Golden Legend* to provide a dramatic account of Mary's history, and incorporates such vivid stage effects as the immolation of the Seven Deadly Sins, consigned to fire by Satan when they fail in their assault on Mary. The play shows Mary turning to a life of sensuality after the death of her father and squandering her inherited wealth on worldly pleasures, before her sudden conversion in the house of Simon the Pharisee. The scene of the conversion begins with Mary waiting in an arbour among precious 'balms', an enclosure of herbs and spices that recalls the fragrant garden of the Canticles. She is waiting for some of her lovers to arrive, but the beloved she finally pursues is the spiritual Bridegroom, Christ, who is dining at Simon's house. Mary's conversion is simply related: as she sleeps in her perfumed bower, the Good Angel wakes her and exhorts her to forsake her life of pleasure: 'Full bitterly this bliss it will be bought'. Mary goes into the house to anoint Christ's feet with 'sweet balms' in an act of submissive penitence. Much later in the play, after many adventures, comes the scene in the garden where Mary meets the risen Christ. She addresses him in language that recalls the spicy odours of the Shulamite:

> Ah, gracious Master and Lord, it is you that I seek!
> Let me anoint you with this sweet balm:
> Lord, long have you hid thee from my spice,
> But now I will kiss you, for my heart's relief [,]

and she tells him that she had mistaken him for Simon the gardener. Christ's reply also recalls the spiritual garden of the Canticles, the holy place where Christ is united with his Beloved, the individual soul, but he extends the Bridegroom's role to embrace the physical tending and nurturing required to make a garden flourish:

> Man's heart is my garden here;
> Therein I sow seeds of virtue all the year;
> The foul weeds and vices, I tear up by the root.
> When that garden is watered with pure tears,
> Then spring virtues, and smell full sweet.

In contrast to the developed narrative and broad-ranging scenes of the Digby play, the mysterious lyric, 'Maiden in the moor lay', miraculously preserved in note form on a battered scrap of manuscript now in the Bodleian Library, is tantalizingly elliptical:

Maiden in the moor lay,
    In the moor lay,
Seven night full,
    Seven night full,
Maiden in the moor lay,
    In the moor lay,
Seven night full and a day.

Well was her meat.
    What was her meat?
The primerole and the –
    The primerole and the –
Well was her meat.
    What was her meat?
The primerole and the violet.

Well was her drink.
    What was her drink?
The cold water of the –
    The cold water of the –
Well was her drink.
    What was her drink?
The cold water of the well-spring.

Well was her bower.
    What was her bower?
The red rose and the –
    The red rose and the –
Well was her bower.
    What was her bower?
The red rose and the lily-flower.

Recent scholarship suggests that this lyric is based on Mary Magdalene's legendary life, and in particular her successful period as a
desert ascetic, described in *The Golden Legend*:

At this time blessed Mary Magdalene, wishing to devote herself
to heavenly contemplation, retired to an empty wilderness, and
lived unknown for thirty years in a place made ready by the

hands of angels. There were no streams of water there, nor
the comfort of grass and trees: thus it was made clear that our
Redeemer had determined to fill her not with earthly viands
but only with the good things of heaven. Every day at the seven
canonical hours she was carried aloft by angels and with her
bodily ears heard the glorious chants of the celestial hosts. So it
was that day by day she was gratified with these supernal delights
and, being conveyed back to her own place by the same angels,
needed no material nourishment.

As David Fowler points out, Mary's desert 'has blossomed as the rose
(Isa. 35:1) and has become a place of beauty resembling the garden
of the Song of Solomon', and he recalls Jesus' image of the garden
of penitence in the Digby play, the garden where, if it is 'watered
with pure tears', virtues will spring up and 'smell full sweet'. The
desert garden is enriched by the symbolism of the flowers that are
Mary's food or her sleeping chamber, flowers that link her with the
Virgin Mary: 'the primrose for her zeal as an apostoless, the violet
for her humility as a confessor, the rose for her constancy as a
martyr, and the lily for her purity as a virgin'. 'Can a former
prostitute ever again be said to be a virgin?' asks Fowler. But the
question is not really in doubt. 'The poet's answer is affirmative.
The final miracle, attributable to the Magdalene's heroic asceticism,
is that she is refined and made pure in the sight of God.'

The appealing image of Mary Magdalene as the Shulamite was
still current in the nineteenth century. In the 1850s, Dante Gabriel
Rossetti chose her conversion as the subject of a highly wrought
drawing, *Mary Magdalene at the Door of Simon the Pharisee*, completed
in 1858 and now in the Fitzwilliam Museum in Cambridge. The
picture shows a voluptuous Mary Magdalene leaving a carnival
group of pleasure-seekers and running up the steps of Simon's
house, impetuously tearing a cluster of roses from her hair, while
her lover clings on to her foot and another young woman attempts
to bar her way. Through a side window of the house, Jesus' head
appears in profile, crudely rayed with light, his expression sad,
contemplative, a little stern, an image of stillness and austerity that
contrasts painfully with the revelry in the street. To accompany the
drawing, Rossetti wrote a poem in which, as in the similar scene in

the Digby play, he exploits the parallel between Mary's resolute attempt to reach Christ and the Bride eagerly searching for the Bridegroom in the Song of Songs. The poem begins with the earthly lover's pleas to Mary to turn back:

> 'Why wilt thou cast the roses from thine hair?
>   Nay, be thou all a rose, – wreath, lips, and cheek.
>   Nay, not this house, – that banquet-house we seek;
> See how they kiss and enter; come thou there.'

But the Magdalene replies:

> 'Oh loose me! Seest thou not my Bridegroom's face
>   That draws me to Him? For His feet my kiss,
>   My hair, my tears He craves to-day . . .
>   He needs me, calls me, loves me: let me go!'

By the mid-nineteenth century the *hortus conclusus*, the enclosed garden evoked by Tennyson in 'Come into the garden, Maud', had become the nexus of a host of conflicting ideas about female sexuality. On the one hand there was the Virgin Mary, the Second Eve, who somehow managed to accommodate intact virginity with perfect motherhood; on the other there were the two penitent women, the fallen Eve thrown out of Eden for sexual misbehaviour, and the penitent whore Mary Magdalene, also known as the New Eve and identified, like the Virgin Mary, with the spiritual Bride of Christ in the Song of Songs. Tennyson could not have chosen a more fruitful image to communicate frustrated sexual desire. The rose garden, with its perfumes and colours and gushing waters, *is* Maud's body, but it is possessed only in her lover's imagination: 'A garden inclosed is my sister, my spouse; a spring shut up, a fountain sealed.' The lily and rose, Mary's flowers, symbols of purity and God's love, breathe a contradictory message of passionate invitation through their musky odours, the falling rills can only lead him to one conclusion. But this is not the visionary garden of the Shulamite, where the lover feeds among the lilies, and Maud's heritage from 'the snow-limbed Eve from whom she came' has ominously been suggested earlier in the poem. What greets her lover at the garden gate is not love about to be triumphantly possessed, but the disillusionment and death of Paradise lost:

> O dawn of Eden bright over earth and sky,
> The fires of Hell brake out of thy rising sun,
> The fires of Hell and of Hate . . .

No sooner has Maud appeared, than her brother, 'That jewelled mass of millinery,/That oiled and curled Assyrian Bull/Smelling of musk and of insolence', arrives with the man who is her formally approved lover. There are angry words, an exchange of blows, one man lies dying and the other flees to a life-in-death exile of madness, grief and regret.

Tennyson's use of Marian vocabulary followed a long poetic tradition in which spirituality was evoked in the heady language of sensual passion, but an additional stimulus was perhaps the revival of interest in religious symbolism during the mid-nineteenth century (*Maud* was published in 1855), when artists and art historians were eagerly rediscovering the great works of the Italian Renaissance. In 1852, the art historian Anna Brownell Jameson published *Legends of the Madonna*, an exhaustive account of representations of the Virgin in the fine arts, which she prefaced with a list of the emblems popularly associated with Mary, including the lily, the rose and the enclosed garden. The Pre-Raphaelite Dante Gabriel Rossetti's first major oil painting was *The Girlhood of Mary Virgin* (1849), an idealized scene of the Virgin at home with her parents Anna and Joachim which draws heavily on traditional symbolism, as his brother William's description makes clear:

> The Virgin, aged about seventeen, is shown working at
> an embroidery under the eye of her mother St Anna. The
> embroidery represents a lily, the emblem of purity, which she
> copies from a plant watered by a child-angel. The father St
> Joachim is behind, trailing up a vine. The Holy Ghost, in the
> form of a dove, is also present . . . The vase containing the lily
> is mounted upon six large volumes lettered with the names of
> virtues, Charity being the uppermost. There are numerous
> other details, each with a symbolic or spiritual meaning . . .

In Rossetti's *Ecce Ancilla Domini* ('Behold the handmaid of the Lord'), exhibited in 1850, Mary's lily-embroidered stole now hangs like an admonitory sampler or ecclesiastical band beside her bed, on which the young girl sits, clad only in her nightdress and half-cowering against the wall, her eyes fixed on the stem of the lily that Gabriel is pointing at her as if about to penetrate her womb, a disturbingly graphic illustration of the virgin conception. In a political climate where Catholics had only recently been enfranchised and were still regarded with suspicion, Anna Jameson had vigorously defended her interest in Romanist iconography: 'I hope it will be clearly understood that I have taken throughout the aesthetic and not the religious view of those productions of Art which in as far as they are informed with a true and earnest feeling, and steeped in that beauty which emanates from genius inspired by faith, may cease to be Religion, but cannot cease to be Poetry; and as poetry only have I considered them.' But for many nineteenth-century artists and writers, the 'aesthetic' use of religious symbolism was a socially acceptable way of balancing the urgencies of male sexuality with contemporary morality, which required women to be chaste guardians of the sexual status quo. The troubadour recognition of the titillating potential of denied desire was fully exploited by the Victorians and is a leitmotif of the art and literature of the period.

But the *hortus conclusus* had further implications for female behaviour. In his essay, 'Of Queens' Gardens', John Ruskin invited the virtuous women of England to step out from the safe enclosure of their own homes and gardens into the wild garden of needy humanity, where 'feeble florets are lying, with all their fresh leaves torn, and their stems broken', waiting to be set 'in order in their little fragrant beds' and fenced 'in their trembling, from the fierce wind'. For Ruskin, the flowers in Maud's garden who cry out so passionately for the beloved represent the voices of suffering humanity, waiting to blossom under a woman's tender care, and the one who waits alone at the gate is Christ himself in the fertile garden of compassion:

Who is it, think you, who stands at the gate of this sweeter garden alone, waiting for you? Did you ever hear, not of a

Maud, but a Madeleine, who went down to her garden in the
dawn, and found One waiting at the gate, whom she supposed to
be the gardener? Have you not sought Him often; – sought Him
in vain, all through the night; – sought Him in vain at the gate of
that old garden where the fiery sword is set? He is never there;
but at the gate of *this* garden He is waiting always – waiting to
take your hand – ready to go down to see the fruits of the valley,
to see whether the vine has flourished, and the pomegranate
budded. There you shall see with Him the little tendrils of
the vines that His hand is guiding – there you shall see the
pomegranate springing where His hand cast the sanguine seed; –
more: you shall see the troops of the angel keepers that, with
their wings, wave away the hungry birds from the pathsides
where He has sown, and call to each other between the
vineyard rows, 'Take us the foxes, the little foxes, that spoil the
vines, for our vines have tender grapes.' Oh – you queens – you
queens! among the hills and happy greenwood of this land of
yours, shall the foxes have holes, and the birds of the air have
nests; and in your cities, shall the stones cry out against you, that
they are the only pillows where the Son of Man can lay His
head?

There are innumerable Victorian paintings of women in gardens,
pinned like chloroformed butterflies against the green baize of grass
and orderly border, constrained by stays and cumbrous skirts and
veiled bonnets while they snip unconvincingly at roses, or perform
some other decorous but inutile task. The sentimental ideal of
nurturing femininity that Ruskin so eloquently advocates in 'Of
Queens' Gardens' expressed itself, in the pictorial garden at least, as a
straitjacket that denied women the freedom to tend their gardens as
they wished, when they wished, dressed as they wished. And behind
this powerful image of a woman in a garden, invoked by Ruskin, by
Tennyson, by Dante Gabriel Rossetti, lay the long tradition of the
hortus conclusus, the enclosed garden of Mary, of Mary Magdalene, of
Eve. But change was in the air. In the early 1900s, the American
horticulturalist, Helena Rutherfurd Ely, offered a refreshingly sympathetic view of Eve's behaviour in the Garden of Eden:

It has always seemed to me that the punishment of the first gardener and his wife was the bitterest of all. To have lived always in a garden 'where grew every tree pleasant to the sight and good for food,' to have known no other place, and then to have been driven forth into the great world without hope of returning! Oh! Eve, had you not desired wisdom, your happy children might still be tilling the soil of that blessed Eden. The first woman longed for knowledge, as do her daughters of to-day. When the serpent said that eating of the forbidden fruit would make them 'as gods,' what wonder that Eve forgot the threatening command to leave untouched the Tree of Life, and, burning to be 'wise,' ate of the fateful apple and gave it to her Adam? And then, to leave the lovely place at the loveliest of all times in a garden, the cool of the day! Faint sunset hues tinting the sky, the night breeze gently stirring the trees, Lilies and Roses giving their sweetest perfume, brilliant Venus mounting her accustomed path, while the sleepy twitter of the birds alone breaks the silence. Then the voice of wrath, the Cherubim, the turning flaming sword!

To have knowledge *and* the garden: it is quite clear where Helena Ely's priorities lay. Perhaps the challenge for women has always been how to rewrite mythology to suit this surely modest ambition.

The *felix culpa*: *The Marble Faun* and *Daniel Deronda*

NATHANIEL HAWTHORNE'S NOVEL, *The Marble Faun*, begins in the sculpture-gallery at the Capitol in Rome, a room whose windows look out over the mélange of modern buildings, Catholic monuments and classical ruins that suggest, in one rapid sweep of the eye, the layered history of the ancient city. What that hasty glance reveals is the confusion wrought by time on civilization and its artefacts, the melding and blending of styles and systems, the collapse of regimes and the jostling of faiths epitomized by the battered triumphal arch of the emperor Septimius Severus, the washer-women hanging out their linen on the stone walls of the obsolete

Forum, the Christian churches crammed literally on top of heathen temples and supported by the selfsame pillars and, outlined against the limpid azure sky of mid-summer Rome, the arches of the abandoned Colosseum, witness to the bloodstained struggle between the old faith and the new. And yet, 'Far off, the view is shut in by the Alban mountains, looking just the same, amid all this decay and change, as when Romulus gazed thitherward over his half-finished wall.'

It is with the same baffled awareness of simultaneous change and continuity that the modern archaeologist of the myth of Eve surveys the jumbled landscape of the Christian centuries. If those lichened stones, the shards of brick and crumbling mortar could speak, what stories would they tell to confound neat summary or cosy conclusion? But Hawthorne reminds his readers that there are themes whose defining features have persisted, however partially, through the obscuring rubble. In the salon of the sculpture-gallery, along with the Dying Gladiator and the yellowed marble of Lycian Apollo, there is 'the pretty figure of a child' clutching a dove while being attacked by a snake, 'a symbol (as apt, at this moment, as it was two thousand years ago) of the Human Soul, with its choice of Innocence or Evil close at hand'. Those two potent symbols, the dove and the snake, did not begin with Christianity, but the interpretation that Hawthorne gives to the classical image derives from the Christian juxtaposition of the evil Tempter in the Garden of Eden with the innocent dove, avatar of the Holy Ghost who miraculously impregnated the young Mary at the Annunciation and who is depicted as the Virgin's companion in countless paintings, testimony to the purity and tenderness that became her essential attributes.

The Marble Faun was written comparatively late in Eve's imaginative history and throws into relief beliefs about women and sin that had been bubbling in the doctrinal cauldron of Christianity for centuries, and which derived in turn from earlier Jewish traditions. Basic to this cultural inheritance is the contrast between two women, whose familiar lineaments, encountered again and again in Western folklore, literature and mythology, recompose those of the two pivotal women of the Christian tradition, the Virgin Mary and the temptress Eve. Hawthorne uses the contrast between his Eve and Mary, passionate Miriam and ice-maiden Hilda, to test the concept of the *felix culpa*, the 'happy fault' praised by the early Church Father, Ambrose, which saw the Fall as the necessary evil that paved the way for the redemptive Virgin Mother and her Son. The idea was to become a persistent part of the Virgin's myth, another reason for worship and celebration; in the words of a beautiful fifteenth-century poem:

> Ne had the apple taken been,
>   The apple taken been,
> Ne hadde never our Lady
>   A been heaven's queen.
> Blessed be the time
>   That apple taken was;
> Therefore we may singen
>   'Deo gratias.'

The concept of the *felix culpa* recalls the conundrum posed by Job, the 'only problem' so brilliantly explored in Muriel Spark's novel of that name: what is the point of misfortune and evil? In Job's case, troubles came unsolicited, while Adam and Eve brought disaster by their own disobedience, but, in a perfect world, what was the purpose of the forbidden fruit? The *felix culpa* offered one solution to the difficulties, but as Hawthorne's inconclusive exploration suggests, the idea created as many moral dilemmas as it solved.

Published in 1860, *The Marble Faun* was the last of Hawthorne's great Romances and his final work of fiction, inspired by a period of liberating European travel. The polarized heroines of the novel are Hilda, a young artist arrived in Rome from New England, and the vivid Miriam. The two women are defined as opposing moral types through their differing looks and heritages, and the disparity in their views of themselves as artists. Miriam's name and rich colouring imply Jewish ancestry: she has 'a complexion in which there was no roseate bloom, yet neither was it pale; dark eyes . . . black, abundant hair, with none of the vulgar glossiness of other women's sable locks; if she were really of Jewish blood, then this was Jewish hair, and a dark glory such as crowns no Christian maiden's head'. Hilda, on the other hand, is a 'fair young girl, dressed in white', a ' "daughter of the Puritans" ', pretty and girlish

with her 'light brown ringlets . . . her sensitive, intelligent, yet most
feminine and kindly face'. While Miriam's dark beauty links her
with explosive passions and dangerous female sexuality, Hilda's
purity and moral probity are emblematically established by her
residence in a tower that soars above the jumbled topography of
Rome, a remote and hallowed eyrie where Hilda acts as guardian
to a Catholic shrine dedicated to the Virgin. In return for her
elevated lodging, Hilda tends the lamp in front of the Virgin's
image, keeping it perpetually burning, and she feeds the many
doves, the Virgin's birds, that wheel round her windows at the
summit of the tower and swoop down like heavenly messengers to
greet her few visitors. She defends her apparently anomalous role by
saying that even a daughter of the Puritans may pay homage to
'"the idea of Divine Womanhood"', and the lofty Hilda typifies
the Virgin's aloofness from human fallibility. As Miriam says to her,
'"in your maiden elevation, you dwell above our vanities and
passions, our moral dust and mud, with the doves and the angels for
your nearest neighbors"'.

Even Hilda's art aligns her with the tradition of selfless female
devotion, the Virgin's humble obedience: 'Behold the handmaid of
the Lord' (Luke 1:38). Although Hilda might have won distinction
in her own right in her native North America, once in Rome she
recognizes her inability to equal the great male artists, and becomes
a copyist, dedicating her unique qualities of sympathy and intuition,
and her technical expertise, not simply to reproducing a work, but
even to fulfilling the artist's incompletely realized intention: 'In such
cases, the girl was but a finer instrument, a more exquisitely effective
piece of mechanism, by the help of which the spirit of some great
departed Painter now first achieved his ideal, centuries after his own
earthly hand, that other tool, had turned to dust.' In her selflessness
and dedication, Hilda epitomizes the self-suppression and deference
to male achievement that were the Virgin's essential attributes and
were held up as ideals for Victorian womanhood, finding their most
notable literary expression in Dorothea Brooke's obeisance to the
dubious scholar Edward Casaubon in *Middlemarch*. Unlike Dorothea,
however, who managed finally to escape the dead hand of her
husband's moribund scholarship, Hilda 'chose the better, and loftier,
and more unselfish part, laying her individual hopes, her fame, her

prospects of enduring remembrance, at the feet of those great departed ones'; she was 'the handmaid of those old magicians, instead of a minor enchantress within a circle of her own'. Those loaded words, 'handmaid' and 'enchantress', had by this period accrued such layers of resonance that Hawthorne's audience would have been in no doubt how they were intended to respond not only to the good 'handmaid' Hilda, but also to the dark 'enchantress' Miriam, whose art, far from perfecting the design of some 'Old Master', so shockingly expresses her own unsubmissive character.

Long before twentieth-century feminists rediscovered the muscular art of the Italian Renaissance painter Artemisia Gentileschi, Hawthorne describes Miriam's vigorous sketches of biblical heroines in terms that suggest he might have come across the Italian artist's work and been struck by her dramatic portrayals of female power and resolution. As in Gentileschi's paintings of *Judith Slaying Holofernes*, Miriam's Judith is caught in the very act of cutting off the general's head, while her Jael wields the hammer to drive the nail through Sisera's brains, and her Salome triumphantly claims the head of John the Baptist in the charger. Hawthorne does not hesitate to spell out the implications of Miriam's troubled drawings and to hint at the dark outcome of his own fable:

> Over and over again, there was the idea of woman, acting
> the part of a revengeful mischief towards man. It was, indeed,
> very singular to see how the artist's imagination seemed to run
> on these stories of bloodshed, in which woman's hand was
> crimsoned by the stain; and how, too – in one form or another,
> grotesque, or sternly sad – she failed not to bring out the moral,
> that woman must strike through her own heart to reach a
> human life, whatever were the motive that impelled her.

Miriam's passionate, personal art is in strong contrast to the saintly Hilda's sensitive renderings of the male artistic status quo, and her shadowy background enhances the enigma of her character and behaviour, and exposes her to sensationalism. Some rumours suggest that she is heiress to a rich Jewish banker and has fled to Rome to set up her studio in order to escape a hated betrothal; others claim that she is a German princess, or the art-loving wife of an English nobleman, who has romantically cast aside wealth and rank in order to pursue her vocation. There is even the caustic hint of 'one burning drop of African blood in her veins'. The truth of Miriam's origins is never fully revealed, but there are suggestions that the dark secret in her past may mirror the tragic story of Beatrice Cenci, a beautiful girl executed for the murder of her incestuous father. The cumulative effect of the innuendo that is slow-released during the course of the novel is to link Miriam with the tradition of dangerous Jewish female temptresses that ran parallel with the cult of the Virgin – a genealogy that began with Eve and included the murderous heroines Judith and Jael, as well as the renowned penitent, Mary Magdalene.

The novel is set among the expatriate artist community in Rome, where Hilda and Miriam have become friendly with Kenyon, a young American sculptor. Miriam has also attracted to their company an Italian nobleman, Donatello, who bears a striking resemblance to the classical sculptor Praxiteles' statue of a faun, and seems to reflect its mythological character as a pagan creature halfway between man and animal with a child's capacity for spontaneous, innocent joy. Donatello is devoted to Miriam, who treats him with half-contemptuous affection. Following a pleasure trip to the catacombs, a sinister monk known only as the Model or the Shadow attaches himself to Miriam as a grim reminder of some unspecified horror in her past. This reptilian stalker is identified with the devil, his influence over Miriam, like that of certain beasts of 'subtle and evil nature', linking him with Satan in his guise as tempting serpent, and both Hilda and Kenyon recognize his facial resemblance to a sketch by the Renaissance artist Guido Reni of the malevolent dragon of Revelation being conquered by the archangel Michael. Goaded by the Shadow's persistent dogging of Miriam, Donatello inadvertently murders him in an attack that is the instinctual response of goodness to evil, as unfettered by moral considerations as Billy Budd's annihilating blow to Claggart's forehead, but the effect of his action is to alienate him from the natural world. Like Adam or the presexual Enkidu in *The Epic of Gilgamesh*, the innocent Donatello had been able to talk to the birds and animals on his family estate at Monte Beni, sharing with them a special language that marked his half-primitive state, but his impulsive killing of the Shadow separates him for ever from that carefree interplay. The wild creatures' rejection of his overtures confirms his fall from grace and he eventually returns to Rome to give himself up to the authorities. The novel ends with Donatello in prison, Miriam free, but feeling herself morally bound to him for life by her tacit encouragement of the murder, while Hilda and Kenyon renounce the foetid air of Rome for the purer breezes of their native America.

In the course of Donatello's metamorphosis from carefree innocence to bitter experience – *Transformation* was the title used for the novel's first publication in England – his friends observe that he seems almost literally to grow a soul, as if the murder were the crucial stimulus that released him from his half-animal state into full humanity. In Kenyon's unfinished bust of his friend, chipped out of white marble some time after the murder, Hilda perceives '"the impression of a growing intellectual power and moral sense . . . a soul is being breathed into him"', and Hawthorne confirms that a percipient observer may identify in this imperfect work, 'the riddle of the Soul's growth, taking its first impulse amid remorse and pain, and struggling through the incrustations of the senses'. It is Miriam who underlines this upbeat reading of Donatello's violence when she asks Kenyon, '"Was the crime – in which he and I were wedded – was it a blessing in that strange disguise? Was it a means of education, bringing a simple and imperfect nature to a point of feeling and intelligence, which it could have reached under no other discipline?"' The cautious Kenyon declines to follow Miriam into these '"unfathomable abysses"', but she persists:

'The story of the Fall of Man! Is it not repeated in our Romance of Monte Beni? And may we follow the analogy yet farther? Was that very sin – into which Adam precipitated himself and all his race – was it the destined means by which, over a long pathway of toil and sorrow, we are to attain a higher, brighter, and profounder happiness, than our lost birthright gave? Will not this idea account for the permitted existence of sin, as no other theory can?'

Kenyon falteringly tries to pursue this idea with Hilda:

'Sin has educated Donatello, and elevated him. Is Sin, then –
which we deem such a dreadful blackness in the Universe – is it,
like Sorrow, merely an element of human education, through
which we struggle to a higher and purer state than we could
otherwise have attained? Did Adam fall, that we might ultimately
rise to a far loftier Paradise than his?'

but the Puritan girl rejects his suggestion with horror: '"Do not
you perceive what a mockery your creed makes, not only of all
religious sentiment, but of moral law, and how it annuls and
obliterates whatever precepts of Heaven are written deepest within
us?"'

Hawthorne's complex and ambiguous novel ends with a questionmark as he appears to renege on his own moral vision by allowing
Hilda, the symbol of spiritual purity, to have the final condemnatory
word on the faun's *felix culpa*. George Eliot's *Daniel Deronda*,
published sixteen years after *The Marble Faun*, also explores the
equivocal relationship between sin and redemption through the
experiences of two contrasting heroines, but, rather than Adam
fallen, the novel tells the story of the Temptation of Eve and the
bitter taste of the fruit of knowledge. Eliot's Gwendolen Harleth
and the Jewish singer Mirah, her sinning Eve and immaculate
Virgin, reverse Hawthorne's visual symbolism, with dark-haired
Mirah all goodness and purity, while the blonde Gwendolen is
marked out as flawed from her first appearance, recklessly playing
the gaming tables in Leubronn. But Mirah, for all the pathos of her
history and Eliot's loving descriptions of her tender, womanly
nature, is as lifeless as the sterile Hilda. It is Gwendolen, with her
narcissism and indolence, who is the focus of interest, and she is
one of George Eliot's most psychologically persuasive creations, her
complex nature painstakingly and sympathetically revealed through
the twists and turns of her difficult history. Gwendolen's connection
with Eve is established in the first pages of the novel when she
appears at an evening party temptingly dressed in sea-green and
silver, the *ensemble du serpent*, as one of the male guests appreciatively
observes: '"Woman was tempted by a serpent: why not man?"', an
identification of Eve with her Tempter that had long been familiar
in art and legend; and it is partly Gwendolen's reliance on her

powers as temptress that persuade her to marry Grandcourt despite her intuitive shrinking from him. She sees him as a compliant husband whom she will be able to manage by her feminine charm and beauty. But it is Gwendolen herself who is tempted, by Grandcourt's wealth and social position, to commit a crime against another woman which has terrible repercussions. By marrying Grandcourt she deprives his long-term mistress Lydia Glasher of the opportunity for public redress, and Lydia's children by Grandcourt remain bastards. At the same time, her knowledge of Lydia's prior claims undermines her authority within the marriage. Instead of controlling an adoring husband, Gwendolen finds herself compelled to accede to his domination, which encroaches on every aspect of her life.

Ennervated by her moral lapse in marrying Grandcourt, Gwendolen becomes increasingly inert and mute, and when she does finally rebel, it is by a small but decisive lack of gesture, a momentary suspension of action. During a sailing holiday, they are alone together in a small boat off Genoa harbour when Grandcourt falls in the water and, as the current tugs him away, calls to Gwendolen to throw him a rope. But '"I held my hand, and my heart said, 'Die!'"' Although she then immediately leaps into the water in a vain attempt to save him, Grandcourt is drowned and Gwendolen has to confront the possibility of her responsibility, in will if not in deed, for her husband's death. It is Daniel Deronda, the young man who has become her unwilling mentor, who suggests a route out of her terrible grief and self-blame in the hope of leading a better life and, as the book closes with Deronda's marriage to Mirah, he receives a valedictory letter from Gwendolen reassuring him that she has remembered his words: '"that I may live to be one of the best of women, who make others glad that they were born."' As with Donatello, Gwendolen's sin, her self-serving marriage with its train of appalling consequences, is to be the means of her redemption; in her case, the *felix culpa* that encourages her to turn from an arid life of self-absorption to the full consciousness that may allow her to ease existence for others. This is no facile victory of good over evil, however; nobody is more aware than Gwendolen how difficult such a life will be, and she acknowledges, '"I do not yet see how that can be"', but there has already been a significant

change – a transformation, in Hawthorne's term – in her view of
the world. Eliot's conclusion, although in some senses as equivocal
as Hawthorne's, leaves the reader in no doubt as to where her
sympathies lie.

IN THE MANY fantasies that exploit the polarities between Eve and
Mary, it is generally the Mary character, the virtuous virgin, who
ends up 'getting her man' and living happily ever after: Hilda and
Mirah both marry with every prospect of leading happy, useful
lives, while Miriam and Gwendolen are left partnerless to brood
over past sins and new resolutions towards good. But once the bride
crosses the threshold of her new home, she almost inevitably metamorphoses into Eve in her role as marital partner, the 'help meet'
for man that God thoughtfully provided for Adam in the Garden of
Eden. Eve's duties as wife are briefly outlined in the Book of
Genesis, but it required the poetic vision of John Milton to give
imaginative life to the promising concept of 'one flesh' – and the
innovative intelligence of Elizabeth Barrett Browning to hypothe-
size an alternative to his masculinist enterprise.

CHAPTER 9

AN HELP MEET FOR ADAM

And the LORD God said, It is not good that the man should be alone; I will make him an help meet for him.

Genesis 2:18

———◆◆◆———

A NEWLY MARRIED COUPLE are honeymooning in a secluded fishing village in the Camargue. Catherine is an heiress, David a writer whose second novel has just been declared a critical success. The hours pass in a sunlit haze of sensual pleasure, but one afternoon Catherine comes back with a new boyish haircut, and in bed that night she undergoes a psychological transformation into the sexually assertive Peter, who claims David as his female lover: ' "You're my wonderful Catherine. You're my beautiful lovely Catherine . . . I'm going to make love to you forever." ' Hemingway's *The Garden of Eden*, published posthumously in 1986, provides a twentieth-century reworking of the Genesis story, in which gender roles and ideas of good and evil are once again questioned. The struggle over who wears the trousers in David and Catherine's sexual relationship reflects a profounder battle over who controls the domestic narrative, again quite literally represented by David's subject matter and words as a writer. In reaching his perhaps predictable conclusions about the appropriate marital partnership for his hero, Hemingway draws heavily on the myth of Eden, with its patriarchal hierarchy, Adam's ambivalent relationship with his father/creator, and the dichotomous female inheritance as destructive 'temptress' and passive 'helpmate'.

At the beginning of the novel, the power relations between the two lovers seem ideally balanced: both are young, healthy, extraordinarily good-looking; Catherine is independently wealthy, and David's writing is beginning to be lucrative. They are madly in love. They share an appetite for sex, food, sunbathing and drink. But conflicts quickly emerge, not simply because of Catherine's cross-dressing and unexpected metamorphosis into Peter, which Hemingway presents as a periodic compulsion, like a man who becomes a werewolf with the changing phases of the moon, but because of her jealousy over David's success as a writer, which eventually is channelled into her wish to control what he writes, to persuade him to work on the day-by-day narrative of their marriage rather than the short stories exploring his boyhood relationship with his father that are beginning to preoccupy David. Matters slowly reach a crisis with Catherine's introduction of Marita, a young woman picked up in a café, into their troubled duo. Pretty, willing, self-effacingly anxious to please, Marita, whose name 'Little Mary' recalls the obedient Virgin Mother of Christianity as well as hinting at the marital qualities that will become so useful later in the novel, at first seems cast as Catherine's partner in sexual experimentation, a useful minder while David is busy at his writer's craft, but as Catherine's behaviour grows increasingly manipulative and paranoid, Marita and David become united first in trying to keep her happy, then in controlling her wilder outbursts, and finally, with relief, in letting her go.

On one level, a sexist tale of what a (male) writer needs to keep him content and productive – Marita is not only beautiful, unselfish and terrific in bed, but she admires and is eager to discuss David's writing and encourages him to work, the ideal helpmate in fact – Hemingway's novel reflects ideas about women that have been available since the Eden myth was first canvassed. Catherine is the prototypical sexual temptress, characteristically preoccupied with her personal appearance and its effect on other people, aiming for maximum shock with her white-bleached cropped hair against sun-blackened skin, and the tailored men's flannels and fishermen's shirts that she increasingly chooses to wear. Hemingway makes it clear that Catherine's cross-dressing and transsexuality identify her as deviant, in contrast with Marita who remains adorably feminine despite her sapphic dalliance with Catherine, which seems to be a marker of amenability rather than of any strong sexual preference. Like Delilah with Samson, Catherine seeks to tempt David away from his serious purposes and weakens him by dangerous sexual play. The reader is warned early in the novel how to 'read' Catherine and David when, in response to David's playful, ' "I'm

the inventive type"', Catherine responds, '"I'm the destructive type
. . . And I'm going to destroy you . . . I'm going to wake up in the
night and do something to you that you've never even heard of or
imagined."' David's pet name for her in her boyish mode is 'Devil',
and in her efforts to reverse conventional sex roles, Catherine
closely resembles the devilish Lilith, who was fantasized by the Jews
of the talmudic period as the first wife of Adam, the woman created
at the same time as the man in Genesis 1. Even in that golden
springtime of human life, there were problems over mastery, Adam
preferring the missionary position for sex, but Lilith objecting to
lying beneath him, pointing out that she was his equal since both of
them had been created from dust. When Adam threatened to
overpower Lilith by force, she uttered the magic name of God and
flew away to the Red Sea, already notorious for shady sexual
practices, where she lived with a horde of lascivious demons and
became renowned for her promiscuity.

But Catherine is also Eve in her wish to challenge the influence
of David's father and to take control of the masculine powerbase of
language. In Genesis 2, God allows Adam to name the animals, a
gift of enormous significance as it gives Adam the right to label
things according to his own perception of the world. Even the
woman created from his rib is named by Adam, first as Woman and
then as Eve, mother of all living. Eve's bid for knowledge, her wish
to become godlike, is a bid for a stake in language, the power to
name the world according to her own image of it. When David
uses his command of language to write an account of their life
together, Catherine grudgingly permits him time to work and even
makes plans to publish the typescript, but when he neglects their
domestic narrative in order to record his early adventures with his
father, stories of hunting and barbarism which exclude women and
predate his experience of her, Catherine is restless and unhappy,
accusing David of neglecting his real life in order to pursue his
fantasies: '"Jumping back and forth trying to write stories when all
you had to do was keep on with the narrative that meant so much
to all of us. It was going so well too and we were just coming to
the most exciting parts. Someone has to show you that the stories
are just your way of escaping your duty."' David's power to step
outside the marital narrative to explore ideas of his own, his claim

to a life independent of their partnership, infuriates Catherine and finally she destroys the stories. By the end of the novel, Catherine has been written off as mad, and David and Marita have set up their own cosy domestic scene in which Marita acts as willing helpmate to David, a loving partner who encourages and enables his work, her own life subordinated to his masculine creativity. In Hemingway's neat fable, David's acquiescence in Catherine's disruptive games, recalling the androgyny or bisexuality which some commentators attributed to God's first human creation in Genesis 1, is barely explored, while the dangerous Catherine, like Bertha Mason, Rochester's West Indian wife in *Jane Eyre*, is denounced as sexually abnormal, culpably narcissistic, a threat to the masculine status quo that can justifiably be labelled insane and therefore repudiated. At the same time, the male right to control the realm of storytelling is confirmed and Marita cheerfully embraces Eve's given role as supportive helpmate. What seems to be at stake is the female right to be sexually adventurous, to make Odyssean voyages; for David Bourne, the docile, unchallenging Marita is a far more comfortable and therefore acceptable marital partner.

Hemingway's *The Garden of Eden* can be read as the fantasies of an ageing writer about male potency, sexual deviance (safely initiated by an 'unstable' or mad, but beautiful woman) and the appropriate conditions for matrimonial harmony, an ironic gloss on the volatile relationship of the first couple, poised from the start on the brink of a dangerous disharmony stimulated by Eve's megalomaniac tendencies, from which they are rescued by God's quick-thinking curse. By reworking the Eden story, Hemingway slots into a long tradition of writers who drew on the familiar events in the Garden of Eden to discuss marriage in narratives that, while assuming traditional, canonical ideas about male/female relationships, knocked against the boundaries of the conventional stereotypes to propose variant interpretations of Adam's partnership with his 'meet help'. The most substantial of these reworkings was John Milton's epic poem, *Paradise Lost*.

'A nail driven into the wall'

IN WRITING HIS POEM, first published in 1667, Milton was able to draw on a substantial and still virile tradition of commentary on Genesis 1–3 and the related New Testament writings on marriage. Theologians and moralists in seventeenth-century Europe continued to scrutinize the story of Adam and Eve for evidence of God's intentions for human sexual and domestic relations, research that had been given new impetus by the Protestant Reform movement. According to Catholic teaching, marriage was an inferior choice to celibacy, although its importance as a prophylactic against lust and an appropriate framework for bringing up children was acknowledged, the Church neatly resolving the twinned problems of desire and its consequences by preaching that the justification for marriage was childbearing, God's gracious remedy for original sin. When Martin Luther nailed his ninety-five theses on the church door at Wittenberg in 1517, a welcome breeze gusted through Christendom whisking the dust off centuries of conservative Catholic teaching and exposing it to the harsh light of the Reformers' critical gaze. Anxious to prove that marriage, rather than a prop for human fallibility, was in fact positively recommended by God, and keen to stress the spirituality of the marriage bond, the Protestant Reformers found justification for their new ideal of marital reciprocity in God's words in Genesis 2:18: 'It is not good that the man should be alone; I will make him an help meet for him.' In his commentary on Genesis, John Calvin interpreted the phrase 'meet for him' as meaning that Eve was 'a kind of counterpart' to Adam, 'for Moses intended to note some equality. And hence is refuted the error of some, who think that the woman was formed only for the sake of propagation'. In Calvin's view, Eve was 'given to' Adam to be 'the inseparable associate of his life', for marriage 'extends to all parts and usages of life', a reading that appeared to grant women a greater degree of reciprocity and influence in the marital relationship.

The doctrinal reforms initiated by Luther and Calvin, who both wrote commentaries on Genesis, offered an opportunity for new approaches to gender roles in marriage, but in the end, their revised readings of the Eden story simply confirmed woman's subordinate status. She might have been created equal to man and even in God's image, although there continued to be debate about this, but in the Reformers' view, Eve sinned and corrupted Adam through her independence, for which she was punished not only by the pain of repeated childbearing, but also by being placed under her husband's domination. In Calvin's crisp summary, 'Thus the woman, who had perversely exceeded her proper bounds, is forced back to her own position. She had, indeed, previously been subject to her husband, but that was a liberal and gentle subjection; now, however, she is cast into servitude.' This sentence was similarly imposed on Eve's daughters, and any attempt by women to rebel against the status quo by asserting personal authority constituted rebellion against God's commandment. In Luther's striking terminology, the woman 'is like a nail driven into the wall'. While the husband 'rules the home and the state, wages wars, defends his possessions, tills the soil, builds, plants, etc.', the wife 'should stay at home and look after the affairs of the household, as one who has been deprived of the ability of administering those affairs that are outside and concern the state. She does not go beyond her most personal duties . . .'. The effect of Luther's arguments was to plunge women back into the generative function that was their marital *raison d'être* in Catholicism. While women were not allowed to 'perform the functions of men: teach, rule, etc.', they were conceded mastery in 'procreation and in feeding and nurturing their offspring'. 'In this way Eve is punished; but . . . it is a gladsome punishment if you consider the hope of eternal life and the honour of motherhood which have been left her.'

Luther's interpretation of Genesis perpetuated traditional views of maternity and child-rearing as instinctive drives that the female of the species, closer to 'nature' than the intellectually evolved male, was well-qualified to fulfil, while men got on with the serious business of developing their minds and running society. The limitations of this point of view were eloquently spelled out, centuries later, by Olive Schreiner in her novel, *The Story of an African Farm*, first published in 1883, where her feminist heroine, Lyndall, talks bitterly about the powerful influence a mother exerts over the development of her tiny child, and weighs the immense social expectations of motherhood against women's lack of training for the role, a late-nineteenth-century protest that testifies to the persistence of ancient ideas about woman's limited role and potential, and the frustration and unhappiness of countless women denied education, autonomy and power:

> 'They say women have one great and noble work left them, and they do it ill. – That is true; they do it execrably. It is the work that demands the broadest culture, and they have not even the narrowest . . . the woman who does woman's work needs a many-sided, multiform culture; the heights and depths of human life must not be beyond the reach of her vision; she must have knowledge of men and things in many states, a wide catholicity of sympathy, the strength that springs from knowledge, and the magnanimity which springs from strength. *We* bear the world, and *we* make it . . . The first six years of our life make us; all that is added later is veneer; and yet some say, if a woman can cook a dinner or dress herself well she has culture enough.'

Luther's prejudices extended beyond his enthusiasm for female domestic confinement; he warned that women were as unwilling to bear restraint from their husbands as they were to suffer the pangs of childbirth, and 'they naturally seek to gain what they have lost through sin. If they are unable to do more, they at least indicate their impatience through grumbling', lazily imprecise accusations that relied on the traditional male consensus that women were prone to mischief and complaint. His apparently casual comments attest to the fear and suspicion of women's unpredictable behaviour commonly voiced by men, and the attempts to denigrate and suppress female speech which were frequently justified by reference to Eve's unfortunate conversation with the serpent. A French nobleman, the Knight of la Tour-Landry, had pointed out the dangers of Eve's indiscriminate speech in a guide to good behaviour that he wrote in the 1370s for his three daughters: 'And know ye that the sin of our first mother Eve came by evil and shrewd acquaintance by cause she held parlement [i.e. conversation] with the serpent which as the History saith had a face right fair like the face of a woman. And spake right meekly . . .'. Humble words are no guarantee of innocence, and the Knight goes on to point out how Eve first put herself at risk by even listening to the serpent's dangerous words, then by gossiping inaccurately about the forbidden fruit, giving bad advice to Adam about eating the fruit and finally, foolishly, trying to justify her bad behaviour to God. The moral is clear; as the Knight tells his daughters, 'if one require you of folly or of any thing that toucheth your honour and worship you may well cover and hide it saying that you thereof shall speak thereof to your lord'. In any situation outside her immediate domestic responsibilities, a woman should have recourse to her husband's wisdom and authority. The idea of male superiority was deeply ingrained in Western Christendom, and a wife's duty to obey her husband was regarded as God-given. The fact that he might be a dolt or otherwise ill-qualified to win her respect was irrelevant; God had set the terms of the marriage contract in Genesis 3:16 when He told Eve, 'thy desire shall be to thy husband, and he shall rule over thee', and a man who, like Hemingway's David Bourne, let his wife 'wear the trousers' was regarded as failing in his responsibilities to God.

The Reformers' arguments reinforced such traditional ideas about appropriate female behaviour and condemned further generations of Protestant women to a life restricted to family duties. Eve's imaginative leap towards independence had yet again been turned on its head and used as an argument to keep her in chains. What is interesting about these panicky attempts to confine women within the safe boundaries of the family home is the power that is attributed to them. It seems that, left to her own devices, Eve is capable of anything, certainly of wrapping Adam round her little finger, and even of disrupting God's serious purposes for humankind. As with the polemic of the early Church Fathers, the Reformists' anxieties suggest that woman is a volcano always on the point of erupting, a bubbling pot whose contents must be carefully contained under a heavily weighted lid. Most of all they imply male susceptibility to womanpower, both at the domestic level of mother or wife, and in the troublesome realm of the imagination, where woman was projected as wicked seductress, adroitly able to shape-shift to accommodate the multiple projections of masculine terror and desire.

'Part of my soul'

MILTON'S *PARADISE LOST* recreates the early history of Adam and Eve and explores the idea of the companionate marriage hinted at by the Reformers and eloquently argued in his own pamphlets calling for a liberalization of the divorce laws. In tackling Christianity's founding myth, Milton consciously assumed the mantle of Moses, the first great Jewish storyteller who was believed to have set down the account of the Creation in Genesis, and thereby placed himself within the long tradition of male theologians and exegetes who had determined the moral codes by which Christian men and women were expected to live, a formidable ancestry whose debates and conclusions underpin the plots and characterization of Milton's poem. Yet for all his lofty purposes, Milton could not help telling a good story, and narrative pace and inventiveness, a pleasing mix of villains and heroes, the compelling portrayal of loss and suffering, not to mention the sheer grandeur and beauty of the poetry, make *Paradise Lost* immensely readable and emotionally persuasive. His account of Adam and Eve's brief sojourn in Paradise traces the history of a love affair, with its manipulations and compromises, its secret agendas and sudden surges of powerful emotion.

Milton's Adam and Eve are a couple in the first stages of partnership still finding their way about their environment, their work and their relationship to one another. Created fully grown, they are in the unique position of having no history. Everything is new to them, and there are no other human beings on whom to model their behaviour. This can lead to misunderstandings; when Eve is first created, she falls in love with her reflection in a pool, preferring her own image to the 'less fair,/Less winning soft, less amiably mild' appearance of Adam, but Adam's eager claiming of her as 'Part of my soul' quickly persuades her to appreciate the superiority of 'manly grace' and 'wisdom' to her feminine beauty. Eve was made for Adam out of his rib, and his love for his wife stems from his sense of her as part of himself, literally bone of his bone and flesh of his flesh, that '*second self, a very self it self*' that Milton construed as God's intention in creating a 'help meet' for

Adam. This symbiotic awareness of Eve makes Adam protective of her, while at the same time he is susceptible to the qualities that make her different from himself, her female beauty and charm. Eve's love for Adam is more volatile, filtered through a self-love which does not identify itself with him. Away from him, she is capable of action of which she knows he will disapprove and which may even harm him. Her own wants come first. Adam is faithful to Eve to the point of apostasy (he puts her before God); Eve is faithful to herself (she consciously puts Adam at risk). It is only through eating the forbidden fruit and experiencing its consequences that Adam and Eve reach a more balanced partnership and can finally set off hand in hand from Paradise to populate the wilderness outside its boundaries.

The taming of damaging excess in both Adam and Eve takes place in a series of set scenes and conversations in Paradise that punctuate the political action of the poem, the drama-packed narrative of Satan's unsuccessful rebellion against the Almighty with one third of the heavenly host, and of his determination to take revenge for his defeat by corrupting God's favoured new creation, Adam and Eve. On their first appearance, spied on by Satan during his reconnoitre of Paradise, Milton defines the power structure between Adam and Eve along apparently conventional lines. What the envious fallen angel sees are two noble and majestic creatures, reflecting their Maker's image in their truth, wisdom and sanctitude, but unequal in other ways. Adam is formed for 'contemplation' and 'valour', Eve for 'softness' and 'sweet attractive grace', but Adam's intellectual leadership and Eve's winning deference are quickly exposed as superficial and even dangerous. Eve's mortified sense of Adam's superiority will be one of the factors that persuades her to eat the forbidden fruit, so that she can equal him in wisdom, while Adam's susceptibility to Eve's 'attractive grace' will similarly over-come his objections to the fruit, even though he rejects Eve's belief in its magic powers. Already, as Satan listens to their conversation, there are hints of these future disruptions. Adam's first speech dwells on God's taboo on eating fruit from the tree of knowledge, an 'easy prohibition' that nevertheless seems to be at the forefront of his mind. Eve has her own preoccupations, charmingly reminding Adam that her lot is the happier, since he is so much the superior partner, but then going on to tell the story of her creation and self-infatuation, a disquieting hint of her potential for narcissism and rebellion. Later when they retire to their bower, Eve is compared to the lovely Pandora, who 'ensnared/Mankind with her fair looks', Jove's revenge for Prometheus' theft of forbidden fire and, as they sleep together after happy enjoyment of 'connubial love', Milton warns them, 'O yet happiest if ye seek/No happier state, and know to know no more'. Soon after, the guardian angels Ithuriel and Zephon find Satan 'Squat like a toad' at Eve's ear, attempting to taint her fancy with subversive dreams.

Eve's status in the human and heavenly hierarchy is defined early in the poem as secondary to Adam's: 'He for God only, she for God in him', a straightforward rendering of Paul's statement that 'the head of every man is Christ; and the head of the woman is the man; and the head of Christ is God' (1 Cor. 11:3). But the fragility of Adam's superiority is exposed when he confesses to the arch-angel Raphael that his feelings for Eve overwhelm his rational understanding of their relative positions. Even though he knows that she is his inferior in mind and 'inward faculties', less closely resembles the image of God and has less authority over other creatures,

> yet when I approach
> Her loveliness, so absolute she seems
> And in her self complete, so well to know
> Her own, that what she wills to do or say,
> Seems wisest, virtuousest, discreetest, best . . .

Adam is enraptured by Eve's beauty, but also by her completeness, that self-involvement which had earlier allowed her to hang lovingly over her own image in a pool of water, and which will later encourage her to make a bid for deification. Although she responds to his claiming of her as his 'other half', he is fascinated by her self-containment. Raphael's frowning response is to warn Adam against the lure of outward attractions. He must build up his self-esteem and guard against the ennervating effects of passion; but Adam persists that it is not Eve's beauty that disarms him so much as her civilities, the daily acts that confirm her affection and compliance, that mark 'Union of mind, or in us both one soul'. In the end, it is this sense of union with Eve, a bonding that exceeds sexual love, that persuades him to throw in his lot with her and eat the forbidden fruit.

Eve's deference to Adam is revealed as mere lip-service. When we first meet her, she is all compliance, naming Adam as her 'author and disposer' and claiming:

> what thou bid'st
> Unargued I obey; so God ordains,
> God is thy law, thou mine: to know no more
> Is woman's happiest knowledge and her praise.

But only a few days later, she disobeys Adam's wishes, insisting on going off to garden on her own, despite his reluctance and sensible arguments about sticking together in case Satan tries to approach them. The plot requires that Eve should be alone so that she can be tempted by Satan, but Milton provides a persuasive psychological motivation for her initiative. What has intervened in the meantime is the flattering dream that Satan had poured into her ear, promising her deity if she dares to partake of the forbidden fruit. In the dream, she does taste and is immediately whisked up into the clouds, a goddess who sees the earth 'outstretched immense' beneath her in a tempting vision of supremacy which echoes Christ's temptation in the wilderness, when the devil takes him to the top of a high mountain and offers him the kingdoms of the world stretched out before him. Adam had soothed Eve's waking distress about the dream, but it appears to have continued its work in her subconscious mind, acting as a counterbalance to her duty to Adam and God, suggesting alluring possibilities of autonomy and power, and softening her up for the encounter with Satan in the guise of the serpent. Eve justifies her determination to garden alone on the grounds of efficiency – they will get more done if not distracted by smiles and conversation, but her persistence suggests that more is at stake, a dangerous if still innocent bid for independence, while her self-appointed task, to prop up the drooping heads of roses with bands of myrtle, hints at the perils she is voluntarily seeking. The rose blooms suggest human frailty and the transience of human happiness, while the myrtle was associated with a goddess's defence of her virtue. Eve's fragile happiness depends on her marital fidelity, but, as Milton points out, she busies herself with the flowers unaware that she herself is the 'fairest unsupported flower,/From her best prop so far, and storm so nigh'. The 'storm' breaks in the seductive form of the serpent, who arrives in splendid guise, his crested head balanced aloft on a massy column of circular folds, his eyes the glowing red of carbuncle and his neck 'burnished . . . of verdant gold'.

Eve's dialogue with the serpent and her tasting of the forbidden fruit confirm the psychological profile that Milton has painstakingly built up. That self-containment Adam so admires in her is revealed as a repository of secret ambitions and desires that are independent of her subordinate relationship to her husband or to God. When Satan promised her deity in her troubling dream, it was what she felt she deserved, and this is the card he successfully plays when, in the guise of the serpent, he comes across her so conveniently alone amidst the tumbled roses. 'Empress,' he calls her, and says she should be a 'goddess among gods, adored and served/By angels numberless'. He claims that his capacity to speak came from eating the fruit of the forbidden tree and, with it, enviable intellectual powers. If he, a humble serpent, could be so enhanced, what may Eve expect? Not death as God had threatened, but no less than deity:

> in the day
> Ye eat thereof, your eyes that seem so clear,
> Yet are but dim, shall perfectly be then
> Opened and cleared, and ye shall be as gods,
> Knowing both good and evil as they know.

Tempted, Eve gorges herself on the fruit, 'nor was godhead from her thought'.

As Milton describes it, Eve shares the fruit with Adam out of selfishness, while Adam eats out of an excess of affection for his wife, a subtext of female treachery and male vulnerability that Christ, God's surrogate, will deal with by imposing the judgement of submission on Eve: 'to thy husband's will/Thine shall submit, he over thee shall rule'. Eve's thoughts, once the initial excitement of eating the fruit is over, reveal her insecurity about being Adam's inferior, the difficulty of being the underdog in the patriarchal hierarchy. First of all, she persuades herself that perhaps God, 'Our great forbidder' as she rather sneeringly calls Him, may not have noticed, preoccupied and remote with all His spies in heaven, but how is she to present herself to Adam? Should she share the fruit with him, or keep its intellectual benefits to herself, making herself more equal to Adam and even at times superior, something which she regards as 'not undesirable . . . for inferior who is free?' But her next thought is that if God *has* seen and she dies as a result, then Adam may simply marry and live happily with another Eve, an idea that determines her to share the fruit – and its consequences – with Adam.

Faced with an excited Eve babbling about a talking serpent, claiming, disingenuously, that she had sought godhead for her husband's sake and urging him to share it quickly as she may not be able to renounce it if he does not eat, Adam is not deceived. He takes in the situation at a glance and, after a few moments of shocked silence, declares simply that since he cannot bear to live without her, 'Certain my resolution is to die'. Adam's fault is to renounce God in favour of Eve, a decision that is determined by his symbiotic bond with his wife:

> no no, I feel
> The link of nature draw me: flesh of flesh,
> Bone of my bone thou art, and from thy state
> Mine never shall be parted, bliss or woe.

This is not the end of *Paradise Lost*. The effect of the fruit is to engender lust in Adam and Eve, an opening of their eyes to mutual sexual exploitation which leads to shame and bitter recrimination, and finally to penitence. Together Adam and Eve sue God for forgiveness, Christ comes to declare judgement on them and the serpent, and Michael shows Adam a healing vision of the future history of humanity, culminating with the coming of the Redeemer, born from the seed of Eve. Replenished by hope and with renewed conjugal amity, Adam and Eve reluctantly leave Paradise, turning on the plain below to look back once more at the eastern gate now

thronged with the 'dreadful faces' and 'fiery arms' of the angels
who guard their former home, the flaming sword of God blazing
above:

> Some natural tears they dropped, but wiped them soon;
> The world was all before them, where to choose
> Their place of rest, and providence their guide:
> They hand in hand with wandering steps and slow,
> Through Eden took their solitary way.

AT THE HEART of Milton's poem is the question, 'What does a man
need in order to be happy?' When he is created, Adam argues that
what he lacks is a companion, to provide 'fellowship' and 'rational
delight' and to multiply his image through childbearing, but after
Eve has been formed from his rib, he becomes enthralled by her to
the point of self-betrayal. Milton uses the Genesis story of Adam
and Eve to give new vigour to the idea that women are unreliable
and mendacious, dangerously independent and self-involved, while
it is their superiority to women that makes men vulnerable. Adam
is disarmed by his unsuspecting delight in Eve's affection and
conjugal compliance, and his compassion for her weakness, and
desire both to protect and indulge her, persuade him to act against
his judgement. God had said in Genesis 2:18 that it was not good
for man to be alone and, in his pamphlet *The Doctrine and Discipline
of Divorce* (1643), Milton interprets God's creation of the 'help meet'
for Adam as an endorsement of the emotional benefits of marriage,
that 'meet and happy conversation' between man and wife that
Milton saw as the 'chiefest and the noblest end of mariage'. But in
Milton's support for marriage as the 'prevention of lonelinesse to
the mind and spirit of man', the emphasis lay on the word 'man' as
referring to the male gender, and in *Paradise Lost* he fell back on
traditional ideas of how the marital partnership should operate. To
maintain the proper balance between the sexes, Eve must be fully
submissive to her husband and her potential for troublemaking
diverted into childbearing, while Adam must unambiguously assert
his authority and love his wife within reasonable bounds.

'Jehovah's daughter'

In *PARADISE LOST*, Milton shows an Eve eager for experience and autonomy, but her initiatives are fettered by a plot that condemns her to rebuff and suppression. Milton takes great care to explain Eve's character and motives, but his reading of Eve was conditioned by his own beliefs and didactic project, and his definition of the 'help meet' for Adam was determined by his privileging of male needs. Mary Wollstonecraft identified some of the defects of Milton's account of Eve in her feminist manifesto, *Vindication of the Rights of Woman*, first published in 1792, pointing out that faulty education kept women in a position of humiliating subservience. Men blame women for their follies and weakness, but at the same time deny them the information and training that would enable them to develop intellectual and emotional maturity. They are kept in a state of ignorance 'under the specious name of innocence', and such life skills as they do receive are corrupting:

> Women are told from their infancy, and taught by the example
> of their mothers, that a little knowledge of human weakness,
> justly termed cunning, softness of temper, *outward* obedience,
> and a scrupulous attention to a puerile kind of propriety, will
> obtain for them the protection of man; and should they be
> beautiful, everything else is needless, for at least twenty years
> of their lives.

This, she points out, is how Milton describes 'our first frail mother', and she continues bitingly,

> when he tells us that women are formed for softness and sweet
> attractive grace, I cannot comprehend his meaning, unless, in
> the true Mahometan strain, he meant to deprive us of souls,
> and insinuate that we were beings only designed by sweet
> attractive grace, and blind docile obedience, to gratify the
> senses of man when he can no longer soar on the wing of
> contemplation.

Guided by his senses, Milton is inconsistent in what he requires of women. Before Eve is created, Adam complains bitterly of his loneliness, with only the animals as his companions:

> Among unequals what society
> Can sort, what harmony or true delight?
> Which must be mutual, in proportion due
> Given and received; but in disparity
> The one intense, the other still remiss
> Cannot well suit with either, but soon prove
> Tedious alike: of fellowship I speak
> Such as I seek, fit to participate
> All rational delight . . .

But when Eve is created to fulfil Adam's need for 'fellowship', far from being his equal in 'rational delight', she defers to him as her 'author and disposer', whose will she claims to obey in everything. To rectify this damaging inequality between men and women, Wollstonecraft proposes a programme for educating women 'in order to co-operate . . . with the Supreme Being'.

In her novel *Shirley* (1849), Charlotte Brontë took up the question of female education, balancing the wretchedness of the dependent woman against her vision of an Eve who, as 'Jehovah's daughter', talked 'face to face' with God, and exploring contrasting ideas of the 'help meet' for Adam. The novel tells the story of two young women, the vivid heiress Shirley Keeldar and gentle, penniless Caroline Helstone. Shirley is mistress of property and land; although an orphan, she can rely on her erstwhile governess Mrs Pryor for companionship, and by her quick wits and self-reliance, but principally the authority of her wealth, commands respect from the local male community of landowners, industrialists and churchmen. Her buoyant self-confidence and optimism are nourished by her financial freedom. Caroline, with little to recommend her except delicate prettiness, intelligence and the social position granted her on account of her uncle, the formidable curate Mr Helstone, is by contrast powerless and lonely, a caged bird beating tender wings against the iron bars of boredom and inutility. Both women are in love: Shirley with the proud, poor tutor Louis

Moore; Caroline with his brother Robert, a hard-nosed manufac-
turer who risks assassination to introduce mechanization into his
factory and callously abandons Caroline in order to pursue the
wealthy Shirley.

The novel falls into two main sections in which the harsh reality
of spinsterhood is contrasted with female financial independence.
The story begins with Caroline Helstone's love for her cousin
Robert Moore and pained recognition that he does not intend to
marry her. As she understands this, she is forced to ask herself, at
the age of eighteen, how to occupy the rest of her life: '"What am
I to do to fill the interval of time which spreads between me and
the grave?"' Like so many young girls in the neighbourhood, the
Misses Sykes, the Armitages, the Birtwhistles, she has '"no earthly
employment, but household work and sewing; no earthly pleasure,
but an unprofitable visiting; and no hope, in all [her] life to come,
of anything better"'. The brothers of these young women find
useful work in business or the professions, but the girls are neglected.
Her uncle's contribution to her education is to encourage her to
'"stick to the needle – learn shirt-making and gown-making, and
pie-crust-making, and you'll be a clever woman some day"', but
although she has no prospects except the annuity which he intends
some time to purchase for her (he is already fifty-five), he discour-
ages her from the 'folly' of marriage, declaring in his assertive way:
'"It is decidedly the wisest plan to remain single, especially for
women."' Thrown back on herself, Caroline takes stock of the
meagre options available to her, visiting the old maids Miss Mann
and Miss Ainley to see how they occupy their lives, but what she
finds is tragic and daunting. She thinks of finding work as a
governess, but Mrs Pryor paints a gloomy picture of hardship and
misery, and prophesies that the strain will lead to early decline.
Indeed, in her heroic attempts to pursue a strict programme of
charitable work, exercise and study, Caroline grows thin and wasted,
and eventually succumbs to a dangerous fever from which she is
rescued by the romantic discovery that Mrs Pryor is the mother for
whom she has pined. Caroline's fate is determined by her heroine
status, the plot dictates her rescue and the resolution of her difficulties; but the other spinsters in the neighbourhood are not heroines
and many will presumably end up eking out sparse and lonely

existences like Miss Mann or Miss Ainley. The only single women
in the novel who find true contentment and a measure of autonomy
are Margaret Hall, who keeps house for her brother, the saintly
Vicar of Nunnely, and Hortense Moore, who similarly looks after
Robert and is allowed free exercise of her individuality and considerable self-esteem in managing his domestic affairs. Both women
rely on their brothers' incomes and good will for their comfort and
financial security. Caroline's plea to the '"men of England"' to
provide opportunities for education and satisfying work for their
daughters and sisters is endorsed by the impoverished lives of many
of the women described in the novel, and, like Mary Wollstonecraft,
she particularly condemns a social system which requires women to
'"scheme"', to '"plot"', to '"flirt"' and manoeuvre in order to win
a husband.

By contrast with Caroline and probably every other woman in
the novel, Shirley Keeldar is wealthy in her own right and, no
longer a minor, has the freedom to administer her own affairs,
although as a beautiful heiress she is also prey to the unmarried men
in the neighbourhood, and as a woman still has to negotiate her
way between the potholes and swamps of male prejudice and
misogyny. Unlike Caroline's practical measuring of the realities of
woman's lot, Shirley's image of female possibilities is expressed in
her rhapsodic interpretation of Eve as the heaven-born mother of
Titans. In a deliberate rejection of the churchmen and their ecclesiastical rituals that dominate the community's social routines, Shirley
chooses one evening to linger in the churchyard instead of attending
the service, to admire the beauty of the quiet graves framed by the
sunset-hued hills of the still rural landscape. Here she sees Nature
'"at her evening prayers: she is kneeling before those red hills . . .
she is like what Eve was when she and Adam stood alone on
earth"'. This is not Milton's domestic Eve, the busy housewife
puzzled about what fruits to offer the visiting Raphael; Shirley's Eve
is a magnificent pagan goddess, the mother of the ancient classical
deities, Saturn and Oceanus and the sun-god Hyperion, and of the
daring transgressor Prometheus. In Shirley's imaginative re-creation,
the beginnings of human history saw the struggle of giants '"to scale
heaven"', and it was Eve, herself '"heaven-born"', who yielded the
daring to '"contend with Omnipotence"':

'the strength which could bear a thousand years of bondage, –
the vitality which could feed that vulture death through
uncounted ages, – the unexhausted life and uncorrupted
excellence, sisters to immortality, which, after millenniums of
crimes, struggles, and woes, could conceive and bring forth a
Messiah . . . vast was the heart whence gushed the well-spring
of the blood of nations; and grand the undegenerate head where
rested the consort-crown of creation.'

Caroline's level-headed response, '"She coveted an apple, and
was cheated by a snake"', suggests a scepticism about mythological
hyperbole that would have done credit to Lucy Snowe, but Shirley
will not be deflected from her vision. She goes on to describe the
'"woman-Titan"' whom she sees kneeling at prayer on the evening
hills, the Eve/Nature whose massive form and draperies embody
the universe:

'her robe of blue air spreads to the outskirts of the heath, where
yonder flock is grazing; a veil white as an avalanche sweeps from
her head to her feet, and arabesques of lightning flame on its
borders. Under her breast I see her zone, purple like that
horizon: through its blush shines the star of evening. Her steady
eyes I cannot picture; they are clear – they are deep as lakes –
they are lifted and full of worship – they tremble with the
softness of love and the lustre of prayer. Her forehead has the
expanse of a cloud, and is paler than the early moon, risen long
before dark gathers: she reclines her bosom on the ridge of
Stilbro' Moor; her mighty hands are joined beneath it. So
kneeling, face to face she speaks with God. That Eve is Jehovah's
daughter, as Adam was his son.'

Caroline dismisses Shirley's Eve as '"vague and visionary"' and
begs her to enter the church for the service that has already begun,
an invitation to join the masculine world of established religion, but
Shirley prefers to linger with her ancestress. But even outside the
church, Shirley's nourishing vision of an Eve who speaks '"face to
face"' with God is undermined. Joe Scott, the foreman at Hollow's
Mill and an unregenerate misogynist, leaves the congregation to

take a breath of air in the churchyard, and seizes the opportunity to put both Caroline and the lofty heiress, his master's employer, in their places with a series of derogatory remarks about women's intellectual abilities, quoting the pseudo-Paul on Adam's rights to authority and leadership, for '"Adam was not deceived; but the woman, being deceived, was in the transgression"'.

Shirley's spirited opposition to Joe's stale arguments, her impassioned sense of Eve's status and power, and her bold, playful interaction with the male members of her community, suggest potentialities for women that lie at the opposite pole to Caroline's bitter assessment of female futility and helplessness, and hint that Adam is finally to be matched with a 'meet help' who offers new possibilities of equality and freedom, an Eve for women to admire and emulate. But Charlotte Brontë's vision did not extend so far. The formative relationship of her adult life, her pupilship in Brussels to the charismatic Constantin Heger, determines the romantic partnerships of her heroines. Jane Eyre, Lucy Snowe, Shirley Keeldar all fall in love with men whom they admire as 'masters', men whose strong, sometimes ruthless personalities and desire for authority are acceptable because of their intuitive understanding and clever management of their lovers. The dominant theme of these relationships is a strong woman's deference to a superior male, who combines the emotional fervour of a lover with the firm and kindly guidance of an omnipotent father.

Shirley makes clear her practical position on sexual equality in an early conversation with Caroline in which she praises '"good"' men as '"the lords of the creation"', '"the sons of God"':

'Moulded in their Maker's image, the minutest spark of His spirit lifts them almost above mortality. Indisputably, a great, good, handsome man is the first of created things.'

'"Above us?"' murmurs Caroline and, in a series of bodily images that recall Adam's welcoming of Eve as 'flesh of my flesh', Shirley says that she would scorn to contend for empire with a man: '"Shall my left hand dispute for precedence with my right? – shall my heart quarrel with my pulse? – shall my veins be jealous of the blood which fills them?"' Caroline persists, '"But are we men's equals, or are we not?"' and Shirley, astonishingly (although perhaps, also, with a touch of her characteristic delight in subverting expectation), breaks faith with her ideology, and unhesitatingly responds, '"Nothing ever charms me more than when I meet my superior – one who makes me sincerely feel that he is my superior ... the higher above me, so much the better: it degrades to stoop – it is glorious to look up."' The difficulty is to find anyone she can so esteem, but here Shirley is being disingenuous. She has already met her 'god', the tutor Louis Moore, once literally her master when, shades of M. Heger, he taught her French, and now the 'lord of creation' to whom her spirit, with some anguish, defers.

Louis' claim to superiority over Shirley appears to lie in his reticence and air of calm authority, which he maintains despite his socially equivocal role as tutor to a rich man's son. However passionate his feelings, which are cautiously revealed to the reader through short extracts from his journal, his external aspect is cool, unruffled and detached, a carapace of self-sufficiency that Shirley is too proud to attempt to penetrate without encouragement. Their courtship is a game in which neither partner is willing to show their hand, a stately dance in which Shirley reluctantly curtseys to Louis' ambiguous lead. His power over her is worryingly symbolized by his skill in winning the devotion of her brutish dog Tartar. In a battle of wills, he draws the usually 'sullen' and 'ruffianly' beast away from Shirley's feet to his own and, as the tamed and besotted Tartar approaches Louis, 'with head lovingly depressed, to receive the expected caress', a 'significant smile' ripples across the tutor's face.

Louis identifies himself as '"Adam's son; the heir of him to whom dominion was given over 'every living thing that moveth upon the earth'"', but both he and his author seem to forget that in Genesis 1 the first man and woman were granted joint dominion. For all her unorthodoxy, in writing about Shirley's relationship to her lover, Charlotte Brontë reneged on the vivacious, independent Shirley of the early section of the novel, and fell back on her personal fantasy of the omnipotent 'master'. Alone with Caroline in the churchyard – '"Cary, we are alone: we may speak what we think"' – the adult Shirley had shared an ecstatic vision of the heaven-born Eve, talking face to face with God on the evening hills, an inspiring image of female deity. But what Louis Moore recalls to her attention is the yearning Eva of 'La Première Femme Savante', 'The First Blue-Stocking', Shirley's girlhood essay written for Louis and a particular favourite with him, read so often that he can still recite it word for word. Shirley's *devoir* was based on the curious passage in Genesis 6 so popular with the early Jewish storytellers, in which the sons of God came down to earth to take wives from among the daughters of men. The seductive fantasy that the beautiful young heiress had offered her tutor was the story of the lonely orphan, Eva, born among an ancient primitive tribe, but neglected by her people, and growing up alone with wild beasts and birds for company and the green wilderness as her nourishing mother. Nature blesses her with beauty, candour and intelligence, but she feels her isolation and craves to know the purpose for which she has been created. One evening, she climbs on to a crag to watch the night descend and, as she kneels before heaven and the world spread out before her, feels her 'spark of soul . . . burning unmarked to waste in the heart of a black hollow'. Passionately she asks whether she exists only to perish, unused and unnoticed; could this be her fate, 'when the flame of her intelligence burned so vivid; when her life beat so true, and real, and potent; when something within her stirred disquieted, and restlessly asserted a God-given strength for which it insisted she should find exercise?' This cry at first finds no response that she can interpret, but as she persists in her agony, she feels 'Something' above relent, and finally a voice sounds from the ether, naming her ' "Eva!" ' It is the voice of the seraph Genius, a son of God who has come to embrace his bride Humanity, ' "to rescue, to sustain, to cherish, mine own" '. It is Genius who supports Eva in the battle against the corrupting serpent and who, with his God-given patience and strength, fights the good fight for humanity through aeons of time:

> and, when Time's course closed, and Death was encountered at
> the end, barring with fleshless arm the portals of Eternity . . .
> Genius still held close his dying bride, sustained her through the
> agony of the passage, bore her triumphant into his own home –
> Heaven; restored her, redeemed, to Jehovah – her Maker; and at
> last, before Angel and Archangel, crowned her with the crown of
> Immortality.

Shirley's essay is a brilliant evocation of the pain and yearning of adolescence, the longing for that recognition by another which confirms existence and identity in an amorphous universe. It also reflects Caroline Helstone's agonized question, '"What was I created for, I wonder? Where is my place in the world?"' But it also establishes the pattern for Shirley's mature relationship with Louis, in which the moral and intellectual authority that had guided her impetuous girlhood is re-established as the controlling framework of her adult life. The way in which their marital relationship will function is made even clearer a little later in the same scene when Louis' pupil Henry Sympson reminds Shirley of a French piece that she used to be able to recite by heart, Jacques-Bénigne Bossuet's 'Le Cheval Dompté', 'The Tamed Horse'. Bossuet compares a horse that is uncontrolled with one that has been taught to recognize his master, and explains that in the case of the latter: 'His ardour has changed to force, or rather, since the force was in some way in that ardour, it is regulated. Notice: it is not destroyed, it is regulated.' Shirley's girlish ardour is to be regulated by the judicious curb of her master Louis.

It is not without cost. Charlotte Brontë was too protective of her own independence and integrity of speech not to feel Shirley's pain in relinquishing her public and private authority to her husband, but she does not question the necessity and seems to experience a masochistic pleasure in Shirley's capitulation, the sexual frisson of female subjection to a dominant male which is fundamental to the romance genre. The woman's resistance is essential to the thrill and Shirley does not give up without a fight. When she finally agrees to marry Louis, a union that many in her social circle would regard as beneath her, she asks him Caroline's question, '"And are we equal then, sir? Are we equal at last?"' But his response falls back, however humorously, on his tutorial role and places her in the position of obligation, '"You are younger, frailer, feebler, more ignorant than I"', and Shirley modifies her claim, modestly asking him to '"Be my companion through life; be my guide where I am ignorant: be my master where I am faulty; be my friend always!"' Under pressure to make plans for her marriage, she feels an ominous depression and reluctance and, when she does finally name a date, her agreement is described in terms of bondage: 'there she was at last, fettered to a fixed day: there she lay, conquered by love, and bound with a vow'. Finally, she deliberately abdicates all power to Louis, who was 'virtually master of Fieldhead, weeks before he became so nominally', and by the closing pages of the novel, it is forecast (by Robert Moore) that, as master of Shirley's estates, Louis will take over her influence and authority in the district, becoming magistrate and general benefactor, while Robert himself will expand his mercantile empire, levelling the Hollow to build a new mill and houses for the workforce, and obliterating Shirley's visionary Nature/Eve with the practical realities of commerce.

A woman's need to marry is the central theme of *Shirley*, but although the novel concludes with the joint wedding of the two heroines, enough doubts are raised in the course of the narrative to make the reader uncertain whether this is truly a happy ending. The marriages already in progress are almost all unhappy. The Rector of Briarfield, Mr Helstone, is outspokenly dismissive of women, and his wife died young, the victim of neglect rather than deliberate ill-treatment. His brother was a villain from whom his young wife fled, abandoning her daughter Caroline because she feared that she would grow up to resemble her father in character. The landowner Mr Yorke still clings to romantic fantasies about his first love, the marmoreal and probably aptly named Mary Cave, who had rejected him only to be ignored by Mr Helstone, and Yorke eventually finds marital satisfaction with a prejudiced, moody and tyrannical wife. Despite all this negative evidence, Caroline's experience indicates that marriage is the only option for her, even as the reader trembles for her happiness with the expedient Robert Moore, while the spirited Shirley's willed surrender of power in favour of the prosy and self-conscious Louis raises questions about the subordinate role of the 'meet help' even as it seems to endorse its necessity.

Building the New Jerusalem

IN HER VERSE-NOVEL *Aurora Leigh* (1857), Elizabeth Barrett Browning confronted Caroline's question of '"What was I created for, I wonder? Where is my place in the world?"' By choosing a heroine who was sure from an early age that her destiny was to be a poet, Barrett Browning was able to open out the debate about the 'help meet' for Adam into a discussion of how a man and a woman could reconcile personal ambition and a strong sense of their individual life's work with a loving partnership. It was a scenario that moved Eve out of her role as wife and mother into the separate realm of Adam's sons who laboured for bread, and which then went on to ask the question, 'But what about love?'

When Barrett Browning first addressed the problem of Eve's destiny, she had focused on Eve's 'allotted grief' immediately after God's curse, the self-sacrifice that had become her portion along with the responsibility for causing 'creation's groan'. 'A Drama of Exile', a long poem published in 1844, imagines Adam and Eve during the terrible hours when they have just been driven out by the flaming sword into the barren wastes of the wilderness. In her Preface to the 1844 *Poems*, Barrett Browning bravely claimed that the subject 'rather fastened on me than was chosen', but it is an uncomfortable and lifeless work which lacks the vigour and self-confidence of her mature poetry. Although she chose to write sympathetically about Eve in exile as a theme 'more expressible by a woman than a man', on her own admission Barrett Browning was unable 'to shut close the gates of Eden' between Milton and herself, and the poem struggles towards grandeur and pathos, but only manages to achieve the embarrassingly fey, with 'groaning creation' represented by bands of tediously wailing spirits, an irritatingly self-abasing Eve as fall guy to loftily magnanimous Adam, and a Christ who, rather ludicrously, visibly metamorphoses from deity 'into humanity and suffering' in the course of half a page of dialogue. But there is a magical moment when Eve slips the noose of the authorized plot and we catch a glimmer of Barrett Browning's true poetic project. Recalling her past glories, Eve says proudly:

> For was I not,
> At that last sunset seen in Paradise,
> . . . was I not, that hour,
> The lady of the world, princess of life,
> Mistress of feast and favour? Could I touch
> A rose with my white hand, but it became

Redder at once? Could I walk leisurely
Along our swarded garden, but the grass
Tracked me with greenness?

What really interested Barrett Browning was not the Eve shuddering
under creation's groan, but Eve glorying in her power and authority,
the 'mistress of feast and favour', the position from which she chose
to eat the taboo fruit. In order to explore the implications of Eve
unfallen and her courageous leap into forbidden knowledge, Barrett
Browning had to abandon the Eden story altogether and invent a
new plot in which an exploratory Eve, the poet Aurora Leigh, sets
out to find her own route towards knowledge and, only then, to
marital concord. But Aurora's quest takes her into the very heart of
male territory, in search of God's creating Word, the mastery of
language which was appropriated to Adam in Genesis 2 and for ever
denied Eve after the Fall because of her misuse of speech in the
encounter with the serpent; the Word that was at the centre of the
power struggle between Catherine and David Bourne. When she
wrote about the biblical Eve, Barrett Browning was working under
the shadow of a great male poet and of the founding myth used by
the Church to keep women under control; in *Aurora Leigh* she was
able to shake off the constraints of ancient story and to write her
own feminist account of a young woman's struggle to find herself
and to take on the male establishment on its own terms. When she
does, finally, bring her heroine to the church door, it is after a
sustained and vigorous argument about work, love and the marital
partnership in which references to the story of Adam and Eve
abound.

Consisting of around 11,000 lines split into nine 'books' or
chapters, *Aurora Leigh* provided the capacious format in which
Barrett Browning could explore a lifetime's ideas about women's
rights and gender relations, and about writing poetry: she was fifty-
one when the poem was published, married to Robert Browning
and the mother of a small boy, and an established poet. The story is
sensationalist, involving several deaths, a forfeited inheritance, rape
and illegitimacy, poetry, passion and lurid scenes of both high and
low society, all described with huge energy and enthusiasm. In
brief, the plot runs as follows: Aurora Leigh is the daughter of a

beautiful Italian woman who dies when her child is four. Her devoted English father brings her up in Italy, teaches, encourages and loves her, but also dies when Aurora is still a young girl, so that she is sent to England to live with her repressive maiden aunt. Despite the punitive hours tamed into young-ladyship with needle and sampler, Aurora secretly educates herself by browsing through her father's stored-away library, and grows up a free spirit determined to be a poet, quarrelling with her cousin Romney Leigh when he asks her to relinquish poetry in order to marry him and join him in his work to help the impoverished masses. Even when her aunt dies and Aurora finds herself homeless and penniless, she still pursues her goal, working tirelessly in a garret in London, until she slowly begins to earn a reputation as a poet. In the meantime, the idealistic Romney, financed by the family estate and fortune, pursues his interest in social reform, in the course of which he rescues a young girl, Marian Erle, from poverty and degradation and finds work for her as a sempstress. Eventually he decides to marry her as a public statement of his commitment to the breaking-down of class barriers, but Marian disappears on the wedding day, leaving a letter to say that she cannot marry him. Some time later, in Paris, Aurora catches a glimpse of Marian with a small boy, and discovers that she had been persuaded out of the marriage by Lady Waldemar, a wealthy aristocrat who wanted Romney for herself, and Marian had then been betrayed into rape by the servant employed to help her make a new life. Abandoned in France, Marian had given birth to her illegitimate child and was again earning her living as a sempstress. Aurora and Marian set up house together with the child in Florence, where they are visited by Romney. It emerges that he is not married to Lady Waldemar, as Aurora had believed, has heard about Marian's plight and is anxious to make amends by marrying her, but Marian refuses. Aurora also discovers that Romney has been blinded in the torching of his home by the ungrateful poor whom he had housed there. Finally, after some negotiation, true love prevails and it is agreed that Aurora and Romney will marry.

Romney's three potential marriages – to Aurora, Marian and Lady Waldemar – span the action of the book and provide an opportunity for an extensive enquiry into the appropriate emotional, social and ideological conditions for marriage, not just the 'help

meet' for Adam, but the suitable partner for Eve. The question is
first raised when Romney proposes to Aurora on her twentieth
birthday. She is still living at her aunt's country house, and has risen
early to revel in the beautiful June day and crown herself in the
garden with a poet's ivy wreath. Embarrassed to be caught in this
act by the censorious Romney, she is further disconcerted to learn
that he has found her poetry notebook. He has not bothered to
read it, feeling sure that she writes as well, and ill, as other young
women, which in his opinion is badly. What he wants to offer her,
he says, is something far more serious and worthwhile than what he
insultingly calls the '"sleek fringes"' of verse that adorn the sun-
shades of the rich. Aurora may be as young as '"Eve with nature's
daybreak on her face"', but she must face the realities of a world
where the '"sweat of labour in the early curse"' has become '"the
sweat of torture"'. There is no time for poetry when all creation
groans, and Romney accuses Aurora, and all women, of being
unable to comprehend the general woe in their narrow fixation on
the personal. A woman's sympathy is won to the hard-luck tale of a
child she sees waiting in the cold, but

> 'does one of you
> Stand still from dancing, stop from stringing pearls,
> And pine and die because of the great sum
> Of universal anguish?'

Women do not understand the world and therefore cannot influence it:

> 'Women as you are,
> Mere women, personal and passionate,
> You give us doating mothers, and perfect wives,
> Sublime Madonnas, and enduring saints!'

but '"We get no Christ from you"', and he brutally concludes his
argument, '"We shall not get a poet, in my mind"'.

Romney's arguments set up the great oppositions that Barrett
Browning tries to resolve in the course of the poem. In the face of
poverty and suffering, what use is poetry compared with practical

action; what value sympathetic female myopia, compared with male vision; or the nurturing of the beggar who happens to arrive on one's doorstep compared with large-scale programmes for alleviating society's ills? And how can women be respected in a world which holds them so cheap? Romney has known Aurora for seven years and yet he still patronizes her as a frivolous girl, incapable of comprehending the important public concerns that preoccupy his mind. But what Romney also says is that women are incapable of Art; they cannot write poetry, and Aurora should accordingly stop wasting her time and join him in his important project of social and political reform.

Painstakingly, Aurora spells out to him the flaws in his argument:

> 'am I proved too weak
> To stand alone, yet strong enough to bear
> Such leaners on my shoulder? poor to think,
> Yet rich enough to sympathise with thought?
> Incompetent to sing, as blackbirds can,
> Yet competent to love, like HIM?'

and she concludes bitterly, '"It's always so./Anything does for a wife."' Romney's argument that if her sex is '"weak for art . . . it is strong/For life and duty"' understandably does little to placate Aurora, and she firmly rejects his proposal:

> 'What you love
> Is not a woman, Romney, but a cause:
> You want a helpmate, not a mistress, sir,
> A wife to help your ends, – in her no end.'

Given that nearly two thousand years of Christian teaching had emphasized that a helpmate was exactly what a man needed and deserved, Romney is understandably disconcerted, but again fails to understand Aurora's point, thinking that she is angry with him for asking her to share a life of love and work rather than flattering her with extravagant declarations of devotion. Yet again, she sets him straight. Men think of women as complementary to themselves, forgetting that everybody, female as well as male, '"Stands single in responsible act and thought"'. Offer a woman work and love that are good for her – '"the best/She was born for"' – and he'll get a fair answer. In her case, she says proudly, '"I too have my vocation"', work that is as necessary as any of the economists', and she goes on to make an impassioned claim for the role of the artist as essential to the success of Romney's task, to '"keep up open roads/Betwixt the seen and unseen"', to burst through Romney's conventions with

> 'The speakable, imaginable best
> God bids him speak, to prove what lies beyond
> Both speech and imagination[.]'

Without the soul, the ideal, Romney will never achieve his reforms; if he can reach the inner life, which is precisely the poet's task, he has a possibility of reforming the outer man.

This is not the end of their discussions. Romney renews his suit, still without understanding that what Aurora requires of him is recognition of her independent, serious purpose, her right to try to be a poet; she refuses him again, the death of their aunt separates the pair, and 'in between us rushed the torrent-world'. Years later Aurora still bitterly recalls the blow Romney dealt to her young idealism:

> the wrong
> And shock he gave my life, in finding me
> Precisely where the devil of my youth
> Had set me, on those mountain-peaks of hope
> All glittering with the dawn-dew, all erect
> And famished for the noon, – exclaiming, while
> I looked for empire and much tribute, 'Come,
> I have some worthy work for thee below.
> Come, sweep my barns and keep my hospitals,
> And I will pay thee with a current coin
> Which men give women.'

How different is the young Aurora's sense of herself from that even of Charlotte Brontë's socially poised Shirley. How modern she seems, how courageous and self-confident in her determination to try her utmost as a poet, setting off with her aunt's modest legacy to live alone in London, eking out an existence with hack writing, and burning the midnight oil while she wrestles with Art. When she does think of Romney, it is not with a sexual thrill at the memory of his masterful ways, but with a corroding sense of injustice, of wanting her work to be understood and valued. In the meantime, Romney continues his search for a mate, turning from Aurora, who had been his heart's choice, however much he failed to understand her, to the pathetic sempstress Marian Erle.

Romney justifies his wish to marry Marian Erle on the grounds of their common humanity. Despite their differences in status, '"standing at the two extremes/Of social classes"', both are fashioned from '"one clay"', the stuff from which God '"made us all"' and to which we must all return; both are dedicated to '"mercy and ministration"', he through his knowledge of the world, his '"conscience"', she through her '"woman's heart"'. Romney's proposal to Marian makes it clear that he has learnt nothing from his quarrel with Aurora; for him, man and woman still inhabit separate spheres of intellect and emotion, but Marian does not question his definition of their partnership. Romney seems to her an angel, whom she worships with doglike devotion, seeing herself as '"fitter for his handmaid than his wife"', a role that recalls the Virgin's quiet acceptance of the Annunciation. Aurora's assumption that this is a love match in conventionally romantic terms is contradicted by both partners. Marian does not question Romney's love for her since she sees it as part of his angelic capacity to love all the world, while Romney, too, has a rather austere notion of generalized love:

> 'We're fallen on days,
> We two who are not poets, when to wed
> Requires less mutual love than common love
> For two together to bear out at once
> Upon the loveless many.'

Romney describes his concept of altruistic love as a '"fall"', a notion of decline that is emphasized by his contemptuous dismissal of poetic romanticism: ' "love's fool-paradise/Is out of date, like Adam's" '. But the reader knows that a more personal love is possible and, despite all its difficulties, desirable, even in these post-lapsarian times. Behind the discussions of different kinds of love in *Aurora Leigh* lingers an echo of the *coup de foudre* that begins the poem, the sudden passion of Aurora's middle-aged father for a beautiful young Italian girl, a storm of feeling that floods through the 'dry lifetime' of the 'austere Englishman', and sweeps him away for ever from his respectable life of 'college-learning, law, and parish talk'. He abandons family and fortune for his wife, and all too soon finds himself living alone with a small child in the Italian mountains, but when he dies, his final words to his teenage daughter are ' "Love, my child, love, love!" ', and Aurora's emotional quest in the poem is to interpret and attempt to fulfil her father's dying injunction without losing her self-respect.

Chilled by Romney's expedient marriage, Aurora withdraws from the wedding preparations, leaving Marian prey to Lady Waldemar, who destroys Marian's innocent acceptance of what Romney is offering her. Marian flees to protect him from the social shame of marrying beneath him, but years later, when he seeks her out to marry her and give her son his name, she again rejects him. Her refusal is no longer based on a sense of her own unworthiness: Marian's struggles have given her a new sense of self-worth and she makes a proud claim for every woman's right to her own identity:

> ' – a woman, poor or rich,
> Despised or honoured, is a human soul,
> And what her soul is, that she is herself,
> Although she should be spit upon of men . . .'

She tells Romney that she has come to understand that slavish subjection to a man is no proof of love, still less a healthy basis for marriage:

> 'What was in my thought?
> To be your slave, your help, your toy, your tool.
> To be your love . . . I never thought of that:
> To give you love . . . still less.'

In an image that recalls and reformulates Romney's earlier claim that they had both been made from common clay, she sees herself as having been quite literally Romney's creation:

> 'I was but only yours – upon my knees,
> All yours, in soul and body, in head and heart,
> A creature you had taken from the ground
> Still crumbling through your fingers to your feet
> To join the dust she came from.'

By giving Romney God-like authority over her, Marian denied her own identity, so that – and the text is ambiguous here – she either spontaneously disintegrated, was never fully formed, or was actually pulverized by Romney's shaping fingers back into the dust from whence she came. In saying that both were made of clay, Romney had perhaps been thinking, not of Adam's creation in Genesis 2, but of the first account of the Creation where man and woman are made together in God's image. In practice, Marian is shaped by Romney, rather as Eve was named by Adam; she ' "let [Romney] write/His name upon her" ', a process of masculine control that Barrett Browning suggests is fatally damaging to a woman's identity. A woman must do her own naming.

In one of her many musings on the poet's role in society, Aurora reflects on the creative power of language:

> Virtue's in the *word*!
> The maker burnt the darkness up with His,
> To inaugurate the use of vocal life . . .

a reference to the creation, when the Spirit of God moved across the face of the deep and spoke into the primeval darkness, 'Let there be light: and there was light' (Gen. 1:3). In what was an extraordinarily bold act for a woman, Aurora/Barrett Browning claims God's creative Word for herself. Her struggle to become a poet has been an attempt to master (and the gendered verb reflects the difficulty of her task) the power of language, which she sees as an influence for good that does more for a man than 'if you dressed him in a broadcloth coat/And warmed his Sunday pottage at your fire'. The (woman) poet's right to language, with its potential for social reform, and his refusal to accept this authority are the basis of her quarrel with Romney.

Unlike Marian or Aurora, Lady Waldemar has no need of suffering or artistic achievement to feel a sense of her own worth. Rich, beautiful and high-born, she offers Romney the allurement of a socially equal marriage with a woman who appears eager to share his humanitarian concerns. But her love is tainted by self-interest, and she is unscrupulous in how she achieves her ends. It is uncertain how far she was responsible for Marian's rape and abandonment, but she callously manipulated Marian's naivety to persuade her to leave Romney, and stands convicted at least of carelessness in her choice of protector for the girl. Aurora, admittedly an interested party, accuses her of a narcissism that uses others for her own selfish purposes. She is 'a woman of the world', 'centre to herself', isolated in 'self-love and self-will', and if she does love at last:

> Her love's a re-adjustment of self-love,
> No more, – a need felt of another's use
> To her one advantage, as the mill wants grain,
> The fire wants fuel, the very wolf wants prey,
> And none of these is more unscrupulous
> Than such a charming woman when she loves.

Lady Waldemar's true function in the plot is to represent the treacherous face of womanhood, a femme fatale whose duplicitous nature is confirmed by her identification with the persuasive, death-dealing serpent of Genesis. Described by Aurora as the 'woman-serpent' and the 'Lamia-woman', she is one of the snaky seductresses, descendants of Eve, so popular in nineteenth-century art and literature. Her machinations provide a sense of tension and drama as she coils ever closer around the unsuspecting Romney, and Barrett Browning is clever enough to suggest genuine feeling in her dedicated pursuit, although it is difficult to see the attraction for any of these women of this fanatical and humourless young man.

Despite her plausibility, Lady Waldemar is not the help meet for

Romney Leigh; that role belongs to Aurora, but only after both she and Romney have had a long period of separation and painful experience in which to work out how to make their two discordant clocks chime in accord. At first Barrett Browning's resolution of the problem of love, marriage and female identity appears to be a capitulation to the dominant ethos of her time: after all her courage and independence, Aurora lapses towards the end of the poem into a melancholy state in which she questions her work and feels the insufficiency of Art. At the root of her problem is grief over the loss of Romney, whom she believes to be married to Lady Waldemar, and anxiety that she should have prevented what she sees as a disastrous partnership for her cousin:

> 'Now, if I had been a woman, such
> As God made women, to save men by love, –
> By just my love I might have saved this man,
> And made a nobler poem for the world
> Than all I have failed in.'

This is something of a volte-face for the self-sufficient artist, Aurora Leigh, as is her new awareness that a life lived solely for Art is insufficient – it needs to be pieced out 'with another's life'. But for all the melodrama that resolves the action of the poem – the fire and Romney's blindness, the on-off news of the marriage to Lady Waldemar, the will-she, won't-she proposal to Marian – when Romney and Aurora do finally come together to negotiate the trade-off between their respective ambitions and their relationship with one another, Barrett Browning struggles through the flimflammery of her own ridiculous plot to an innovatory interpretation of the meet help which defines both partners in the marital relationship, and attempts to accommodate romantic love with self-fulfilment, Art with practical social reform. The years since Romney's first proposal have modified the cousins' polarized positions. Romney has seen his social experiments fail and, powerfully persuaded by Aurora's latest book of poems, finally acknowledges her high claims for the artist's role in society. He accepts that he took too much on himself, working as Adam did,

> 'as if the only man on earth,
> Responsible for all the thistles blown
> And tigers couchant, struggling in amaze
> Against disease and winter, snarling on
> For ever that the world's not paradise[,]'

and resolves henceforth to be more realistic in his ambitions. Aurora recognizes that in her pursuit of poetry, she neglected her needs as a woman, and now she shifts the focus of her ambition from emulating God's creating Word to recognizing the breath of life with which He animated Adam, and which she defines as Love:

> 'A handful of the earth
> To make God's image! the despised poor earth,
> The healthy, odorous earth, – I missed with it
> The divine Breath that blows the nostrils out
> To ineffable inflatus, – ay, the breath
> Which love is.'

and she humbly acknowledges:

> 'Art is much, but Love is more.
> O Art, my Art, thou'rt much, but Love is more!
> Art symbolises heaven, but Love is God
> And makes heaven.'

In their new, united vision of the world, they agree that after God's love, comes ' "the love of wedded souls" ', which Romney sees as its counterpart and which he defines as the rose of Sharon, symbol of Christ's love for his spouse, the Church, in the Song of Songs:

> 'Sweet shadow-rose, upon the water of life,
> Of such a mystic substance, Sharon gave
> A name to! human, vital, fructuous rose . . .'

But there is nothing solipsistic about this rose: it contains and nourishes all the varieties of love available to humanity:

'Loves filial, loves fraternal, neighbour-loves
And civic – all fair petals, all good scents,
All reddened, sweetened from one central Heart!'

What Romney proposes to Aurora is a mutually supportive and
complementary partnership, but one that reverses his original balance between feminine feeling and masculine intellect. Now that
he is disabled by blindness, she is to work for both of them, her
poetry the '"silver key"' that will help humanity to unlock the
door between body and spirit, while he will supply the love:

'Shine out for two, Aurora, and fulfil
My falling-short that must be! work for two,
As I, though thus restrained, for two, shall love!'

The poem concludes with an inspirational vision of the New
Jerusalem that they will build together:

faint and far,
Along the tingling desert of the sky,
Beyond the circle of the conscious hills,
Were laid in jasper-stone as clear as glass
The first foundations of that new, near Day
Which should be builded out of heaven to God.

As the blind Romney turns instinctively towards this radiant horizon, Aurora, his '"compensation"', his '"dear sight"', reminds him
of the jewelled foundations of the heavenly city described in the
Revelation of St John the Divine and now reflected in the glowing
colours of the new dawn that they face together, like Milton's
Adam and Eve, hand in hand:

'Jasper first,' I said;
'And second, sapphire; third, chalcedony;
The rest in order: – last, an amethyst.'

Aurora Leigh was Barrett Browning's answer to Milton's epic
account of Adam and Eve and, in working out Aurora's relationship

with Romney, she redefined the role of the 'meet help' to embrace both partners in a pact of mutuality which released Eve from her traditional subjection to Adam and gave her access to Adam's right to work. At the end of the verse-novel, Aurora is to give birth to poems rather than babies and, despite the elitist idealism of the conclusion, Barrett Browning's courageous new definition of the marital relationship endorses women's right to self-respect. Wifely obedience has been replaced with complementarity, the generous pooling of skills between people with different abilities but similar goals, a beneficent interpretation that may well have reflected the reality of many Victorian marriages, even though their public face was better represented by the ironic lines of Christina Rossetti's 'A Helpmeet for Him' (written *c.* 1887):

> Woman was made for man's delight;
>   Charm, O woman, be not afraid!
> His shadow by day, his moon by night,
>   Woman was made.
>
> Her strength with weakness is overlaid;
>   Meek compliances veil her might;
> Him she stays, by whom she is stayed.

THE EVE WHOM Barrett Browning explored in her portrait of the poet Aurora Leigh was the brave adventurer determined to taste the forbidden fruit whatever the cost, a resolute woman who emerges from her odyssey with a compliant husband, an established reputation as a poet, mistress of God's creative word, and a programme of fulfilling work to lead her into the future. What her character does not embrace is sexuality. There is much talk of love in the poem, but Aurora's sexual rapport with Romney, if it exists, is barely whispered. As in Hemingway's *The Garden of Eden*, there is a split between Adam's 'meet help' and the beautiful, dangerous woman who offers sexual temptation. The seductive face of Eve is represented in Barrett Browning's poem by Lady Waldemar, the wily 'Lamia' who is roundly condemned as an unacceptable partner for Romney/Adam. But Eve's snaky daughters played a major role in the developing mythology of Woman, offering a tantalizing projection of forbidden pleasure that was almost inevitably deadly to the male, a juicy fruit that men must bite and bite again even as it turned, like the fruit of the tree of knowledge when consumed by the rebel angels, to dust and ashes in the mouth.

CHAPTER 10

TEMPTING WOMEN: MERMAIDS, LILITHS AND LAMIAS

It may be that vice, depravity and crime are nearly always . . .
attempts to eat beauty, to eat what we should only look at. Eve
began it. If she caused humanity to be lost by eating the fruit, the
opposite attitude, looking at the fruit without eating it, should be
what is required to save it.

SIMONE WEIL

＊◆＊

FACING A QUIET FLORENTINE square near the Boboli
Gardens is the tranquil church of Santa Maria del Carmine
where, in the early fifteenth century, the artist known as
Masolino painted a classically beautiful Eve. The young woman's
finely modelled body is lit by pearly light, her perfect mouth is
highlighted by an elegant mole, and her striking brown eyes and
blonde hair could identify a Diana or Aphrodite. In her right hand
she holds a fig, plucked from the tree under which she and the
equally sculptural Adam stand; around its trunk trails the long
sinewy form of the serpent, but the head poised over the couple,
watching their every move, is that of a young girl, whose dark eyes,
modelled features and mass of blonde hair link her unmistakably
with Eve.

The identification of Eve with her Tempter goes back very
early in Eve's history. Her possible ancestry in the reptilian Tiamat,
the primordial mother goddess of the *Enuma Elish*, is one strand in
the chain that binds the two together; another is the name that
Adam gives his wife: Eve, Hawwah, which he defines as 'mother of
all living'. Scholars puzzling over the etymology of this term have
linked it with Aramaic *ḥiwyā'* and Arabic *ḥayyatun*, both of which
mean 'serpent', an association which the Rabbis had toyed with,
but which did not become current in religious exegesis until the
Middle Ages, when the tradition was established by the scholar
Peter Comestor (died 1179). Nicknamed the 'feeder' because of his

love of studying, Comestor mentions in his *Historia Scholastica*, a collection of stories from the Bible which was widely read throughout the period, the by now conventional association of the serpent with Satan, but then goes on to say that 'he chose a kind of serpent . . . which had a face like a maiden's, since like approves of like'. This idea delighted medieval commentators, who argued that the serpent's female face made it a particularly suitable vehicle for Satan's temptation of Eve, an idea that chimed with popular beliefs about women's love of gossip and pleasure in subverting male authority, and it appears in many subsequent writings. In the Chester play of the Temptation and Fall, the devil says he is going to assume the form of a local snake, which has a bird's wings, an adder's feet and a 'maydens face', and the stage direction specifies that the serpent should be 'forma puella', that is, in the shape of a woman; and Christ in *Piers the Ploughman* accuses Satan of deceiving humanity, 'disguised as a reptile with a woman's face'. The blonde, female-headed serpent is represented in many paintings of the Fall, sometimes with just a human head planted on a reptile's body, as in Masolino's portrayal, sometimes with a fully formed female torso, as in Michelangelo's Temptation, or even standing erect, as in Hugo van der Goes' Fall, where the serpent balances on scaly legs that end in dragon-like claws. But although van der Goes' serpent has a face that recognizably mirrors Eve's, it is Eve after the Fall and some years into her wilderness experience: strained and hollow-eyed, with lank, meagre locks instead of the luxuriant brown tendrils that drift almost to the unfallen Eve's ankles. In the Tempter's time-worn visage the young Eve may read her fate, but she chooses not to look and instead plucks a second apple to hand to the waiting Adam – the first she already holds in her hand, its flesh noticeably toothmarked by her rebellious bite.

Eve's association with the serpent became one of the most fruitful strands in the many fantasies that proliferated about her, branching off into multiple stories about reptilian monsters as well as snaky seductresses, manifestations of the female in her most repulsive and alluring forms, but having in common the troubling notion of menacing carnality. As the earlier story of Tiamat and the Jewish elaborations of the 'daughters of men' narrative in Genesis 6 illustrate, female sexuality can be a two-edged sword. Along with

fleshly pleasures and the bonus of legitimate heirs, sons to carry on
the family name and daughters to sweeten the attenuations of old
age, it offers the potential for spawning monsters. Tiamat gives birth
to a brood of demons, the reptilian Viper, the Dragon, Mad-Dog
and Scorpion-Man, whose sharp teeth and terrific roars are graphically described, and only the superhero Marduk can kill the mother
and trample her progeny underfoot. The attractive 'daughters of
men' are wily temptresses, whose honeyed words and lascivious
glances can seduce even God's angels away from the paths of
righteousness, and they bear cannibalistic giants who bring destruction and terrible suffering on humanity. In these narratives, the
vagina/birth canal which is the object of heterosexual male desire
and the womb from which every man emerges are seen as potentially lethal weapons in the female armoury, which the early
Christians dismantled by the drastic but simple expedient of
abstinence.

The male's horrified fascination with the female sexual organs,
the theme of so much early Jewish and Christian homily, has
persisted in Western society until the present day. The Jungian
psychologist Erich Neumann explained it as a fear of returning to
the preconscious chaos of the womb in terms that echo the repellent
symbolism of the ancient storytellers:

> For the ego and the male, the female is synonymous with the
> unconscious and the nonego, hence with darkness, nothingness,
> the void, the bottomless pit . . . Mother, womb, the pit, and hell
> are all identical . . . every female . . . threatens the ego with the
> danger of self-noughting, of self-loss – in other words, with death
> and castration.

One way to cope with female sexuality was by rigid social hierarchies and rules controlling women, such as the Jews and Greeks
and Romans imposed; another was by inventing stories in which its
fearful aspects could be contained or exorcized. The monstrously
productive woman and the alluring temptress are two of the fantasies
through which societies have come to terms with the threatening
feminine for literally thousands of years; both are expressed through
the image of woman as a dangerous reptile.

Monstrous women

In the *Theogony*, Hesiod describes the horrific Echidna, a monster whom the gods have confined for all eternity in an underground cave. Her beautiful nymph's face cannot disguise that from the waist down she has the gross and ravening body of a serpent. Mated with the fearsome Typhaon, a brute with a hundred cacophonous snake-heads, she brings forth terrible offspring: multi-headed Cerberus, guard-dog of Hades; the Hydra, a serpent whose heads spontaneously regenerate as soon as they are cut off; and the triple-headed Chimaera, lion, goat and serpent in one, and mother to the Sphinx. This grotesque snake-woman epitomizes all that the gloomy Reuben and the shrinking Church Fathers dreaded in the female: the tempting face and sexually rapacious body hidden in the chthonic cave of uncontrollable desire. This potent image of alluring nastiness, sex with a sting in its twitchy tail, survived the Dark Ages to re-emerge in the Anglo-Saxon epic of *Beowulf*, where the eponymous hero kills the water-monster Grendel, a direct descendant of the first murderer Cain, and then Grendel's avenging mother, a 'brawny water-hag', the 'she-wolf of the water'. Beowulf slaughters Grendel in the King's great feast-hall, but he seeks the mother in the watery deeps of the lake where she has made her home, a place of malevolence that glows with lurid light, and he finally beheads her with a giant sword, the phallic weapon used again and again to destroy or at least render harmless the threatening female.

Beowulf is a Christian account of a proto-cosmic struggle between good and evil that recalls the destruction of the great dragon in Revelation; but Grendel's mother's seamy lair could equally have belonged to the Greek Echidna. In Spenser's *The Faerie Queene*, a Christian knight again sets out to fight a great dragon, but pauses en route to battle with a noxious serpent-woman. The Red Cross Knight encounters vile Error very early in his quest, coming across her cave in labyrinthine woods where he has inadvertently strayed. When he enters the 'darksome hole' that she inhabits, he sees an ugly monster, half-woman, half-serpent, whose massive tail fills her den, its multiple knots and coils armed with poisonous darts. Here she lies feeding her thousand whelps, each as ugly as herself;

but as soon as the light from the knight's glistening armour falls on them, they creep into her mouth to hide. At his approach, Error rushes forward on the attack, only to draw back daunted by the Red Cross Knight's shimmering light, but when he strikes her, she turns at bay and wraps her tail closely round him. Urged on by his fair companion, the saintly Una, the knight manages to free one hand and starts to strangle the monster, at which she spews out a great flood of foul-smelling poison littered with gobbets of flesh from earlier meals, and full of the books and papers of ungodly learning. Almost choked by the stench, the knight falls back and Error now vomits her serpent brood, who swarm around his legs and further hinder him. Goaded beyond endurance, he aims a mighty blow with his sword and refts the monster's head from her body; her ungrateful progeny rush to gorge on her blood, but it overswells their bellies and they literally burst to death.

'Mother, womb, the pit, and hell' – Neumann's ominous definition of the female is corroborated by Spenser's terrible Error, whose repellent odours and filthy effluent recall the Rabbis' obsession with woman's 'stink', and whose disproportionately elongated tail and hordes of loathsome children emphasize her evil female appetites. Once again, she lurks in a dark, dangerous cave, the treacherous womb which the hero discovers after a journey through threatening territory, the mazy pathways of the 'wandring wood', in which he runs the risk of losing himself in the moral as well as the physical sense.

Error's most egregious successor is Milton's Sin, a similarly endowed hybrid engendered by Satan when he was still in heaven, bursting from his head in an act of spontaneous parthenogenesis, 'a goddess armed', like Athene from the head of Zeus. Winning favour with the angelic hosts by her 'attractive graces', she most particularly delighted her parent, who was narcissistically drawn to his offspring and secretly impregnated her. When Satan and his remnant were routed, Sin fell with them and was made portress of the gates of hell. Here Satan re-encounters her on his journey to spy out God's new creation, sitting in front of the massive 'thrice threefold' portals. She is a 'formidable shape', the now familiar combination of woman and serpent. Unlike Error, Sin's face and female torso are beautiful, but her nether parts are similarly 'foul', '[v]oluminous and vast', and she is again armed with a 'mortal sting'. Her whelps are a pack of barking hell hounds, who retreat back into her womb when anything disturbs them. Guarding the gates with her is the fearful 'shadow', the ravenous Death, a featureless shape who shakes his 'dreadful dart' at Satan, so that Sin has to rush between them to prevent a fight. She reminds Satan who she is and tells him of the birth of their son, the grisly king who now accompanies her. He too had been born fully formed and his first act was to rape his mother, engendering the hell hounds who now prey upon her, gnawing her vitals for nourishment.

There is no mistaking the implication of these obscene images of the feminine, whose insatiable bodies spawn monsters and whose snaky tails identify them as figures of lust: the Luxuria whom medieval artists loved to depict with serpents gnawing her breasts, or else lewdly cuddling up to the devil. When Lear goes mad and runs amok with flowers in his hair, he praises lust which may produce more faithful offspring than 'lawful sheets' had managed: 'To 't, Luxury, pell-mell!' Raving about female duplicity, the 'riotous appetite' of the 'simp'ring dame' who parades her virtue, he claims:

> Down from the waist they are Centaurs,
> Though women all above:
> But to the girdle do the Gods inherit,
> Beneath is all the fiend's: there's hell, there's darkness,
> There is the sulphurous pit – burning, scalding,
> Stench, consumption . . .

and he calls for 'an ounce of civet' to 'sweeten' his imagination and presumably the 'stench' that pollutes his nostrils. 'Mother, womb, the pit, and hell': in the topsy-turvy world of the insane, an embittered old man reveals his terror of women, the threat of 'self-noughting' and 'self-loss', of the 'death and castration' symbolized by the powerful king stripped of his rank, his wealth and his self-respect by scheming, sexually potent daughters.

Bronzino's sumptuous *An Allegory with Venus and Cupid*, dating to around 1546 and now housed in the National Gallery in London, offers persuasive visual testimony to the deceptive glamour of women and its terrible consequences. The centrepiece of the painting is Venus herself, a stunningly beautiful nude who holds in one hand Cupid's arrow, in the other a tempting golden apple. Next to her, half-kneeling on a scarlet cushion, a familiar symbol of lechery and idleness, is her son Cupid, a ravishing adolescent boy, also naked and leaning forward to embrace his mother. With his left hand he supports her jewelled head as their lips touch in an intimate kiss; with his right he tenderly palpates her breast in a gesture that is rather amorous than filial. To the left of the couple is a gleeful putto, the figure of Pleasure who smilingly tosses roses and tinkles an anklet of tiny bells; but the illusory nature of the joys he offers is suggested by the two masks that lie at his feet: the face of a young woman next to a frowning hooknosed man with a libertine's fleshy lips. Symbols of 'worldliness, insincerity and falsehood', the masks spell out the contrasts that the painting encapsulates: between youth and age, beauty and ugliness, health and the corroding sicknesses of body and soul. Just behind and to the right of the loving couple is an agonized figure clutching its hair and seeming to shriek in anguish. Vasari defined this tortured creature as Jealousy, but more recent scholarship has identified the characteristic symptoms of syphilis, an interpretation that redefines the shrieker as a reminder of the destructive consequences of lust.

These oppositions between love's transitory pleasures and more lasting pains are summed up in the ambiguous figure of a girl who crouches behind the happy putto. Her blandly pretty face tops a fish-scaled body with a serpent's tail and dragon claws. In one hand she offers a honeycomb, but the other conceals a threatening little animal, and her hands have in any case been reversed, the right hand placed on her left wrist and vice versa. In a symbolic system that equates the right hand with goodness and the left with evil, the 'good' of the nourishing honeycomb and the 'bad' of the poisonous beast are called into question, a confusion of moral values that is at the heart of lust. At the rear of the tableau, Time with his wings and hourglass and a female figure who may represent Truth between them hold a curtain, but again their action is fraught with contradiction: are they struggling for possession of the veil, have they just drawn it back, or are they about to cover over these shameless figures? In his analysis of the painting, the art historian Erwin Panofsky defined it as 'Luxury, surrounded by personifications and symbols of treacherous pleasures and manifest evils', a duality that is summarized by the serpent-girl, the furthest figure from the viewer, but the only one of the group who looks out of the painting, her balanced hands seeming to weigh the dubious pros and cons of what is on view. 'What else is woman' wrote St John Chrysostom, 'but . . . a necessary evil, a natural temptation, a desirable calamity, . . . a delectable detriment, an evil nature, painted with fair colours?' Bronzino's enticing Venus with her golden apple is Tertullian's Eve, 'the devil's gateway', and Hesiod's Pandora, the 'beautiful evil' with whom Zeus permanently blasted mankind, all over again; and her defining symbol is a serpent-woman offering ambiguous gifts.

Fishy tales

THE SCALY-TAILED WOMAN is not always obviously threatening, although danger is generally the sub-text of her story. One of her most intriguing manifestations was the fairy Melusine, whose legend was recorded by Jean d'Arras in the fifteenth century. Melusine was a daughter of King Elinas of Albania and the mysterious fairy Pressina, whose legacy to her daughter was the curse of transformation: one day a week she would metamorphose into a creature half-human, half-serpent and, should any lover happen to see her in demi-reptile form, she would be forced to relinquish her humanity for ever. One moonlit night, the young lord Raimondin caught sight of Melusine near a spring of the natural waters with which she became associated. He fell passionately in love with the beautiful girl and she finally agreed to marry him on condition that they would never meet on a Saturday. Of course, he broke the taboo, peeking at his wife, according to the legend, as she took her weekly bath, and seeing her splendid snaky tail. Despite his pleadings, Melusine was obliged to flee, throwing herself out of a window to join the winds in whose company she was condemned to wander the earth for all eternity.

Melusine was a Celtic fertility goddess, linked with the natural freshwater sources that enrich the soil and bring about a bounteous harvest and, as mother of many children, the guarantor of human fecundity, Eve in her benign telluric aspect. But, like Eve's identification with her Tempter, Melusine's serpent's tail also connected her with the subterranean world of female sexual secrets, an association which A. S. Byatt brilliantly exploits in her novel *Possession* (1990), where the legend of Melusine becomes a teasing metaphor for a love affair stifled by Victorian pieties. Byatt's heroine, the reclusive poet Christabel LaMotte, introduces her narrative poem about the fairy Melusine by recalling her female ancestresses – snake-haired Medusa, witchy Scylla, the Hydra, the sirens and the clever Sphinx, monstrous women who are punished for their supernatural powers by isolation and even death, just as Christabel's illicit passion cuts her off from the human sympathies that would have nurtured and sustained her. Christabel's cousin, Sabine de Kercoz, is similarly well-versed in folkloric warnings about female seductresses; she lives in a region of Brittany associated with Dahud, a sorceress who is terribly punished for her sexuality. Her sensual excesses lead to her city, Is, being swallowed up by her lover, the Ocean, and buried for ever under water. Studying the legend in a learned edition, Sabine reads that the story of Is encapsulates '"the terror of ancient pagan cults and the terror of the passion of the senses, let loose in women . . . Paganism, woman and the Ocean, these three desires and these three great fears of man, are mingled in this strange legend"', but she angrily rejects this misogynous reading: 'Why should desire and the senses be so terrifying in women? Who is this author, to say that these are the fears of man, by which he means the whole human race? He makes us witches, outcasts, *sorcières*, monsters . . .' For all her feisty feminism, Sabine's story ends tragically: she marries a dull and melancholy obsessive, many years older than her, and perishes in childbirth, and her two surviving daughters die when barely in their teens.

What Melusine and her serpentine precursors appear to embody is a horrified male fascination with female sexuality, the slithery tail suggestive of a sensuality that threatens to engulf and drown even as it allures. Mermaids played a similar role in popular fantasy: sea-maidens with fishy lower parts, they lured men to their doom by their sweet songs and fair faces. Robert Graves links the mermaid with Mary of Egypt, originally a pagan sea-goddess, but in Christian legend famed for working her passage to the Holy Land by sexual favours to the boat's entire crew; and in churches all over England, mermaids lurk on misericords and at the ends of benches with their combs and mirrors, symbols of vanity and heartlessness and a warning to sailors of the perils of female beauty. They were frequently identified with that other soul-stealer, the siren, and in a Boston church a mermaid charms a boatload of mariners with her music. At Exeter, two mermaids hold a small drum over the head of a man they have dragged to the bottom of the ocean; while another triumphantly wields a fish, a Christian soul gripped by lust. A mermaid in Bristol Cathedral socializes with the devil and an evil dragon: a deadly trio waiting to entrap the unwary.

The dangerous powers of mermaids and sirens, their sexuality and artifice, were closely linked with those of Eve. The *Malleus Maleficarum*, written in 1486 by two Dominican friars and an important document in the Church's drive against witchcraft, attributed female carnality, which was considered far to exceed that of the male, to Eve, 'the first temptress', who was also responsible for the widespread female tendency to dupe and lie. These moral defects were due to an initial flaw in her creation:

> it should be noted that there was a defect in the formation of the
> first woman, since she was formed from a bent rib, that is, a rib
> of the breast, which is bent as it were in a contrary direction to
> a man.

Because of this deficiency, she is 'an imperfect animal' and 'always deceives'. As for female carnality, it has exposed the world to untold dangers, and they quote Valerius, who compared woman to the Chimaera, that smelly monster in the classical bestiary with a whippy, poisonous tail:

> its face was that of a radiant and noble lion, it had the filthy belly
> of a goat, and it was armed with the virulent tail of a viper.

As the cautious monks remind their readers, this confirms that a woman 'is beautiful to look upon, contaminating to the touch, and deadly to keep'. A woman's voice is similarly tainted:

as she is a liar by nature, so in her speech she stings while she
delights us. Wherefore her voice is like the song of the Sirens,
who with their sweet melody entice the passers-by and kill them.

Like the bird-bodied siren, like the mermaid, like 'temptress' Eve:
as Sabine de Kercoz points out, it is male anxiety that fantasizes
women as 'witches, outcasts, *sorcières*, monsters . . .' The reality for
the majority of women throughout the early modern period when
these beliefs were so prevalent was marriage and the pains and risks
of childbirth.

What is so extraordinary about the mermaid's reputation for
sexual allure is that her anatomy actually implies the baulking of
lust: what phallus could penetrate that slippery scaly surface? Where
is the mermaid's vagina and how does she reproduce? It is a subject
that Carol Shields wittily addresses in her novel *The Republic of Love*
(1992), in the fictitious paper that her heroine Fay, an expert in
mermaid lore, places before the Minneapolis Regional Folklore
Association:

> The mermaid . . . is thus, an emblem of sexual ambiguity.
> Traditionally, women were regarded as lesser versions of men,
> with abbreviated sex organs, but the mermaid preceded even
> that image, being a female whose development was arrested at an
> early stage of evolution. She is erotic but passionless, a culturally
> charged gender model whose seductive capacity is valued over
> her reproductive capacity. In her double-tailed version she may
> call to mind the old Celtic sheila-na-gig, or the Indian Kali,
> aggressively squatting and displaying her yoni. In her far more
> familiar single-tailed version, though, she is closer to an Eve
> figure overlaid with the cult of the Virgin, a sealed vessel
> enclosing either sexual temptation or sexual virtue, or some
> paradoxical and potent mixture of the two.

In Helen Dunmore's novel *Zennor in Darkness* (1993), a carving of
a mermaid survives in the local church in Zennor in Cornwall, a
quasi-pagan symbol of the superstition at the heart of this introspec-
tive community. Her significance is recognized by the outsider,

D. H. Lawrence, a chance wartime resident of Zennor whom the locals eventually reject as a potential enemy agent:

> 'She doesn't belong. She's half and half. They laugh at her on
> land, and hate her. And when she's in the sea, she can't breathe.
> So what's left for her? She can only sit on her rock, neither on
> land nor in the sea, and wait, and drive men mad. So they hate
> her all the more, all the time they're pretending to love her
> and want her . . . Because she makes people think that there's
> something more – something they haven't been told about.
> And they'll never have it.'

This sense of the sea-enchantress's potential, that she represents something desirable, fearful and unattainable, is explored in Giuseppe di Lampedusa's short story 'The Professor and the Siren' (1957). Unlike the cautious Christian commentators droning through the centuries the dreary catalogue of female sexual crime, di Lampedusa's anti-hero, an illustrious classical scholar, had once embraced a siren, abandoning himself to the jouissance of unencumbered sensuality. But the professor's brief idyll with the beautiful girl, mermaid rather than siren, and one whose female torso melds conveniently *below* her crutch into a fish's scaly tail, offers far more than fulfilled passion. His nymphet embodies the life-force itself: pagan, energizing and without shame, an eternally flowing current into which all life merges and from whence it issues forth. But this is an unusually unfettered response to the siren's call. Hans Andersen metamorphosed his little mermaid into a human girl at the terrible cost of the loss of her beautiful voice, of knife-sharp pain with every step she took with her pretty new legs, and finally the sacrifice of her immortal soul. His mermaid's story ends, like Melusine's, with her joining the daughters of the air, although in this case three hundred years of virtuous deeds may restore her to God. Andersen's moralistic fable reverses the popular legend of the mermaid, so that she herself falls prey to impossible longings, and is denied salvation in a characteristically Christian narrative in which female suffering and self-denial are valued over sensual pleasure.

In the instructive iconography of the misericords, the mermaid's haunting song may lead a man astray and damn his soul for all eternity; but the enchantress has another, more inspirational role. Yeats' 'The Song of Wandering Aengus' tells of a man who one night catches a silver trout in a stream. When he brings it home, it turns into a girl crowned with apple blossom who calls his name and then runs away, drawing him on a lifelong journey in search of her. What Yeats' Aengus so movingly evokes is the passionate yearning to taste the golden apples of the creative imagination, tempting fruit proffered by the teasing muse, the elusive White Goddess tracked by Robert Graves through the groves and thickets of ancient poetry.

Liliths and Lamias

IN THE LATE 1880s, the artist John Collier painted a voluptuous standing nude: a young woman whose head and shoulders are framed by the abundant red-gold hair characteristic of the seductress. The girl's ample body is entwined by a huge snake, whose tail trails on the grass at her feet while its head is cradled on her shoulder beneath her caressing chin. This extraordinary image is named as Lilith, Adam's assertive first wife, whom Jews of the talmudic period imagined to have quarrelled with her husband over equal sexual rights and fled to the Red Sea, where she lived promiscuously with demons and gave birth daily to a hundred or more evil spirits. According to her legend, the world became overrun with Liliths, malevolent night spirits who were feared as a particular threat to newborn babies and caused nocturnal emissions in men, and were guarded against by amulets and incantations. Lilith's monstrous fertility links her with Tiamat and Echidna and the loathsome Error; her powers of seduction declare her sister to the Watchers' wives and Milton's Sin, women who combine sexuality with prodigious motherhood. The snake who entwines Collier's Lilith recalls Eve, the first temptress and mother, and also the Greek Lamia, associated with Lilith by her reputation for child-snatching and her dangerous sexual powers, through which she lured virile young men, enjoyed their bodies and then drank their blood and consumed their flesh like an early version of the vampire. As

Collier's painting demonstrates, the attributes of Lilith and Lamia became confused and intermeshed with stories about other enchantresses, a potent mix on which artists and poets drew freely for their images of woman.

For the Romantic poets the demon-woman represented the endlessly desirable other, a dangerous seductress who was irresistibly 'beautiful to look upon, contaminating to the touch, and deadly to keep'. Her image was particularly fruitful for that aesthete of the unobtainable, Samuel Taylor Coleridge, and she haunts and illuminates his most beautiful and mysterious poems. In 'Kubla Khan' her spirit lurks in the savage chasm, confirming it as a site of mystery and enchantment; in *The Rime of the Ancient Mariner*, she is the nightmare Life-in-Death, a red-lipped, yellow-haired ghoul with leprous-white skin, who dices with Death for the Mariner's soul; in 'Christabel' she casts a spell on a young girl and turns her doting father against her by viperish tricks. The sorceress's ravishment of the pure Christabel is figured in the minstrel's dream of a bright green snake strangling the tender dove that Sir Leoline has named for his beloved daughter – the Christian tussle between Innocence and Evil that Hawthorne identified in the sculpture-gallery in Rome – and Geraldine is clearly a type of Lamia, whose small snake eyes and hissing malice are unwittingly reflected by the hapless Christabel. In a sullen atmosphere of suspense and threat, the wily interloper casts her erotic spell over daughter and father alike, exposing the one to some undefined horror and then bewitching her so that she cannot reveal, can indeed barely recall, the deathly experience that has contaminated her, while Sir Leoline is deceived into a welcome that warmly embraces what it had better shun.

Coleridge never completed his poem, so it is unclear whether Christabel's virtue would have triumphed over Geraldine's demoniac blight. In Keats' quasi-pagan *Lamia*, morality is subordinate to pleasure; although the enchantress – and her handsome Corinthian – are vanquished by a philosopher's gimlet gaze, the reader's sympathies, if they are engaged at all, are drawn towards the lovers' plight. The poem, first published in 1820, is a story of deception and enchantment which again begins with a woman's plaintive voice begging for help in a secluded glade, but where 'Christabel' evokes the superstitious medieval north, a chilly landscape of bare trees and thinly moonlit towers, of mastiff and minstrel and drafty arras-hung chambers, fit setting for a spooky sorceress, *Lamia* takes place in Crete and Corinth, the dusty sunlit territories that border the Aegean and where nymphs and satyrs, dryads and fauns still inhabit the woods. Hot in pursuit of a nymph, the god Hermes is distracted by the sound of lament and discovers a dazzlingly decorated snake half-hidden in the undergrowth. Her brilliance cannot disguise that there is something dangerous about this creature, who may be elf, 'demon's mistress, or the demon's self', and her honeyed voice speaks amorously through a woman's shapely mouth. She promises to reveal the nymph if Hermes will restore her to human female shape and, their transaction completed, the god fleets away to enjoy his lover leaving Lamia to tortured rebirth – a pyrotechnical transformation in which Lamia's vivid green and argent body is overwhelmed lava-like by a 'deep volcanian yellow', which convulses her in 'scarlet pain' and finally liberates her into delicious womanhood. Lamia's purpose is to win the young Lycius with whom she has fallen in love, and she waylays him as he returns alone to Corinth one evening. Captivated by her siren voice and remarkable beauty, he hides away in her secret palace in the city where the couple enjoy a Paradise of love. Lamia's downfall comes when Lycius' mentor, the arid philosopher Apollonius, invites himself to their wedding feast and names Lamia for what she is – a serpent. The cold touch of reality destroys the witch, who vanishes with a terrible scream, but Lycius, too, dies of the shock.

Keats based his poem on a narrative in Burton's *Anatomy of Melancholy*, using the simple story of the original as a vehicle for voluptuous scene-setting and some rather schoolboy jokes. There is little that is sinister about his Lamia and her illusory joys, and she even consciously shakes off her Peri nature in order to captivate Lycius, guessing that he 'could not love in half a fright'. Her lover's mistake was not in enjoying Lamia, but in wanting to show her off and thereby exposing his love to a withering logic which even an enchantress could not withstand. Far more eerie than this cheerfully sumptuous narrative was Keats' 'La belle dame sans merci', in which a young knight is seduced by 'a faery's child', who sings elfin songs and feeds him on wild honey and manna and then, like Aengus' apple-blossom girl, abandons him to a longing that will wear out his life. In both these poems it is a woman's voice, as with persuasive Eve and the hypnotic sirens, that weaves the spell: the faery's enchanted melodies and Lamia's whispered 'woman's lore' that entices Lycius to 'unperplex'd delight and pleasure known'.

The snaky sorceress was hugely popular with male Victorian writers and artists, an image of threatening female desirability which was exploited with at times pornographic enthusiasm and which drew on a rich vocabulary of religious and secular symbolism. Kenyon Cox's *Lilith* (*c.* 1892) mimics the impressively enthroned Virgin surmounting a miniature Temptation and Fall so popular in Renaissance religious painting, but instead of chaste Mary with her redemptive child, Cox displays a fleshy seated Lilith, her naked body closely entwined by a snake whose forked tongue caresses her parted lips; in the smaller panel below, it is she, half-serpent, half-woman, who encircles the tree of knowledge and offers the forbidden fruit to Eve. In these paired paintings woman and snake are confirmed as akin to the point of becoming one, their erotic entanglement implying bodily incorporation, literally 'flesh of my flesh'. What Cox suggests is that Lilith-Eve's erotic fascination is with herself rather than with Adam, the powerful female narcissism identified by Milton and one of the most maddening characteristics of the temptress. Rossetti acknowledged its allure, describing his *Lady Lilith*, as 'gazing on herself in the glass with that self-absorption by whose strange fascination such natures draw others within their own circle' and, as Swinburne recognized in his rapturous response to the painting, the subject's dreamy self-involvement embodied the idea of primordial female threat:

> [she] draws out through a comb the heavy mass of hair like thick
> spun gold to fullest length: her head leans back half sleepily,
> superb and satiate with its own beauty ... The sleepy splendour
> of the picture is a fit raiment for the idea incarnate of faultless
> fleshly beauty and peril of pleasure unavoidable.

Tennyson tamed the temptress in 'The Lady of Shalott', where his heroine, like Andersen's little mermaid, falls victim to a forbidden love – Sir Launcelot glimpsed in her magic mirror, symbol of woman's vanity and guile, but here the medium of her betrayal –

and after singing a last melancholy hymn, she floats, an exquisite corpse, down the river to towered Camelot in a barge that skims along on top of the water: a neat reversal of the mermaid's traditional role. The fairy Lady is mysteriously killed off before she has the opportunity to exploit her 'cheerly' song and magic web, but many Victorian sorceresses do terrible damage in narratives that lovingly record their evil machinations and inevitable downfall. The ingenious Becky Sharp thrives in the vicious world of *Vanity Fair*, but Thackeray finally exposes his sandy-haired witch as a 'siren' whose monstrous tail is barely disguised underwater:

> Those who like may peep down under waves that are pretty
> transparent, and see it writhing and twirling, diabolically hideous
> and slimy, flapping amongst bones, or curling round corpses . . .
> They look pretty enough when they sit upon a rock, twangling
> their harps and combing their hair, and sing, and beckon to you
> to come and hold the looking-glass; but when they sink into
> their native element, depend on it those mermaids are about
> no good, and we had best not examine the fiendish marine
> cannibals, revelling and feasting on their wretched pickled
> victims.

Thackeray attributes a Harpy-like cannibalism to his repulsive siren-mermaid: this rapacious creature will literally consume any unfortunate man who falls into her clutches, and it is Becky's winning ways and clever manipulations, her honeyed words and feminine deceitfulness – the wiles of Eve – that disarm her victims.

The familiar iconography of the blonde serpentine beauty was cleverly exploited by George Eliot to create two of her most interesting temptresses: Gwendolen Harleth in *Daniel Deronda*, with her serpent's livery of green and silver, her 'Lamia beauty' and gracefully winding neck, and Rosamond Vincy in *Middlemarch*, who seduces Lydgate with the delicate curves of her sinuous nape and her carefully arranged golden curls. Mr Farebrother refers to Rosamond as a 'siren', Lydgate calls her a 'mermaid', and true to her calling she sings and plays with taste and some talent, but she draws Lydgate less by her cooing voice than by what it implies, a dovelike womanliness that becomes irresistible in combination with her beauty and the quiet attentiveness which he mistakenly attributes to a refined intelligence. George Eliot's sensitive dissection of the seductress exposes the suffering which results from ill-judged fantasy: Gwendolen and Rosamond are bitterly punished for their projection on to their lovers of their own narrow narcissism, and Lydgate too is ensnared as much by his imagination and desires as by Rosamond's wiles.

Keats' Lamia suffered 'scarlet pain' in the metamorphosis from snake to woman, but emotional pain became increasingly an attribute of the enchantress, although her anguish was typically far removed from ordinary human experience. In Rider Haggard's *She*, the great white queen Ayesha, 'She-who-must-be-obeyed', despotic ruler of a remote African tribe, embodies the seductress's essential characteristics of irresistible sexuality and ruthlessness: that devastating combination noted by Swinburne of 'faultless fleshly beauty and peril of pleasure unavoidable'. Like Lilith, she appears to be immortal; like the Watchers' wives, she is mistress of arcane lore that gives her formidable powers of healing; like the sirens, she has a charming voice whose bell-like cadences may temporarily obscure its sinister meanings. But for all her beauty, intelligence and irrefutable authority, she has suffered centuries of torment. Her pain is revealed to the narrator, the sceptical English scholar Holly, when he unexpectedly comes across her alone one night engaged in a ritual which exposes her savagery and violence. Dressed in a clinging, low-cut white gown with a belt whose 'barbaric double-headed snake' so appropriately represents Ayesha herself, and with her black hair (Ayesha is pure-blooded Arabian) flowing down her back in a heavy torrent, she is cursing the Egyptian woman who had been her rival for the affections of the priest Kallikrates two thousand years previously. In her jealousy and rage, Ayesha had murdered Kallikrates, but her desire for him has endured the centuries and irretrievably tainted her happiness. Peering through the curtains at the entrance to Ayesha's secret cavern, Holly spies on 'the agony, the blind passion, and the awful vindictiveness' of the half-naked woman, and observes the way in which the leaping flames of the fire follow her upflung arms – clear evidence of sorcery – as she malevolently hisses her curses. George MacDonald's Lilith, in the novel of that name, similarly suffers appalling agony, in her case acute physical pain caused by a cancerous wound, symbol of her evil, that eats into her side, withering her bosom just as Geraldine's maleficent purposes had horribly destroyed her living flesh in 'Christabel', a 'sight to dream of, not to tell'.

Both Rider Haggard and MacDonald exploit the erotic potential of feminine evil and describe their heroines' unhappiness with a relish that smacks of sadism, and neither woman is allowed to prolong her wickedness beyond the end of the narrative. Titillatingly naked except for her magnificent hair which is cinched around her body by the snaky belt, displayed for her lover 'as Eve might have stood before Adam', Ayesha is confirmed as the embodiment of the (deadly) eternal feminine; but the revolving pillar of flame, source of her immortality, destroys her at the moment of triumphal union with the reincarnated Kallikrates, metamorphosing the blooming Eve into a hideous shrunken mummy. MacDonald's Lilith, another despotic queen who uses her beauty to manipulate and deceive and, like her namesake, a destroyer of tiny babies, is eventually captured and held in the House of Bitterness to repent if she can. Lilith's terrible inner struggle is described in voyeuristic scenes of physical onslaught: a white-hot serpent bores into her terrible wound, opening her to the hell of self-knowledge, and her writhing soul lies 'naked to the torture of pure interpenetrating inward light'. She is finally rendered harmless by mutilation, her clenched fist, last remnant of her evil, again phallically lopped off by Adam with a sword given him by the avenging angel, and she is consigned to Adam's house of death to 'sleep the sleep' until her final awakening into heavenly goodness.

Perhaps unsurprisingly, the enchantress found her way into children's literature, and both Hans Andersen and C. S. Lewis wove her into versions of the Eden story. Andersen's 'The Garden of Paradise' tells of a young prince who yearns for the delights of the Garden of Eden and is finally carried there by the Eastwind. He is greeted by the Fairy of the Garden, a beautiful young woman who introduces him to all the wonders of her magic realm. The Prince is so happy that he wants to stay in the garden for ever, but the Fairy warns him that he can only do this if he obeys one small prohibition. Every evening, she will beckon him to follow her, but he must resist because she will lead him to the hall where the tree

29. Modest Mary dispenses the host to the elect, while an opulently naked Eve deals death. Berthold Furtmeyer, *Tree of Life and Death*, *c.* 1478–89.

30. Mary Magdalene as a reformed whore, identified by her alabaster pot and penitent's tears. Rogier van der Weyden, fifteenth century.

31. Mary Magdalene abandoning her sinful life to follow Christ. Dante Gabriel Rossetti, *Mary Magdalene at the Door of Simon the Pharisee*, 1858.

32. William Blake, *Satan, Sin and Death*, 1808. Sin, with multiple reptilian fanged tails, guards the gates of Hell, while the fearful shadow Death threatens Satan with his dart.

33. A mermaid with a fish in her grasp, symbolizing a human soul caught by the enchantment of evil. Misericord in Exeter Cathedral, *c.* 1230–70.

34. A mermaid socializing with the devil and an evil wyvern, on a sixteenth-century misericord in Bristol Cathedral.

35. The serpent
with leathery wings
and claws eagerly watches
as Adam remonstrates with
Eve. Rembrandt van Rijn,
Adam and Eve, 1638.

36. Laura trades
innocence for the
goblins' forbidden fruits.
Dante Gabriel Rossetti,
'Buy from us with a
golden curl', drawing
for Christina Rossetti's
Goblin Market, 1862.

37. A reptile-tailed girl with reversed hands offers an ambiguous commentary on love's transitory pleasures. Agnolo Bronzino, *An Allegory with Venus and Cupid*, c. 1550.

38. Lilith lovingly caresses a snake, symbol of woman's dangerous eroticism. The Hon. John Collier, *Lilith*, 1887.

39. Annette Kellerman with a mermaid's scaly tail and flowing locks in Kate Carew's caricature of silent-cinema vamps with a moneybags victim, early twentieth century.

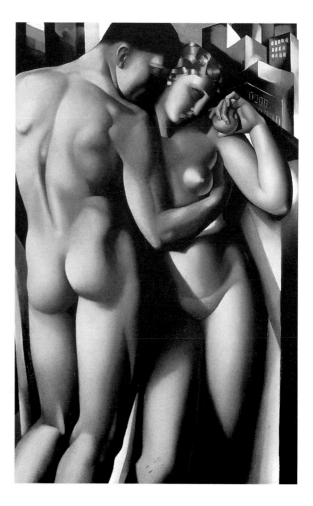

40. The Fall transposed to the dangerous glamour of an urban landscape. Tamara de Lempicka's moodily erotic *Adam and Eve*, 1932.

of knowledge grows and, if he bends to kiss her lips as she sleeps beneath the tree, Paradise will vanish, ' "Sorrow and labour will be your lot." ' But the Prince follows the shimmering girl when she calls him and creeps with her under the branches of the tree, confident at every moment that he is still strong enough to draw back, until finally he bends, sees that her eyes are wet with tears, and kisses her on the mouth. Like Keats' knight, he awakens to darkness and cold; the Fairy and Paradise are gone, and black-winged Death tells him that he must wander the earth for a time to expiate his sins, and then may regain the garden if he is ' "good and holy" ', but

> 'if his thoughts are wicked and his heart still full of sin, he will
> sink deeper in his coffin than Paradise sank, and I shall only go
> once in every thousand years to see if he is to sink deeper or to
> rise to the stars, the twinkling stars up there.'

Andersen's version of the temptress is essentially benign: her function is to test the hero and she weeps at his failure, although paradoxically it is her tears that finally goad him to the forbidden kiss. Lewis' beautiful witch is selfish and greedy, a powerful catalyst for evil. In *The Magician's Nephew*, the first of a series of novels that explore the Christian theme of loss and redemption, the great lion Aslan sings the empty land of Narnia into being, summoning all variety of plant and animal life just as God created the universe by his vivifying word, but even at this promising beginning, evil enters the new kingdom in the form of the beautiful but terrible Queen Jadis. It is she, not Eve, who eats a silver apple from the magic tree and as a result gains Lilith's legendary qualities of 'unwearying strength and endless days like a goddess', although, again, the suggestion is that her magical powers will do her no good. She flies away to the north of the world, where she grows 'stronger in dark Magic', but as Aslan points out, ' "length of days with an evil heart is only length of misery and already she begins to know it" '. Like MacDonald's Lilith, she is condemned to suffer the inner scourge of her own wickedness and must ache accordingly.

Forbidden fruit

MASOLINO PAINTED EVE with a fig (*fico*), as did Michelangelo, perhaps a visual pun on *fica*, the vulgar Italian term for the female genitalia, but it was an identification of the forbidden fruit that would have pleased some Rabbis. Rabbi Jose told the story of the royal prince who had sinned with a slave girl, and who was consequently banned from court by the king. The young man went from door to door, begging the slave girls for shelter, but they all refused him, until finally he knocked on the door of the girl who had been his partner in sin. She opened her door and took him in. The Rabbi argued that this confirmed that the forbidden fruit was a fig: only the fig tree was prepared to donate its leaves to cover the nakedness of the guilty pair. But other Rabbis thought it might have been grapes, a citron, even wheat or bread, the staff of life. In the Middle Ages, the fruit was widely believed to be an apple, perhaps because Latin *malus* could mean apple or evil, but also because of the amorous connotations of apples in classical and Christian tradition. That prodigious traveller John Mandeville described 'apples of Paradise', the local name for bananas, growing in Egypt: they were sweet and delicious and when cut open revealed the figure of the Cross; melons were known as 'Adam's apples' and had a toothmark in the side like a man's bite. In the seventeenth century Linnaeus endorsed the Arab tradition by naming the banana *Musa paradisiaca* and the plantain *Musa sapientum*, reflecting the fruit's origins and its reputation for donating wisdom, although, as Jane Grigson points out in her *Fruit Book*, he probably took the *sapientum* from Pliny who wrote that the wise men of India lived off the banana. Rose Macaulay was sure that the only fruit that could have provided the 'magnificently inebriating effects wrought by its consumption on both our parents' must have been a mango.

Whatever the identity of the original fruit in the garden of Eden, what it came to represent in the Christian tradition was the power of sexual desire, and it was woman herself who became the forbidden fruit, the tempting object that must be resisted. In a culture which equated sexual abstinence with morality, women were blamed for male straying: it was their fault if men were irresistibly drawn to sexual sin. What was denied women was any expression of their own sexuality, their own desire. Christianity developed a prohibitive folklore on the subject of female rapacity, insatiability and so on, characteristics that were fictionally represented by adventuresses such as Defoe's Moll Flanders and Thackeray's Becky Sharp. But such women exploit their sexual attractiveness for gain, trading their bodies for income and, if possible, social status. When 'desire' alone is at stake, women often seem immobilized, unable to speak out without impropriety or the risk of losing the beloved through 'unwomanly' behaviour. Jane Austen's chaste heroines are forced to suppress their feelings, or to make them known only through stratagems that may not succeed. Marianne Dashwood is cruelly punished for her open passion for Willoughby, with social opprobrium, sickness almost to death and finally a respectable marriage to the quiet, reliable Colonel Brandon, although from some perspectives he might seem to be a better bet than the too-charming, worldly Willoughby. Similarly in George Eliot, female sexual desire is negated or deflected on to the man so that it becomes his responsibility. When Maggie Tulliver and Stephen Guest are overcome by mutual attraction in a conservatory, Stephen is driven mad by Maggie's bare arm and rushes to kiss her wrist while she draws back shocked. There can be no doubt that his warm flesh exerts a profound influence over her nerves and senses, but George Eliot does not permit her openly to acknowledge this. The lush, overheated atmosphere and the mere fact of Stephen's powerful presence have to speak for her. When Stephen rows Maggie down the river, she lapses into trance, induced apparently by sexual languor, but again she is acted upon rather than proactive – she allows herself to be run away with and, when forced to acknowledge what has happened, she withdraws from Stephen and her tacit acceptance of him as her lover. She parts from him and goes home, to find her character wrecked.

Dorothea in *Middlemarch* is similarly constrained from admitting her passion for Ladislaw, and some readers have been unable to understand why the beautiful, wealthy, talented Dorothea should have married this rather drifting, undynamic young man. Dorothea's physical agony – she literally writhes on the floor – when she thinks that Will is having an affair with Rosamond makes it quite clear what Dorothea wants from Will: she is sexually in thrall to him and has had enough of 'intellectual' bonding. Her marriage to the 'dry stick' Casaubon has taught her the terrible cost of denying the body's claims – a sacrifice which was recognized by her family and friends long before she understood it herself. In *Daniel Deronda*, George Eliot puts a subtly different emphasis on female sexual desire – or its lack. Gwendolen's fastidious distaste for sex expresses her recoil from its implications for women – subjection in marriage to a husband's will. Again and again she stresses her wish to be free, unimpeded, allowed to do what she wants, and she only marries Grandcourt because she thinks in her girlish way that she can subject him. We can only guess at her husband's epicene intimacies, but there are hints of a sexual sadism that would have been particularly repellent to fastidious Gwendolen, who can hardly bear even her mother's touch. George Eliot is very clever at showing the cost of failing to listen to one's instincts: Gwendolen's body had told her in a myriad tiny recoils that she did not like Grandcourt, that it was deeply dangerous to her essential self to allow him to approach too near her.

What made Thomas Hardy's *Tess of the d'Urbervilles* so unusual for its period – it was published in book form in 1891 – was that it examines the implications of female sexual desire, not through the passionate vaunting of parity between male and female that Charlotte Brontë placed on Jane Eyre's lips when she declared herself equal with Rochester at the feet of God, but through Hardy's sympathetic exploration of the power of 'nature'. The early section of the novel tells of the brief liaison between the country girl Tess Durbeyfield and the red-lipped Alex d'Urberville, an encounter which leaves her pregnant and shamed before her family and the tiny rural community among whom they live. Tess meets Alex when her impoverished parents persuade her to seek kin with the wealthy d'Urbervilles, a mother and son newly settled in the neighbourhood. Although Tess's own family have far more claim to the ancient d'Urberville name, Alex's father having simply annexed it when he made his fortune, Alex enjoys the charade and hires Tess to tend his mother's poultry, attracted by her precocious voluptuousness, 'a luxuriance of aspect' and 'a fulness of growth, which made her appear more of a woman than she really was'. In a novel which will dwell in loving detail on the contrast between the lush Froom Vale, scene of a passionate courtship that occupies a lavishly fecund spring and summer, and the wasteland of Flintcomb-Ash where Tess endures a bitter winter's exile, this description is particularly meaningful. What Hardy is saying is that Tess is ripe for the plucking, a tempting fruit that the sensual, greedy Alex cannot resist. Late one evening Alex offers Tess a lift home on horseback from a dance and allows his horse to wander in the mist out of their path. Nested in a sheltered woodland, Tess falls asleep and succumbs 'to adroit advantages he took of her helplessness'. Gossip recalls reports of sobbing in the woods that night, and Tess very quickly leaves Alex and returns home, but she does first spend a few days with him, 'temporarily blinded by his ardent manners'. Later she bitterly reproaches herself, feeling that her lack of love for him only makes her behaviour the more inexcusable: '"My eyes were dazed by you for a little, and that was all."'

Tess has learnt the bitter lesson that 'the serpent hisses where the sweet birds sing' and '[a]n immeasurable social chasm was to divide [her] personality thereafter from that previous self of hers', but her simple mother's final response to the situation is, '"'Tis nater, after all, and what do please God"', which is precisely Hardy's view of the matter. As the pregnant Tess hides herself away at her parents' home, feeling that the natural world around her participates in her story, the moaning wind reproaching her and the rain 'the expression of irremediable grief at her weakness in the mind of some vague ethical being', Hardy robustly rebuts her fancies as 'based on shreds of convention' and 'a cloud of moral hobgoblins':

> It was they that were out of harmony with the actual world, not she. Walking among the sleeping birds in the hedges, watching the skipping rabbits on a moonlit warren, or standing under a pheasant-laden bough, she looked upon herself as a figure of Guilt intruding into the haunts of Innocence. But all the while she was making a distinction where there was no difference. Feeling herself in antagonism she was quite in accord. She had been made to break an accepted social law, but no law known to the environment in which she fancied herself such an anomaly.

Hardy's point is that Tess's sexual capitulation to Alex only matters because of society's 'moral hobgoblins'. In the world of nature, mating and reproduction are instinctual and Tess's prematurely ripe body had fulfilled its 'natural' outcome, however mistaken her choice of partner. Once she has recovered from her morbid self-absorption and her baby's death, Tess's spirits rise once more, an ebullience as spontaneous as 'the sap in the twigs': 'It was unexpended youth, surging up anew after its temporary check, and bringing with it hope, and the invincible instinct towards self-delight.' Like a plant revitalized in springtime, Tess puts her past behind her and moves to the luxuriant landscape of the Valley of the Great Dairies, where 'milk and butter grew to rankness', only to find her 'nature' unexpectedly opposed once more by 'moral hobgoblins' in the person of Angel Clare.

When Hardy offered the novel for serialization in *Macmillan's Magazine*, the editor responded frankly: 'You use the word *succulent* more than once to describe the general appearance & condition of the Frome [*sic*] Valley. Perhaps I might say that the general impression left on me by reading your story . . . is one of rather too much succulence.' The love affair between Tess and Angel Clare develops among scenes of almost preternatural fecundity in which Tess becomes implicated, her mellow sexuality seeming to participate in the burgeoning landscape as if she were some latter-day fertility goddess. When she first arrives at Mr Crick's dairy, she finds a group of 'prime milchers' waiting to be milked in the yard. '[N]ourished by the succulent feed which the water-meads supplied at this prime season of the year', they are bursting with milk: 'Their large-veined udders hung ponderous as sandbags, the teats sticking out like the legs of a gipsy's crock; and as each animal lingered for her turn to arrive the milk oozed forth and fell in drops to the ground.' Tess's breath will become sweetly perfumed with all the butter and milk and honey that she consumes during her stay at the farm, and this physical nourishment plumps out her flesh and makes her all the more desirable to Clare, as does the environment in which they daily meet. Their first significant encounter is in a wild part of the garden one June evening, a spot which is 'damp and rank with juicy grass which sent up mists of pollen at a touch' and which seems to absorb Tess into its clammy profusion: she creeps through the brimming undergrowth, 'gathering cuckoo-spittle on her skirts, cracking snails that were underfoot, staining her hands with thistle-milk and slug-slime, and rubbing off upon her naked arms sticky blights'. Surrounded by such brimful generation, Tess becomes absorbed into it, a human embodiment of its seductive secretions and branchy entanglements, but its purpose is that relentless drive towards mating and reproduction that has already cost her dear. As the temperature heats up, so do passions at the farm and, amid 'the oozing fatness and warm ferments of the Froom Vale, at a season when the rush of juices could almost be heard below the hiss of fertilization', the other young dairymaids fall in love with Angel. They too are victims of their instincts and writhe 'feverishly under the oppressiveness of an emotion thrust on them by cruel Nature's law – an emotion which they had neither expected nor desired ... each was but portion of one organism called sex'.

Even Angel Clare is not immune to plashy Nature and her cruel law, but the sensitive Tess had soon perceived in Angel 'something educated, reserved, subtle, sad, differing', and his passions are leavened by the harsh sexual code of the faith he has renounced and his narrow idealism. Although he eventually succumbs to the pagan atmosphere of the dairy as personified by Tess, his discomfort with sexuality, the conventional morality which eventually destroys his relationship with her, is never entirely absent from their encounters. Angel apostrophizes Tess as ' "a fresh and virginal daughter of Nature" '; she is 'a visionary essence of woman' whom he gaily names as Artemis and Demeter without perhaps recalling all the attributes of these deities, but other definitions of the female are available to a young man brought up in the Christian tradition. One summer's day he returns to the dairy after a visit to his parents to tell them about his intention to marry Tess. As he begins to descend to the 'fat alluvial soil' in the valley below, there is a deepening of the atmosphere: 'the languid perfume of the summer fruits, the mists, the hay, the flowers, formed therein a vast pool of odour which at this hour seemed to make the animals, the very bees and butterflies, drowsy'. Everyone is asleep at the dairy, the essential afternoon nap of farmworkers who rise before dawn, but Tess has just come down to attend to the skimming and he catches her yawning, sees 'the red interior of her mouth as if it had been a snake's'. His brain primed with rational justifications for his physical response to Tess, his body tensely attuned to her in the heady atmosphere of the drowsing vale, Clare subconsciously sees her as the serpent, the Tempter in the Garden of Eden. She has become Swinburne's primordial female: 'her head leans back half sleepily, superb and satiate with its own beauty . . . the idea incarnate of faultless fleshly beauty and peril of pleasure unavoidable', and a little later Hardy himself compares her to Eve.

When Tess eventually confesses her affair with Alex d'Urberville, even though Angel has just told her of his own shortlived dissipation with a stranger, she becomes transformed in his eyes from the 'fresh and virginal daughter of Nature' to a woman whom he cannot respect and whose history will bring opprobrium on their children. What he has failed to understand, despite his instructive experience of the Valley of the Great Dairies, is that 'Nature' is not virginal, that her drive is towards sexual consummation, and that she is careless how this aim is achieved. As Hardy wrily comments when Tess first meets Alex:

> in the present case, as in millions, it was not the two halves of a
> perfect whole that confronted each other at the perfect moment;
> a missing counterpart wandered independently about the earth
> waiting in crass obtuseness till the late time came. Out of which
> maladroit delay sprang anxieties, disappointments, shocks,
> catastrophes, and passing-strange destinies.

In *Tess*, Hardy explores these disappointments and destinies, the chance meetings and missings that prevent or delay the Platonic reunion of the two ruptured halves and, in the process, claims the validity of the sexual instinct for women as well as men. Tess may be the forbidden fruit incarnate, but she cannot be blamed for her sexuality, nor for her beauty which she makes every attempt to use responsibly, and Hardy demonstrates that Angel Clare is equally tempting, but less cautious how he uses his powers. As a result of his marriage to Tess, one young girl is driven to drink, another to attempted suicide and the third becomes severely depressed. What is at fault is not desire, but the 'moral hobgoblins' that condemn men and women when their sexuality, 'cruel Nature's law', leads them astray, and Hardy's summing-up of his blighted heroine appears in the subtitle to the novel: 'A Pure Woman'.

Tess is an Eve twice tempted, first by Alex's flattering attentions and then by her love for Angel, and what she experiences during the latter's ardent courtship is the anguish of the divided will that St Augustine wrote about so passionately in the *Confessions*. In his case, the choice was between sensual pleasures and abstinence; in her case, between marrying Angel under false pretences or not marrying him at all. For both, the desire for gratification wrestles with the moral requirement for renunciation. Christina Rossetti's *Goblin Market*, first published in 1862, vividly dramatizes this struggle in her story of two sisters and their very different approaches to the goblins' forbidden fruit and, in doing so, like Hardy, returns the Eden myth to its origins as a story of female temptation and fall. In place of the fevered images of wily woman's 'faultless fleshly beauty' so favoured by her brother and his friends, she tells a piquant tale of a young girl who, like Eve, cannot resist the 'peril of pleasure unavoidable'.

The poem is set in a fairy world where two young girls live alone together in a little house which they keep immaculately clean. Every day, they milk cows, churn butter and cream, bake wheat cakes and fetch in honey, and at night they sleep together in their curtained bed, like 'two blossoms on one stem'. But their happiness is disturbed by the goblin men who morning and evening troop through the glen calling their wares, the most tempting, juicy fruits imaginable:

> 'Plump unpecked cherries,
> Melons and raspberries,
> Bloom-down-cheeked peaches,
> Swart-headed mulberries . . .
> Figs to fill your mouth,
> Citrons from the South . . .'

But these are fairy fruits and who knows what dubious soil may feed their 'hungry thirsty roots', while the goblins themselves, despite their dove-like voices, are diversely bizarre:

> One had a cat's face,
> One whisked a tail,
> One tramped at a rat's pace,
> One crawled like a snail . . .

Sensible Lizzie resists their enticements, but one evening Laura exchanges a golden curl for a taste of their enticing fruits:

> [She] sucked their fruit globes fair or red:
> Sweeter than honey from the rock,
> Stronger than man-rejoicing wine . . .
> How should it cloy with length of use?
> She sucked and sucked and sucked the more . . .
> She sucked until her lips were sore . . .

When she returns home, Lizzie reminds her of poor Jeanie who had met the goblin men by moonlight, eating their fruit and wearing their flowers, mysteriously grown in bowers where it is eternally summer. Jeanie never saw the goblin men again, pined away and very quickly died, a fate which seems likely to overcome Laura, for from that day she cannot see or hear the goblin men, although Lizzie is as aware of them as ever. Ravished by the unique savour of the fruit, Laura yearns for a second taste; her hair turns grey, and she dwindles and neglects her household tasks until finally Lizzie resolutely sets off to encounter the goblins and purchase some fruit.

The goblin men are delighted to take her silver penny, but will not allow her to carry the fruit away, insisting that she must eat it there and then. When she refuses, they begin to jostle and claw her, hissing and barking, and pressing the fruit against her tightly closed lips until the juices:

> syrupped all her face,
> And lodged in dimples of her chin,
> And streaked her neck which quaked like curd.

Worn out by her stubborn resistance, they eventually disappear and Lizzie rushes home to Laura:

> 'Hug me, kiss me, suck my juices
> Squeezed from goblin fruits for you,
> Goblin pulp and goblin dew.
> Eat me, drink me, love me . . .'

But when Laura kisses her pulp-smeared sister, the juice turns to wormwood on her tongue and she is struck by a terrible seizure which leaves her unconscious. Her life seems to hang in the balance, but when morning comes, she awakens refreshed and restored. Later, the sisters marry and have children of their own, and Laura tells them the story of her loss and recovery, bidding them to cling closely together:

> 'For there is no friend like a sister
> In calm or stormy weather;
> To cheer one on the tedious way,
> To fetch one if one goes astray . . .'

Like Andersen's 'The Garden of Paradise' and Lewis' *The Magician's Nephew*, this ambiguous poem may be read on one level as a classic Christian narrative of Fall and Redemption. The tempting serpent becomes the goblin men with their seductive dove-like voices, the fruit they offer seems paradisiacal in its fresh succulence, their flowers are plucked from bushes that are ever-blooming like the trees in Paradise, and the effect of eating the fruit is exclusion (Laura can no more hear the goblin men or buy their fruit), pining and death. Laura is redeemed by her sister's willing self-sacrifice, a confrontation with the evil goblins in which she is reviled and buffeted as Christ was beaten by his tormentors before the crucifixion, but which pulls Laura back from the grave and restores her to the fullness of life before her 'fall'. The outcome for both sisters is Eve's destiny of marriage and motherhood. It is also an extremely erotic poem, in its voluptuous descriptions of the fruit, in Laura's eager consumption of it, her gorging and sucking and excited licking of her fruit-stained sister, and in the furry capering of the wheedling goblins. There is a suggestion that what the goblin men offer is sexual. Jeanie had fallen ill and died 'for joys brides hope

to have', and Laura's grief and dwindling might be the sickness of a
seduced and abandoned girl.

But the poem also suggests the tension between desire and
abstention, the fractured will that had so troubled Augustine, and
Rossetti's Laura and Lizzie seem to represent violent internal oppositions, two antagonistic sides of one personality, that can only be
resolved through self-sacrifice and the calming rituals of an ordered
life. Christina's forbidden longing, the fruit she desired to gorge,
may have been sexual, although it is unlikely that she would have
written about it so openly; but it was probably for a more generalized pleasure, the indulgence of appetites for attention and praise
that her severe moral code censured, and the poem symbolically
acknowledges her difficult struggle for self-suppression, a conflict
that she addressed more openly in many of her shorter poems. It
was dedicated to Maria, Christina's sister, a devout Christian who
eventually became a nun, the 'calm' to Christina's 'storm', and
William Rossetti acknowledged that the final tribute to sisterhood
might well imply that Maria had helped Christina through some
'spiritual backsliding'.

GOBLIN MARKET is light in tone despite Laura's trouble, one of
Rossetti's most assured and bewitching poems, rich, strange and
ambiguous, Laura living through temptation and fall to enjoy a
happy motherhood which yet looks wistfully back to the 'pleasant
days long gone/Of not-returning time'. By re-connecting the Eden
story with its core narrative, a young woman's greedy eating of
dangerous, tantalizing fruit, and allowing her to be redeemed
through a sister's love, Rossetti liberated woman from her role as
wicked temptress while restoring her to her central place in the
drama. Rossetti was not alone in her revisionist treatment; many
other women writers have explored aspects of Eve's history in
narratives that extend the boundaries of the popular myth of the
'tempting woman' into sometimes surprising new territory.

CHAPTER 11

EVE TELLS HER OWN STORY

[T]here is no fruit in the garden of knowledge it is not our determination to eat.

OLIVE SCHREINER, *Woman and Labour*

———•◆•———

O LIVE SCHREINER'S short story 'Three Dreams in a Desert', published in 1891, is a powerful and moving evocation of visionary experience. Her narrator, whose sex is not revealed, is travelling by horseback across an unnamed African plain. Overcome by the burning sun, s/he falls asleep and in a dream sees a woman stretched out on the ground, a great burden tied to her back and her body piled high with the sand that has for centuries flowed over it. This ancient woman is attached by a broad cable to a man who stands beside her, gazing out across the desert. As the narrator watches, the woman is released from the band of Inevitable Necessity that binds her burden to her and begins with great difficulty to struggle to her knees, although she is still hampered by the man. In a second dream, the narrator sees a woman advance out of the desert to the steep banks of a river, where she is met by the old man Reason. He tells her that the only route to the Land of Freedom is by climbing down the banks of Labour and through the deep waters of Suffering, but first she must cast off her garments of Ancient-received-opinions and her shoes of dependence, and must cross the river clothed only in the white robe of Truth. As she tries to set off, the old man delays her; he has seen something hidden beneath her robe. It is the tiny winged child, Passion, whom she wants to take with her to the land of Freedom, where he will grow into Friendship. But Reason will not allow her to take the precious child; left on the bank, he will fly to the other side of his own accord and welcome her as the adult Love. The woman, now white-haired with age, still lingers on the bank and cries out in anguish, '"Oh, I am alone! I am utterly alone!"' But,

coached by Reason, she hears the sound of thousands of feet beating
a path at her heels, the multitudes who will follow her and whose
stacked bodies will bridge the waters of Suffering to make a path for
the entire human race. And so the woman grasps her staff and turns
to walk down the dark path to the river. Again the narrator dreams,
and this time sees an idyllic vision of heaven on earth, a place where
men and women walk together without fear . . .

Schreiner's vision of the ancient, suffering woman, whose body
is the first building block of the bridge across which humanity will
eventually trek to freedom, recalls Shirley Keeldar's titanic Eve,
with her 'strength which could bear a thousand years of bondage',
and proposes a new world of truth and equality between the sexes,
where men and women, no longer yoked together and burdened
by the past, are able to walk freely hand in hand. The power of
Schreiner's vision lies in its evocation of the woman's suffering and
her determination to endure for the good of humankind. She is
never named as Eve, but the identification is suggested by her
immense antiquity, her original freedom to wander at will with the
man now tied to her, and the burden of childbearing that made her
subjection a necessity in the age when muscular force predominated.
Schreiner's beautiful fable recalls woman's age-old endurance, her
long-suffering and courage, and proposes a wistful vision of future
accord with man, who is seen as similarly a victim of custom and
prejudice.

Schreiner wrestled out her revisionary feminism with considerable mental and physical suffering, and her work offers a unique
vision of human isolation and the cost of the struggle for a more
truthful coexistence. The story of Eve has attracted commentary by
many other women, writing in different times and contexts, and has
inspired a great variety of response. Since early times, women have
engaged in the long-standing theological debate about the meaning
and interpretation of the Genesis account of Adam and Eve and,
more recently, novelists and poets have developed an imaginative
dialogue with the story of the Garden of Eden. The brief account
given below indicates some of the ways in which women writers
have looked afresh at Eve's story and its implications, breaking away
from conventional interpretations to explore new ways of looking
at the problems of gender roles and procreation, of language and

power, of good and evil, and of the relationship between the values of Christianity and the classical tradition that has so profoundly influenced Western culture. In 'Code-breaking in the Garden of Eden', the afterword to her collection *The Raw Garden* (1988), the poet Helen Dunmore suggests that, 'Perhaps the Garden of Eden embodies some yearning to print down an idea of the static and the predictable over our knowledge that we have to accept perpetual changeability', and she proposes a new idea of the Garden as existing 'moment by moment, fragmented and tough, cropping up like a fan of buddleia high up in the gutter of a deserted warehouse'. In the poems that make up *The Raw Garden*, Dunmore turns her back on the 'prelapsarian state of grace' to celebrate 'resilience, adaptability, and the power of improvisation' in humanity's relationship with the natural world, qualities that have long been characteristic of women's lives and are hearteningly present in their fantasies of Eden.

Voices from the past

'SUBVERSION' IS A POPULAR and useful word in feminist studies, implying a knowing naughtiness and willingness to take on the male Establishment that is indeed reflected in the writings of some women about Eve; for others, the effort to rebel even faintly and to propose alternative views was painful and serious, requiring the courage to face disparagement, ridicule, or even legal penalties. What emerges from looking at the commentary of women writers on Christian teaching about the Garden of Eden is a willingness to question received opinion about Eve's behaviour, and to propose interpretations that better corresponded to their own experience and ideologies. One of the earliest surviving accounts of Eve by a woman was the series of commentaries written by the visionary Abbess Hildegard of Bingen (1098–1179). Described by the medievalist Peter Dronke as 'an overpowering, electrifying presence', Hildegard combined formidable scholarship with an intense spirituality and independence of thought. Her meditations on Adam and Eve continued throughout her life; like many of her contemporaries, she reflected on the Garden of Eden as a guide to the meaning of life and God's purpose in creating humanity, and as a means of examining the relationships of man and woman with one another and with God and Satan. Her views on Eve were consistent with her holistic view of woman, an analysis which took account of gynaecology, erotic love and the marriage relationship, and which interpreted Eve's actions and destiny in terms which offered women dignity and hope.

At a period which took an increasing interest in man as the physical representation of God, literally the *imago Dei*, Hildegard radically argued that it was woman rather than man who expressed the humanity of Christ, while man signified his divinity. As Barbara Newman explains in her careful study of Hildegard's theology:

> Adam symbolizes, but does not share, the divine nature. In contrast, Eve both symbolizes and bestows the divine humanity, insofar as she prefigures Mary. It is not by her appearance but by her gift that the woman represents Christ's human nature and bears the stamp of his image . . . Woman's primary significance in the divine scheme of things is to reveal the hidden God by giving him birth. In the meantime, she gives birth to his image in every child that she bears.

Just as man came from the earth and is committed to tilling the soil, so woman labours at his earthly garment in both the figurative and literal sense, she gives birth to him and she covers his body with the garments she has woven and stitched for him; in return he protects her in her weakness. Hildegard uses the image of the mirror to evoke the reciprocity of man and woman: Adam sees his own image and likeness in Eve, but in their mutual gaze are reflected the generations to come, as two facing mirrors endlessly duplicate any object that stands between them and, in procreation, the role of man and woman is complementary:

> in one activity they perform one act, just as the air and the wind work together . . . The wind stirs the air and the air enfolds the wind, so that every green plant in their sphere is under their sway . . . Woman cooperates with man, and man with woman . . .

Hildegard's sympathetic view of human relations extended to her explanation of sexuality in Eden. Where the Church Fathers, following Augustine, believed that if Adam and Eve had not fallen they would have procreated for the sole purpose of reproduction, and regarded the enjoyment of sexuality as a sign of evil or God's punishment for disobedience, Hildegard restored the idea of love and of pleasure in love to the act of generation:

> Adam experienced a great love in the slumber that God sent
> upon him. And God made a form for the man to love, and
> thus woman is the love of man. And as soon as the woman was
> formed, God gave the man the power of creation that by his
> love, who is woman, he might beget children.

In her benign interpretation, the first parents would have lain side by side, gently perspiring, and Eve would have become pregnant from Adam's sweat, imagined as a kind of heavenly dew, giving birth painlessly from her side, as she had been brought forth from Adam.

It is impossible to do justice to the range and complexity of Hildegard's thought in a brief narrative, but until her writings are more widely available in translation, most readers can only explore her ideas through the work of scholars who have studied and attempted to explicate her texts. This marginalization of one of the great religious thinkers of the Christian Church, whose humanity and breadth of practical as well as scholarly knowledge made her work so particularly relevant to any debate about the status and function of women, suggests the difficulties which female religious commentators have faced in developing a counter tradition to the typically misogynous readings of the Church Fathers. The occasional voice speaks out, only to vanish again, and there is a lack of the continuity and cross-referencing to one another's work by early feminist theologians that is so characteristic of their male counterparts.

The world of the writer Christine de Pizan (1365 – c. 1430) could not have been more different from that of Hildegard. She was born in Venice, but the family moved to France after her father, a physician and astrologer, had been appointed to the court of

Charles V. Christine was brought up in the artistic, intellectual environment of the French court and when she was about fourteen married Etienne de Castel, a notary and secretary. The marriage was a love match and produced three children, but then Christine's life, so far idyllically happy, was struck by the double misfortune of the deaths of both father and husband, the latter in 1389, leaving Christine and her young family almost destitute. With great presence of mind, she took the unprecedented course for a woman of becoming a professional writer, looking for patrons to support her work. Her long literary life produced lyrical and love poetry, and a number of substantial allegorical and political works which commented on contemporary issues. Christine was spirited in the defence of women and when Jean de Montreuil, provost of Lille, misguidedly praised the *Roman de la Rose*, an allegorical poem about a young man's search for love which includes a misogynous second half written by Jean de Meun, Christine enthusiastically put her own point of view in an exchange of letters with leading male humanists of the period, the first salvos in the centuries-long debate on the status of women known as the *Querelle des femmes*.

Christine's upbeat ideas about Eve were set out in *The Book of the City of Ladies*, a work in which Christine explains how, browsing through her library, she is disheartened and even partly persuaded by the harsh criticisms of women by centuries of male authors. At this point, three female figures, Reason, Rectitude and Justice, appear and encourage her to build the City of Ladies, founding a new tradition of writing that celebrates female achievement. Eve is among the important women rehabilitated by Christine, who construes her formation from Adam's rib as proof that 'she should be at his side as a companion and not at his feet like a slave, and also that he should love her as his own flesh'. The circumstances of Eve's creation were as favourable as possible: woman 'was made by the supreme craftsman. And in which place was she made? In the earthly paradise. And of what? Of vile matter? No, but from the noblest matter that had ever been created: it was from the body of man that God made her.' She was similarly robust in asserting that Eve was formed equally with Adam in the 'image of God', which she interprets as referring not to the material body, but to the soul: 'God created this soul and put completely equal souls, one as good and noble as the other, into the female and male bodies.' As for the claim that man was exiled from Paradise because of Eve, Christine points out that 'it is through woman that man reigns with God'. Man 'has gained a higher good through Mary than he lost through Eve, when humanity was joined to the Deity, which would have never happened if Eve's misdeed had not occurred'. Men and women should both be happy about a fault which has, paradoxically, brought them honour: 'For as low as human nature fell through the created beings, the higher it was lifted up by the Creator.'

The Renaissance humanist, Isotta Nogarola (1418–66), also took up cudgels on Eve's behalf. In a series of letters exchanged with another distinguished humanist, the Venetian Ludovico Foscarini, she argued the relative responsibility of Adam and Eve for the Fall, defending Eve against Ludovico's accusations that she was clearly the guiltier party because she was more severely punished, acted out of pride, and caused Adam to sin. Isotta's response was that Eve sinned less than Adam because she was by nature weaker than Adam, lacking his intellect and constancy, which was why the serpent decided to approach her. In any case, God had given the responsibility not to eat the forbidden fruit to Adam rather than Eve. As for the question of the harsher punishment, Adam received hard labour and death while Eve was only sentenced to pain in childbirth. Isotta's retaliation did not end the debate, which continued to rage furiously through a number of letters and ended without either side acknowledging defeat. What is interesting is that Isotta apparently felt no reticence about defending Eve on the grounds of her inferiority to Adam, while Ludovico's arguments, conversely, tend to stress Eve's ability to be accountable for her own acts and to influence Adam. Unlike Christine de Pizan, Nogarola seems to have swallowed the long tradition of woman's weakness, and uses this double-edged instrument in Eve's defence.

The debate about the nature and worth of women was continued in England during the late sixteenth and seventeenth centuries in a series of pamphlets which attacked and (less frequently) defended women in verse and prose. *Jane Anger her Protection for*

Women, published in 1589, cites the two-part creation of Genesis 2 to prove woman's superiority:

> The creation of man and woman at the first (he being formed
> *in principio* of dross and filthy clay) did so remain until God saw
> that in him his workmanship was good, and therefore, by the
> transformation of the dust which was loathsome unto flesh, it
> became purified. Then, lacking a help for him, God making
> woman of man's flesh – that she might be purer than he – doth
> evidently show how far we women are more excellent than men.

But it is not just the greater purity of women's material bodies that gives them the edge; women's bodies are fruitful 'whereby the world increaseth', and by their 'wonderful' care 'man is preserved'. Women have benefited the world spiritually through the Virgin, Mary Magdalene and Eve: 'From woman sprang man's salvation. A woman was the first that believed, and a woman likewise the first that repented of sin.' Anger would not have agreed with Isotta Nogarola on the question of woman's inconstancy; on the contrary: 'In women is only true fidelity: except in her, there be [no] constancy', and she goes on to extol all the benefits to men of female 'huswifery', a list that may resonate with many women today:

> In the time of their sickness we cannot be wanted [i.e. done
> without], and when they are in health we for them are most
> necessary. They are comforted by our means; they nourished [*sic*]
> by the meats we dress; their bodies freed from diseases by our
> cleanliness . . . Without our care they lie in their beds as dogs
> in litter and go like lousy mackerel swimming in the heat of
> summer. They love to go handsomely in their apparel and
> rejoice in the pride thereof, yet who is the cause of it, but our
> carefulness to see that everything about them be curious [i.e. neat
> and fastidious]?

And yet, she continues triumphantly, 'They confess we are necessary, but they would have us likewise evil.'

One of the most famous attacks on women was Joseph

Swetnam's *Arraignment of Lewd, idle, froward and unconstant women*, printed in 1615 under the unconvincing pseudonym of Thomas Tel-troth. Swetnam's pamphlet was hugely popular and regularly reprinted for another hundred years, but, ill-written, nasty and derivative, it provoked a furious response from women pamphlet-eers. Rachel Speght was probably the daughter of a Yorkshire clergyman who held parishes in London from 1592. Her *A Mouzell [Muzzle] for Melastomus, The Cynical Bayter of, and foul mouthed Barker against Evahs Sex*, was written in 1616 when she was still under twenty, but it is an impressively learned work in which she carefully lists the traditional Bible-based arguments against women in order to knock them down, one by one, like a gaggle of male Aunt Sallies. To the accusation that woman brought death and misery by listening to Satan, she points out that Satan approached woman first as the weaker vessel, but that Adam was equally guilty. In eating the fruit, he too was ambitious to become like God; he too was unfaithful in believing Satan rather than God ('Ye shall not surely die'); and if he had really disapproved, he could have simply reproved Eve and reminded her of God's commandment. As a result of his disobedience 'the whole earth was cursed', while Eve only brought punishment to the female sex. Adam and Eve were not aware of their nakedness until Adam had eaten the fruit, 'as if sin were imperfect and unable to bring a deprivation of a blessing received, or death on all mankind, till man (in whom lay the active power of generation) had transgressed'. God's promise to Eve that by her seed the serpent would be crushed and Adam's naming of her as 'Hevah, Life' proves that 'he is a Saviour of believing women no less than of men'. At the end of her rebuttal of the complaints against Eve, Speght goes on to list woman's excellencies and to explain her purpose, making a spirited attack on those husbands who defined 'helper' to justify their laying 'the whole burden of domestical affairs and maintenance on the shoulders of their wives'. Just as the male pigeon is happy to take his turn at egg-sitting, or among smaller birds the cock is a willing partner in constructing the nest, so much the more should man and woman, 'which are reasonable creatures, be helpers each to other in all things lawful'. It might be a programme for the late-twentieth-century 'New Man'.

The poet Aemilia Lanyer (1569–1645) is perhaps best known today through the historian A. L. Rowse's still-disputed identification of her as the Dark Lady of Shakespeare's sonnets. Daughter of an Englishwoman and an Italian musician, she was brought up and well educated in a noble household. She appears to have married unwisely; her husband, the musician Alfonso Lanyer, reportedly 'consumed her goods', and in 1611, in order to raise money, she published *Salve Deus Rex Judaeorum*, ('Hail God, King of the Jews'), a collection of poetry in which the central poem concerns Christ's death. Lanyer demonstrates her interest in female patronage by dedicating nine of the poems to aristocratic women and, in writing about Christ's passion, she emphasizes the positive role played by women in supporting Christ and his own tender interest in their welfare during his ministry. It was men who betrayed him to his death, and she contrasts this great sin with Eve's comparatively minor fault:

> Our Mother Eve, who tasted of the Tree,
> Giving to Adam what she held most dear,
> Was simply good, and had no power to see,
> The after-coming harm did not appear:
> > The subtle Serpent that our Sex betrayed,
> > Before our fall so sure a plot had laid.

Some of Eve's staunchest supporters were American woman writing in the nineteenth century, early voices in the fledgling women's movement which assert a new independence in their confident revision of familiar Bible texts. Sarah Grimké (1792–1873) published her *Letters on the Equality of the Sexes* in 1838. A fervent abolitionist and for many years a Quaker, Grimké was influenced by the Puritan belief in the validity of personal interpretation of the Bible and the *Letters* astutely argue the case for a scriptural basis for sexual equality. In her letter of 11 July 1837, Grimké discusses the early chapters of Genesis, pointing out that male and female were created equally in the image of God and were jointly given dominion over other creatures but not over each other: 'Created in perfect equality, they were expected to exercise the vicegerence intrusted to them by their Maker, in harmony and love.' In Genesis 2, when God created woman as a help meet for the man, it was to give him an equal companion:

> All creation swarmed with animated beings capable of natural
> affection . . . it was not, therefore, merely to give man a creature
> susceptible of loving, obeying, and looking up to him, for all
> that the animals could do and did do. It was to give him a
> companion, *in all respects* his equal; one who was like himself *a
> free agent*, gifted with intellect and endowed with immortality . . .

When the woman was tempted by the serpent, she 'was exposed to temptation from a being with whom she was unacquainted' and was beguiled by the serpent's subtlety; Adam however was tempted by his 'equal', subject to the same divine constraints as himself, and she uses the same argument as Speght, that Adam could have admonished Eve rather than following her example:

> Had Adam tenderly reproved his wife, and endeavored to lead
> her to repentance instead of sharing in her guilt, I should be
> much more ready to accord to man that superiority which he
> claims . . .

According to the facts set out by the 'sacred historian', Adam showed as much weakness as Eve: 'They both fell from innocence, and consequently from happiness, *but not from equality*.'

Sarah Josepha Hale (1788–1879) published her *Woman's Record* in 1853, a phenomenal 2500-entry encyclopaedia of distinguished women from the creation of Eve to 1850. Hale was not interested in sexual equality and she opposed female suffrage; her platform was woman's superiority to man as 'God's appointed agent of *morality*, the teacher and inspirer of those feelings and sentiments which are termed the virtues of humanity', a role which she was best suited to carry out through her domestic responsibilities as wife and mother. In the Preface, Hale explains that the Fall had an adverse effect on man, rendering him incapable of cultivating, without assistance, any of his good qualities:

Left to himself, his love becomes lust, patriotism, policy, and religion, idolatry. He is naturally selfish in his affections; and *selfishness* is the sin of depravity.

Woman, by contrast, was intrusted by the Creator with 'the mission of disinterested affection; her "desire" was to be to her husband – not to herself'. Through her seed, Christ, Good 'would make war with the Evil, and finally overcome Sin, Death, and the Grave'. She points out that in Genesis 1:28: 'the term *man* included *woman*; the twain in unity, the female being the complement of the male, formed the perfect being made in the "likeness of God"', and she cites the rib story in Genesis 2 as evidence that 'there was a care and preparation in forming woman which was not bestowed on man'. Woman was 'the crown' of creation, 'the *last*, and must therefore have been the *best* in those qualities which raise human nature above animal life'. She could help man in those areas 'where he was deficient': not in his earth-bound task of subduing the world, but by 'her intuitive knowledge of heavenly things'.

These arguments are augmented in Hale's biography of Eve, where she says that Adam and the woman were together when visited by the tempting serpent, which confirms that 'she was the spiritual leader, the most difficult to be won, and the serpent knew if he could gain her the result was sure'. The woman took the decision to eat because of her 'higher faculties of mind', the 'desire for knowledge and wisdom', while the man 'had no higher motives than gratifying his sensuous inclinations'. Adam ate 'because his wife gave him the fruit' and Hale continues with brisk dismissiveness: 'Precisely such conduct as we might expect from a lower nature towards a higher; compliance without reason or from inferior considerations.' God's punishment of the guilty pair is similarly favourably interpreted, with the woman promised the hope of prevailing over the tempter through her seed, while Adam's sentence 'was in accordance with his character, addressed to the material rather than the spiritual in human nature': he was condemned '[l]ike a felon . . . to hard labour for life'. In her robust defence of Eve, Hale demolished the long tradition of Adam's spiritual and intellectual superiority and established Eve as moral arbiter, the hope of humanity's future weal, to be expressed through her given role as mother of all living:

> Thus was motherhood predicated as the true field of woman's
> mission, where her spiritual nature might be developed, and her
> intellectual agency could bear sway; where her moral sense might
> be effective in the progress of mankind, and her mental triumphs
> would be won.

The dissatisfaction of American women with the way in which the Bible was used to endorse female subjection culminated at the end of the century in the publication of *The Woman's Bible* (1895), a collection of 'women's commentaries on women's position in the Old and New Testaments'. Put together by a team of exegetes, it was the first systematic attempt by women to produce their own readings of the Bible narratives that had for centuries been used against them, and the writers drew freely on contemporary scholarship to support their revisionist ideas. Elizabeth Cady Stanton's discussion of Eve's encounter with the serpent and its repercussions demonstrates a characteristic flexibility, wit and common sense. Given the recent discovery of the 'missing link' between ape and man, she says that the Darwinian theory of human evolution is more 'hopeful and encouraging' than the biblical story of the Fall, which gave rise to the doctrine of original sin with 'woman the author of all our woes'. Whatever the status of the Eden story, however, whether allegory or historical fact, Stanton is equally pleased with the woman's behaviour, which shows 'courage', 'dignity' and 'lofty ambition'. The serpent recognized her 'high character' and instead of tempting her with jewels, frocks, luxuries and so on, 'he roused in the woman that intense thirst for knowledge, that the simple pleasures of picking flowers and talking with Adam did not satisfy', and Stanton echoes Hale's schoolmarmish demotion of Adam: 'Compared with Adam [Eve] appears to great advantage through the entire drama.'

As for God's 'curse' of pain in childbearing, Stanton suggests that it was inserted to justify woman's 'degradation and subjection to man' and she continues with a practical self-help programme for the pregnant woman that would make acceptable reading today:

With obedience to the laws of health, diet, dress, and exercise,
the period of maternity should be one of added vigor in both body
and mind, a perfectly natural operation should not be attended
with suffering. By the observance of physical and psychical laws
the supposed curse can be easily transformed into a blessing.

'Some churchmen,' she sniffs, 'speak of maternity as a disability, and
then chant the Magnificat in all their cathedrals round the globe',
and her final word on motherhood is that 'Through all life's shifting
scenes, the mother of the race has been the greatest factor in
civilization.' Stanton's splendidly practical approach to Eve's curse
would have been invaluable to generations of Christian women if,
from the early days of Christianity, such a document could have
been published and promoted in parallel with the punitive admonitions of the Church Fathers. What had made it possible, finally, for
her so freely to criticize ideas that had been regarded for centuries
as God's actual words, written down by his prophet Moses, was the
change in attitude to biblical truth brought about by the Darwinian
revolution. At the end of Sarah Josepha Hale's biography of Eve,
she solemnly noted that 'Adam and Eve were created on Friday,
October 28th, 4004 B. C.' Forty years later, Elizabeth Cady Stanton
was applauding Darwin's theory as preferable to the biblical 'allegory' of Eden, dismissing God's curse on Eve as the insertion of a
malicious scribe, and mocking the hypocritical attitude of churchmen to maternity.

The arguments of these three vigorous supporters of Eve offered
women a new, positive sense of their inheritance from the first
woman and of their own powers and possibilities, but the reality of
how many American women continued to see their lives was
perhaps better represented by the self-sacrificing Marmee in Louisa
May Alcott's *Little Women* (1868), or the taming of the rebellious
Katy in Susan Coolidge's *What Katy Did* (1872), a story which re-
enacted the Eden myth for a contemporary audience and still attracts
a substantial readership. These fictional narratives demonstrated the
mythologies that still governed women's lives, however cleverly
they might be rejected by courageous polemicists. For many young
women the story of Eve's disobedience and punishment in the
Garden of Eden echoed the familiar experience of puberty: the

undermining of the intellectual curiosity and physical freedom of young girlhood by the female biological destiny in which the mind's liberty is constrained by the demands of the body and the imposition of social rules. Eve's painful transition from active girlhood to adult social responsibilities was skilfully reworked in the story of the tomboy Katy Carr, the eldest of six motherless children, whose greatest pleasure in life is to escape to 'Paradise', a dense thicket near the house which in summer is 'full of delightful things, wild roses, and sassafras, and birds' nests':

> it was comforting to remember that Paradise was always there;
> and that at any moment when Fate and Aunt Izzie were willing
> they had only to climb a pair of bars – very easy ones, and
> without any fear of an angel with flaming sword to stop the way
> – enter it, and take possession of their Eden.

But Eden proves surprisingly easy to lose – for Katy, at least – and through an act of wilful disobedience. Like her alter ego Jo March in *Little Women*, Katy is impulsive, untidy, often harsh and tactless with the siblings whom she is supposed to mother, always in trouble for some imaginative act of rebellion, endlessly penitent, but unable to resist the enjoyment of sinning again. When her authoritarian Aunt Izzie puts the new swing in the woodshed out of bounds (but, like God, fails to explain the reason for the taboo), Katy cannot resist tasting this forbidden pleasure. Dreamily she propels herself higher and higher on the swing, more and more daring in her sweeps until she seems to be flying through the air, but at the peak of her climb one of the staples holding the ropes into the roof gives way and Katy is thrown violently to the ground. What follows are years of paralysis during which the eager Katy, immobilized in bed, is gradually tamed into the arts of young-womanhood, learning patience and self-denial, and with exemplary fortitude taking over the management of the household and the children when Aunt Izzie dies of a fever. For Katy – and the thousands of girls who read her history – the message is clear: Katy lost her easy access to Paradise by her disobedience in the woodshed, the tomboyish act of rebellion whereby she literally fell from irresponsible girlhood into the confining and self-sacrificing life of mature femininity, her body constrained to inactivity, her mind disciplined by suffering and self-suppression into an appropriate docility, and channelled into the care for others still characteristic of adult female life. Katy's reward in this seductively written fable is the love and approval of her family and the social community, and Susan Coolidge persuasively endorses the traditional message of the Eden story. Other women novelists reworked the familiar elements of the tale to explore more innovative, although not necessarily more optimistic, views of female – and male – destiny.

'In solitude what happiness?'

MARY SHELLEY'S *Frankenstein*, first published in 1818, explores the human cost of pursuing hidden or forbidden knowledge. Both the scientist Frankenstein and the monster he creates identify at various times with Adam and with Milton's fallen angel, but Eve is absent or marginalized, leaving an emotional and moral void that shapes the plot. Loneliness is the novel's leitmotif, a cry of profound human desolation that anticipates the anguish of Schreiner's Eve as she contemplates the wearisome route across the deep waters of Suffering, 'Oh, I am alone! I am utterly alone!', but, like Adam unpartnered in the garden, it is the male protagonists who yearn for fellowship: the ambitious explorer Walton who rescues Frankenstein from the icy waste at the North Pole, the scientist himself, cut off from family and friends by the knowledge of horrific responsibility, and his monstrous creation, the giant whose loathsome features repel all human sympathy. Again and again, the words 'solitude', 'solitary', 'alone', 'desolate' reverberate chillingly through the text, the bleak keynote of destinies in which human affections are marginalized by vaunting ambition, guilt and the obsession with revenge.

Like Frankenstein, Walton is isolated by his own aspirations, and the novel begins with the letters to his sister Margaret in which he confesses his longing for a friend to share the joys and despairs of his perilous voyage to what he names as '"the land of mist and snow"', an identification with Coleridge's Ancient Mariner that forebodingly recalls the Mariner's severance from divine and human love after he murders the innocent albatross, and his solitary confinement in the torturing landscapes of hostile nature. Even this early in the plot, the reader is instructed in its tragic trajectory: the flouting of nature's laws entails horrific suffering and, in particular, an anguished isolation from one's fellow-creatures. Walton's 'want' of a companion is temporarily assuaged by his chance encounter with Frankenstein, adrift in the freezing waters on a free-floating block of ice, but the scientist's history is a monitory tale of the evil consequences of overreaching. Like Walton, Frankenstein has dared to explore new territory, but in his case, '[c]uriosity', Eve's legendary flaw, has led him to investigate hidden or forbidden knowledge, to aspire to know the 'secrets of heaven and earth', and to pursue 'nature to her hiding-places'. At the height of his powers and ambition, he planned to uncover the best-kept secret of all, to 'unfold to the world the deepest mysteries of creation', the source of life itself. But the cost of his challenge to God, the first and omnipotent Creator, is to find himself cut off from the people he loves, first by the all-absorbing demands of his research, and then by his failure to look after his invention. His negligence leads to the deaths of the people he most loves and to the desperate situation in which Walton finds him, adrift and companionless in an icy wasteland.

At the heart of Frankenstein's narrative is the misery of being cut off from the love and sympathy of one's own kind. Horrified by what he has made in his 'workshop of filthy creation', Frankenstein abandons the monster, who is left to make his way in a world of whose social customs and language he is as ignorant as a newborn baby, and where his massive form and blasted countenance arouse extremes of loathing and abhorrence in the people he timidly approaches for help and companionship. Even more isolated than Frankenstein, he is eventually driven by loneliness and despair into horrific acts of revenge against his creator, which in turn further alienate the scientist from his family and friends. After the death of Frankenstein's brother William, strangled by the monster, and the execution of the innocent Justine for the murder, Frankenstein's 'only consolation' is a 'deep, dark, deathlike solitude' in which he shuns 'the face of man'. Weighed down by the albatross promise to create a companion for his creature, he can take no joy in plans for marriage to his childhood sweetheart Elizabeth and, when in a recoil of repugnance he destroys the monster's female mate at the very threshold of life, he experiences again a terrible alienation, wandering around the remote island where he has based his second workshop 'like a restless spectre, separated from all it loved, and miserable in the separation'. The monster takes a savage revenge, killing Elizabeth on her wedding-night, and Frankenstein is plunged once more into a desolation which finds relief in temporary lunacy and 'a solitary cell'. The end of his story charts his 'destructive and almost endless journey across the mountainous ices of the ocean' as he pursues the monster, an environment and a quest that reflect the wasteland of alienation from God and human affections to which he seems now to be irrevocably committed. Walton's friendship cannot redeem him from this extremity of solitude; his only remaining link with life is to '"pursue and destroy the being to whom I gave existence"'. This ambition is denied him and he dies, at last able to rejoice in the prospect of being reunited with his '"beloved dead"', and advising Walton to '"[s]eek happiness in tranquillity, and avoid ambition"'.

Frankenstein's alienation is the penalty of attempting to annex the divine prerogative to create life and of his failure to nurture his botched manufacture, reflective of a more general inability appropriately to nurture his emotional relationships. The monster's loneliness is the more pitiable because it is involuntary, the result of a physical repulsiveness which makes him universally shunned. Even the child William, whom he seizes with the idea that he is too young to be afraid of deformity and can be educated to be his companion, rejects him as the child-eating ogre of fairy tale. When he finally meets Frankenstein at the edge of the glacier below Montanvert, the monster pleads that it is isolation that has made him wicked, a corruption of his natural goodness caused by despair:

> 'Believe me, Frankenstein: I was benevolent; my soul glowed
> with love and humanity: but am I not alone, miserably alone?
> You, my creator, abhor me; what hope can I gather from your
> fellow-creatures, who owe me nothing? they spurn and hate me
> . . . Shall I not then hate them who abhor me? I will keep no
> terms with my enemies. I am miserable, and they shall share my
> wretchedness.'

The tale he then tells Frankenstein confirms his claim to
primordial goodness: it is the history of the terrible months after he
fled from the workshop, his refuge in the wooden shack next to the
remote cottage of a French family living in exile in Germany, his
struggle to understand and use language and to socialize himself by
spying on the De Lacey family, and of their overwhelming rejection
of him when he finally dares to attempt their friendship and
compassion. In the course of this courageous attempt at self-
education, the monster reveals his essential benignity by his
emotional responsiveness to the family, to their sad history, the
loving kindness they show one another, the music they play and
sing together, and by his acts of benevolence, the secret replenishment of their woodstore and his self-control in feeding off roots and
berries rather than stealing from their meagre stores. But the sense
of his own difference is continually brought home to him:

> 'I was . . . endued with a figure hideously deformed and
> loathsome; I was not even of the same nature as man . . . When
> I looked around, I saw and heard of none like me. Was I then a
> monster, a blot upon the earth, from which all men fled, and
> whom all men disowned?'

His awareness of personal isolation increases as he learns more about
customary social and domestic affections:

> 'But where were my friends and relations? No father had
> watched my infant days, no mother had blessed me with smiles
> and caresses . . . I had never yet seen a being resembling me, or
> who claimed any intercourse with me.'

Like Brontë's solitary spinster Caroline Helstone, a less extreme
'type' of social deformity, he is forced to question his own existence
and destiny: '"Who was I? What was I? Whence did I come? What
was my destination?"'
    One day he chances on a copy of *Paradise Lost* and recognizes
parallels with his own situation in Adam's solitariness as the first
human creature: '"Like Adam, I was apparently united by no link

to any other being in existence"', but Adam's situation was far preferable to his own.

> 'He had come forth from the hands of God a perfect creature,
> happy and prosperous, guarded by the especial care of his
> Creator; he was allowed to converse with, and acquire
> knowledge from, beings of a superior nature: but I was wretched,
> helpless, and alone.'

God made man '"beautiful and alluring, after his own image"', but the monster's form is '"a filthy type"' of Frankenstein's, '"more horrid even from the very resemblance"', and he acknowledges that his true relationship is with the fallen Satan, '"for often, like him, when I viewed the bliss of my protectors [his self-deluding term for the De Lacey family], the bitter gall of envy rose within me"'. Later, when his 'Eve' is destroyed, '"the fallen angel"' will become '"a malignant devil"', whose watchword, like Milton's Satan, is 'Evil be thou my good'. But even Satan has the advantage over the monster, as he points out to Frankenstein: '"[He] had his companions, fellow-devils, to admire and encourage him; but I am solitary and abhorred."' '"Increase of knowledge"' only heightens the monster's sense of being an outcast, rather as eating the fruit of the knowledge of good and evil forces Adam and Eve into exile, and whenever he allows his thoughts to '"ramble in the fields of Paradise"', he recognizes that his fantasies of '"amiable and lovely creatures"' to console and cheer him are but a dream: '"no Eve soothed my sorrows, nor shared my thoughts; I was alone."'

The monster's identification with Milton's Adam and Satan suggests the answer to the riddle of his existence, the troublesome '"Who am I? What is my destination?"' that is stimulated by his close observation of the De Lacey family. When he first encounters Frankenstein on the glacier, he reminds him of his responsibilities towards him and indicates how his malevolence can be controlled:

> 'Remember, that I am thy creature; I ought to be thy Adam; but
> I am rather the fallen angel, whom thou drivest from joy for no

misdeed. Every where I see bliss, from which I alone am
irrevocably excluded. I was benevolent and good; misery made
me a fiend. Make me happy, and I shall again be virtuous.'

What he needs is a companion and he begs Frankenstein to create a
female '"with whom I can live in the interchange of those sympathies necessary for my being"'. His modest requirement is for
'"one as deformed and horrible as myself"' and, while he has few
anticipations of happiness, he and his mate will at least live '"harmless"' lives, free from the misery he now experiences. The creature
demands his mate, '"as a right which you must not refuse to
concede"' and claims that when he lives '"in communion with an
equal"', he will '"feel the affections of a sensitive being, and
become linked to the chain of existence and events, from which I
am now excluded"'. With this companion, he promises that he will
'"quit the neighbourhood of man, and dwell as it may chance, in
the most savage of places"'. Frankenstein reluctantly agrees, but the
monster's Eve only partially materializes. She is almost finished,
botched together from parts of cadavers rather than constructed
from the monster's rib, but at the crucial moment of galvanization
Frankenstein draws back, reflecting that 'she, who in all probability
was to become a thinking and reasoning animal, might refuse to
comply with a compact made before her creation' (which had,
indeed, been the case with the original Eve). Fearing the woman's
possible malignancy, dreading her fertility, the potential for propa-
gating a race of devils to torment humanity, Frankenstein destroys
his female giant, tearing her apart and placing the pieces in a bag
which he fills with stones and casts into the depths of the sea, paving
the way for the monster's final act of revenge: '"I shall be with you
on your wedding-night"'.

Mary Shelley subtitled her novel 'The Modern Prometheus',
identifying her Faustian overreacher Frankenstein with the Greek
hero's theft of Zeus' fire, the forbidden knowledge that he brings to
mankind in a narrative in which revenge similarly plays a crucial
role, but the subtitle also links Frankenstein with a later tale that
credits Prometheus with the creation of man by animating a figure
fashioned out of clay, a similar appropriation of the father god's
powers. Prometheus is not the only mythological anti-hero whom

Mary Shelley links with Frankenstein. Like the monster, his history parallels Adam's; in his case, not the pristine Adam of Eden, but Adam fallen and exiled in the wilderness. As he contemplates his marriage to Elizabeth after so many people he loves have already died, he recognizes that it is too late for 'paradisiacal dreams of love and joy': 'the apple was already eaten, and the angel's arm bared to drive me from all hope'. His 'fall' also recalls the protracted, breath-taking plunge of the rebel angels from the lofty heights of 'the ethereal sky' to the unfathomable depths of 'bottomless perdition'. Walton mentions Frankenstein's awareness of the 'greatness of his fall', and he himself laments his fall from a high destiny, '"never, never again to rise"' in an explicit identification with the over-ambitious Satan: '"like the archangel who aspired to omnipotence, I am chained in an eternal hell"'. The question Mary Shelley suggests but never actually poses is whether he could have avoided that hell by taking better care of his monster, by teaching and protecting him, and eventually providing him with a mate. Such a Utopian outcome seems to have been unthinkable from the moment Frank-enstein first saw 'the dull yellow eye' of his creature open, and understood with 'breathless horror and disgust' the difference between his dream and its hideous realization; and his purpose throughout his experiments appears to have focused on creating life with little thought of how to deal with the outcome, a characteristic lack of empathy that will eventually destroy him. In a final self-justification to Walton, he exonerates himself from blame, but it is difficult to see what Frankenstein did to assure the '"happiness and well-being"' of his creation. As the novel closes, it is the terrible plight of the monster that lingers in the memory, the last torrent of passionate explanation that he pours out to Walton as he hangs over Frankenstein's dead body, and his dignified decision to seek his own death among the 'torturing flames' of the funeral pile:

> 'The light of that conflagration will fade away; my ashes will be swept into the sea by the winds. My spirit will sleep in peace; or if it thinks, it will not surely think thus. Farewell.'
>
> He sprung from the cabin-window, as he said this, upon the ice-raft which lay close to the vessel. He was soon borne away by the waves, and lost in darkness and distance.

These concluding lines eerily anticipate Percy Bysshe Shelley's death at sea, four years after Mary Shelley first published *Frankenstein*, and the conflagration on the seashore about a mile from Viareggio on the western Italian coast when his body was burnt in a funeral modelled on ancient Greek ritual. By a further horrible coincidence, again the random aping of literature by life, the terrible loneliness that permeates the novel's pages and its unanswered questions about human destiny are painfully echoed in Mary Shelley's diary entries in the months following Shelley's death: 'When in utter solitude I weep to think how alone I am . . .', she writes on 21 October 1822, and again on the same date, 'the utter solitude in which I would fain immure myself'; two months later on 19 December, 'Sorrow – Sorrow – Why am I here?', and then with painful resignation,'The extreme solitude in which I now live . . . I felt as if I had already entered my grave – my dreary, companionless but peaceful grave . . .' (17 February 1823). She was twenty-five years old.

Mary Shelley's absentee Eve is the crucial void in her novel, the 'thinking and reasoning animal' who might act independently of her mate, refusing to hide in savage, uninhabited places, or whose prodigious fertility might overrun the earth, as had rebellious Lilith, with demons. The sisters, wives, daughters, female servants who are permitted fictitional life in *Frankenstein* are ciphers, uniformly virtuous and loving, subordinate to masculine authority and dependent on their male relatives for financial support, perhaps a subconscious reflection of Mary Shelley's own situation as a penniless runaway daughter, in an environment where the emphasis was on male activity and creativity. The novel focuses on male needs and aspirations, while the women remain shadowy figures, occasionally highlighted for their fortitude in adversity, or capacity for loving kindness. Mary Shelley's three narrative voices are male, and even her female authorship of *Frankenstein* has been challenged by critics who claim the novel as Percy Bysshe Shelley's work. The Eve who might speak or act for herself is suppressed, denied the vital spark of life, her body dismembered and sunk beneath the waves, weighted down with stones.

Mother Eve

MARY SHELLEY'S *Frankenstein* offers an alternative creation story about the horrific penalties of failing to balance the search for knowledge with living as a social being. In *The Professor's House* (1925), the American novelist Willa Cather similarly examines the creative male's conflict between aspiration and emotional experience in a novel that looks back nostalgically to the pre-sexual, paradisiacal innocence of boyhood, and in which another suppressed and voiceless Eve, this time known as Mother Eve, a murdered woman whose corpse has been preserved for centuries in an abandoned village high up in the New Mexican mesa, is the central, enigmatic symbol of female sexual sin.

The professor of the title is Godfrey St Peter, a man in his early fifties, who has worked all his professional life at the university of Hamilton near Lake Michigan, where he lives with his wife Lillian and their two daughters in an ugly rented house. In the attic which he shares with Augusta, the German woman who looks after the family sewing, he has produced his great work, the eight volumes of the *Spanish Adventurers in North America*, written at night after a regular day's teaching, in a room without the convenience of filing cabinets and storage systems, heated by a potentially lethal gas stove, and lit by a kerosene lamp or the harsh glare of a naked bulb. All his life, St Peter has been sustained by delight, the twin romances of heart and imagination which have illuminated his marriage and his research, but as his project finally draws to a close after fifteen years' hard labour, he finds himself in crisis, the familiar patterns of his life disrupted and his energies dwindling. The apparent cause of the change is the building of a new house, made possible by prize money won by his scholarly publications. His daughters Rosamond and Kathleen have already married and left home, and St Peter is due to join Lillian in the elegant new home with its beautiful downstairs study specially fitted out for him. But as the moment to move arrives, he finds he cannot bear to leave the familiar study at the top of the old house, with its tantalizing glimpse through the window of the 'long, blue, hazy smear' of Lake Michigan, the inland sea where he grew up and whose loss, when his parents took

him away to central Kansas at the age of eight, was the greatest
anguish of his life. He arranges to rent the house for another year
with the excuse that he must have continuity for the final stages of
his work. But what St Peter really wants is solitude and, in the silent
room, the busy domestic life of his children's growing-up stripped
away from the empty house beneath him, he slowly comes to terms
with the changes that the years have wrought in his family and in
his own view of his life. This new understanding nearly destroys
him.

Cather charts the professor's movement towards self-knowledge
through a series of incidents and negotiations, some of which remain
unresolved by the end of the novel, but which reveal subtle changes
in St Peter's thinking and in his relationship with the small community of friends and family within which he operates. One such
incident occurs very early in the novel, in the curious battle over
Augusta's 'forms'. Despite his attempts to immure himself from his
family, St Peter has always had evidence of the presence of his wife
and little girls in the dressmaker's 'forms' that Augusta keeps in the
study, and in her sewing patterns, stored with his manuscripts at
each end of a trunk where the leaves of their separate ' "life work" '
gradually meet and comfortably intermingle in the middle of the
box. When Augusta arrives to move her sewing equipment to the
new house, St Peter helps her to sort out the patterns, the documen-
tary evidence that records the changing physiques of his wife and
daughters, but he resolutely opposes her taking the 'forms'. There
are two of these dummies, one aptly named the 'bust' and the other
a full-length female figure made of wire. The 'bust' looks tantalizingly soft and accommodating, a comforting haven where a weary
head could rest in safety, but in reality it is astonishingly hard and
solid, with 'a dead, opaque, lumpy solidity, like chunks of putty, or
tightly packed sawdust', that somehow always fools the onlooker
into thinking it more approachable than it is. The second 'form', by
contrast, is a wire shell around an inner blank, although when
decked out in a new frock for one of the girls, it acquires a giddy
air, like a lady of light behaviour.

St Peter's clinging to these 'forms' hints at his nostalgia for the
now-past family life, but they also symbolize his physical revulsion
from and disappointment in the living bodies they have so often

mimicked. He tells Augusta that he has never complained about the 'forms' themselves, only of '"certain disappointments"' or '"cruel biological necessities"' that they suggest, and the unexpected unyieldingness of the maternal figure foreshadows his growing awareness of his wife's forceful and active personality, which he comes to see emblematically as 'a hand . . . holding flaming arrows – the shafts of her violent loves and hates, her clear-cut ambitions', and finally as 'a stamp upon which he could not be beaten out any longer'. Similarly, the frivolity and rapacity of the young wire flirt prefigure the greed and worldliness of the newly wealthy Rosamond, made rich when her husband Louie Marsellus develops the patent for a new gas discovered by the young scientist Tom Outland and willed to Rosamond when Tom dies fighting in Flanders. Rosamond's selfish exploitation of her riches is endorsed by her mother, and Kathleen too is corrupted, her jealousy of her elder sister literally casting the ugly green hue of envy across her pale complexion. Looking back on a past in which his house was enlivened by happy children, 'full of pretty fancies and generous impulses', St Peter's regret is shockingly savage: 'Was there no way but Medea's, he wondered?' But if lost innocence cannot be recalled, there is a way to escape the depradations of adult women, as St Peter reminds himself after a particularly bruising shopping expedition with Rosamond. Recollecting Euripides' withdrawal in old age to a cave by the sea, he tells Lillian, '"it was thought queer, at the time. It seems that houses had become insupportable to him. I wonder whether it was because he had observed women so closely all his life."' Later, the equivalent of Euripides' retreat to the cave, his own inner retreat from his family, will seem to him the only way in which he can continue with his life.

St Peter's reference to the '"cruel biological necessities"' embodied by the 'forms' suggests an equivocal response to human sexuality and its accompanying domestic drama that crystallizes at this transitional period into a vivid remembrance of two key stages in his life, the St Peter of his early youth in the Solomon Valley in Kansas, and the intense friendship with the young explorer and scientist Tom Outland which marked the beginning of the rift with Lillian. Alone one long summer while Lillian is on holiday with Rosamond and Louie Marsellus in France, St Peter lies by his beloved lake and lets his mind drift in a kind of waking dream in which he returns to a time which predated marriage, children and academic success, and in which he now feels he was more truly himself than in any of these subsequent stages. In this sustained reverie, he recalls a period when the primitive St Peter was linked into the chain of existence, at one with the earth and woods and water in a state of elemental Truth and Desire which excluded marriage and fatherhood, in which all that mattered was solitude and finally the return to the earth from which he came. This primary being, Adam before the existence of Eve, was the real St Peter, and all that has happened since has been 'the work of this secondary social man, the lover . . . Because there was Lillian, there must be marriage and a salary. Because there was marriage, there were children. Because there were children, and fervour in the blood and brain, books were born as well as daughters.'

As an adult, St Peter's principal link with nature, apart from his swimming and boating trips, is within the walls of the French garden which he had constructed for himself at the rented house, a place of refreshment and retreat made after Rosamond's birth, 'when his wife began to be unreasonable about his spending so much time at the lake and on the tennis court'. But this is not the fecund enclosed Garden of Eden; instead of the fruit-bearing trees favoured by his landlord Applehoff, St Peter lovingly cultivates 'glistening, barren shrubs', plants whose lack of apparent fertility may symbolize the quiescence of pre-pubertal innocence or even the deliberate asceticism of the founding Christian Fathers (according to popular legend, the original St Peter was married but relinquished sexual relations with his wife). His favourite companion in his garden is not the assertive Lillian, whose name recalls Adam's disquieting first wife Lilith, but Tom Outland, with whom St Peter spent many agreeable evenings during an earlier summer when his family had left him alone with his research. It is not, however, in St Peter's garden, but on a rainy night in front of the domestic dining-room fire that he at last hears the painful story of Tom Outland's great adventure, the journey into the heart of the mesa to find a series of cliff villages where once had flourished an ancient civilization that cultivated the arts of peace.

Tom's story is an account of his own fall from innocence into a betrayal of friendship that he will regret for the rest of his short life. It is a boy's tale of daring and hardihood, which has many parallels with St Peter's own research into the Spanish adventurers, and similarly records the painful acquisition of experience. The sixteenth- and seventeenth-century voyages of discovery led to the destruction of sophisticated cultures by greedy, well-armed Spaniards, who ironically justified their activities in the name of the religion that gave St Peter his name; Tom's own exploration recovers an ancient culture that seems to have been destroyed by warlike barbarians, only to lose it to a twentieth-century plunderer, the German Fechtig, who buys up and carries off to Europe all his artefacts while Tom is away in Washington trying hopelessly to persuade the corrupt officials at the Smithsonian to take an interest in what he has found. The effect of his discovery is to tutor him in the persistence of human indifference and greed masked as 'civilization', and in his own lack of generosity when he blames his friend Roddy Blake for selling their finds. The glorious adventure in the mesa cliff dwellings costs Tom this friendship and also, in one of the persistent reminders of Eden that Cather slips into her story, involves the rapid and horrible death of their other companion, the old man who cooks for them, by snakebite.

Henry's death takes place at the time of the new moon, the planet associated in many cultures with female sexuality, the powers of life and death, and with the lunacy to which it gave its own name. As the old man stands on Tom's shoulders, scrabbling to find purchase on the floor of a cavern above their heads so that they can climb up to a new cluster of ruins, a rattlesnake lashes out from the ledge and strikes him in the forehead. Within minutes his face has turned purple and he is out of his wits; two hours later he is dead. The tragedy occurs while Tom, Blake and Henry are plundering the secret domestic strongholds of a society which seems to have been wiped out when most of the population were away from home, perhaps summering on the plains below to tend their crops and flocks. As Father Duchene, the local missionary, interprets the findings, the mesa people had developed their own complex patterns of life beyond the simple need for food and shelter, valuing the domestic and creative arts, weaving and ceramics, over those of '"brute strength and ferocity"', and respecting religious ceremony.

Cather's layered use of symbolism invites a reading that Henry and his friends are punished for probing into forbidden knowledge involving the hidden, domestic, feminine spaces of the mesa people. Within the Christian culture represented by Tom and his friends, the death-dealing rattlesnake recalls the treacherous serpent in the Garden of Eden, but it may also suggest the legendary sacred serpent of the pueblo Indians, kept hidden in the mountains and brought out for secret religious ceremonies, which no outsider is allowed to view.

The story of Mother Eve is similarly suggestive. One of the few bodies they find in the mesa dwellings is the mummy of a young woman, her body preserved by the pure, dry air. The woman has a great wound in her side and her mouth is open in a scream of agony; it is Henry who names her as Mother Eve. Later Father Duchene attributes her murder to sexual infidelity, a liaison with a lover discovered and punished by a jealous husband. While Tom is away in Washington, Blake sells Mother Eve along with all the rest of their 'finds' to Fechtig, but, as he eventually tells Tom, Mother Eve refused to leave them. She had needed a particularly wide box which had forced the mule that carried her too far out from the canyon wall; both had plunged to the bottom.

Mother Eve has multiple possible meanings in the novel. For Tom she represents his heritage, the inheritance of poor boys '"that have no other ancestors to inherit from"'. As he tries to explain to Blake, she is part of the trust '"preserved through the ages by a miracle, and handed on to you and me, two poor cow-punchers, rough and ignorant . . . I'd as soon have sold my own grandmother as Mother Eve"'. But she also symbolizes St Peter's reservations about female sexuality; its power to despoil male innocence, its persistence and durability. Father Duchene does not believe that Mother Eve had anything to do with the fall of the mesa civilization, but her astonishing survival acts as a mute reminder of the sexual sin at the heart of Eden, or perhaps as a hint from Cather that St Peter's attempt to wipe out the effects of sexuality, to return to the innocent singularity of his boyhood, is impossible. Mother Eve's corpse stubbornly remains even when all vestige of her life and beauty has been savagely destroyed.

The wound in the murdered woman's side mirrors Adam's wound when the rib was removed in the Garden of Eden, a reversal of the normal process of birth whose mythical origins scholars have never satisfactorily explained. In a rare reference to the Genesis story, Sigmund Freud endorsed Otto Rank's suggestion that the rib narrative deliberately reverses the details in order to conceal an unpalatable reality. In Rank's view, the 'real' story was that Adam was created from the primal mother Eve and then seduced her, and Freud concludes that Genesis records 'the mother incest so familiar to us, the punishment and so on'. The suggestive gash in Mother Eve's side may implicate both St Peter and Tom Outland in an oedipal immaturity, and there are further clues to support this. While Mother Eve is being carted down the canyon on the back of a mule, Tom is in Washington where his sole friend and sympathizer is a young woman significantly named Virginia, a reminder of the unspoiled territories first colonized by the Europeans across the Americas, but also of the pristine state in which the young boy, according to Freud, at first desires to keep his mother. While his wife and daughter travel in France, St Peter insists on keeping the female 'forms' with their reminder of 'cruel biological necessities' under his eye in his study, the scene of his adult achievement, but he spends the summer by the lake dreaming of the single-minded Truth and Desire of his pre-pubertal boyhood. In both these stories, mature female sexuality is counterpoised by innocent boyish dreams. And even his grown-up daughters do not avoid St Peter's nostalgia and revulsion: 'Was there no way but Medea's . . .'. On the day that he hears that his wife and daughter are rushing home from Europe because Rosamond is pregnant, the irrefutable proof of her active sexuality, St Peter narrowly escapes death from the faulty gas stove, and it is unclear how far he had attempted to rescue himself. The story of Mother Eve suggests that there is no escape from sexuality and its consequences.

But this is only one of several possible readings. *The Professor's House* is a complex novel that draws freely on the symbolism of Eden to produce a narrative with multiple, sometimes contradictory and incomplete meanings. St Peter's pain and his falling out of love with his worldly wife are part of a mosaic that incorporates, among other themes, Lillian's jealousy and anguish at love betrayed, the bitter awareness of ageing, and the struggle of any artist and thinker to pursue creative work in the teeth of domestic demands and worldly pressures. The overall effect is a profound sadness and resignation, the pain of accepting a life 'without delight' that may have mirrored Cather's own pessimistic sense of the dwindling of life's possibilities as she reached her mid-fifties. But it is not the end of the professor's life; as the novel closes he can face the future with fortitude, even though he has been forced to 'let something go . . . something very precious'. What remains is the grim awareness of 'the ground under his feet', the generative earth that as a young boy he had known he must, like Adam, ultimately re-enter, the first and final house built for him, in the words of an Anglo-Saxon poem that he remembers reading in one of his mother's books:

> For thee a house was built
> Ere thou wast born;
> For thee a mould was made
> Ere thou of woman camest.

The archaic smile of the kouroi

THE NOVELIST ANITA BROOKNER is similarly aware of the pain of living 'without delight'. In a series of novels that explore the cost of the getting of experience, she develops an opposition between Christian and pagan behaviour, in love and in life, to present a low-toned, resigned critique of the Christian equation of sensuality with sin and a fatal loss of innocence. In the moral atmosphere of her novels, knowingness and the indulgence of pagan appetites are far more beneficial to the individual than the post-Fall squeamishness of fastidious Christians, whose tentative bite of the apple sticks remorselessly in the moral gullet and, like the rebel angels' dust and ashes, atrophies what it was intended to nourish.

The heroine of *A Misalliance*, published in 1986, is appropriately named Blanche, symbolic of an innocence and chastity that have to do with a lack of wordliness rather than sexuality, and linking her with the cautious medieval religiosity which she comes to understand is her natural spiritual element. Preparing for bed one night, she sees that her face 'had the anxious look, the lugubrious bleached look, of an inhabitant of mediaeval Flanders', while below her long

white nightdress, 'her ribbed Gothic feet shone palely'. Even at her
wedding, she had felt reproached for abandoning her mother, the
latter's friends having decreed for her 'a life of forbearance, prudence, fortitude, humility: all the Christian virtues, in fact' and, as
she embarks on married life with Bertie, she makes the mistake of
trying to please him, forgetting his boredom with obedience. It is
only when she loses Bertie to a younger woman, a thoroughly
modern, technologically skilled temptress deceptively nicknamed
Mousie, that she is forced to understand the speciousness of the
Christian bargain with fate: good behaviour will not necessarily be
rewarded. The resourceful Mousie inveigles Bertie into cohabitation
and divorce by arts that are alien to Blanche, but which she comes
to recognize as the stock-in-trade of the successful: 'For . . . the
world respects a predator, . . . will be amused by, interested in,
indulgent towards the charming libertine.' Blanche's own 'timorous
decency' facilitates Bertie's decampment and marks her as 'part of
the fallen creation, doomed to serve, to be faithful, to be honourable, and to be excluded'. Waiting alone in her well-ordered and
silent flat in the hope of a chance visit from Bertie, she sees herself
as embodying that fallen creation: 'mournful in its righteousness,
uncomforted in its desolation, and living in expectation'.

Blanche's getting of wisdom is expedited by two events, her
visits to the National Gallery and a chance meeting with the feckless
Sally Beamish and her stepdaughter Elinor. With time on her hands
after Bertie's departure, she turns to art for answers to the nagging
question: 'how is it possible that my life has slipped through the net
in this way?' She feels faint in the British Museum when she
encounters 'the archaic smile of the kouroi', life-sized marble statues
of Greek maidens, but in their enigmatic expressions she identifies
'an essential secret knowledge that had always escaped her', a
'certainty' and 'fulfilment' that she then looks for in the nymphs
and goddesses of the National Gallery, which she visits several times
a week. What she learns from the nymphs' 'patrician' smiles is the
arbitrary and mysterious nature of love. 'Love was the passing favour
dispensed by the old, cynical, and unfair gods of antiquity; it was
the passport to the landscape where the sun shone eternally and
where cornucopias of fruit scented the warm air', the Mediterranean
heat and fragrance for which Blanche yearns, for she agrees with

Turner that 'The sun is God'. But 'for those whom the gods disdained, and Blanche felt herself to be one of them, the world was the one after the Fall, where only effort and mournfulness might lead to a promise of safety . . . where nothing gratuitous could be hoped for, and no lavishness bestowed'. Despite this chilling recognition, Blanche persists in her visits to the gallery, looking for a sign that will initiate her into the secret mysteries from which she has so far been excluded, but the sign comes from a more mundane environment, the canteen of the hospital where she does voluntary work and where she first sees three-year-old Elinor, patiently chasing a piece of Battenburg cake around her plate with a spoon in a stoic attempt at self-reliance with which Blanche immediately identifies.

In the 'blind and undifferentiated' smile of Sally Beamish, Elinor's stepmother, Blanche recognizes the 'true pagan' smile that she has been scrutinizing so carefully on the walls of the National Gallery. She sees that Sally 'would operate according to the laws of the old gods rather than huddle in the mournful companionship of the fallen world' and, in the weeks that follow, Blanche is able to watch the pagan world in action. Left behind in London to look after the child while her husband Paul pursues an ill-defined role as companion to wealthy Americans in Paris, Sally lives in elegant squalor in a basement flat, happy to receive whatever discreet monetary donations Blanche cares to leave in a teapot in the kitchen 'to tide her over' while she waits for the good times to roll again. Blanche is not Sally's only benefactor; Blanche's old friend and erstwhile admirer, the fastidious bachelor Patrick, is also drawn in by Sally's airy expectation that pleasure is her due while the burden of adult responsibilities will inevitably be assumed by other, duller people.

Seduced into helping Sally by her fantasy of being of use to the dumb child, whose refusal to talk Blanche interprets as a resolute attempt to maintain self-possession in a hostile environment, Blanche reflects on the chasm that divides womankind, the good women like herself and her neighbour Phyllis Duff, who so closely resembles the virtuous wife in Proverbs, and Sally and Mousie, the 'movers and shakers, careless and lawless', for whom men reserve their 'primitive and half-conscious energies'. Blanche's mistake has been to assume 'the uncomplaining and compliant posture of the Biblical wife when all the time the answer was to be found in the scornful and anarchic posture of the ideal mistress'. It is a question of language, of storytelling; she has read the wrong kind of fiction, been 'shackled by the wrong mythology'. Like Kitty Maule, the heroine of Brookner's *Providence*, and Ruth Weiss in *A Start in Life*, she has chosen a defective narrative for herself, ending up with futility and inertia, while clever Sally's delinquent fictions, her reminiscences of a fun-filled past and careless expectations of an exciting future, breed effectiveness and vitality. As Blanche sets off on her ill-judged visit to the Demuths to plead for Paul who has fallen from favour, the comforting Christian images of compassion-ate mother and humble saints abandon her, and instead the heavens fill with pagan deities, gods and nymphs who 'sail, impervious to mortal needs, above the world of just deserts'. In this piercing vision, product of the gimlet thrusts of migraine, Blanche sees that what is at stake is a huge conflict of principle between, on the one hand, the gods 'striding with all their ideal muscularity into new liaisons, or smiting, wrestling, rising, setting, identifying with the cosmos of which they are embodiments, and bearing in their faces the ardour of the beginning of the world', and on the other 'the confusion of Adam and Eve, mawkishly, stupidly, ashamed, half-heartedly instinctive, and instantly, massively, rebuked'. Despite the ruthlessness and lack of care of the pagan deities, their transformative 'energy and bliss' may in the end be less questionable than that state of cautious timidity in which, like Adam and Eve, 'eternal children with a problematic parent they were too inexperienced to chal-lenge', fallen creation waits anxiously for 'a sign of forgiveness'.

In the end, Blanche understands that her relationship with Sally and Elinor was a 'misalliance', an attempt to go against her true nature; but at the same time, she has learnt from the experience, as she explains to Bertie, that '"there *are* no bad. Indifference to the good is all that is needed."' Aware that it is too late to change the past, to rewrite the role she had cast herself for, she can still attempt to live '"a little more carelessly. Artlessly. That is to say, without art. Art can be very subversive."' As the novel concludes, Blanche, her newly cropped hair making her feel as 'weightless' as one of the nymphs in the National Gallery or the quasi-mythic Sally Beamish, lies in bed in her flat on the eve of her flight to the pagan, southern sun. Night after night during her months of solitude she has heard the tinkle of the cat's bell as it stalks across the lawns outside her window in search of prey, but tonight, for once, the predatory cat, a popular medieval symbol of the fall of the animal kingdom from harmony to mutual slaughter when Adam and Eve ate the forbidden fruit, is silent. Just for one moment, we expect, we hope, that Blanche Vernon has stepped out of the fallen world and into the alternative mythology of the kouroi's archaic smile. But Brookner is too skilled in disappointment and ambiguity for an unequivocally happy ending and, with Bertie's eleventh-hour return, Blanche's transformation from post-lapsarian anxiety to pagan indifference remains in doubt.

Eden revisited

THE SITUATION OF Brookner's Blanche Vernon, forced into unwelcome knowledge by the ways of a world which she had never previously found it necessary to comprehend, apparently has little in common with that of the unnamed heroine of Daphne du Maurier's *Rebecca* (1938), a chilling thriller about the acquisition of damaging knowledge. But the naive girl who becomes Maxim de Winter's bride, successor to the polished socialite Rebecca, is similarly ill-equipped to judge her own behaviour or that of her more worldly-wise husband, and likewise suffers a painful rite of passage from innocence to experience. Brookner's elegant and intelligent fable offers a sophisticated dissection of the Fall; the roots of *Rebecca* lie in romantic fairy tale, a never-never land where things may just possibly turn out for the best, but where, like Psyche or Jane Eyre, the heroine is forced to undergo a series of trials before she can enjoy her princely lover. The novel tells the story of a young orphan, paid companion to a wealthy and vulgar American widow, Mrs Van Hopper. On holiday in Monte Carlo, the girl meets and is unexpectedly courted by the handsome Maxim de Winter, an Englishman whose exotically foreign name hints at the mysterious moodiness which Mrs Van Hopper attributes to the premature death of his beautiful first wife, Rebecca. After their marriage, the girl is taken by Maxim to Manderley, a stately house hidden behind high walls and closed gates, and reached by a serpentine drive that twists through dense foliage before emerging among monstrous blood-red rhododendrons. It is the familiar walled estate of the Sleeping Beauty, of the yearning Beast, of Cupid's secret hideaway for Psyche, or the primordial garden. All is not peaceful in this Cornish Eden, however, and the ingenuous girl undergoes an emotional *rite de passage* from joy at being chosen by Maxim as the new Mrs de Winter, through shame and unease at a social ineptitude that contrasts unfavourably with the savoir faire of her brilliant predecessor, to the terrible knowledge that Rebecca's apparent death by drowning was the result of her murder by the husband who detested her. The novel ends with Manderley in flames, incinerated by Rebecca's vengeful housekeeper Mrs Danvers.

In her portrait of Maxim de Winter, Daphne du Maurier astutely diagnoses the original Adam's need for conformity. Maxim's excessive respect for the status quo, in this case, the familial and social pieties of the wealthy middle class, and for his own comfort and authority within that norm are what lead to his difficulties. Like Adam, who was prepared to accept the passive role of unquestioning obedience that would guarantee a pleasant, undemanding life in Eden as God's gardener and intellectual companion, Maxim is equally protective of Manderley and the position that the inheritance of this grand house offers him. In his case, swallowing the tempting fruit of knowledge – keeping silent about Rebecca's secret life and thereby implicitly condoning it – enables him to remain in Paradise, but Rebecca's indiscretions increasingly threaten Maxim's country idyll and finally, goaded by her taunt that she will pass off a child fathered by her unpleasant cousin Jack Favell (or one of her other lovers) as lawful heir and inheritor of the Manderley estate, Maxim murders his wife. His collusive silence has led to her physical and his moral death.

But this is not the end of the story. Like Lilith, that earlier first wife whom she in some ways resembles, Rebecca's power to implicate other people in her evil schemes operates even when she has apparently vacated the stage. As she had intended, there is no release for Maxim after her death: his life is now polluted by the knowledge of his own violence and his fear of discovery, and Rebecca has left behind her creatures, the slithery Mrs Danvers to act the serpent's part within the walls of Manderley, and her vulpine cousin Jack Favell, who is similarly determined that Maxim shall have no joy of his privileged existence as chatelain of Paradise. Maxim's attempt to return to the prelapsarian garden, his choice of an innocent (and nameless) bride, ends with the loss of Manderley which is reduced to dust in the great fire, and even his ingénue bride is corrupted. When he is finally forced to confess the murder to her, she is fluent in arming him with verbal justifications for his false identification of Rebecca's body, and she doggedly supports him through the inquest and Favell's subsequent attempts at blackmail. During the crisis, Maxim tells her, '"It's gone forever, that funny, young, lost look that I loved"', and her innocence has indeed been wiped out by the need to deal with the crisis that threatens Maxim and their future together. In the extremity of her love, she tempts Maxim all over again with the apple of secrecy, and the de Winters' later relationship will inevitably be tainted by their collusion in deception. At best, like Adam and Eve, they will limp along in mute acceptance of their common humanity, but the bride's prized innocence has been lost for ever. Rebecca's bitter fruit has contaminated everyone and there can be no happy ending. While Rebecca embodies many of the characteristics of the legendary Lilith, refusing to obey Maxim, exerting her sexual authority and haunting his afterlife, the girl is a version of Eve, innocent, receptive, resourceful, an apt partner for exile when the couple seeks sanctuary from society's raised eyebrows in an anonymous European resort, where they drink tea and discuss the English cricket results, convalescents from the cataclysm that has destroyed Maxim's world even as it has finally provided the bride with the 'meet help' role that she had lacked at Manderley.

Saved in childbearing

THE NOVELS DISCUSSED so far have explored persistent questions relating to the myth of Adam and Eve, ideas about good and evil, innocence and experience, and the comparative moralities of the Christian and pagan worlds, but Eve's central biblical function, her destiny as the mother of all living, has played only a minor, equivocal role. *Frankenstein* features a male creator who fabricates his progeny out of scraps from the charnel house; *The Professor's House* again focuses on a male protagonist, who turns away from wife and children to look back nostalgically to a pre-sexual, paradisiacal boyhood. In *Rebecca*, the birth of a child, ironically, threatens male dynastic ambitions, but obversely the lack of children may fatally canker Maxim's second marriage. His murder of Rebecca was to protect the family inheritance, and her triumph is complete when he learns soon after the inquest into her death that she was physically unable to bear a child, but her malevolence towards her husband overshadows his second attempt at happiness. Legitimate children, the goal and solace of the propertied male, seem unlikely once de Winter's *raison d'être* has been destroyed with the burning of his family home, and he and his young bride take refuge in the stagnation and suppressions of a premature retirement.

Brookner's *A Misalliance* also hints at dynastic disappointments. The Demuths' lack of heirs is the main reason that Paul Beamish is able to prey on the couple. Sally is as yet childless, although, as Blanche tartly comments to herself, 'nymphs are not known for their maternal feelings', a criticism that is borne out by Sally's random mothering of her stepchild Elinor. That devoted daughter and wife, Blanche's attentive neighbour Mrs Duff, has no doubt about her yearning for children, and even the subversive Blanche comes to see that a child would have been 'an eternal agent of reconciliation' between herself and Bertie, and would have acted as a channel for her own childish fantasies, 'the last hope of a good outcome in a world flawed by false expectations', but for unexplained reasons, neither Blanche nor Mrs Duff can have children. The young are indifferent to the joys of motherhood; while Sally daydreams about the good times to come, Mousie occupies herself with her career and a noisy social life. But Blanche and Mrs Duff belong to an older generation of stay-at-home wives, and fill empty hours with impeccable grooming and good housekeeping, and in that modest care for others, the anxious service offered by the timid to propitiate fate, that Brookner pinpoints as a marker of fallen creation.

In these novels, motherhood is a more or less significant absence; Eve's central function is subordinate to other more pressing questions about Eden and its equivocal messages, but other fictions bring maternity centre stage in order to question conventional teaching about Eve's role as childbearer and her subjection to her husband Adam. In *Herland* (1915), the American feminist Charlotte Perkins Gilman imagined a Utopian female community devoted to the selective bearing and raising of children which they achieve without the aid of men. A similarly robust celebration of female power and autonomy is Enid Bagnold's *The Squire* (1938), a sensuous evocation of pregnancy and motherhood in which men are again marginalized. Bleaker and more pessimistic in tone, the Canadian novelist Margaret Atwood's *The Handmaid's Tale* (1985), utilizes the Bible-based Christian tradition of motherhood to denounce a totalitarian regime with its masculinist ideologies of inheritance and the related emphasis on women as childbearers. All three novels challenge the received wisdom of male superiority and endorse the solidarity and continuity of female relationships, as mothers, daughters and friends, a network of support and shared experience that makes it possible for society to fulfil its important task of child-raising.

Herland delightfully and outrageously exploits the idea of parthenogenesis, with one woman who is quite literally Mother (or at least Originator) of All Living. The story tells of three young American men who discover a community of women living hidden behind a remote mountain range to which they gain access by biplane. To their astonishment, they find a well-organized society, able to feed, house and educate itself to an exceptionally high standard without male assistance. The community derived in the ancient past from a two-sexed society in which the male population was gradually eliminated by natural catastrophe and warfare. Left to themselves, the women developed the necessary skills of construction, cultivation and mutual cooperation in which a peaceful community could flourish, and eventually one woman spontaneously gave birth to a succession of children, five girls, who in turn bore five daughters each, a pattern which was then repeated to found a new dynasty as the survivors from the old civilization gradually died out. By trial and error over the centuries, the community has established the optimum level of population that can comfortably be accommodated on the land available to them, and voluntary abstention from motherhood has become as important as giving birth, but lifelong motherhood is the sole aim and end of the group, an ideal that is realized by methods of childcare and education that allow everyone to play a role in the rearing of the young.

In the interplay between the three young Americans and their ever-courteous interlocutors, for the women prove eager to discover all that they can about the workings of American society, Gilman wittily exposes the flaws in a system which privileges male aspirations and abilities, encourages rivalry and warfare, and keeps wealthy women under-educated and trapped in the home under the pretext of being ' "loved – idolized – honored" ', while poorer women, generally burdened with larger families, are compelled to work for their livings. As Vandyck Jennings, the most perceptive of the three Americans, comes to understand during the months he spends in Herland, customary male attitudes to women are hypocritical and patronizing: 'We talk fine things about women, but in our hearts we know that they are very limited beings'. His experience of the Herland women demonstrates that motherhood – sentimentalized and idealized by Western males, and secretly despised – is highly valued and protected by this female community, who at the same time carry out all the other functions of administering a population of several million people. In achieving this, they have reversed the gender perspectives which he and his companions have always taken for granted, attitudes that are encoded in language:

> When we say *men, man, manly, manhood,* and all the other
> masculine derivatives, we have in the background of our minds
> a huge vague crowded picture of the world and all its activities.
> To grow up and 'be a man,' to 'act like a man' – the meaning
> and connotation is wide indeed. That vast background is full of
> marching columns of men, of changing lines of men, of long
> processions of men; of men steering their ships into new seas,
> exploring unknown mountains, breaking horses, herding cattle,
> ploughing and sowing and reaping, toiling at the forge and
> furnace, digging in the mine, building roads and bridges and high
> cathedrals, managing great businesses, teaching in all the colleges,
> preaching in all the churches; of men everywhere, doing
> everything – 'the world.'

In contrast to this great welter of masculine activity and achievement: 'when we say *women*, we think *female* – the sex'. But for the citizens of Herland, who have similarly survived two thousand years of their own 'feminine civilization', 'the word *woman* called up all that big background ... and the word *man* meant to them only *male* – the sex'. The implications of this reversal of psychological perspective are demonstrated, with humour and empathy, throughout the novel; the further difference, which by now Van does not need to spell out, is that the women have ignored many of the competitive, aggressive and wasteful activities he lists as characteristic of 'the world', choosing to develop instead a harmonious society where the emphasis is on the production of attractive housing and gardens, with ample nourishment for all, and the cultivation of mind, body and spirit in an atmosphere of mutual support and respect. Above all, it is a society which reveres the original Mother of All Living and regards motherhood in all its plenitude of roles as the most important human function.

Enid Bagnold's *The Squire* is not Utopian. Although it describes a micro-society in which a powerful woman has the upper hand, and is again an energetic celebration of motherhood and female abilities, in this highly stratified social group all women are far from equal. The squire of the title is mistress of the Manor House, an ample country residence which fronts a village green. The master of the house is a merchant who has departed for his annual three-month trip to Bombay, leaving his wife to await the birth of their fifth child and to oversee the activities of a teeming household of children and servants. Reeking of the snobbery and class-consciousness of its period, and sometimes florid and sentimental, *The Squire* is nevertheless a compelling portrait of a mature and well-grounded woman, sure of herself and her place in the world, reflecting on her sexual past and her current identity, and finding energy and consolation in the idea of herself as part of a continuity of women, generations which flow from mother to daughter in a steady stream of resilient femaleness. On a day-to-day level, the squire is busy running a large household, with a surly, misogynous butler, sulky maids and a drunken cook, and four young children – including the ultra-sensitive Lucy – to be cared for and reassured as the birth approaches. But her real preoccupation is with herself, a long, slow meditation on the physical and emotional changes of her life which she teases out in discussions with the midwife and her attractive, unmarried friend, the '"love-woman"' Caroline. Unlike the modern Mousie with her briefcase and technological know-how, or the women of Herland with their wide range of expertise and activities, the squire's life has been almost exclusively devoted to her own sexuality. What Bagnold communicates is an engagement with the body that is its own justification, since it enables the continuation of the human race. Once her child has been born, the squire feels 'a calm, a stoic pleasure in *procession*'; she is '"a pipe through which the generations pass"'. Nursing her baby, she thinks of herself as taking her place 'in a line of women like a figure on a roll of film, her mother before her, her children behind . . . "Lucy," whispered the squire, and had an odd sense that Lucy was herself, that she herself was her own mother, that these three women were one'. Behind this comforting sense of procession, there is a persistent awareness of death, which Bagnold claims as particularly female, a sense of the inexorable life cycle that is reinforced by the rituals of childcare, the routine preparation of meals and organization of schedules. '"Death is the matter with life,"' says the squire, a sentiment echoed by ten-year-old Lucy with her agonized sense of transitoriness, '"Axed – my babyhood! . . . Axed – my life"', and her anxious question to her mother, '"How old are you?"' Only childbirth itself can, momentarily, arrest this cycle: 'a child in the womb or at the breast stops time. Time stands still. Death recedes.' With her 'body already a little threadbare', the squire is ready to enter the female continuum and to see 'her own end as endurable'.

The changes in the squire's body mark the transition from her role as lover to that of wife and childbearer: 'She who had once been thirsty and gay, square-shouldered, fair and military, strutting about life for spoil, was thickened now, vigorous, leonine, occupied with her house, her nursery, her servants, her knot of human lives'. What Bagnold describes is a metamorphosis into asexuality which the squire willingly embraces. To her lovers she was once 'female', but 'now what was left standing at the core was the rock of neutral human stuff, neither male nor female'. Watching Caroline arriving by car at her house on the opposite side of the village green, late at night, with 'the white shirt-front of a man' beside her, the squire thinks, '"I can take nothing of that sort any more."' Caroline is a '"love-woman"', '"made to please"', but the squire is getting '"older and tougher . . . more male"'. She is '"saying the farewell to sex . . . looking to a future in which I shall find again what life is made of, bare life, without mirage, without props"'. While Caroline remains in thrall to her sexuality and the often tortuous relationships with her lovers, the squire is committed to the passionate engagement with her husband and children, a role in which sex has become superfluous, although procreation continues. Again it is a question of language. As Van Jennings had recognized in Herland, the word 'woman' has a specific meaning for men. '"You're the thing that man sees when he says 'woman'"', the squire tells pretty, well-dressed Caroline, but she allocates herself to a new category which she names as '"wumen"': '"hard-working, faulty, honest, female males – trudging down life, pushing the future before them in a wheelbarrow"'. The squire is not the only woman in the novel whose behaviour does not conform to conventional male ideas of 'woman'. The squire's midwife, an idealistic and committed 'priestess' of her trade, whose ideologies were based on those of Bagnold's own midwife Ethel Raynham Smith, believes that a baby's future health depends on optimum birth conditions and, in her dedication to achieving these for mother and baby, she has made her own '"farewell to sex"'. The resourceful squire is quick to find a new name for her as well: '"You're a drone"', she says jubilantly, '"a grand, a gallant, a formidable and nearly divine drone. You and those like you have become a third sex."'

Although Bagnold's squire acknowledges the power and influence of male aspiration and domination, she does not allow masculine ambitions to impinge on her own sense of herself and her goals. At one stage she gave up a love affair '"because I wanted myself for myself"'. This experience changed her: '"It developed the male in me, the *choosing* streak in me."' When she finally married, it was because she had felt moved by compassion for a fellow-being caught up in the cycle of life and death:

'When you learn that another creature is pitiful, is doomed . . .
then you enter with him a ring fence from which you never can

come out. Marriage is like that . . . From battles and intimacy
and love, through the passage of time and the carrying on of a
common life, there springs up a fellow-pity, from the very base
of the heart . . .'

Her tenderness and empathy for her husband are the foundation of
their marriage, the 'battles and intimacy and love' that make up
what appears to be a supportive partnership, although we hear very
little of the husband's role or attitudes. The appetite and energy of
the squire's life, her 'male' ability to enjoy and to discard lovers, and
the self-confident management of her marital household are contrasted with Caroline's vulnerability and susceptibility, qualities
which make her attractive to men and also their victim. Assertive-
ness and autonomy, the 'choosing streak' that the squire regards as a
masculine quality, have facilitated her mastery, literally, of her life
and paradoxically enabled her to fulfil her destiny as mother, so that
'with a deep, female pride, she felt herself an archway through
which her children flowed; and cared less that the clock in the
arch's crown ticked Time away'. In Bagnold's triumphal paean to
motherhood, Eve's curse of childbearing becomes a blessing, the
miraculous passing of life from generation to generation that defeats
time and death, which was surely the original meaning of the story.
For Mother Eve, renamed as 'wuman', Bagnold offers the possibility
of transformation through the experience of marriage and childbearing into something rock-like, finally, essentially, herself; while Eve's
subordination to her husband is redefined as a partnership in which
the squire, with her thickening, vigorous, leonine body, her strong
hands with their blunt fingers, her shrewd and watchful eyes, plays
at least an equal role.

In contrast to Bagnold's vibrant model of upper-middle-class
motherhood Thirties-style, Margaret Atwood's *The Handmaid's Tale*
is a deeply pessimistic study of a society dominated by procreation
and the control of sexuality. Set in the totalitarian Republic of
Gilead, in some unspecified but not too far distant future, the novel
describes an interlude in the life of a young woman whose real
name is never revealed, but who is known as Offred, the Handmaid
of Fred, the Commander whose house she temporarily inhabits. In
a reaction against a breakdown of law and order in which the army

took control, the inhabitants of Gilead have been organized into a stratified society in which each group has its own uniform and strictly regulated codes of behaviour, and the republic is committed to a moral purge in which indiscriminate coupling is taboo and the conception and birth of children is closely monitored. Decimated by civil war and pollution, the population of Gilead urgently needs replenishment, but the men regarded as suitable fathers, the privileged senior officials known as the Commanders, tend to be married to elderly or otherwise infertile wives. In order to boost the population and maintain moral standards, the republic's leaders have drawn on biblical precedent, the barren Rachel's offering of her handmaid Bilhah to Jacob as surrogate childbearer. Nubile young women are selected to be trained as Handmaids and then placed with a Commander and his Wife, and the Handmaid's conduct is modelled on the pseudo-Paul's instructions about seemly female behaviour: the modest apparel, the good works, the silence and deference to male opinion:

'For Adam was first formed, then Eve.

'And Adam was not deceived, but the woman being deceived was in the transgression.

'Notwithstanding she shall be saved by [sic] childbearing . . .'

At the Handmaid's most fertile phase each month, she and the Commander perform a mating ceremony in which the Wife is also, for form's sake, involved; if the Handmaid is fortunate enough to conceive and carry the Commander's child to term, she then gives birth, with the aid of a specially designed Birthing Stool, on to the Wife's knees, in order to fulfil Rachel's words, 'she shall bear upon my knees, that I may also have children by her' (Gen. 30:3). The birth itself is carried out without medical intervention: no drugs or anaesthetics, no inducing, cutting or stitching, in fulfilment of God's words to Eve, 'I will greatly multiply thy sorrow and thy conception; in sorrow thou shalt bring forth children' (Gen. 3:16). Boy children are particularly valued, but whatever the sex of her baby, the parturient Handmaid is quite literally 'saved in childbearing'. Assuming that the child is healthy, she will be allowed to nurse the baby for a few months before being transferred to another Commander to see if she can repeat her success. Unlike the Handmaids who fail to bear, she will never be sent to the Colonies, penal areas whose inhabitants suffer terrible hardships and die prematurely from pollution or disease.

The strict controls do not prevent sexual misdoing, but although men are executed for rape and similar misdemeanours, often in the horrific Salvagings in which an accused man is handed over to a group of Handmaids who are goaded literally to tear him apart like the Maenades dismembering Orpheus, it is the women who come under greatest pressure. The law says that there is no such thing as a sterile man, 'only women who are fruitful and women who are barren', and the requirement for the Handmaids to bear children to Commanders who may in fact be infertile exposes them to blackmail from the doctors who routinely check their wombs and ovaries for signs of disease or pregnancy. When she does not immediately get pregnant by the Commander, Offred's doctor offers to mate with her to provide her with the desired baby, but if she agrees, he may turn out to be a spy, working for the Eyes, the dreaded secret service; if she refuses, he may falsify his report on her fertility and get her shipped off to the Colonies. In the end she has sex, with the connivance of the Commander's Wife, with the household odd-job man, the Guardian Nick, who is too low in status to have a woman of his own. Still pining for her husband Luke and their young daughter, who disappeared when she was arrested, Offred turns to Nick with an appetite that is whetted by the danger of discovery, just as the Commander gets his kicks out of meeting her for illicit games of Scrabble, and eventually takes her, dressed in the tawdry spangles and feathers of prohibited female glamour, to a nightclub where the Commanders mingle with prostitutes, a sexual servicing that is licensed by the state on the grounds that '"Nature demands variety, for men."'

Atwood's novel recreates the conflicts for women of living in a society where their bodies are at the service of the state and where fertility is the supreme goal of a woman's life. There are echoes of the plight of women in early Judaism, with its emphases on female chastity and seclusion, the pressure to bear children, and subjection to rules closely monitored by a group of senior men, but Judaism valued and cared for its women as essential to family and social cohesion and wellbeing. Perhaps the closest contemporary resemblance to the situation in Gilead would be the sexual policing of fundamentalist Islam.

Gender-bender

IN URSULA K. LE GUIN's short story, 'She Unnames Them', Eve and the animal kingdom decide to relinquish the generic names given them by Adam at the beginning of creation. Once the animals have understood that, henceforth, naming can be an entirely personal matter, relinquishing 'the lowercase . . . generic appellations "poodle," "parrot," "dog," or "bird,"' becomes easy, and the immediate effect of the unnaming from Eve's point of view is that she feels much closer to the animals. The distinctions between hunter and hunted, eater and eaten, are removed, and the mutual fear and attraction between different species can be more intimately experienced and enjoyed. Returning her name to Adam, a gift which '"doesn't exactly seem to fit very well lately"', Eve steps out into her new life with 'them', aware of the tremendous possibilities of a language in which nothing is taken for granted: 'My words now must be as slow, as new, as single, as tentative as the steps I took going down the path away from the house, between the dark-branched, tall dancers motionless against the winter shining.'

'Unnaming' is one way of dealing with the patriarchal legacy. Naming defines us, but words have acquired an accretion of meanings which can distort truth, an idea that is explored in A. S. Byatt's Babel Tower (1996), a novel concerned with language and its contexts, and in which, for example, a young woman finds that her positive self-definition as an emancipated female intellectual is rewritten by the divorce court to brand her as promiscuous, unreliable, a 'bad' wife and potentially a negligent mother. Like Blanche Vernon, Frederica finds herself in the wrong mythology, but in her case the public, masculine narrative of the law negates her private life story. As Frederica's experiences show, language is deeply implicated in the social code; the words 'wife' and 'mother' traditionally carry with them a range of expectations and behavioural norms that 'husband' or 'father' have not been expected to accommodate. But is gender simply a matter of naming? In *Babel Tower*, Byatt recalls the legend of the Ur-language, 'the original speech of God, spoken by Adam in Eden, and indeed by God, the Word Himself, when he called the universe into being out of chaos, simply by naming it'. In this original speech, words and things were integrated, '*one*, as a man and his shadow perhaps are one, or a man's mind and his brain', but this cohesion was shattered into multiple, mutually incomprehensible tongues by the presumption of the builders of Babel, and 'the languages of men' became opaque, mysterious, idiosyncratic. One of the questions explored by Angela Carter in *The Passion of New Eve* (1977) is whether gender works in a similar way. Is there a unifying 'Ur-gender' beneath the accreted meanings of words such as 'man', 'woman', 'whore', and even the sexual apparatus that physically identifies 'male' and 'female'? Is differentiated gender behaviour simply a function of the culture and systems of naming that we have inherited?

The New Eve of the title was originally Evelyn, a callous, exploitative young man whose female icon is the glamorous Tristessa, heroine of countless Hollywood movies in which she appears, passive and suffering, doomed to the 'solitude and melancholy' that are a woman's life. Newly arrived in New York, Evelyn is lured home by Leilah, a sexual temptress who becomes Evelyn's plaything and victim, a beautiful woman trapped by her own narcissism and passivity. When an abortion goes horribly wrong, Evelyn flees the city and finds himself in the desert, 'the abode of enforced sterility, the dehydrated sea of infertility, the post-menopausal part of the earth', where he is captured by the women of the biblically named Beulah, Isaiah's new Israel, whose totem is a broken penis and whose leader is a gigantic black woman, the multi-breasted Mother who recalls the savage mother goddesses of the ancient world, Cybele whose priests castrate themselves in bloody rituals, mighty Artemis, Astarte and Ishtar. But Mother's breasts are the result of scientific intervention, a miracle of grafting, and she plans to use her technological skills to transform the aggressively masculine Evelyn into Eve, and impregnate her with her own seed in order to '"reactivate the parthenogenesis archetype"'. Eve will become creatrix and Virgin Mary all in one, producing 'the authentic

Messiah ... born of a man', a mingling of mythologies in which
Evelyn will also be Oedipus/Adam, fulfilling his archetypal yearning
to mate with his mother, for the seed used to impregnate the New
Eve will be Evelyn's own, randomly spurted when he is ignomi-
niouly raped by Mother in the final sexual act of his life as a man.
But although Mother believes that ' "sexuality is a unity manifested
in different structures" ', she and her girls, led by the appropriately
named Sophia, archetype of wisdom in the classical and early biblical
world, attempt to brainwash the newly castrated and remodelled
Eve with a programme of feminization that includes persistent
exposure to every movie made by Tristessa, 'every kitsch excess of
the mode of femininity', and to prepare her for motherhood, they
show her reproductions of the Virgin and Child 'blown up to larger
than life-size, accompanied by a sound track composed of the
gurgling of babies and the murmuring of contented mothers'.
But 'does a change in the coloration of the rind alter the taste of
a fruit?' The New Eve, metamorphosed into a *Playboy* centre-
fold, finds that 'the cock in my head, still, twitched at the sight of
myself'.

   Eve's psycho-sexual conditioning is expedited after she runs away
on the eve of her impregnation, only to be captured once more, this
time by the misanthropic, one-legged poet Zero, who keeps a stable
of wives whom he abuses. Eve is repeatedly raped, a first-person
experience of male domination that is particularly confusing, as an
image of herself as violator intervenes at the moment of penetration,
like an act of 'seppuku, a ritual disembowelment I committed upon
myself'. But, by the end of three months with Zero, 'as savage an
apprenticeship in womanhood as could have been devised for me',
she has 'become almost the thing I was'. Zero's rage towards women
is compounded by his sterility, for which he blames Tristessa, whom
he believes 'blasted his seed' via the cinema screen, because he was
'Masculinity incarnate'; but when he finally tracks her down, living
in retirement in a house protected by high walls and a tree-filled
park, Zero is astonished to find that Tristessa, goddess and feminine
icon, is a man. He now forces Eve to marry Tristessa, both in drag, a
partnership whose sexual ambiguities are truly mind-boggling. As
Eve says, 'My bride will become my child's father', but as for the true
sexual status of either partner:

Masculine and feminine are correlatives which involve one
another. I am sure of that – the quality and its negation are locked
in necessity. But what the nature of masculine and the nature of
feminine might be, whether they involve male and female, if they
have anything to do with Tristessa's so long neglected apparatus
or my own factory fresh incision and engine-turned breasts, that
I do not know. Though I have been both man and woman,
still I do not know the answer to these questions.

By the end of the novel, Mother has become obsolete as history
overtakes mythology in the form of a gang of boy terrorists led by
her own daughter Leilah, a.k.a. Sophia, a.k.a. Lilith. Eve too, the
perfect archetype, is an anachronism, and she retires first to a cave by
the sea where, as she worms her way through the innards of the earth
to the beginning and end of time, she recognizes that 'Mother is a
figure of speech and has retired to a cave beyond consciousness'.
Finally, believing that she is pregnant with Tristessa's child, she sets
out alone in a small boat to cross the ocean to the place of birth, a
journey that may or may not be illuminated by her reflection that
'The vengeance of the sex is love.'

CARTER'S WITTY AND incisive exposé of the mythologies that have
dogged women since Genesis is a fitting place to end this brief
chronicle of female fantasies about the Garden of Eden. Despite the
negative image of Eve developed very early in her history, women
have been prepared to think innovatively about the Genesis account
of origins, opposing unhelpful theology with fresh arguments that
put Eve in a better light, and writing stories that offer new perspectives on good and evil, innocence and experience, and human sexual
behaviour. Eve's story has affected the lives of millions of women
and cannot lightly be discarded, but it can be freed from the 'naming'
of the past, opening up the possibilities for imagination and storytelling suggested by Le Guin's Eve: 'My words now must be as slow,
as new, as single, as tentative as the steps I took going down the path
away from the house, between the dark-branched, tall dancers
motionless against the winter shining.'

AFTERWORD

INTO THE FUTURE

And when the woman saw that the tree was good for food, and
that it was pleasant to the eyes, and a tree to be desired to make
one wise, she took of the fruit thereof, and did eat . . .

Genesis 3:6

———————◦•◦———————

IN HER NOVEL *The Silent Duchess*, the Italian writer Dacia
Maraini tells the story of the Duchess Marianna, a deaf-mute
whose life nevertheless follows the customary pathways of the
wealthy aristocrats of mid-eighteenth-century Sicily. Married at
thirteen to her uncle, a man as trapped by his own fear of
demonstrating affection as his wife is by her inability to speak and
hear, Marianna pursues the traditional female plot of wife and
mother. She watches her children grow up and become independent, and is a faithful and respectful wife to her elderly husband, but
when he dies, her predictable course begins to go awry. She takes a
young lover and then resolutely puts him aside, and rejects the
courtship of a cultivated man of her own age. In her early forties,
she abandons the respectable widowhood that is her only option if
she remains in Sicily, and starts out on a new life of restless travel,
the difficult journey in search of herself.

Marianna's plunge into unexplored territory is the adventure
that Eve embarked on at the beginning of history. In Eve's case,
her step into the unknown predated the conventional female roles
of wifehood and childbearing; she tried to become like God, but
instead found herself trapped within her biological destiny, unable
to get out. And there she and her daughters stayed, locked in
a preordained narrative until very recent times. Even now, the
structure of any alternative narrative is uncertain: like Maraini's
Duchess, women are still trying out plots at different stages of
their lives. There is no definitive path to tread, just multiple
possibilities.

Eve's stunted story is useful as an example of how narrative can catch us out, bind us down, trap us into destinies that we may find desperately uncomfortable. Angela Carter wrote bracingly in *The Sadeian Woman*, 'All the mythic versions of women, from the myth of the redeeming purity of the virgin to that of the healing, reconciling mother, are consolatory nonsenses', invented to obscure 'the real conditions of life', but the myth of Eve was developed to manipulate and control women rather than to console them, however reassuring the versions may have been for men. Read positively as a story about a woman's enterprise and willingness to explore and take risks, it could have been helpful to women, and even the 'curse' of childbearing might have been construed as a gift, a promise of renewal and continuity that compensates for disappointments and betrayals, and all the other ills of life, including mortality. But, except for a few isolated female voices, Eve's story has been read against rather than for women. For over two thousand years, male commentators have plundered her history in an attempt to discover and pin down the nature of Woman, and in Eve's many faces we have a unique record of the male imagination at work, wrestling with the female other. But there is no longer any need for women to live under her shadow. Demystifying Eve – understanding where she came from and how her character evolved – is one way of leaving her behind, but the questions that still remain open for women are the riddles that men as well as women have confronted since the Garden of Eden. They are questions that each generation must ask anew as circumstances change and beliefs are readjusted. Who are we? Who do we want to be? And how do we reconcile our human biology with the plots that attract us – the multifarious ways of living our lives?

Eve's story still has something to offer women. It is a reminder of the difficult choices and compromises of adult life, the requirement to balance exploration and individuation with social and family demands. And Eve had excellent reasons for eating the forbidden fruit: it looked good and was nourishing, and it promised her the priceless gift of wisdom. She took and ate, and was rewarded with the opportunity to pass on her knowledge to future generations. The modern Eve may interpret that destiny in any number of ways; children are not the only gift that a woman can offer the future.

Perhaps what is most important is Eve's recognition of the need to challenge boundaries, to make the imaginative leap, however difficult, unpredictable and even dangerous, into a new phase of existence.

NOTES

Editions of works cited in the Notes are listed in the Select Bibliography.

CHAPTER 1: THE GARDEN OF EDEN

10 **'I taste of death and knowledge'**: Mann, p33.

10 **So God created man**: all biblical quotations from the Authorized King James Version of the Holy Bible, unless otherwise indicated.

12 **a rhetorical device known as aposiopesis**: see Fox (1995), p21, translation of Gen. 3:1 and footnote.

12 **Geneva Bible of 1560**: quoted in *The Shorter Oxford English Dictionary*, vol. 1, Oxford 1983, under headword 'Breech'. The Geneva Bible was known as the 'Breeches Bible', although this rendering of Gen. 3:7 had already been used by Wyclif.

13 **Hawwah**: it is Adam who explains that this means 'the mother of all living', but the etymology and meaning of the Hebrew *ḥawwāh* has puzzled scholars. It is phonetically similar to the Hebrew verbal root *ḥayah* ('to live'), but also to Aramaic *ḥiwyā'*, meaning 'serpent'. See Phillips, pp40–1; Alter (1996), p15.

14 **Dates and authorship of Y and P**: for discussion, see Evans, pp11–13; Pagels (1988), pxxii; Forsyth, p149. Dates have been referred to as BC and AD for the benefit of the general reader, who may be unfamiliar with the more neutral BCE (Before Common Era) and CE (Common Era).

16 **Judea, Samaria and Galilee**: see Meyers, pp51, 122.

16 **far from being 'a land flowing with milk and honey'**: see Meyers, p59.

16 **poor soil . . . a difficult topography**: see Meyers, p51.

16 **deep cisterns . . . the year-round water requirements**: see Meyers, pp54–5.

16 **day-in, day-out routines . . . food production**: see Meyers, pp61–3.

17 **a large family of boys . . . a liability**: see Bird, p55.

17 **Population loss through . . . disease**: see Meyers, pp64–71.

17 **mortality rate for children and adolescents**: see Meyers, p112.

17 **childbirth . . . was risky . . . for mother**: see Meyers, pp112–13.

17 **troubled Israel . . . real suffering**: see Bird, p62.

18 **a lapse of duty**: see Bird, p53.

19 **The Rabbis . . . misogynous jokes**: for rabbinic jokes about women and the rib, see ch. 2 below.

19 **NIN.TI . . . *tsela***: see Evans, p16; Phillips, p28.

19 **Adam had intercourse with the animals**: see Graves and Patai, p65; some Rabbis interpreted Adam's words, 'This is now bone of my bones, and flesh of my flesh', to imply that he had first tried out every beast and animal, but found no satisfaction until he had intercourse with Eve, *Babylonian Talmud, Yebamoth* I, 63a, p420.

19 **Jewish Bible**: renamed by Christians as the Old Testament.

19 **animals are to be dominated**: Vawter, p59, points out that naming and ownership are synonymous, i.e. possession (and domination) of the animals is implicit. Commenting on Genesis 2:18–25, Swidler writes, p26: '[The animals] were to have been understood by, and placed under, the authority of the man – they were not to have been worshipped, even symbolically, as they were in Canaanite and Egyptian cults.'

19 **'. . . yet I have none'**: *Midrash Rabbah, Genesis* I, 17:4, p136.

19 **'This-time, she-is-it!'**: see Fox (1995) translation of Genesis 2:23, pp20–1. See, too, Trible (1992), p95: 'This, finally, bone of my bone/ and flesh of my flesh'; Cassuto, p126: 'This, at last,/is bone of my bones/ and flesh of my flesh'.

19 **St Augustine interpreted the rib story**: Augustine, *City of God*, XII:28, p508: 'the fact that a woman was made for the first man from his own side shows us clearly how affectionate should be the union of man and wife'.

19 **'Heaven's last best gift'**: John Milton, *Paradise Lost*, V:19.

19 **'a companion corresponding to' Adam**: Trible (1992), p90; and see, too, Cassuto, pp127–8; Meyers, pp84–5.

20 **a man leaving his parents and siblings**: see Cassuto, p137, who comments on Genesis 2:24: 'Some commentators regard this verse as an echo of the system of matriarchy, in which the woman was the head of the family. But in the epoch of the Torah this system had long disappeared, and the words that occur later on in our section, *and he shall rule over you* (iii 16), suffice to show that, according to the narrative before us, it is the man who is deemed the family head. The meaning of the verse is simply this: whilst a man is single, he forms part of his father's family, but when he takes a wife, he founds a new family; so long as he is in his father's house, all his love is dedicated to his father and mother, but when he marries, his love for his wife transcends that for his parents.' See, too, Bird, p48, who points out that patrilineal descent and patrilocal residence were the norm.

20 **feminist commentators**: see, for example, Meyers, pp114–17; Trible (1992), pp127–8.

22 **girdled with serpents**: see Baring and Cashford, p459; for Canaanite goddesses, see ibid., pp454–60.

22 **carved wooden images or** *asherim*: Baring and Cashford, pp454–6; Patai, p38.

22 **to be worshipped well into the Temple period**: Patai, p38. Solomon's Temple was dedicated in approximately 964 BC.

22 **Solomon . . . married a Sidonian princess**: see ibid., pp39–41, for Solomon's political marriages.

22 **Solomon introduced the cult of Asherah into royal worship**: ibid., p41.

22 **it lodged . . . three centuries**: ibid., p50.

23 **Asherah's son**: Baal was popularly identified with Yahweh, see ibid., p50.

23 **small clay figurines**: ibid., p39.

23 **the** *Enuma Elish*: I have used the translation by E. A. Speiser in Pritchard, pp60ff.

24 **her reptilian nature**: Tiamat was depicted as a huge snake or even a winged creature rather like a dragon, see illustration 13, and Baring and Cashford, pp273ff, figs 1–3. For the evolution of the dragon battle in Ancient Near East myth, see Forsyth.

25 **the struggle . . . to overcome the hitherto dominant female principle**: see Baring and Cashford for an account of the dethronement of the Goddess.

25 **'tohu-wa-bohu'**: Phillips, p5.

25 **tehōm . . . Tiamat**: ibid., p5; Forsyth, p48.

25 **'Somewhere . . . act of creation'**: Phillips, p5.

26 **'Lock up your daughters'**: for attitudes towards female sexuality in early Judaism, see ch. 2 below.

26 **slippery, upright serpent**: the idea that Eve had sex with the serpent was a later rabbinic intervention: see ch. 3 below.

26 **the serpent had seen Adam and Eve making love**: *Midrash Rabbah*, *Genesis* I, XVIII:6, p147.

26 **Adam had fallen asleep**: ibid., XIX:3, p149.

27 **nakedness . . . had strong connotations of public humiliation**: see Epstein, who comments, p26, that 'throughout the Bible, nakedness is primarily conceived as shameful and only secondarily as immodest'.

27 **It has been suggested**: see Williams, p43, who explains that the Hebrew words for 'good' and 'evil' (*ṭōbh* and *rā'*) refer primarily to humanity's

physical wellbeing, in the sense of things that are useful or beneficial, and those that are harmful. 'The knowledge, therefore, of "good" and "evil", that is of "beneficial" and "noxious" things . . . would appear to be what we should call "scientific" knowledge rather than moral illumination. [Yahweh] does not wish them to know anything of the arts of civilisation, or of the sciences which make society and culture possible: he desires to keep them in happy, child-like ignorance . . . safeguarded from the sorrows which the increase of knowledge brings in its train.' Evans supports this view, p18, arguing that Adam and the woman had an ethical sense from the beginning: they knew, for example, that they were not supposed to eat the forbidden fruit.

27 **the early books of Genesis**: with reference to Genesis 1–11, the books that lead up to the rainbow covenant with Noah and its immediate aftermath (Genesis 12 begins the story of Abraham), Forsyth points out, pp149–50: 'Each of the stories seems designed to illustrate the human propensity to violate the limits imposed by the covenant with Yahweh, even though they are set in the primordial time before any formal covenant existed. Each story, in fact, establishes the need for the covenant, at least in general moral terms'.

29 **Christina Rossetti's 'Eve'**: composed 20 January 1865; text, Crump, vol. 1, pp156–7. **'twelvefold-fruited'**: see Rev. 22:2, where the tree of life 'bare twelve manner of fruits, and yielded her fruit every month'. For discussion of Rossetti's view of Eve, see Diane D'Amico.

29 **the combination of forbidden knowledge with immortality**: Barr, p64, makes the point that, rather than death, disobedience opens up 'the glimmering distant vision of immortality': 'Within the story, most probably, it was assumed that man was going to die in any case. Man was mortal, only gods were immortal, as in all the ancient orient . . . The problem that is opened up by the "Fall" is the possibility of eternal life for man.'

29 **trees in the garden of the goddess Siduri**: Cassuto, p74, points out that the *Epic of Gilgamesh* also uses the phrase 'good to look upon', and he cites these similarities between the two narratives as 'definitely point[ing] to an established poetic tradition in the ancient East, in which Israel shared'.

29 **serpent's theft**: see Evans, p16.

30 **Hebrew ideas . . . considerable change and modification**: for a summary of early Jewish ideas on the afterlife, see McDannell and Lang, ch. 1.

30 **food and veneration . . . blessings**: ibid., pp3–7.

30 **The dead . . . cut off from God**: ibid., p10.

31 **Sin began . . .**: *The Wisdom of Ben Sira*, also known as *Ecclesiasticus*, 25:24, in *The Jerusalem Bible* (1974).

31 **persistent verbal echoes**: for parallels between Creation and Noah narratives, see Fox (1995), pp34, 40.

33 **His 'rushing-spirit'**: Fox (1995) translation of Gen. 1:2, p13, and cf. Gen. 6:3, ibid., p33.

CHAPTER 2: THE VIEW THROUGH ONE PAINTED EYE

40 **The woman, says the Law . . . by God to the man**: Josephus, *Apion*, II:201, quoted in Swidler, p142.

40 **At the cathedral of Saint-Lazare in Autun, France, a melancholy stone Eve**: see O. K. Werckmeister, 'The Lintel Fragment Representing Eve from Saint-Lazare, Autun', in *Journal of Warburg and Courtauld Institutes*, vol. XXXV, 1972.

41 **'the devil's gateway'**: Tertullian, *On Female Dress*, I:I, in Thelwall, vol. I, p304.

43 **it 'was only when the material . . . older than the documents'**: Goldberg and Rayner, p211.

43 **the two magnificent . . . winged figures**: for the Temple cherubim, see Patai, pp70ff.

43 **scholars are now looking at a broader spectrum of archaeological and inscriptional sources**: Kraemer, pp93ff.

45 **the disobedient termagant . . . the York and Towneley biblical cycles**: Muir, p73, and see pp210–11, footnote 59.

45 **some early European religious dramas followed an Eastern legend**: ibid., p73, and see p210, footnote 58.

45 **personal growth, vegetarianism and female bonding**: Michèle Roberts, *The Book of Mrs Noah*, Methuen 1988, ch. 14, pp71–89.

45 **'the ghost in the library . . . sacred texts'**: ibid., p89.

45–6 **a familiar folkloric tradition . . . an old couple**: Fox (1995), p74.

46 **named Isaac, 'He Laughs'**: ibid., p73, for meaning of 'Isaac', and see footnote to Gen. 17:17.

46 **God's renaming of her . . . character and destiny**: ibid., pp70, 73. They begin as Abram and Sarai; both are renamed by God, see Gen. 17:5, 15. As Fox (1995) points out, p70, Abram's name is changed preparatory to becoming the father of Isaac, and also of nations. Sarai is similarly renamed to mark the birth of her son. The act of renaming was 'of the utmost significance in the biblical world. Since a person's name

was indicative of personality and fate, the receiving of a new one signified a new life or a new stage in life.' Sarah is the only woman in the Bible whose name is changed by God, see ibid., footnote to Gen. 17:15, p73; her new name means 'Princess'.

47 'four matriarchs' were buried . . . entombed together: *Midrash Rabbah, Genesis* II, LVIII:4, pp510–1.

47–8 Another rabbinic story . . . Sarah was even more beautiful than Eve: *Midrash Rabbah, Genesis* I, XL:5, p329.

48 his sister: she is, in fact, his half-sister, see Gen. 20:12.

49 tricky Jacob, the Heel-Holder: Fox (1995), p115, translation of Gen. 25:26, and footnote.

50 He who has no wife . . . without atonement: *Midrash Rabbah, Genesis* I, XVII:2, p132.

50 'if he is fortunate, she is a help; if not, she is against him': ibid., XVII:3, p133. The literal translation of *ʿēzer kᵉnegdô*, 'a help meet' (for Adam), is 'a help against him'.

50 gloomy stories about a Rabbi: ibid., XVII:3, pp133–5.

50 'all depends . . . and made him righteous': ibid., XVII:7, p138.

52 the allegorical figure of Wisdom: see Swidler, pp35–6, who makes the point that positive remarks about women in the book of Proverbs are 'really not about women . . . as human beings, but only about women in their relationship to men'.

53 'The procedure . . . of a woman's sexual function': Wegner, p42.

53 The customary *ketubah* . . . for non-virgins: *Mishnah, Ketuboth* ('Marriage deeds') 1:2, in Danby, p245. All text references to Danby's translation. The term *ketubah* refers to the document in which the husband pledged a sum of money to the wife in the event of death or divorce, or to the sum assigned, see ibid., Appendix I, p794.

53 the Mishnah provided legal redress . . . in this matter: ibid., *Ketuboth* 1:1, p245; Wegner, pp21ff.

54 In the case of female slaves . . . other form of sexual intercourse: *Mishnah, Ketuboth* 1:2, 4, p245; Wegner, p22.

54 unmarried girls . . . were virgins: *Mishnah, Ketuboth* 1:2, p245; Wegner, p22.

54 women divorced . . . fetch a lower remarriage jointure: *Mishnah, Ketuboth* 1:4, p245; Wegner, pp22–3.

54 if a man was convicted . . . or an equivalent fine: Exod. 22:16–17; Deut. 22:28–9.

54 women who were presumed not to be virgins . . . no sum was payable: *Mishnah, Ketuboth* 3:2, p248.

55 no fine was applicable . . . paid for her virginity: ibid., *Ketuboth* 3:8, p249; Wegner, pp24–5.

55 the bride-price . . . payable on divorce or widowhood: *Mishnah*, *Ketuboth* 4:2, p249; Wegner, p27.

55 the use for her lifetime . . . she might possess: *Mishnah*, *Ketuboth* 6:1, p253.

55 'Even the poorest . . . wailing woman': ibid., *Ketuboth* 4:4, p250.

55 a wife's maintenance . . . of fig-cake': ibid., *Ketuboth* 5:8, p252; Wegner, pp74–5; for measurements, see ibid., p231, footnotes 132–3.

55 'He must also give her a bed . . . every year': *Mishnah*, *Ketuboth* 5:8, p252.

55 The clothes . . . more clement: ibid., *Ketuboth* 5:8, p252.

55 'The *duty of marriage* . . . sailors': ibid., *Ketuboth* 5:6, p252.

55 Students of the Law . . . Torah study in the academy: ibid., *Ketuboth* 5:6, p252; *Babylonian Talmud*, *Ketuboth*, 62b, quoted in Swidler, pp111–12.

55 Labourers were only allowed a week's abstention: *Mishnah*, *Ketuboth* 5:6, p252.

56 purpose of sex . . . affection: Swidler, pp139–40.

56 refusal of sexual intercourse . . . forced to abstain: *Mishnah*, *Ketuboth* 5:7, p252.

56 routine duties . . . taking her ease: ibid., *Ketuboth* 5:5, p252.

56 'idleness leads to lowness of spirit': ibid., *Ketuboth* 5:5, p252.

56 'Even if she brought him . . . leads to unchastity': ibid., *Ketuboth* 5:5, p252.

56 The proceeds of a wife's work belonged to her husband: ibid., *Ketuboth* 6:1, p253.

56 Failure to do this . . . honour and status: ibid., *Ketuboth* 5:9, p253.

56 widows, divorced women, and unmarried daughters who had reached their majority: see Wegner, ch. 5, pp114ff.

56 a woman 'continues within . . . the husband at marriage': *Mishnah*, *Ketuboth* 4:5, p250.

57 Louisa May Alcott's *Little Women*: first published in North America in 1868.

57 ' "*That* woman was a manager . . . most faithful prop in age': Brontë, *Shirley*, ch. 22, pp378–9.

58 prostitution, slavery, or a subordinate role: see Bird for alternative roles for women.

58 It may be written with anything . . . (. . . the slave): *Mishnah*, *Gittin* ('Bills of divorce') 2:3, p308.

59 'Lo, thou art free to marry any man': ibid., *Gittin* 9:3, p319.

59 'By three means . . . the death of her husband': ibid., *Kiddushin* ('Betrothals') 1:1, p321.

59 the patrician Shammaite group . . . the more liberal, plebeian Hillelites: Swidler, p160.

59 The School of Shammai say . . . *in* anything: *Mishnah, Gittin* 9:10, p321.

59 'Even if he found . . . *no favour in his eyes* . . .': ibid., *Gittin* 9:10, p321.

60 the Mishnah gives examples . . . he was unaware: ibid., *Ketuboth* 7:7, p255.

60 And these are they . . . she will enervate him: ibid., *Ketuboth* 7:10, p255.

60 childlessness was included as a ground . . . look after her in old age: *Babylonian Talmud, Yebamoth* I, 65b, pp436–40; Swidler, p162.

60 personal preference . . . monetary considerations: Swidler, p162.

60 husband not the wife . . . bill of divorcement: see I. Abrahams, *Studies in Phariseeism and the Gospels*, Cambridge 1917, p72, quoted in Swidler, p162.

61 for behaviour as trivial . . . '. . . stay with her husband': *Babylonian Talmud, Gittin*, 89a, quoted in Swidler, p155.

61 I would sooner keep house . . . get rid of her: *Ecclesiasticus*, 25:16–17, 24–6, in *The Jerusalem Bible* (1974), pp932–3.

61 'A perfect wife . . . his life in peace': ibid., 26:2, p933.

62 The grace of a wife will charm her husband . . . a good wife in a well-kept house: ibid., 26:13–16, p933.

62 Like the lamp shining on the sacred lamp-stand . . . are shapely legs on firm-set heels: ibid., 26:17–18, p933.

62 'it is the nature of a man . . . On the contrary!': *Babylonian Talmud, Yebamoth* I, 65b, p437.

62–3 'A man is commanded concerning procreation, but not a woman': ibid., *Yebamoth* I, 65b, p436; *Midrash Rabbah, Genesis* I, VIII:12, p63.

63 'He who does not engage . . . he sheds blood': *Babylonian Talmud, Yebamoth* I, 63b, p426.

63 'If a man took a wife . . . he shall divorce her': ibid., *Yebamoth* I, 64a, p428; Swidler, p140.

63 the responsibility for barrenness . . . 'In private matrimonial affairs . . . he is not in a position to know it': *Babylonian Talmud, Yebamoth* I, 65a, p435.

63 'all rejoice' . . . 'everybody is upset': *Babylonian Talmud, Niddah*, 31b, pp218–9.

63 'As soon as a male comes into the world . . . nothing with her': ibid.,
   Niddah, 31b, p218.

64 she is rushed out of the Temple Court so as not to defile it: *Mishnah*,
   Sotah ('The suspected adulteress') 3:4, p296.

64 her symptoms . . . probably illegitimate: Fox (1995), p681, footnote to
   Num. 5:21.

64–5 A priest lays hold on her garments . . . *to do after your lewdness*:
   Mishnah, Sotah 1:5–6, pp293–4.

65–6 Ben Azzai recommends . . . '. . . the selfsame death': ibid., *Sotah*
   3:4–5, p296.

66 'teach Scripture to his sons and to his daughters': ibid., *Nedarim*
   ('Vows') 4:3, p269.

66 the exclusion of women . . . including communal study of the Torah:
   Wegner, p146, and see pp145ff for discussion.

66 various categories of exemption: for women's observance of positive
   and negative precepts, see Wegner, pp150–3.

66–7 the *shofar*, the ram's-horn, which was sounded on prescribed
   occasions in the Temple and in the synagogue service: *Mishnah*,
   Appendix I, p796.

67 the *mezuzah*: ibid., Appendix I, p795.

67 such as study of the Torah: Wegner, pp147, 155.

67 [Woman's] value as enabler . . . cultic and religious duties of the
   Israelite: ibid., p151.

67 'For three transgressions . . . lighting of the [Sabbath] lamp': *Mishnah*,
   Shabbath ('The Sabbath') 2:6, p102.

68 Concerning menstruation . . . the precept about lighting the
   (Sabbath) lamp: *Palestinian Talmud, Shabbath*, 2:5b, 34; quoted in
   Swidler, pp86–7; see *Midrash Rabbah, Genesis* I, VII:8, p139, for variant
   version. Adam was God's Hallah, the sacred portion that He separated
   out when He poured water on to the dust of the ground, see ibid.,
   XIV:1, footnote 2, p111.

68 Jewish pseudepigraphic narratives: see ch. 3 below.

68 'And do you not know that you are [each] an Eve?': Tertullian, *On
   Female Dress*, 1:1, in Thelwall, vol. I, p304.

68 incumbent on men: Wegner, p155.

69 meals at home . . . unclean objects: ibid., p163.

69 Greek notions of women as 'imperfect' or 'undeveloped' men: see
   ch. 5 below.

69 the purity laws . . . discriminatory against women: see Cohen,
p291.

69 'Praised be God that . . . an ignoramus!': *Tosephta, Berakoth* 7:18, quoted in Swidler, p80.

69 'because the woman is not obliged to fulfill the commandments': ibid.

69 'He who is commanded and does . . . not commanded and does': *Babylonian Talmud, 'Abodah Zarah*, 3a, p6.

70 The Sages spoke in a parable about woman . . . any rights over her: *Mishnah, Niddah* ('The menstruant') 5:7, p751.

70 the right 'to own and dispose of property, to conduct business, to engage in litigation, and most important to choose her own husband from among her suitors': Wegner, p39.

70 a daughter passed to the control of her husband once she was married: *Mishnah, Ketuboth* ('Marriage deeds') 4:5, p250.

71 Rabbi Gamaliel gave his daughter in marriage . . . "woe that he has not gone to school"': *Midrash Rabbah, Genesis* I, XXVI:4, pp212–13.

71 Over thy daughter keep a strict watch . . . a disgraceful daughter poureth forth disgrace: *The Book of Sirach (Ecclesiasticus/The Wisdom of Ben Sira)*, 42:11–14, in Charles, vol. 1, pp470–1, a particularly eloquent translation of this section of Ben Sira.

71–2 In her youth, lest she pass the flower of her age . . . lest she be barren: ibid., 42:9–10, p470.

72 'the man must master his wife . . . will eventually come to grief': *Midrash Rabbah, Genesis* I, VIII:12, p63.

72 'this evil . . . set his eyes upon her': *Ancren Riwle*, quoted in Rogers, p71.

73 'that place of horror . . . an old woman's': Mann, pp119–20.

73 Early Jewish legend . . . to Dinah's brother Joseph: C. Burchard, introduction to *Joseph and Aseneth*, in Charlesworth (1985), p183.

73 Country women . . . carefully indoors: Swidler, p119.

73 'Their women are kept . . . their closest relations': Philo, *Flaccus*, 89, quoted in Swidler, p120.

73 they were to avoid the busy market hours when the streets were teeming with shoppers and traders: Philo, *De specialibus legibus*, III, 171, quoted in Swidler, p120.

73–4 'These are they that are put away . . . or speaks with any man': *Mishnah, Ketuboth* 7:6, p255.

74 Rabbi Berekiah said . . . Her arm became exposed: *Midrash Rabbah, Genesis* II, LXXX:5, p738.

74 the death penalty for women convicted . . . in certain conditions: Swidler, pp148–51.

75 the exotic Watcher angels . . . feminine wiles and lust: see ch. 3 below.

75 'women are evil, my children . . . by means of their looks': H. C. Kee, trans., *Testament of Reuben*, 5:1, in Charlesworth (1983), p784.

76 a man falling from a raised bench . . . to be beneath him: *Babylonian Talmud, Yebamoth* I, 54a, p358; and see Swidler, p129.

76 warnings against walking behind a woman: *Babylonian Talmud, Berakoth*, 61a, p384.

76 crossing a river with a woman . . . (. . . 'A woman's leg is a sexual incitement'): ibid., *Berakoth*, 24a, p145.

76 against talking with women: *Babylonian Talmud, Nedarim*, 20a, p57.

76 looking closely at a beautiful woman . . . a woman's 'gaudy garments': *Babylonian Talmud, 'Abodah Zarah*, 20a–b, p105.

76 'it is as if he gazed at her secret place': *Babylonian Talmud, Berakoth*, 24a, p145.

76 'the early Sages ruled: . . . [a menstruous woman] . . . he will divorce her!': *Babylonian Talmud, Shabbath* I, 64b, p307.

76 stibium to paint one eye: ibid., *Shabbath* I, 80a, pp380–1.

76 an elaborate arrangement . . . down to the chin: Swidler, p122.

77 Instead of scent, a stink . . . brand marks instead of beauty: Isa. 3:24, in *The Jerusalem Bible* (1974), p976.

78 twentieth-century misogyny: see Joan Smith, *Misogynies*, London 1989, for examples of male revulsion at the female body.

78 if you consider what is stored up inside those beautiful eyes, and that straight nose . . . the storehouses and depositories of these things?: John Chrysostom, 'An Exhortation to Theodore After His Fall', quoted in Rogers, p18.

79 ' "By recognizing . . . may lead to a quarrel" ': R. J. H. Shutt, trans., *Letter of Aristeas*, 250, in Charlesworth (1985), p29.

79 seductively as a bride . . . to entertain the newlyweds: *Midrash Rabbah, Genesis* I, XVIII:1, pp140–1; Ginzberg, vol. I, p68.

80 a reference in Exodus . . . '. . . nullify the Torah': Rabbi Dr S. M. Lehrman, M.A., PH.D., trans., *Midrash Rabbah, Exodus*, XXVIII:2, London 1939, p332.

81 Said He: . . . yet she is a gadabout: *Midrash Rabbah, Genesis* I, XVIII:2, pp141–2.

81 'this is she . . . all night': ibid., XVIII:4, p142, and see footnote 5; also Ginzberg, vol. I, p68.

81–2 'And why must a woman . . . in front of the corpse . . .': *Midrash Rabbah, Genesis* I, XVII:8, pp138–9.

CHAPTER 3: ANGELIC LUST, DEVILISH ENVY

86 successive modifications by a series of editors: see Forsyth, pp152–9.

86 *1 Enoch*: also known as the *Ethiopic Apocalypse of Enoch*.

86 a tradition developed . . . in the course of its history: E. Isaac, in Charlesworth (1983), p5.

86 'looked like . . . travels and reaches afar': *1 Enoch*, 32:3–4, E. Isaac, trans., ibid. All text references to Isaac's translation unless otherwise indicated.

86 'Book of the Watchers': *1 Enoch*, chs 1–36.

86 the 'Watchers' . . . as God's spies or agents: see Forsyth, pp166–7, and Daniel 4:13, 17, 23.

87 'on account of this matter . . . beliefs with pen and ink': *1 Enoch*, 69:9–10.

87 Azaz'el teaches . . . '. . . tinctures and alchemy': ibid., 8:1.

87 'to the degree . . . blood and oppression': ibid., 9:9.

88 a 'terrible place' . . . the offending angels: ibid., 18:10–19:1.

88 ' "shall become sirens" ': *1 Enoch*, 19:2 in Charles' translation, vol. II, p201, and see footnote. See, too, Forsyth, p181.

88 'There is no home-coming . . . at their father's return': Homer, *The Odyssey*, XII, p190.

88–9 'Their cries, their flowering meadow . . . Pure desire, pure death': Vernant, p104.

89 the Watcher angels . . . by God's decree: *Jub.*, 5:6. All references to translation by O. S. Wintermute, in Charlesworth (1985).

89 to teach humanity . . . law and order: ibid., 4:15.

89 In the course of time . . . into cannibalism: ibid., 5:1–2.

89 The Watchers . . . destroy one another: ibid., 5:3–11.

89 demoniac spirits survive . . . into evil ways: ibid., 7:27, 10:1.

89 Noah points out . . . ' ". . . Satan upon the earth" ': ibid., 10:3–11.

89 *Jubilees* . . . the Eden story: see ibid., 3:17–31 for the Fall.

89 the mating of the Watcher angels . . . the origin of evil on earth: ibid., 4:22, 5:1–2, 7:20–5.

90 ' "leads the young person . . . over a cliff" ': *Testament of Reuben*, 2:9; all references to translation by H. C. Kee, in Charlesworth (1983).

90 The story Reuben tells . . . to do with Bilhah: ibid., 3:11–15, 4:4.

90 ' "women are evil . . . means of their looks" ': ibid., 5:1.

90–91 if their good looks are not persuasive . . . ' "by decking themselves . . . take them captive" ': ibid., 5:2–4.

91 ' "harlot's manner" ' . . . Watcher angels: ibid., 5:4–6.

91 the angels were overcome . . . gave birth to giants: ibid., 5:6.

91 ' "destined for eternal punishment" ': ibid., 5:5.

91 whoever or whatever a woman fantasizes about . . . well into the early modern period: see Fletcher, pp72–3.

91–2 'Victim to his libido' . . . intrinsically dangerous: Helena Kennedy, *Eve Was Framed: Women and British Justice*, London 1993, pp119–20.

92 ' "So guard yourself . . . senses from women" ': *Test. Reub.*, 6:1.

92 *Judith*: all text references to *The Jerusalem Bible* (1974).

92 she washed all over . . . every man who saw her: *Judith*, 10:3–4.

92 ' "Who could despise . . . "Better not . . . their fingers!" ' ': ibid., 10:19.

92 ' "We shall be disgraced . . . everyone will laugh at us!" ': ibid., 12:12.

93 'it was not the sons of Titans . . . the scimitar cut through his neck!': ibid., 16:6, 9.

94 Sin began with a woman . . . die: *Ecclesiasticus*, 25:24, *The Jerusalem Bible* (1974), and see chs 1 and 2 above for references to Ben Sira.

94 This might apply . . . it was Eve whom Ben Sira had in mind: Forsyth, pp222–3.

94 Gader'el who 'misled [i.e. seduced] Eve': *1 Enoch*, 69:6.

94 PIERO DELLA FRANCESCA'S fresco: painted in the mid-fifteenth century, the cycle is based on the True Cross narratives in *The Golden Legend* (c. 1260). In this version, Seth is refused the oil of mercy, but is given a branch from the tree of knowledge which he plants on Adam's grave at the time of his death. The tree that grows on the grave eventually supplies the wood for the cross on which Christ is crucified. See 'The Finding of the Holy Cross' in Jacobus de Voragine, vol. 1, ch. 68, pp277ff.

95 ' "the enemy" ': *Apoc. Mos.*, 7:2. All text references are to M. D. Johnson's translation, Charlesworth (1985), unless otherwise indicated.

95 'My lord Adam . . . troubles and pains': ibid., 9:2.

95 ' "and I will anoint myself and rest" ': ibid., 9:3.

95 'O Eve . . . because of you': ibid., 11:1.

95–6 ' "Why have you . . . all our race?" ': ibid., 14:2.

96 The devil: for the evolution of Satan in early Jewish and Christian narrative, see Forsyth and Pagels (1996).

96 ' "May God live! . . . the glory of the tree" ': *Apoc. Mos.*, 18:1.

96 ' "poured upon the fruit . . . and I ate" ': *Apoc. Mos.*, 19:3: L. S. A. Wells' translation in Charles, vol. II, p146.

97 ' "O evil woman! . . . from the glory of God" ': *Apoc. Mos.*, 21:6, in Johnson, op. cit.

97 ' "Why are you dying and I live?" ': ibid., 31:2.

97 'I have sinned, O God; . . . come about through me': ibid., 32:2.

97–8 ' "do not separate me . . . so also let no one separate us [now]" ': ibid., 42:5–7.

98 'when his rib would return to him': ibid., 42:1.

98 the influence of the Watcher stories . . . between angels and human women: see Forsyth, pp233–4, who notes Eve's encounter with the serpent/Satan as 'the final fusion of the Watcher angel tradition of lust between women and angels with the Eden story. Literal seduction by an angel is here combined with the story of the tree and its fruit.'

98 ' "Lord, Lord, save me . . . to your husband" ': *Apoc. Mos.*, 25:3–4, in Johnson, op. cit.

98 ' "all sin in creation has come about through me" ': ibid., 32:2.

98 In *1 Enoch*, the tree of good and evil is called the tree of wisdom: *1 Enoch*, 32:3–6.

99 The father of the world . . . to subjugate all things: *The Book of Wisdom*, 10:1–2, in *The Jerusalem Bible* (1974).

99 thought by some commentators to refer to Adam: but see Evans, pp27–8.

99 Jewish tradition endowed Adam . . . all seventy of the known languages: Ginzberg, vol. I, pp59–62.

99 The Christian Fathers . . . '. . . of a tortoise': Lewis (1960), p117.

99 'fruit that alone . . . ripe': John D. Sinclair, trans., *The Divine Comedy of Dante Alighieri*, III: *Paradiso*, XXVI:91–2, New York 1961, pp376–7.

100 'not deceived,/But fondly overcome with female charm': John Milton, *Paradise Lost*, IX:998–9.

100 an earlier Hebrew source: M. D. Johnson, in Charlesworth (1985), p251; Forsyth, p228, suggests a Hebrew or Aramaic original.

100 ' "My lord, would you kill me? . . . the Lord God is angry with you" ': *Vita*, 3:1. Translation used is M. D. Johnson, in Charlesworth (1985).

100 ' "What have we done . . . pursue us with deceit?" ': ibid., 11:2.

100–101 ' "If he be wrathful with me . . . like the Most High" ': ibid., 15:3.

101 ' "So with deceit I assailed . . . from my glory" ': ibid., 16:3.

101 'You live on, my lord . . . stay there until I die': ibid., 18:1–2.

101 Cain, her 'lustrous' son . . . dalliance with the devil: see Forsyth, p237, note 63. The tradition of Cain as the devil's son was developed in

other Jewish sources and linked with the Watcher legend. See Evans, p55.

101 **female sexual desire and credulity . . . use for evil purposes**: see Kramer and Sprenger; Hufton, pp341–2.

102 **whose origins . . . primeval deep itself**: see Forsyth, ch. 2.

103 **Through the later association . . . an alternative name for the devil**: see Forsyth, p136, and ibid., ch. 6, for the development of the rebel tradition.

103 **Prometheus was another overreacher . . . forge weapons**: see Hesiod, *Theogony*, p.20; Forsyth, pp86–7, on Prometheus/Satan overlap.

103 **Phaethon, the ambitious youth . . . plunges into the river Eridanus**: see Ovid, *Metamorphoses*, pp50–9; see Forsyth, pp132–3, for possible influence on the Satan tradition.

103–4 **The devil . . . adversarial in the Old Testament**: for the Old Testament development of the Satan figure, see Forsyth, pp113ff; Pagels (1996), pp39ff.

103 **'one who opposes . . . adversary'**: ibid., p39.

104 **this shadow aspect of God**: Forsyth, p109, comments: 'The ambivalence of God, the presence in him of a destructive as well as creative side, Job challenges, and only in the final revelation does he get free from his anguish and allow the monstrous and fearful side of God.'

105 **Edmund Gosse recalled . . . the texts predicted**: see Edmund Gosse, *Father and Son: A Study of Two Temperaments*, London 1907, pp75–6.

106 **'the world presented, instantly . . . life had long existed'**: ibid., p120.

106 **Sir Thomas Browne thought not . . . 'She had no navel'**: quoted in Jorge Luis Borges, Ruth L. C. Simms, trans., *Other Inquisitions 1937–1952*, Texas 1964; see, too, James Joyce, *Ulysses*, Harmondsworth 1971, p43; Stephen Jay Gould, 'Adam's Navel', in *The Flamingo's Smile*, Harmondsworth 1987.

106 **'would certainly possess hair . . . to a mother'**: Gosse, op. cit., p121.

106 **'that God hid the fossils in the rocks . . . into infidelity'**: ibid., p120.

106 **'give up the painful . . . superfluous lie'**: quoted ibid., p122.

106 **'Among us the chief . . . examining our writings'**: quoted in Forsyth, p305.

107 **A dungeon horrible . . . That comes to all**: John Milton, *Paradise Lost*, I:61–7.

107 **Farewell happy fields . . . a hell of heaven**: ibid., I:249–55.

108 **'erect/Amidst his circling spires, that on the grass/Floated redundant'**: ibid., IX:501–3.

108 carnal desire . . . finally, sexual dalliance: ibid., IX:1013–16.

108 'very long, red, and spotted fatal snake': Ruth Finnegan, *Limba Stories and Story-telling*, Oxford 1967, p268, note 2.

108 'travelled far in that love': ibid., p268.

108 an aetiological myth . . . for the Limba people: ibid., p267.

108 the rabbinic story: see ch. 1 above.

108–9 Rabbi Johanan ben Zackai . . . three different sections of the *Babylonian Talmud*: Swidler, p47; and see, for example, *Yebamoth* II, 103b, p711: 'When the serpent copulated with Eve, he infused her with lust.'

109 'I was a chaste maiden . . . I stayed with my husband': *4 Maccabees*, 18:7–9, H. Anderson, trans., in Charlesworth (1985), p563.

109 the haunt of evil spirits and demons . . . staying quietly at home: ibid., notes 18b–c, p563.

109 For when he transgressed . . . these things: *2 Baruch*, 56:6–7, A. F. J. Klijn, trans., in Charlesworth (1983), p641.

109 ' "For the first Adam . . . descended from him" ': *4 Ezra*, 3:21, B. M. Metzger, trans., in Charlesworth (1983), p529.

109 the *yēçer ha-ra'* . . . at birth: see Williams, p59; and ibid., pp37ff, for 'The Adam-story and the "Evil Imagination" '.

110 Commenting on Genesis 1:31 . . . '. . . beget children': *Midrash Rabbah*, *Genesis* I, IX:7, p68.

110 WITH THE DISAPPEARANCE of Jewish millennial hopes . . . through Christ: see Evans, p26; for the evolution of Fall theory, see Williams.

CHAPTER 4: CURIOUS WOMEN: EVE, PANDORA AND PSYCHE

113 If there ever was a certain Pandora . . . flowers about the temples: Tertullian, *De corona militis*, VII, quoted in Panofsky, p12.

114 a brief account in the *Theogony*: references to Hesiod's *Theogony* and *Works and Days* are to M. L. West's translation, unless otherwise indicated.

114 the stem of a giant fennel . . . carrying fire: see ibid., p70, l567 note.

114 'the likeness of a modest maiden': Hesiod, *Theogony*, p20.

115 'beautiful evil': ibid., l585, H. G. Evelyn-White, trans., Cambridge 1950, reprinted in Panofsky, p6. West has 'pretty bane', p20.

115 'it is an ill without a cure': Hesiod, *Theogony*, p21.

115 Diogenes Laertius . . . to face in life: see R. D. Hicks, trans., *Lives of Eminent Philosophers*, London 1959, I:167, cited in Rogers, p26.

115 On the one hand loneliness . . . how the children will turn out:

Valerius Maximus, Karl F. Kempf, ed., Pike, trans., *Factorum et Dictorum Memorabilium Libri*, Germany 1888, p327, quoted ibid., p26.

116 **'phlegm, blood, bile, rheum'**: John Chrysostom, 'An Exhortation to Theodore After His Fall', quoted in Warner (1985), p58.

117 **Lady of the Beasts, the Great Mother goddess**: see Baring and Cashford for evolution of myth of the Great Mother.

117 **'broad-breasted Earth'**: Hesiod, *Theogony*, p6.

117 **'the familiar scene . . . Ge [Gaia]'**: Harrison (1991), p280.

117 **'Pandora rises . . . all gifts'**: ibid., p281.

117 **Hephaestus . . . spring forth**: ibid., p282.

117–18 **'the grandmotherly deposits in Hesiod's mind'**: West, intro. to Hesiod, pxv.

118 **'a bitch's mind and a knavish [thieving] nature'**: Hesiod, *Works and Days*, p39. Commenting on 'bitch', Lefkowitz (1986) points out that the Greeks saw dogs as 'shameless, amoral, without judgment', p114.

118 **'the woman unstopped the jar . . . upon mankind'**: Hesiod, *Works and Days*, p39.

119 **a jar . . . even honey**: Walcot, p61, says it was probably a bronze jar.

119 **Erasmus of Rotterdam**: see Panofsky, pp15–19.

120 **the long tradition of Babylonian myth**: see Walcot for links between Greek and Babylonian literatures.

120 **Narru, king of the gods . . . the human race**: *Theodicy*, ll276–9, quoted in Walcot, p56; and see Pritchard, p440. See Walcot, pp55–7, for Babylonian accounts of the formation of humanity out of clay.

120 **'So the goddess . . . wilderness'**: *Epic of Gilgamesh*, pp62–3; and see Walcot, p56.

120 **the Sumerian *Myth of Enki and Ninmah***: Walcot, p56.

120 **the Babylonian *Epic of Atrahasis***: see 'Creation of Man by the Mother Goddess', E. A. Speiser, trans., in Pritchard, pp99–100; and see Walcot, pp56–7.

120 **the *Enuma Elish***: Tablet 6, ll1–36, E. A. Speiser, trans., in Pritchard, p68; and see Walcot, p57.

121 **Pandora's opening of the jar . . . within the jar/womb**: see Zeitlin, pp59–60, who contrasts the 'negativity' of Hesiod's account of Pandora and Epimetheus with the 'union of male and female in joint sex and procreation' of the biblical account of Adam and Eve.

121 **Paul Klee**: see Panofsky pp111–13.

122 **the Rabbis added menstruation . . . an additional penalty**: *Babylonian Talmud*, 'Erubin, 100b, p697.

122 Ovid's *Metamorphoses*: Ovid, *Metamorphoses*, pp31–40.

123 her fabled tomb at Cynus . . . tourist attraction: Bell, p389.

123 According to the Hippocratic Corpus: see ch. 5 below for Greek medical theories about women's bodies.

124 a 'thing apart': Semonides, 7:2, Pomeroy (1994), p49; for translations of Semonides, see Marylin Arthur, ibid., pp49–52, and Richmond Lattimore, in Fantham, et al., pp42–3.

124 The man is lucky . . . underneath her touch: Semonides, 7:83–5, Lattimore, ibid., p43.

124 For women . . . a ball and a chain: Semonides, 7:115–16, ibid., p43.

125 'What else is woman . . . painted with fair colours?': John Chrysostom, *In Mattheum homili*, xxxii, *Ex Capite* xix (a), Migne, *Patrologiae Graecae*, vol. 56, p803, quoted in Phillips, p22.

125 Zeus' two jars . . . in the *Iliad*: Homer, *The Iliad*, XXIV, p451; and see Panofsky, pp49ff and p66. Panofsky, p66, comments that Cousin's Pandora, 'closes the "vase of good" with her left hand while having opened the "vase of evil"; its lid is conspicuously thrown back and permits a cloud of evil spirits to escape.'

125 'We men are wretched things . . . the very pattern of our lives': Homer, *The Iliad*, XXIV, p451.

125 'when Zeus serves . . . by gods and men alike': ibid., p451.

126 Cleopatra . . . dangerous sexuality: for the development of the myth of Cleopatra, see Lucy Hughes-Hallett, *Cleopatra: Histories, Dreams and Distortions*, London 1990.

126 Dora and Erwin Panofsky have suggested . . . the Magdalene with her pot of ointment: Panofsky, pp17–18.

126–7 Erasmus may have been sidetracked . . . her lover's vengeful mother: ibid., p18.

127 Lucius Apuleius' *The Golden Ass*: I have followed the Robert Graves/Michael Grant translation.

127 'a dire mischief', a 'winged pest': ibid., p69.

129 The Rabbis argued . . . in their prime: *Midrash Rabbah, Genesis* I, XIV:7, p114.

130 'suffering, guilt, and loneliness': Neumann, p82.

130 'heeding . . . higher consciousness': ibid., p74; Cassuto, p142, suggests that Eve's conversation with the serpent represented an inner dialogue between wiliness and innocence.

130 an essay on Ulysses' stay-at-home wife: see Heilbrun, p108.

130 As soon as her reason . . . path to moral freedom: adapted from Schiller, *Thalia*, 398–9, quoted in Phillips, p80.

131 **many possible readings**: see, for example, Neumann, and discussion in Warner (1994), pp273ff.

133 ' "O brothers . . . of the unpeopled world" ': John D. Sinclair, trans., *The Divine Comedy of Dante Alighieri*, I: *Inferno*, XXVI:112–17, New York 1961, pp326–7.

134 **an arch wherethrough . . . when I move**: Tennyson, 'Ulysses', ll19–21.

CHAPTER 5: THE TRAGIC PASSIONS OF WOMANHOOD

136 **I am alone . . . in this extremity**: Euripides, *Medea*, p25: all text references to Vellacott's translation.

136 **'the wooden horse . . . futile though it was'**: Augustine, *Confessions*, I:13, p35: all text references to Pine-Coffin's translation.

136 **'who killed herself for love'**: ibid., I:13, p33.

136 **'that a tender and plastic nature . . . the indecencies of comedy'**: St Gregory of Nyssa, *The Life of St Macrina*, p22: all text references to Lowther Clarke's translation.

138 **For well-heeled notables of the Roman Empire . . . a priority**: see Brown (1992) for an excellent brief introduction to the social and sexual mores of late antiquity.

138 **Unstable bodies, febrile minds**: for information on medical attitudes to male and female bodies during the classical period, I found the following particularly useful: Gillian Clark (1994), pp63–93; Dean-Jones (1991, 1995, 1996); Ann Ellis Hanson, 'Continuity and Change: Three Case Studies in Hippocratic Gynecological Therapy and Theory', in Pomeroy (1991); King (1993, 1995); Rousselle; and Sissa.

139 **'burnt hair . . . bed bugs'**: quoted in Dean-Jones (1995), p199.

139 **'the female is . . . the principle of Soul'**: Aristotle, *Generation of Animals*, II:3, p175: all text references to Peck's translation.

139 **'The female always . . . a particular body'**: ibid., II:4, p185.

140 **'The fact is . . . of more retentive memory'**: Aristotle, D'Arcy W. Thompson, trans., *History of Animals*, Princeton, New Jersey 1984, quoted in Dean-Jones (1995), p192.

141 **Augustine's thinking on original sin . . . to the foetus**: see Gillian Clark (1994), p73.

141 **Soranus found it positively harmful . . . an indication of a diseased uterus**: Dean-Jones (1995), p198.

141 **a passage in *On Dreams* attributed to Aristotle . . . a woman's gaze**: Aristotle, *On Dreams*, 459b–460a, in Lefkowitz and Fant, p89.

141 'capability of withering plants . . . and driving dogs mad': Dean-Jones (1995), p198, who points out that Pliny's description of the effects of menstrual blood was used by the Inquisition to identify witches.

142 '[d]enying that your womb . . . stops the treatment': King (1995), p144.

142 'Great men said . . . ideas about the feminine': Sissa, p51.

142 'it appears that much of men's [public] talk . . . was a calculated bluff': Winkler, p4.

143 collusive patterns of role-playing . . . behind the scenes: see Meyers, pp42–3.

144 a woman . . . support and guidance: see Hall (1997), for attitudes to gender roles in Athenian tragedy.

145 'His death itself . . . but sorrow and tears': Homer, The Odyssey, I, p31: all text references to Rieu's translation.

145 ' "in her private messages . . . intention of keeping" ': ibid., II, p39.

146 'her skill in fine handicraft . . . her way': ibid., II, p40.

146 ' "Make voyages! – Attempt them!" ': Tennessee Williams, Camino Real, Block 8, p180, in Tennessee Williams, The Rose Tattoo and Other Plays, Harmondsworth 1976.

146 ' "let him come late . . . trouble in his home" ': Homer, The Odyssey, IX, p154.

147 ' "feasting on meat galore and mellow wine" ': ibid., X, p168.

147 ' "happy in his marriage" ': ibid., IV, p69.

147 ' "may the gods grant you . . . delighting their friends" ': ibid., VI, p107.

149 ' "weaving . . . goddesses love to make" ': ibid., X, p160.

149 ' "my wise Penelope's looks . . . to reach my home" ': ibid., V, p93.

150 Samuel Butler . . . written by a woman: Samuel Butler, The Authoress of the Odyssey, London 1897.

150 ' "for brutality and infamy . . . contemplate such deeds" ': Homer, The Odyssey, XI, p182.

150 ' "now, in the depth . . . for all time to come" ': ibid., XI, p183.

150 ' "Let this be a lesson . . . is in your mind" ': ibid., XI, p183.

150 ' "Do not sail openly . . . no longer to be trusted" ': ibid., XI, p183.

151 'Unconquerable Odysseus! . . . every honest woman in it': ibid., XXIV, p356.

152 'in whose woman's . . . nurses hope': Aeschylus, Agamemnon, p41: all text references to Vellacott's translation.

154 If a man grows tired . . . than bear/One child: Euripides, Medea, pp24–5.

155 'My misery . . . not relent': ibid., p49.

156 But what they knew . . . heart into foreboding: Virgil, *The Aeneid*, V, ll7–9, p125: Fitzgerald's translation.

156 'if . . . our husband does not struggle . . . death is better': Euripides, *Medea*, p24.

157 *Joseph and Aseneth*: all text references to C. Burchard, trans., *Joseph and Aseneth*, in Charlesworth (1985).

159 the 'paradise of delight' . . . the Garden of Eden: ibid., 16:14, and note n., p229.

159 'like flowers of life': ibid., 16:16, p229.

161 'the single vibrant word . . . heads': David Malouf, *Remembering Babylon*, London 1994, p141.

161 'not just . . . *why* they were': ibid., p141.

161 'If she could escape . . . to be an angel': ibid., pp140–1.

161 She just had time . . . It is: ibid., p142.

CHAPTER 6: THE TERRIBLE FLESH

164 'Our life has been . . . the curse of Adam!': Thomas Hardy, *Jude the Obscure* [1895], London 1966, part 6:III, p356.

164 'the sin, the misery, the destructiveness': Pullman, ch. 21, p377.

165 a radical new approach to human sexuality: for early Christian attitudes to sexuality, see Brown (1990).

166 that ancient story of Adam and Eve in the Garden of Eden: for a detailed account of early Christian ideas about Adam and Eve, see Pagels (1988).

170 Women in the Corinthian congregation . . . at religious gatherings: see Brown (1990), p52.

170–71 in their looks divine . . . she for God in him: John Milton, *Paradise Lost*, IV:291–9.

171 in wanton ringlets waved . . . reluctant amorous delay: ibid., IV:306–11.

171 Robert Graves' . . . hair-fetichist Milton: see Robert Graves, *Wife to Mr Milton* [1942], Harmondsworth 1954.

172 And Adam was not deceived . . . in the transgression: Christian and Jewish commentators had difficulty accepting that the intellectually superior Adam could have been deceived by the serpent, and came up with a variety of explanations as to why he should have sinned 'with his eyes open'. See pp191–2 below.

172 *'[E]l papa resta assai ben sodisfato'*: Michelangelo to his father Lodovico, early October 1512, quoted in Johannes Wilde, *Michelangelo*, Oxford 1978, p67.

175 'In the Old Testament . . . becomes clear': Augustine, quoted in Norman Cohn, *Noah's Flood: The Genesis Story in Western Thought*, New Haven and London 1996, p23.

176 Corinth, where consorting . . . for young men: Brown (1990), p51.

176 A weak thing in itself . . . pitted against the spirit of God: ibid., p48.

178 the Encratites: I am indebted to Peter Brown's commentary on the Encratites: Brown (1990), pp90–99.

178 'For it makes human nature weaker . . . copied them': Clement of Alexandria, *On Marriage*, ch. XVII:102, p88. All text references to Chadwick's translation.

178 'sustenance': see ibid., ch. VI:45, p61, where Clement opposes continence.

178 the noblewoman Mygdonia . . . bed-curtain: see *Acts of Thomas*, 98, in James, p407.

179 'those . . . who under a pious cloak . . . the holy Creator': Clement of Alexandria, op. cit., ch. VI:45, p61.

179 *Gospel According to the Egyptians*: see James, pp10ff.

179 When Salome asked the Lord . . . 'As long as you women bear children': quoted in Clement of Alexandria, op. cit., ch. VI:45, p61.

179 'the ordinary course of nature . . . by death': ibid., ch. VI:45, p61.

179 'Thou know'st 'tis common . . . to eternity': William Shakespeare, *Hamlet*, I:2, ll72–3.

179 They say that the Saviour . . . birth and corruption: Clement of Alexandria, op. cit., ch. IX:63, p69.

179 'Has this destruction . . . referred to as "female" ' ': ibid., ch. IX:63, p69.

180 In general . . . self-controlled marriage: ibid., ch. 12:86, p80.

180 'we ought to share suffering . . . If you burn, marry': ibid., ch. I:4, p42.

180 'he was no ordinary man . . . after the flesh': ibid., ch. VI:49, p63.

180 Paul had had a wife . . . without causing scandal: ibid., ch. VI:53, pp64–5.

180 Adam and Eve . . . 'by nature': ibid., ch. XVII:102, p88.

180 they rushed . . . for disobeying God's will: ibid., ch. XIV:94, p84, and ch. XVII:103, p89.

180–81 For having been created . . . from that time onwards: Irenaeus, *Libris Quinque Adversus Haereses*, 3:22:4, quoted in Pagels (1988), p28.

181 the 'coats of skins' . . . physical bodies: Clement of Alexandria, op. cit., ch. XIV:95, pp84–5.

181 'birth is holy' . . . 'came in the flesh': ibid., ch. XVII:103, p89.

181 'knowledge' . . . the tree of life: ibid., ch. XII:81, p78; ch. XVII:104, p89.

181 The responsibility was Adam's . . . ' "And Adam knew . . . the name of Seth" ': ibid., ch. XII:81, p78; and see Gen. 4:25.

181 'if the flesh were hostile to the soul . . . of its passions': ibid., ch. XVII:104, p89.

181 'The human ideal of continence . . . to experience desire at all': ibid., ch. VII:57, p66.

181 'must practise continence . . . chaste and controlled will': ibid., ch. VII:58, p67.

181 'the law intended husbands . . . of begetting children': ibid., ch. XI:71, p73.

182 what sexual acts . . . could sexually come together: Clement of Alexandria, *Paidagogos*, 2:97ff; quoted in Pagels (1988), p29.

182 Eve 'first began transgression': Clement of Alexandria, *On Marriage*, ch. IX:65, p70.

182 How can a newborn baby . . . not in itself sinful: ibid., ch. XVI:100, p87.

182–3 Eve was called 'Life' . . . 'the mother of righteous . . . or disobedient': ibid., ch. IX:65, p70. Her name Eve/Hawwah (Gen. 3:20) can be translated as 'Life-giver', see Fox (1995), p23.

183 reminding battered wives . . . obey her husband: Augustine, *Confessions*, IX:9, p195: all text references to Pine-Coffin's translation.

183 'proof that she . . . brought into the world': ibid., V:8, p101.

184 'a blow . . . I loved her dearly': ibid., VI:15, p131.

184 'a slave of lust': ibid., VI:15, p131.

184 an iron chain . . . ' . . . my soul apart': ibid., VIII:5, p164.

184 'the drowsy words . . . "Let me wait a little longer" ': ibid., VIII:5, p165.

184 'For the rule of sin . . . its own accord': ibid., VIII:5, p165.

184 he told him . . . themselves to God: ibid., VIII:6, pp167–8.

184 ' "Give me chastity and continence, but not yet" ': ibid., VIII:7, p169.

184–5 In turmoil . . . to do good: ibid., VIII:8–9, pp170–2.

185 ' "Are you going . . . for ever and ever" ': ibid., VIII:11, pp175–6.

186 whether virgin, married or widowed . . . the same rewards in heaven: Jerome, *Against Jovinianus*, I:3, in Fremantle, p348. Jovinian's words have survived in Jerome's polemic, which both quotes and vigorously refutes his arguments. All text references to Fremantle's

translation. For discussion of Jovinian, see Pagels (1988), pp91–7, and Elizabeth A. Clark, 'Heresy, Asceticism, Adam, and Eve: Interpretations of Genesis 1–3 in the Later Latin Fathers' in Clark (1986), pp358ff.

186 First of all, [Jovinian] says . . . 'Be fruitful, and multiply, and replenish the earth': Jerome, *Against Jovinianus*, 1:5, p348.

186 'the hissing of the old serpent . . . from Paradise': ibid., 1:4, p348.

186 they who, while naked . . . clothe themselves withal: ibid., 1:4, p348.

186 And as regards Adam and Eve . . . immediately married: ibid., 1:16, p359.

187 grudgingly allowed marital intercourse . . . '. . . all sexual intercourse is unclean': for both positions, see ibid., 1:20, p361.

187 'For myself, however . . . in creating male and female': Augustine, *City of God*, XIV:22, p584: all text references to Bettenson's translation.

187 'There is no denying . . . of begetting children': ibid., XIV:22, p584.

187–8 'if there had been no sin . . . children to be loved': ibid., XIV:23, p585.

188 'commit in sleep . . . sensual images': Augustine, *Confessions*, X:30, p234.

188 'Without doubt, the marriage in paradise . . . guilt of disobedience': Augustine, *City of God*, XIV:23, p586.

188 'injunction forbidding . . . so brief to remember': ibid., XIV:12, p571.

188 a 'misuse of free will . . . chain of disasters': ibid., XIII:14, p523.

188 'a novel disturbance in their disobedient flesh': ibid., XIII:13, p522.

188 'human nature . . . was vitiated and altered': ibid., XIII:3, p513.

189 'it was I who willed . . . by Adam, my first father': Augustine, *Confessions*, VIII:10, p173.

189 'original perversion . . . at the root': Augustine, *City of God*, XIII:14, p523.

189 'For we were all in that one man . . . in any other condition': ibid., XIII:14, p523.

189 'the whole human race . . . that was thus begotten': ibid., XIII:3, p512.

189 'We bring with us, at our birth, the beginning of our death': ibid., XIII:13, p523.

189 'too pleased with himself': ibid., XIV:13, p571.

189 'falling away from the work of God': ibid., XIV:11, p568.

189 Self-regard was the original evil that cost Adam Paradise: ibid., XIV:13, p573.

189 'that when it reaches its climax . . . are overwhelmed': ibid., XIV:16, p577.

189 'the genital organs have become . . . the eyes of beholders in embarrassment': ibid., XIV:19, p581.

189–90 'exaggerated sense' . . . 'the less dignified anatomy . . . an increase of power': Rebecca West, *St Augustine*, Edinburgh 1933, p44.

190 ' "From this moment . . . for ever and ever" ': Augustine, *Confessions*, VIII:11, pp175–6.

190 'the man would have sowed the seed . . . and had not been excited by lust': Augustine, *City of God*, XIV:24, p587.

190 'Moreover, although we cannot prove this . . . the flux [i.e. the menstrual flow] is ejected': ibid., XIV:26, p591.

190–91 a person's future prospects . . . to elect for special privileges: ibid., XIV:26, pp591–2.

191 the power and authority of the Church . . . through the Eucharist: see Henry Chadwick, *Augustine*, Oxford and New York 1986, pp110–11.

191 'the inferior of the human pair': Augustine, *City of God*, XIV:11, p570.

191 subject to her husband: ibid., XV:7, p606.

191 'in the physical sense, woman has been made for man' . . . to think clearly or act morally: Augustine, *Confessions*, XIII:32, p344.

191 marriage must have existed in Eden . . . as Adam's helpmate: Augustine, Peter Holmes, D.D., F.R.A.S., trans., *On Original Sin*, II:40, in Rev. Marcus Dods, D.D., ed., *The Works of Aurelius Augustine, Bishop of Hippo*, vol. XII, *The Anti-Pelagian Works of St Augustine*, vol. II, Edinburgh 1874, p82.

191–2 'the arrogant angel . . . involved sharing her sin': Augustine, *City of God*, XIV:11, pp569–70.

192 for with thee . . . bliss or woe: John Milton, *Paradise Lost*, IX:906–16.

193 'God created fully innocent natures . . . their will': Augustine, *Opus Imperfectum*, 3:82, quoted in Pagels (1988), p139, and see ibid., pp130–49, for discussion of Augustine's controversy with Julian.

193–4 'Augustine's theory of Adam's fall . . . into the center of western history': Pagels (1988), p126.

CHAPTER 7: DAUGHTERS OF EVE

196 And do you not know . . . the Son of God had to die: Tertullian, *On Female Dress*, I:1, in Roberts and Donaldson (1869), pp304–5.

196 'if the mirror, too, already had licence to lie so largely': ibid., I:1, p305.

197 'walking about as Eve mourning and repentant': ibid., I:1, p304.

197 '[Then] take some spiritual wife . . . pleasing to God': Tertullian, *On Exhortation to Chastity*, XII, in Roberts and Donaldson (1870), p17.

197 Just as someone captures . . . the souls of these men: John Chrysostom, *Instruction and Refutation Directed Against Those Men Cohabiting With Virgins*, 11, quoted in Elizabeth A. Clark, 'Devil's Gateway and Bride of Christ: Women in the Early Christian World', in Clark (1986), pp26–7.

198 And yet ought I not to weep and groan . . . sirens' sweet and deadly songs?: Jerome, letter XXII, in Wright, pp89, 91.

198 You must not be subject . . . '. . . consecrated in the persons of Mary and of Christ': ibid., p91.

198 'Eve in Paradise . . . you were born': ibid., p93.

199 'The command to increase . . . produces fruit a hundredfold': ibid., pp91, 93.

199 'I praise wedlock . . . produce me virgins': ibid., p95.

199 Scarcely had they turned . . . no sexual coupling either: John Chrysostom, *On Virginity*, in O'Faolain and Martines, p138.

200 'she kept watch . . . immeasurable self-control': *Life of Olympias*, 13, quoted in Clark, op. cit., p28.

200 But though in my fear of hell . . . my flesh was as good as dead: Jerome, letter XXII, in Wright, pp67, 69.

201 ' "real solemn history . . . women at all" ': Jane Austen, *Northanger Abbey* [1818], ch. XIV, Oxford 1930, p113. Catherine actually said: 'the men all so good for nothing'.

202 many Gnostics . . . necessary for *gnosis*: see Pagels (1988), p66. For information on the Gnostics, see Pagels (1990); for Gnostic interpretations of Adam and Eve, see Pagels (1988), ch. III.

202 And the spirit-endowed woman . . . '. . . who has given birth': *The Hypostasis of the Archons*, 89:11–17, in Robinson, p164.

203 their imperfection . . . upon their loins: ibid., 90:15–19, p165.

203 'mankind might be . . . the holy spirit': ibid., 91:9–11, p165.

203 After the day of rest . . . '. . . given me life': *On the Origin of the World*, 115:30–116:8, in Robinson, p182.

203 When Eve was . . . into being: *The Gospel of Philip*, 68:22–4, in Robinson, p150.

203–4 . . . Christ came . . . longer be separated: ibid., 70:13–20, p151.

205 Blessed are the bodies . . . his Son: *Acts of Paul*, II:6, in James, p273. All text references are to James' translation.

205 'bound with him, in affection': ibid., II:19, p276.

205 'Burn the lawless one . . . midst of the theatre': ibid., II:20, p276.

206 'the handmaid . . . God': ibid., II:37, p280.

208 'a patently antisocial . . . heroism': Kate Cooper, *The Virgin and the Bride: Idealized Womanhood in Late Antiquity*, Cambridge, Mass. and London 1996, p67.

208 it is essentially . . . the heroine's allegiance: ibid., p55.

208–9 Marcus Aurelius . . . *concordia*: Brown (1990), p16.

209 'a man little of stature . . . face of an angel': *Acts of Paul*, II:3, p273.

209 'like a spider . . . maiden is captured': ibid., II:9, p274.

210 local doctors . . . source of her power: see Karen Armstrong, *The End of Silence: Women and the Priesthood*, London 1993, p99.

211 Holy Thecla's . . . despite all my unworthiness: *Egeria's Travels*, 23:2–6, in John Wilkinson, trans., *Egeria's Travels to the Holy Land*, Jerusalem and Warminster, 1981, pp121–2.

211 'Let . . . Thecla teach you . . . offered': Ambrose, *On Virginity*, II:III:19, in De Romestin, p376.

212 Caroline Bynum . . . medieval anorectics: see Bynum, *Holy Feast and Holy Fast*.

212–13 'You call to mind Blaesilla's companionship . . . less than your deserts': Jerome, letter XXXIX:4, in Fremantle, pp52–3.

213 *The Martyrdom of Saints Perpetua and Felicitas*: I am indebted to Peter Dronke's translation of this work for my summary of the narrative; see Dronke, pp2–4.

214 'still chewing . . . sweet': ibid., IV, p2.

214 'we understood . . . hope in the world': ibid., IV, p2.

215 ' "I am a Christian" ': ibid., VI, p3.

215 'And I saw the immense, astonished crowd': ibid., X, p4.

216 'And I knew . . . the victory would be mine': ibid., X, p4.

216 'a priceless document': Chadwick (1993), p91.

218 'satisfactory marriages': see St Gregory of Nyssa, *The Life of St Macrina*, introduction, p7.

219 'to prevent such a life . . . shades of useless oblivion': ibid., pp18–19. All text references to Lowther Clarke's translation.

219 'for I do not know . . . surpassed her sex': ibid., p18.

219 'a famous Macrina . . . of the persecutions': ibid., p19.

219 'some one in form . . . addressed the child': ibid., pp20–1.

220 'inspired Scripture': ibid., p22.

220 'considerable proficiency in wool-work': ibid., p23.

220 'on behalf of the wronged': ibid., p24.

220 'absent only, not dead . . . who was away': ibid., p25.

220 'two spirits bound on earth . . . giving in marriage': Emily Tennyson, quoted in Ann Thwaite, *Emily Tennyson: The Poet's Wife*, London 1996, p573.

220 'would often say . . . she ever carried her about': St Gregory of Nyssa, *The Life of St Macrina*, p26.

221 'the great Basil' . . . 'puffed up beyond measure with the pride of oratory': ibid., p27.

221 ornately decorated and staffed by numerous servants and slaves: see Elm, p80.

221 'lofty character': St Gregory of Nyssa, *The Life of St Macrina*, p29.

222 'thrown to the ground . . . like some noble athlete hit by an unexpected blow': ibid., p32.

222 'like an invincible athlete . . . the assault of troubles': ibid, p41.

222 'martyrs' relics': ibid., p42.

222 'by putting her hands . . . due to my rank': ibid., p44.

223 'as if she discerned . . . with the greater eagerness': ibid., p54.

223 ' "Thou hast saved . . . – the devil" ': ibid., p55.

223 'she drew a great deep breath . . . her prayer together': ibid., p57.

223 ' "She knew of one store-house . . . treasure in heaven" ': ibid., p63.

223 ' "God of healing" ': ibid., p67.

224 '[h]ealings of diseases . . . predictions of the future': ibid., p78.

CHAPTER 8: THE SECOND EVE

230 I sing of a maiden . . . her son she chose: anonymous, Sloane 2593, f.10b, British Library: text modernized.

231 'as a dove that is nurtured . . . hand of an angel': *Book of James, or Protevangelium*, VIII:1, in James, p42. All text references to James' translation.

231 'As the Lord my God liveth . . . not a man': ibid., XV:3, p45.

232 the Hebrew word . . . physical virginity: see Warner (1985), p19. Marina Warner's *Alone of All Her Sex*, first published in 1976, remains the most complete account of the cult of the Virgin Mary.

232–3 'In the old days . . . life has come through Mary': Jerome, letter XXII, in Wright, p99.

233 the Council of Chalcedon . . . the First Lateran Council, in 649: see Warner (1985), pp65–6.

233 the dogma of the Assumption . . . received papal warranty: see ibid., pp92–3.

234 **And just as it was . . . received life:** Irenaeus, *Proof of the Apostolic Preaching*, 33, quoted in Pelikan, p42.

234 **'Eve [had necessarily to be restored] in Mary . . . virginal disobedience by virginal obedience':** ibid., p43.

234 **'It was absolutely essential . . . in the case of Mary':** ibid., p43.

234–5 **She did not answer . . . great good hath come to us:** *The Goodman of Paris*, Article 6, in Power, p93. All text references to Power's translation.

235 **by disobedience . . . the word of God:** ibid., pp93–4.

235 **before she sinned . . . their husbands would:** ibid., p94.

236 **That angel who greets you . . . the falling sinner came:** quoted in Kraus, p84.

236–7 **Now she can sing . . . it did not belong to her:** Susan Wicks, 'First Coming', in *Open Diagnosis*, London and Boston 1994.

237 **'the means by which . . . shining attributes of Mary':** Phillips, p135.

238 **I am Eve . . . no terror but for me:** anonymous, Old Irish, in David Greene and Frank O'Connor, eds and trans., *A Golden Treasury of Irish Poetry A.D. 600 to 1200*, London 1967, p158.

238 **'The door closed by Adam . . . the Virgin':** Trapp, p226.

240 **a fully clothed, dignified figure:** the paintings of Mary breastfeeding the infant Jesus emphasize her maternity: the breast's function is to nurture and console.

241 **Julia Margaret Cameron . . . vulnerable flesh and blood:** as pointed out by Carol Mavor in her perceptive study of Julia Margaret Cameron's Madonna photographs: see Mavor, pp43–69.

243 **'the woodbine spices . . . rose is blown':** Tennyson, *Maud*, part I, XXII, I:854–5.

243 **'Queen rose . . . in one':** ibid., XXII, IX:902, 905.

244 **. . . long by the garden lake . . . dearer than all:** ibid., XXII, VI:884–7.

244 **. . . the rose was awake . . . the dawn and thee:** ibid., XXII, VIII:898–901.

244–5 **There has fallen a splendid tear . . . in purple and red:** ibid., XXII, X:908–XI:923.

245 **'It is hard . . . added to the other':** Jerome, letter XXII, in Wright, p89.

245 **' "By night . . . soul loveth" ':** ibid., p89, and see Song of Solomon 3:1.

245–6 **Let the seclusion . . . '. . . a fountain sealed':** Jerome, letter XXII, in Wright, p109.

246 **' "I sought . . . no answer" ':** ibid., p109.

246 It [i.e. virginity] loves to grow . . . the modesty of consecrated virginity in the rose: Ambrose, *Concerning Virgins*, I:IX:45, in De Romestin, p370.

246 Ambrose . . . 'a garden inclosed': cited in 'The Uses of the Song of Songs: Origen and the Later Latin Fathers', in Clark (1986), p406.

247 that sealed fount . . . some secret unknown: Adam of St Victor, Digby Wrangham, trans., *The Liturgical Poetry of Adam of St Victor*, London 1881, II, 229, quoted in Stewart, p41.

247 *The Virgin was a Garden . . . which was never sowne*: Henry Hawkins, *Partheneia Sacra* (1633), pp13–14, quoted in Stewart, pp43–4.

248 In his preparatory section to the *Partheneia Sacra . . .* the Garden of Eden: see Stewart, pp44–5.

248 The origins of the Paradise garden: see Penelope Hobhouse, *Plants in Garden History*, London 1994, pp18–19.

248 the famed Spring Carpet of . . . Chosroes: see ibid., pp19–20.

249 The garden was surrounded . . . with marvellous bas-reliefs: Giovanni Boccaccio, *The Decameron*, Third Day, in G. H. McWilliam translation, p232.

249 'all began to maintain . . . any other form': ibid., p233.

249 'liberally stocked . . . perfectly charming animals': ibid., p233.

249 'the earthly paradise': Guillaume de Lorris and Jean de Meun, *The Romance of the Rose*, ch. 1, in Horgan translation, p11.

250 And this was on the sixte morwe . . . beautee with plesaunce: Geoffrey Chaucer, *The Franklin's Tale*, ll906–17, in Robinson, p137.

251 *Garden of Paradise* by an unknown Rhenish artist: I am indebted to Anthony Huxley's interpretation of this painting in *The Painted Garden: The garden through the artist's eye*, London 1988, p26.

254 ' "By night, I sought him . . ." . . . is fulfilled in Martha and Mary': quoted in Haskins, p64, and I am indebted to Haskins, pp64–6, for the commentary on Hippolytus.

254 [And] so that the apostles . . . Eve has become apostle: ibid., p65.

255 Mary as the New Eve: see Haskins for Mary Magdalene's multiple roles and the development of her legend.

255 Jesus loved Mary . . . in front of them all: *The Gospel of Philip*, 63:32–64:2, in Robinson, p148.

255 'I am afraid of him . . . the female race': *Pistis Sophia*, 36:71, quoted in Pagels (1990), p85.

256 She whom Luke calls the sinful woman . . . consumed with tears: Gregory the Great, *Homily XXXIII*, quoted in Haskins, p96.

257 'to every sort of voluptuousness' . . . 'false and frivolous': Jacobus de Voragine, *The Golden Legend*, ch. 96, in Ryan, vol. 1, p382.

258 'Full bitterly this bliss it will be bought': the Digby play of *Mary Magdalene*, part I, scene 13, l589, in F. J. Furnivall, ed., *The Digby Plays*, London 1896, p77: text modernized.

258 Ah, gracious Master and Lord . . . for my heart's relief: ibid., part II, scene 25, ll1070–73, p96.

258 Man's heart is my garden . . . smell full sweet: ibid., part II, scene 25, ll1081–5, p96.

259 Maiden in the moor lay . . . the lily-flower: anonymous, MS Rawl. D. 913 (13679), f.1b, Bodleian Library, Oxford: text modernized.

259 Recent scholarship: discussed in Fowler (1984), pp113, 300–301.

259–60 At this time blessed Mary Magdalene . . . no material nourishment: Jacobus de Voragine, *The Golden Legend*, ch. 96, in Ryan, vol. 1, p380.

260 'has blossomed as the rose . . . the Song of Solomon': Fowler (1984), p113.

260 he recalls Jesus' image of the garden of penitence: ibid., pp113–14.

260 'the primrose . . . her purity as a virgin': ibid., p114.

260 'Can a former prostitute . . . in the sight of God': ibid., p114.

261 'Why wilt thou cast . . . let me go!': Dante Gabriel Rossetti, p356.

261 'the snow-limbed Eve from whom she came': *Maud*, part I, XVIII, III:626.

262 O dawn of Eden . . . Hell and of Hate: ibid., part II, I, I:8–10.

262 'That jewelled mass of millinery . . . and of insolence': ibid., part I, VI, VI:232–4.

262 The Virgin, aged about seventeen . . . a symbolic or spiritual meaning . . .: William Michael Rossetti, in *The Pre-Raphaelites and their World*, London 1995, p48.

263 'I hope it will be clearly understood . . . as poetry only have I considered them': Anna Brownell Jameson, quoted in Weaver, p18.

263 'feeble florets are lying . . . from the fierce wind': Ruskin, p140.

263–4 Who is it, think you . . . the Son of Man can lay His head?: ibid., pp142–3.

265 It has always seemed to me . . . the turning flaming sword!: Helena Rutherfurd Ely, *A Woman's Hardy Garden*, New York 1903, pp4–5.

266 'Far off . . . half-finished wall': Hawthorne, *The Marble Faun*, ch. 1, p7.

266 'the pretty figure . . . a symbol . . . of Innocence or Evil close at hand': ibid., p7.

267 praised by . . . Ambrose: in his Hymn for Easter Eve, '*Exsultet jam angelica turba caelorum*', see Warner (1985), p60.

267 Ne had the apple taken been . . . 'Deo gratias': 'Adam lay y-bounden', anonymous, Sloane 2593, f.11b, British Library.

267 'a complexion . . . no Christian maiden's head': Hawthorne, op. cit., ch. 5, p39.

267 'fair young girl, dressed in white': ibid., ch. 6, p43.

267 ' "daughter of the Puritans" ': ibid., p44.

268 'light brown ringlets . . . most feminine and kindly face': ibid., ch. 7, p50.

268 ' "the idea of Divine Womanhood" ': ibid., ch. 6, p44.

268 ' "in your maiden elevation . . . for your nearest neighbors" ': ibid., p44.

268 'In such cases, the girl . . . had turned to dust': ibid., p48.

268-9 'chose the better . . . circle of her own': ibid., p49.

269 Over and over again . . . the motive that impelled her: ibid., ch. 5, p36.

270 'one burning drop of African blood in her veins': ibid., ch. 3, p20.

270 'subtle and evil nature': ibid., ch. 11, p73.

271 ' "the impression of a growing . . . being breathed into him" ': ibid., ch. 41, p302.

271 'the riddle of the Soul's growth . . . incrustations of the senses': ibid., p303.

271 ' "Was the crime . . . reached under no other discipline?" ': ibid., ch. 47, p344.

271 'The story of the Fall of Man! . . . as no other theory can?': ibid., p344.

272 'Sin has educated Donatello . . . a far loftier Paradise than his?': ibid., ch. 50, p364.

272 ' "Do not you perceive . . . written deepest within us?" ': ibid., p364.

272 ' "Woman was tempted by a serpent: why not man?" ': George Eliot, *Daniel Deronda*, book 1, ch. 1, p41.

272 an identification of Eve with her Tempter . . . art and legend: see ch. 10 below.

273 ' "I held my hand, and my heart said, 'Die!' " ': George Eliot, op. cit., book 7, ch. 56, p761.

273 ' "that I may live to be . . . glad that they were born" ': ibid., book 8, ch. 70, p882.

273 ' "I do not yet see how that can be" ': ibid., p882.

CHAPTER 9: AN HELP MEET FOR ADAM

276 ' "You're my wonderful Catherine . . . I'm going to make love to you forever" ': Hemingway, p17.

277–8 ' "I'm the inventive type . . . heard of or imagined" ': ibid., p5.

278 the devilish Lilith: see Patai, pp221ff, and ch. 10 below.

278 ' "Jumping back and forth . . . your way of escaping your duty" ': Hemingway, p190.

279 the androgyny or bisexuality . . . in Genesis 1: some Rabbis interpreted the change from singular to plural in Genesis 1:27 as meaning that God created Adam and Eve as a unity, a hermaphrodite consisting of two bodies, male and female, which were then separated: see *Midrash Rabbah, Genesis* I, VIII:1, p54.

280 John Calvin interpreted . . . 'meet for him': John Calvin, Rev. John King, M.A., trans., *Commentaries on The First Book of Moses called Genesis*, vol. 1, Edinburgh 1847, II:18, pp130–1.

281 'Thus the woman . . . she is cast into servitude': ibid., III:16, p172.

281 'is like a nail driven into the wall . . . the honour of motherhood which have been left her': Martin Luther, *Lectures on Genesis*, 116, 202–3, quoted in Phillips, p105.

282 'They say women . . . she has culture enough': Olive Schreiner, *The Story of an African Farm* [1883], London 1989, part 2, ch. 17, pp176–7.

282 'they naturally seek to gain . . . their impatience through grumbling': Luther, op. cit., quoted in Phillips, p105.

282 'And know ye that the sin . . . And spake right meekly . . .': William Caxton, trans., M. Y. Offord, ed., *The Book of the Knight of the Tower*, London, New York and Toronto 1971, XXXIX, pp62–3: text modernized.

283 'if one require you . . . speak thereof to your lord': ibid., XL, p63: text modernized.

283 a man who . . . failing in his responsibilities to God: see Sommerville, pp210–17, on subjection in marriage. For various views of marriage in the early modern period, see Davis, Fletcher, Hufton, Laurence, Leyser, Sommerville, Stone (1990).

284 his own pamphlets calling for a liberalization of the divorce laws: for

useful discussion of Milton's ideas about marriage and divorce, see Halkett and Nyquist.

284 a formidable ancestry . . . the plots and characterization of Milton's poem: for the sources of *Paradise Lost*, see Evans.

284 'less fair . . . less amiably mild': John Milton, *Paradise Lost*, IV:478–9.

284 'Part of my soul' . . . 'manly grace' and 'wisdom': ibid., IV:487, 490–1.

284–5 *'second self, a very self it self'* . . . 'help meet' for Adam: John Milton, *Tetrachordon*, in Sirluck, p600.

285 'contemplation' and 'valour', Eve for 'softness' and 'sweet attractive grace': Milton, *Paradise Lost*, IV:297–8.

285 an 'easy prohibition': ibid., IV:433.

286 'ensnared/Mankind with her fair looks': ibid., IV:717–18.

286 'connubial love': ibid., IV:743.

286 'O yet happiest if ye seek . . . to know no more': ibid., IV:774–5.

286 'Squat like a toad': ibid., IV:800.

286 'He for God only, she for God in him': ibid., IV:299; and see ch. 6 above, pp170–71.

286 'inward faculties': Milton, *Paradise Lost*, VIII:542.

286 yet when I approach . . . wisest, virtuousest, discreetest, best: ibid., VIII:546–50.

286 'other half': ibid., IV:488.

287 'Union of mind, or in us both one soul': ibid., VIII:604.

287 'author and disposer' . . . knowledge and her praise: ibid., IV:635–8.

287 'outstretched immense': ibid., V:88, and see Matthew 4:8.

288 Eve's fragile happiness depends on her marital fidelity: see Fowler's edition of *Paradise Lost* (1971), pp451, 463, for the symbolism of Eve's flowers.

288 'fairest unsupported flower . . . and storm so nigh': Milton, *Paradise Lost*, IX:432–3.

288 the serpent . . . 'burnished . . . of verdant gold': ibid., IX:495–503.

288 'Empress,' . . . 'goddess among gods . . . angels numberless': ibid., IX:568, 547–8.

288 in the day . . . good and evil as they know: ibid., IX:705–9.

288 'nor was godhead from her thought': ibid., IX:790.

288 'to thy husband's will . . . he over thee shall rule': ibid., X:195–6.

289 'Our great forbidder': ibid., IX:815.

289 'not undesirable . . . for inferior who is free?': ibid., IX:824–5.

289 Adam is not deceived: cf. pseudo-Paul, 'And Adam was not deceived,

but the woman being deceived was in the transgression', 1 Timothy
2:14, and see ch. 6 above.

289 'Certain my resolution is to die': Milton, *Paradise Lost*, IX:907.

289 no no, I feel . . . bliss or woe: ibid., IX:913–16.

290 'dreadful faces' and 'fiery arms' of the angels: ibid., XII:644.

290 Some natural tears . . . took their solitary way: ibid., XII:645–9.

290 to provide 'fellowship' and 'rational delight': ibid., VIII:389, 391.

290 to multiply his image through childbearing: ibid., VIII:424.

290 Milton interprets . . . 'chiefest and the noblest end of mariage': *The
Doctrine and Discipline of Divorce* (1643), II, in Sirluck, p246.

290 'prevention of loneliesse to the mind and spirit of man': ibid.,
p246.

291 'under the specious name of innocence' . . . the wing of
contemplation: Wollstonecraft, ch. 2, pp100–101.

292 Among unequals . . . All rational delight . . .: John Milton, *Paradise
Lost*, VIII:383–91.

292 'author and disposer' . . . obey in everything: ibid., IV:635–6.

292 'in order to co-operate . . . the Supreme Being: Wollstonecraft, ch. 2,
p102.

292 as 'Jehovah's daughter', talked 'face to face' with God: Charlotte
Brontë, *Shirley*, ch. 18, p316.

293 ' "What am I to do . . . me and the grave?" ': ibid., ch. 10, p190.

293 ' "no earthly employment . . . of anything better" ': ibid., ch. 22,
p377.

293 ' "stick to the needle . . . a clever woman some day" ': ibid., ch. 7,
p122.

293 the annuity which he intends . . . (he is already fifty-five): ibid., ch.
11, p204.

293 ' "It is decidedly . . . especially for women" ': ibid., ch. 7, p124.

294 Caroline's plea to the ' "men of England" ' . . . to ' "scheme" ', to
' "plot" ', to ' "flirt" ': ibid., ch. 22, pp376–9, and see ch. 2 above.

294 ' "at her evening prayers . . . Adam stood alone on earth" ': Charlotte
Brontë, *Shirley*, ch. 18, p314.

294 the struggle of giants . . . ' "contend with Omnipotence" ': ibid., ch.
18, p315.

295 'the strength which could bear . . . the consort-crown of creation':
ibid., ch. 18, p315.

295 ' "She coveted an apple, and was cheated by a snake" ': ibid., ch. 18,
p315.

295 the ' "woman-Titan" ' . . . embody the universe: ibid., ch. 18, p315.

295 'her robe of blue air . . . as Adam was his son': ibid., ch. 18, pp315–16.

295 ' "vague and visionary" ': ibid., ch. 18, p316.

296 quoting the pseudo-Paul . . . ' ". . . in the transgression" ': ibid., ch. 18, p322.

296 ' "good" ' men . . . ' "the sons of God" ': ibid., ch. 12, pp225–6.

296 'Moulded in their Maker's image . . . the first of created things': ibid., ch. 12, p226.

296–7 ' "Above us?" ' . . . ' ". . . it is glorious to look up" ': ibid., ch.12, p226.

297 'sullen' and 'ruffianly' beast: ibid., ch. 26, p430.

297 'with head lovingly depressed . . . significant smile': ibid., ch. 26, p430.

297 ' "Adam's son . . . '. . . that moveth upon the earth' " ': ibid., ch. 26, p433.

297 ' "Cary, we are alone: we may speak what we think" ': ibid., ch. 18, p314.

298 'spark of soul . . . a black hollow': ibid., ch. 27, p457.

298 'when the flame of her intelligence . . . she should find exercise?': ibid., ch. 27, pp457–8.

298 she feels 'Something' above relent . . . ' "Eva!" ': ibid., ch. 27, p458.

298 ' "to rescue, to sustain, to cherish, mine own" ': ibid., ch. 27, p459.

298 and, when Time's course closed . . . the crown of Immortality: ibid., ch. 27, p460.

299 ' "What was I created for . . . place in the world?" ': ibid., ch. 10, p190.

299 'His ardour has changed . . . it is regulated': Charlotte Brontë and Emily Brontë, Sue Lonoff, ed. and trans., The Belgian Essays, New Haven and London 1996, plxxiii.

299 ' "And are we equal then, sir? Are we equal at last?" ': Charlotte Brontë, Shirley, ch. 36, p578.

299 ' "You are younger, frailer, feebler, more ignorant than I" ': ibid., ch. 36, p579.

299 ' "Be my companion through life . . . be my friend always!" ': ibid., ch. 36, p580.

299–300 'there she was at last . . . bound with a vow': ibid., ch. 37, p592.

300 'virtually master of Fieldhead . . . became so nominally': ibid., ch. 37, p592.

301 Eve's 'allotted grief' . . . 'creation's groan': Preface to 1844 edition of Elizabeth Barrett Browning's poems, in Browning (1894), pviii.

301 'rather fastened on me than was chosen': ibid., pviii.

301 'more expressible by a woman than a man': ibid., pviii.

301 'to shut close the gates of Eden': ibid., pviii.

301 'into humanity and suffering': 'A Drama of Exile', ibid., p52.

301–2 For was I not . . . Tracked me with greenness?: ibid., p34.

304 the ' "sleek fringes" ' of verse . . . of the rich: Elizabeth Barrett Browning, *Aurora Leigh*, 2:138–41.

304 ' "Eve with nature's daybreak on her face" ': ibid., 2:159.

304 ' "sweat of labour in the early curse" ' has become ' "the sweat of torture" ': ibid., 2:166, 168.

304 'does one of you . . . Of universal anguish?': ibid., 2:206–9.

304 'Women as you are . . . ". . . in my mind" ': ibid., 2:220–5.

305 'am I proved too weak . . . like HIM?': ibid., 2:359–64.

305 ' "It's always so./Anything does for a wife" ': ibid., 2:366–7.

305 ' "weak for art . . . it is strong/For life and duty" ': ibid., 2:372, 374–5.

305 'What you love . . . in her no end': ibid., 2:400–403.

306 ' "Stands single in responsible act and thought" ': ibid., 2:438.

306 ' "the best/She was born for" ': ibid., 2:442–3.

306 ' "I too have my vocation" ': ibid., 2:455.

306 ' "keep up open roads/Betwixt the seen and unseen" ': ibid., 2:468–9.

306 'The speakable, imaginable best . . . speech and imagination': ibid., 2:471–3.

306 'in between us rushed the torrent-world': ibid., 2:1245.

306 the wrong . . . '. . . Which men give women': ibid., 2:531–41.

307 ' "standing at the two extremes/Of social classes" ': ibid., 4:138–9.

307 ' "one clay" ' . . . ' "made us all" ': ibid., 4:109.

307 ' "mercy and ministration" ' . . . ' "woman's heart" ': ibid., 4:141–3.

307 ' "fitter for his handmaid than his wife" ': 4:227.

307 'We're fallen on days . . . Upon the loveless many': ibid., 4:329–33.

308 ' "love's fool-paradise/Is out of date, like Adam's" ': ibid., 4:339–40.

308 the 'dry lifetime' of the 'austere Englishman': ibid., 1:66, 65.

308 'college-learning, law, and parish talk': ibid., 1:67.

308 ' "Love, my child, love, love!" ': ibid., 1:212.

308 ' – a woman, poor or rich . . . spit upon of men . . .': ibid., 9:328–31.

308 'What was in my thought? . . . still less': ibid., 9:369–72.

309 'I was but only yours . . . the dust she came from': ibid., 9:374–8.

309 ' "let [Romney] write/His name upon her" ': ibid., 6:911–12.

309 Virtue's in the *word*! . . . the use of vocal life: ibid., 6:218–20.

309 'if you dressed him in a broadcloth coat/And warmed his Sunday pottage at your fire': ibid., 6:224–5.

310 'a woman of the world', 'centre to herself', isolated in 'self-love and self-will': ibid., 4:513, 514, 516.

310 Her love's a re-adjustment of self-love . . . Than such a charming woman when she loves: ibid., 4:522–7.

310 the 'woman-serpent': ibid., 6:1102.

310 the 'Lamia-woman': ibid., 7:152.

310 the snaky seductresses, descendants of Eve: see ch. 10 below.

311 to make their two discordant clocks chime in accord: *Aurora Leigh*, 4:421–8.

311 'Now, if I had been a woman . . . Than all I have failed in': ibid., 7:184–8.

311 'with another's life': ibid., 7:914.

312 'as if the only man on earth . . . the world's not paradise': ibid., 8:727–31.

312 'A handful of the earth . . . the breath/Which love is': ibid., 9:651–6.

312 'Art is much . . . And makes heaven': ibid., 9:656–9.

312–13 ' "the love of wedded souls" ' . . . sweetened from one central Heart!': ibid., 9:882, 884–6, 888–90.

313 the ' "silver key" ' . . . body and spirit: ibid., 9:916–21.

313 'Shine out for two . . . for two, shall love!': ibid., 9:910–12.

313 faint and far . . . out of heaven to God: ibid., 9:952–7.

313 ' "compensation" ', his ' "dear sight" ': ibid., 9:907.

313 'Jasper first . . . last, an amethyst': ibid., 9:962–4, and see Revelation 21:19–20.

314 Woman was made . . . by whom she is stayed: Christina Rossetti, in Crump (1986), p169.

315 like the fruit of the tree of knowledge . . . the rebel angels: John Milton, *Paradise Lost*, X:547–72.

CHAPTER 10: TEMPTING WOMEN: MERMAIDS, LILITHS AND LAMIAS

318 It may be that vice, depravity and crime . . . what is required to save it: Simone Weil, 'Forms of the Implicit Love of God', in Emma Craufurd, trans., *Waiting for God*, quoted in Bynum, p297.

318 Scholars puzzling over the etymology . . . both of which mean 'serpent': see Cassuto, pp170–71.

319 'he chose a kind of serpent . . . since like approves of like': Peter

Comestor, *Historia Scholastica*, Lib. Gen. XXI, quoted in Evans, p170. Comestor cites Bede as his authority, but as Evans explains, the reference to the serpent's maiden face appears in none of the extant works of Bede.

319 **delighted medieval commentators, who argued . . . for Satan's temptation of Eve**: see Evans, pp181–2; for the origins of the convention, see Phillips, pp61–2.

319 **a bird's wings, an adder's feet . . . the shape of a woman**: R. M. Lumiansky and David Mills, eds, *The Chester Mystery Cycle*, London, New York and Toronto 1974, vol. 1, p21.

319 **'disguised as a reptile with a woman's face'**: William Langland, J. F. Goodridge, trans., *Piers the Ploughman*, Harmondsworth 1966, Book XVIII, p226.

320 **For the ego and the male . . . with death and castration**: Erich Neumann, *The Origins and History of Consciousness*, Princeton, New Jersey 1995, pp157–8.

321 **the horrific Echidna . . . with a hundred cacophonous snake-heads**: Hesiod, *Theogony*, in West, p12, and see p27, for Typhoeus, whom West equates with Typhaon, see note to l306, p67.

321 **she brings forth terrible offspring . . . mother to the Sphinx**: ibid., p12.

321 **a 'brawny water-hag'**: *Beowulf*, XXII, in S. A. J. Bradley, *Anglo-Saxon Poetry*, London and Vermont 1991, p451.

321 **the 'she-wolf of the water'**: ibid., p451.

321 **Spenser's *The Faerie Queene***: Error's Den appears in Book 1, Canto i, stanzas 13–26, in Edmund Spenser, A. C. Hamilton, ed., *The Faerie Queene*, London and New York 1980, pp33–7.

322 **'a goddess armed'**: John Milton, *Paradise Lost*, II:757.

322 **'attractive graces'**: ibid., II:762.

322 **the massive 'thrice threefold' portals**: ibid., II:645.

322 **a 'formidable shape'**: ibid., II:649.

322 **her nether parts are similarly 'foul'**: ibid., II:651.

322–3 **'[v]oluminous and vast', and she is again armed with a 'mortal sting'**: ibid., II:652–3.

323 **the fearful 'shadow' . . . shakes his 'dreadful dart'**: ibid., II:669, 672.

323 **'lawful sheets'**: William Shakespeare, *King Lear*, act IV, scene VI, l119, in Kenneth Muir, ed., London 1964.

323 **'To 't, Luxury, pell-mell!'**: ibid., l119.

323 **the 'riotous appetite' of the 'simp'ring dame'**: ibid., ll125, 120.

323 Down from the waist they are Centaurs . . . Stench, consumption . . .: ibid., ll126–31.

323 'an ounce of civet' to 'sweeten' his imagination: ibid., ll132–3.

324 Symbols of 'worldliness, insincerity and falsehood': Erwin Panofsky, *Studies in Iconology: Humanistic Themes In the Art of the Renaissance*, New York 1972, p89. I am indebted to his commentary on this painting, pp86–90.

324 Vasari defined this tortured creature as Jealousy: ibid., p87.

324 the ambiguous figure of a girl: ibid., pp89–90.

324 Time with his wings and hourglass . . . who may represent Truth: ibid., p90.

324–5 'Luxury, surrounded by personifications . . . manifest evils': ibid., p90.

325 'What else is woman . . . painted with fair colours?': see note to p125, ch. 4 above.

326 Melusine's serpent's tail . . . female sexual secrets: see Chadwick (1985), pp141–2, for discussion of Melusine and her influence on the Surrealists; Warner (1994), ch. 1, for other legends about snaky female charmers.

326 snake-haired Medusa, witchy Scylla . . . by isolation and even death: Byatt (1990), p292.

326 ' "the terror of ancient pagan cults . . . in this strange legend" ': ibid., p349.

326 'Why should desire . . . outcasts, *sorcières*, monsters . . .': ibid., p349.

326 Sabine's story ends tragically: ibid., p380.

326–7 Robert Graves . . . the boat's entire crew: Robert Graves, *The White Goddess: A historical grammar of poetic myth*, London 1961, pp394–5.

327 in churches all over England . . . to entrap the unwary: see Francis Bond, *Wood Carvings in English Churches: I Misericords*, Oxford 1910, pp8–12; J. C. D. Smith, *A Guide to Church Woodcarvings*, Devon 1974, pp89–92.

327 Eve, 'the first temptress' . . . to dupe and lie: Heinrich Kramer and James Sprenger, Montague Summers, trans., *Malleus Maleficarum: The classic study of witchcraft*, London 1996, part I, question 6, p44.

327 it should be noted . . . a contrary direction to a man: ibid., p44.

327 'an imperfect animal' and 'always deceives': ibid., p44.

327 its face was that of a radiant and noble lion . . . the virulent tail of a viper: ibid., p46.

327 'is beautiful to look upon, contaminating to the touch, and deadly to keep': ibid., p46.

328 as she is a liar by nature . . . the passers-by and kill them: ibid., p46.

328 The mermaid . . . some paradoxical and potent mixture of the two: Shields, p97.

329 'She doesn't belong . . . they'll never have it': Dunmore (1994), pp219–20.

329 Guiseppe di Lampedusa's . . . 'The Professor and the Siren': Archibald Colquhoun, trans., in Guiseppe Tomasi di Lampedusa, *The Siren and Selected Writings*, London 1995.

329 Hans Andersen: 'The Little Mermaid', first published in 1837.

330 Yeats' 'The Song of Wandering Aengus': in *The Collected Poems of W. B. Yeats*, London, Melbourne and Toronto 1950.

330 the elusive White Goddess: see Graves, op. cit. For a female poet's response to the difficulties of being a muse, see Eavan Boland, *Object Lessons: The Life of the Woman and the Poet in Our Time*, Manchester 1995. The debate is continued in her poetry: see *Collected Poems*, Manchester 1995.

330 Lilith . . . fled to the Red Sea: for Lilith, see ch. 9 above. For an account of Lilith in Jewish tradition, see Patai, pp221ff.

331 a potent mix on which artists and poets drew freely for their images of woman: for an exploration of the iconography of feminine evil in fin-de-siècle culture, see Dijkstra.

331 'Christabel': in Coleridge, pp213ff.

332 'demon's mistress, or the demon's self': John Keats, *Lamia*, I:56, in Roe, p221.

332 'deep volcanian yellow' . . . 'scarlet pain': ibid., I:155, 154, p223.

332 Keats based his poem on a narrative in Burton's *Anatomy of Melancholy*: reprinted in ibid., pp323–4.

332 'could not love in half a fright': ibid., 1:335, p228.

333 'woman's lore' . . . 'unperplex'd delight and pleasure known': ibid., 1:325, 327, p228.

333 Kenyon Cox's *Lilith*: see Dijkstra, pp308–9.

333 'gazing on herself in the glass . . . within their own circle': Dante Gabriel Rossetti, in a letter of 1870, quoted in Andrew Wilton and Robert Upstone, eds, *The Age of Rossetti, Burne-Jones and Watts: Symbolism in Britain 1860–1910*, London 1997, p102, and for a reproduction of *Lady Lilith*, see ibid., p103.

333 [she] draws out through a comb . . . faultless fleshly beauty and peril of pleasure unavoidable: Swinburne, 'Notes on Some Pictures of 1868' in *Essays and Studies*, 1875; quoted ibid., p24.

333 Tennyson tamed the temptress: Tennyson, 'The Lady of Shalott'.

334 Those who like may peep down . . . revelling and feasting on their wretched pickled victims: W. M. Thackeray, *Vanity Fair*, London n.d., ch. LXIV, pp877–8.

334 her serpent's livery of green and silver . . . gracefully winding neck: George Eliot, *Daniel Deronda*, book 1, ch. 1, pp40–1.

334 Mr Farebrother refers to Rosamond as a 'siren': George Eliot, W. J. Harvey, ed., *Middlemarch*, Harmondsworth 1985, book 3, ch. 31, p333.

334 Lydgate calls her a 'mermaid': ibid., book 5, ch. 43, p475.

335 'barbaric double-headed snake': Rider Haggard, *She*, ch. 14, p162.

335 'the agony, the blind passion, and the awful vindictiveness': ibid., p163.

336 'sight to dream of, not to tell': Coleridge, 'Christabel', op. cit., part 1, l253.

336 'as Eve might have stood before Adam': Rider Haggard, op. cit., ch. 26, p291.

336 'naked to the torture of pure interpenetrating inward light': MacDonald, *Lilith*, ch. 39, p203.

336 phallically lopped off . . . given him by the avenging angel: see Gilbert and Gubar (1989), ch. 1, for commentary on *She* and *Lilith* and 'The Agon of the Femme Fatale'.

337 ' "Sorrow and labour will be your lot" ': 'The Garden of Paradise', in H. C. Andersen, *The Garden of Paradise and Other Stories*, London 1923, no page numbers.

337 ' "good and holy" ': ibid.

337 'if his thoughts are wicked . . . the twinkling stars up there': ibid.

337 'unwearying strength and endless days like a goddess': Lewis (1990), p162.

337 'stronger in dark Magic': ibid., p161.

337 ' "length of days . . . she begins to know it" ': ibid., p162.

338 *fica*, the vulgar Italian term for the female genitalia: Phillips, p68.

338 Rabbi Jose told the story . . . to cover the nakedness of the guilty pair: *Midrash Rabbah*, *Genesis* I, XV:7, pp123–4.

338 other Rabbis thought . . . bread, the staff of life: ibid., pp122–4.

338 In the Middle Ages . . . in classical and Christian tradition: see Phillips, p85.

338 'apples of Paradise': C. W. R. D. Moseley, trans., *The Travels of Sir John Mandeville*, Harmondsworth 1983, ch. 7, p65.

338 melons were known as 'Adam's apples': ibid., p65.

338 Linnaeus endorsed the Arab tradition . . . the wise men of India lived off the banana: Jane Grigson's *Fruit Book*, Harmondsworth 1983, p50;

and on the banana as the fruit of knowledge, see Marina Warner, 'Diary', *London Review of Books*, 25 May 1995, p25.

338 'magnificently inebriating effects . . . on both our parents': Rose Macaulay, 'Eating and Drinking', in *Personal Pleasures*, London 1936, p179.

340 equal with Rochester at the feet of God: Charlotte Brontë, *Jane Eyre* [1847], London and Glasgow 1953, ch. 23, p289.

340 'a luxuriance . . . more of a woman than she really was': Thomas Hardy, *Tess of the d'Urbervilles*, ch. V, p38.

341 'to adroit advantages he took of her helplessness': ibid., ch. XII, p84.

341 'temporarily blinded by his ardent manners': ibid., p84.

341 ' "My eyes were dazed by you for a little, and that was all" ': ibid., p79.

341 'the serpent hisses where the sweet birds sing': ibid., p78.

341 '[a]n immeasurable social chasm . . . that previous self of hers': ibid., ch. XI, p75.

341 ' "'Tis nater, after all, and what do please God" ': ibid., ch. XII, p85.

341 'the expression of irremediable grief . . . vague ethical being': ibid., ch. XIII, p88.

341 'based on shreds . . . moral hobgoblins': ibid., p88.

341 It was they that were out of harmony . . . in which she fancied herself such an anomaly: ibid., p88.

342 'the sap in the twigs': ibid., ch. XV, p104.

342 'It was unexpended youth . . . the invincible instinct towards self-delight': ibid., p104.

342 'milk and butter grew to rankness': ibid., ch. XVI, p106.

342 'You use the word *succulent* . . . rather too much succulence': Mowbray Morris, quoted in Peter Keating, *The Haunted Study: A Social History of the English Novel 1875–1914*, London 1991, p261.

342 '[N]ourished by the succulent feed . . . this prime season of the year': Hardy, ch. XVI, p110.

342 'Their large-veined udders hung ponderous . . . fell in drops to the ground': ibid., p110.

342 'damp and rank with juicy grass which sent up mists of pollen at a touch': ibid., ch. XIX, p128.

343 'gathering cuckoo-spittle on her skirts . . . naked arms sticky blights': ibid., p128.

343 'the oozing fatness and warm ferments . . . the hiss of fertilization': ibid., ch. XXIV, p154.

343 'feverishly under the oppressiveness . . . one organism called sex':
    ibid., ch. XXIII, p152.

343 'something educated, reserved, subtle, sad, differing': ibid., ch. XVII,
    p116.

343 ' "a fresh and virginal daughter of Nature" ': ibid., ch. XVIII, p125.

343 'a visionary essence of woman' whom . . . Artemis and Demeter:
    ibid, ch. XX, p136.

343 'fat alluvial soil': ibid., ch. XXVII, p174.

343 'the languid perfume of the summer fruits . . . the very bees and
    butterflies, drowsy': ibid., pp174–5.

344 'the red interior of her mouth as if it had been a snake's': ibid., p175.

344 a little later Hardy himself compares her to Eve: ibid., p176.

344 in the present case, as in millions . . . shocks, catastrophes, and
    passing-strange destinies: ibid., ch. V, p39. Hardy was evidently
    referring to the idea discussed in Plato's *Symposium* that human beings
    initially consisted of two people joined together into one body. The two
    halves were separated by the gods as a punishment for humanity's pride
    and insolence and, as a result, each half yearned for and sought out its
    severed part.

345 Christina Rossetti's *Goblin Market*: all text references to Crump, vol. 1,
    pp11ff. The poem has received wide critical comment: for interesting
    modern interpretations, see Gilbert and Gubar (1984); Maureen Duffy,
    The Erotic World of Faery, London 1972; Ellen Moers, *Literary Women*,
    London 1977; Jan Marsh, *Christina Rossetti: A Literary Biography*, London
    1994.

345 'two blossoms on one stem': *Goblin Market*, l188.

345 'Plump unpecked cherries . . . Citrons from the South . . .': ibid.,
    ll7–10, 28–9.

345 'hungry thirsty roots': ibid., l45.

346 One had a cat's face . . . One crawled like a snail . . .: ibid., ll71–4.

346 [She] sucked their fruit globes . . . She sucked until her lips were
    sore . . .: ibid., ll128–30, 133–4, 136.

346 syrupped all her face . . . which quaked like curd: ibid., ll434–6.

347 'Hug me, kiss me, suck my juices . . . drink me, love me . . .': ibid.,
    ll468–71.

347 'For there is no friend like a sister . . . if one goes astray . . .': ibid.,
    ll562–5.

347–8 'for joys brides hope to have': ibid., l314.

348 her difficult struggle for self-suppression: see Kathleen Jones, *Learning
    not to be first: The Life of Christina Rossetti*, Oxford 1992.

348 the 'calm' to Christina's 'storm': among the Rossetti family, Dante Gabriel and Christina were known as 'the storms', Maria and William as 'the calms': see Georgina Battiscombe, *Christina Rossetti: A Divided Life*, London 1981, p16.

348 **William Rossetti . . . through some 'spiritual backsliding'**: see Marsh, op. cit., p237.

348 **'pleasant days . . . not-returning time'**: *Goblin Market*, ll550–1.

CHAPTER 11: EVE TELLS HER OWN STORY

350 **[T]here is no fruit . . . it is not our determination to eat**: Olive Schreiner, *Woman and Labour*, London and Leipsic 1911, p167.

350 **'"Oh, I am alone! I am utterly alone!"'**: Schreiner, 'Three Dreams in a Desert', p81.

351 **'strength which could bear a thousand years of bondage'**: Charlotte Brontë, *Shirley*, ch. 18, p315.

351 **her work offers a unique vision . . . for a more truthful coexistence**: see, for example, Waldo's vision of the search for truth interpreted to him by the stranger in *The Story of an African Farm*, London 1989, ch. 15, pp141–55.

352 **'Perhaps the Garden of Eden embodies . . . resilience, adaptability, and the power of improvisation'**: Dunmore (1988), p60.

352 **'an overpowering, electrifying presence'**: Dronke, p144.

353 **Adam symbolizes, but does not share . . . in every child that she bears**: Newman, p93. For my brief summary, I am indebted to her careful analysis of Hildegard's thought in ch. 3, 'The Woman and the Serpent', pp89ff.

353 **Just as man came from the earth . . . any object that stands between them**: ibid., pp95–7.

353 **in one activity they perform . . . Woman cooperates with man, and man with woman . . .**: Hildegard, *Scivias*, I.2.12, quoted in ibid., p99.

354 **Adam experienced a great love . . . he might beget children**: Hildegard, *Causae et curae*, 136, quoted in ibid., p112.

354 **as a kind of heavenly dew**: Newman, p111, quotes Peter Dronke, who notes in *Poetic Individuality*, p157, that for Hildegard *sudor* (sweat): 'has the associations not of the sweat of effort but of the distillation of a perfume, a heavenly quality, out of anything that is fertile or beautiful on earth'.

354 **the work of scholars . . . to explicate her texts**: see Newman and

Dronke; see also Sabina Flanagan's biography: *Hildegard of Bingen, 1098–1179: A Visionary Life*, London and New York 1989.

354 **there is a lack of the continuity and cross-referencing . . . early feminist theologians**: see Lerner, ch. 7, 'One Thousand Years of Feminist Bible Criticism', pp138ff, in which she points out the 'continuing tradition of women's religious writing', along with 'the lack of continuity and the absence of collective memory on the part of women thinkers', p139. Lerner's chapter provides a useful summary of women writers' responses to traditional interpretations of the biblical view of women.

355 **'she should be at his side . . . as his own flesh'**: Christine de Pizan, *The Book of the City of Ladies*, in Blumenfeld-Kosinski, p132.

355 **'was made by the supreme craftsman . . . the body of man that God made her'**: ibid., p132.

355–6 **'God created this soul . . . the female and male bodies'**: ibid., p132.

356 **'it is through woman . . . it was lifted up by the Creator'**: ibid., pp132–3.

356 **The Renaissance humanist, Isotta Nogarola . . . the Venetian Ludovico Foscarini**: for a brief introduction and English translation of the letters, see King and Rabil, pp57ff.

357 **The creation of man and woman . . . women are more excellent than men**: *Jane Anger her Protection for Women*, in Shepherd, p39. Jane Anger was possibly a pseudonym for a probably female author; Shepherd, however, p30, notes a number of possible Jane or Joan Angers who could have been responsible for the pamphlet, and remarks that a pseudonym would probably have been more elaborate and possibly Italian- or Latinate at this period.

357 **'whereby the world increaseth . . . the first that repented of sin'**: ibid., p39.

357 **'In women is only true fidelity: . . . everything about them be curious?'**: ibid., p39.

357 **'They confess we are necessary, but they would have us likewise evil'**: ibid., p39.

358 **when she was still under twenty**: see Shepherd, p58.

358 **'the whole earth was cursed'**: Rachel Speght, *A Mouzell [Muzzle] for Melastomus, The Cynical Bayter of, and foul mouthed Barker against Evahs Sex*, London 1617, in Shepherd, p66.

358 **'as if sin were imperfect . . . had transgressed'**: ibid., p67.

358 **'he is a Saviour of believing women no less than of men'**: ibid., p67.

358 'the whole burden of domestical affairs and maintenance on the shoulders of their wives': ibid., p70.

358 'which are reasonable creatures . . . in all things lawful': ibid., p70. For a further riposte to Swetnam which includes an energetic and persuasive defence of Eve, see Ester Sowernam, *Ester hath hang'd Haman*, London 1617, in Shepherd, pp85–124.

359 'consumed her goods': see Blain, Clements and Grundy, entry on Lanyer.

359 Our Mother Eve . . . our fall so sure a plot had laid: Aemilia Lanyer, *Salve Deus Rex Judaeorum*, stanza 96:3–8, quoted in Hannay, p217. I have modernized the text.

359–60 'Created in perfect equality . . . in harmony and love': Sarah Grimké, Letter I, in Bartlett, p32.

360 All creation swarmed . . . endowed with immortality . . .: ibid., p32.

360 'was exposed to temptation . . . consequently from happiness, *but not from equality*': ibid., p33.

360 'God's appointed agent of *morality* . . . the virtues of humanity': Hale, pxxxv.

361 Left to himself, his love becomes lust . . . and *selfishness* is the sin of depravity: ibid., pxxxvi.

361 'the mission of disinterested affection . . . not to herself': ibid., pxxxvi.

361 'would make war with the Evil . . . Sin, Death, and the Grave': ibid., pxxxvi.

361 'the term *man* included *woman* . . . made in the "likeness of God"': ibid., pxxxvi.

361 'there was a care and preparation . . . not bestowed on man': ibid., pxxxvi.

361 'the crown' of creation, 'the *last* . . . above animal life': ibid., pxxxvi.

361 'where he was deficient' . . . 'her intuitive knowledge of heavenly things': ibid., pxxxvii.

361 'she was the spiritual leader . . . compliance without reason or from inferior considerations': ibid., p39.

361 'was in accordance with his character . . . to hard labour for life': ibid., p39.

362 Thus was motherhood predicated . . . mental triumphs would be won: ibid., p39.

362 'women's commentaries on women's position in the Old and New Testaments': Stanton, p9.

362 'missing link' . . . 'woman the author of all our woes': ibid., p24.

362 'courage', 'dignity' and 'lofty ambition' . . . 'high character': ibid., p24.

362 'he roused in the woman . . . through the entire drama': ibid., p25.

362 'degradation and subjection to man': ibid., p25.

363 With obedience to the laws of health . . . transformed into a blessing: ibid., p25.

363 'Some churchmen . . . the greatest factor in civilization': ibid., p25.

363 'Adam and Eve were created on Friday, October 28th, 4004 B. C.': Hale, p39.

363 Forty years later: Elizabeth Cady Stanton was not, of course, the last feminist to revise conventionally negative readings of Eve. For some interesting modern readings, see Bal, Meyers, Nyquist and Trible (1976, 1992); also Mary Daly, *Beyond God the Father*, London 1986.

364 'full of delightful things, wild roses, and sassafras, and birds' nests': Coolidge, ch. 2, p15.

364 it was comforting to remember . . . take possession of their Eden: ibid., p22.

365 'In solitude what happiness?': see John Milton, *Paradise Lost*, VIII:364–5.

365 Mary Shelley's *Frankenstein*, first published in 1818: the text used follows the revised 1831 edition: see Joseph, pxv. All text references are to Joseph's edition.

365 ' "the land of mist and snow" ': Mary Shelley, *Frankenstein*, letter II, p21, quoting Samuel Taylor Coleridge, *The Rime of the Ancient Mariner*, l134.

366 Walton's 'want' of a companion: Mary Shelley, op. cit., letter II, p19.

366 '[c]uriosity': ibid., ch. II, p36.

366 'secrets of heaven and earth': ibid., p37.

366 'nature to her hiding-places': ibid., ch. IV, p54.

366 'unfold to the world the deepest mysteries of creation': ibid., ch. III, p48.

366 'workshop of filthy creation': ibid., ch. IV, p55.

366 'only consolation' . . . 'the face of man': ibid., ch. IX, p90.

367 'like a restless spectre . . . miserable in the separation': ibid., ch. XX, p169.

367 'a solitary cell': ibid., ch. XXIII, p198.

367 'destructive and almost endless journey . . . ices of the ocean': ibid., ch. XXIV, p206.

367 the wasteland of alienation from God . . . to be irrevocably

committed: again, an identification with the Ancient Mariner seems clearly intended.

367 ' "pursue and destroy the being to whom I gave existence" ': ibid., ch. XXIV, p212.

367 ' "beloved dead" ' . . . ' "[s]eek happiness in tranquillity, and avoid ambition" ': ibid., ch. XXIV, p217.

367 'Believe me, Frankenstein . . . and they shall share my wretchedness': ibid., ch. X, p100.

368 'I was . . . endued with a figure . . . and whom all men disowned?': ibid., ch. XIII, p120.

368 'But where were my friends and relations? . . . who claimed any intercourse with me': ibid., ch. XIII, p121.

368 ' "Who was I? What was I? Whence did I come? What was my destination?" ': ibid., ch. XV, p128.

368-9 ' "Like Adam, I was apparently united by no link to any other being in existence" ': ibid., p129.

369 'He had come forth . . . I was wretched, helpless, and alone': ibid., p129.

369 ' "beautiful and alluring, after his own image" ': ibid., p130.

369 ' "a filthy type . . . even from the very resemblance" ': ibid., p130.

369 ' "for often, like him . . . the bitter gall of envy rose within me" ': ibid., p129.

369 ' "the fallen angel . . . a malignant devil" ': ibid., ch. XXIV, p221.

369 'Evil be thou my good': Milton, *Paradise Lost*, IV:110, and see Frankenstein's words: ' "Evil thenceforth became my good" ', Mary Shelley, op. cit., ch. XXIV, p220.

369 ' "[He] had his companions . . . but I am solitary and abhorred" ': ibid., ch. XV, p130.

369 ' "Increase of knowledge" ' . . . ' "no Eve soothed my sorrows, nor shared my thoughts; I was alone" ': ibid., p131.

369-70 'Remember, that I am thy creature . . . and I shall again be virtuous': ibid., ch. X, p100.

370 ' "with whom I can live . . . necessary for my being" ': ibid., ch. XVII, p144.

370 ' "one as deformed and horrible as myself" ': ibid., ch. XVI, p144.

370 ' "harmless" ' lives: ibid., ch. XVII, p146.

370 ' "as a right which you must not refuse to concede" ': ibid., p144.

370 ' "in communion with an equal . . . from which I am now excluded" ': ibid., p147.

370 ' "quit the neighbourhood of man . . . in the most savage of places" ': ibid., p147.

370 'she, who in all probability . . . made before her creation': ibid., ch. XX, p165.

370 ' "I shall be with you on your wedding-night" ': ibid., p168.

370 a later tale . . . fashioned out of clay: see Joseph, introduction, pvi, and Appendix B, 'Shaftesbury on Prometheus', pp228–9.

371 'paradisiacal dreams . . . to drive me from all hope': Mary Shelley, op. cit., ch. XXII, p189.

371 'the ethereal sky' . . . 'bottomless perdition': John Milton, *Paradise Lost*, I:45, 47.

371 'greatness of his fall': Mary Shelley, op. cit., ch. XXIV, p210.

371 ' "never, never again to rise . . . I am chained in an eternal hell" ': ibid., ch. XXIV, p211.

371 'the dull yellow eye' . . . 'breathless horror and disgust': ibid., ch. V, p57.

371 ' "happiness and well-being" ': ibid., ch. XXIV, p217.

371 'The light of that conflagration . . .' . . . and lost in darkness and distance: ibid., ch. XXIV, p223.

372 'When in utter solitude I weep . . . I would fain immure myself': Paula R. Feldman and Diana Scott-Kilvert, eds, *The Journals of Mary Shelley 1814–1844*, vol. II: *1822–1844*, Oxford 1987, pp440–1.

372 'Sorrow – Sorrow – Why am I here?': ibid., p446.

372 'The extreme solitude in which I now live . . . but peaceful grave . . .': ibid., p451.

373 St Peter has been sustained . . . heart and imagination: Cather, p258.

373 'long, blue, hazy smear' of Lake Michigan: ibid., p29.

374 Augusta's 'forms': ibid., p17.

374 the leaves of their separate ' "life work" ' . . . in the middle of the box: ibid., pp22–3.

374 'a dead, opaque, lumpy solidity . . . tightly packed sawdust': ibid., p18.

375 ' "certain disappointments" ' or ' "cruel biological necessities" ': ibid., p21.

375 'a hand . . . her clear-cut ambitions': ibid., pp274–5.

375 'a stamp . . . beaten out any longer': ibid., p274.

375 'full of pretty fancies . . . but Medea's, he wondered?': ibid., p126.

375 ' "it was thought queer . . . he had observed women so closely all his life" ': ibid., p156.

376 'the work of this secondary social man, the lover . . . books were born as well as daughters': ibid., p265.

376 'when his wife began to be unreasonable . . . on the tennis court': ibid., p14.

376 'glistening, barren shrubs': ibid., p52.

377 ' "brute strength and ferocity" ': ibid., p220.

378 the legendary sacred serpent of the pueblo Indians: referred to in Cather's *Death Comes for the Archbishop* (1927), book 4, Snake Root.

378 ' "that have no other ancestors to inherit from" ': ibid., p242.

378 ' "preserved through the ages by a miracle . . . I'd as soon have sold my own grandmother as Mother Eve" ': ibid., p244.

379 'the mother incest so familiar to us, the punishment and so on': Sigmund Freud, letter to Jung dated 17 December 1911, in William McGuire, ed., *The Freud/Jung Letters*, Princeton, New Jersey 1974, p288, quoted in Phillips, p89.

379 only one of several possible readings: see, for example, commentary in Byatt and Sodré, Lee, Gilbert and Gubar (1989).

380 'without delight': Cather, p282.

380 'let something go . . . something very precious': ibid., p282.

380 'the ground under his feet': ibid., p283.

380 For thee a house was built . . . thou of woman camest: ibid., p272. Longfellow's translation of an Anglo-Saxon poem, misquoted by Cather: see A. S. Byatt introduction, final page.

380 'had the anxious look . . . an inhabitant of mediaeval Flanders': Brookner, p21.

381 'her ribbed Gothic feet shone palely': ibid., p21.

381 'a life of forbearance . . . the Christian virtues, in fact': ibid., p69.

381 'For . . . the world respects a predator . . . the charming libertine': ibid., p79.

381 'timorous decency': ibid., p79.

381 'part of the fallen creation . . . and to be excluded': ibid., p79.

381 'mournful in its righteousness . . . living in expectation': ibid., p79.

381 'how is it possible . . . in this way?': ibid., p15.

381 'the archaic smile of the kouroi': ibid., p9. Kouroi or korai, full-size standing marble statues of young maidens, date from the mid-seventh century to the early fifth century BC.

381 'an essential secret . . . escaped her', a 'certainty' and 'fulfilment': ibid., p9.

381 'Love was the passing favour . . . scented the warm air': ibid., p20.

382 'The sun is God': ibid., p7.

382 'for those whom the gods disdained . . . and no lavishness bestowed': ibid., p20.

382 a sign that will initiate her into the secret mysteries: ibid., p9.

382 'blind and undifferentiated' smile of Sally Beamish: ibid., p39.

382 the 'true pagan' smile: ibid., p40.

382 'would operate according to the laws . . . of the fallen world': ibid., p40.

382 Phyllis Duff . . . the virtuous wife in Proverbs: ibid., p14.

382 'movers and shakers, careless and lawless': ibid., p63.

382 'primitive and half-conscious energies': ibid., p64.

382–3 'the uncomplaining and compliant posture . . . posture of the ideal mistress': ibid., p64.

383 she has read the wrong kind of fiction: ibid., p94.

383 'shackled by the wrong mythology': ibid., p108.

383 'sail, impervious to mortal needs, above the world of just deserts': ibid., p147.

383 'striding with all their ideal muscularity . . . the beginning of the world': ibid., p147.

383 'the confusion of Adam and Eve . . . massively, rebuked': ibid., p147.

383 their transformative 'energy and bliss': ibid., p148.

383 'eternal children . . . too inexperienced to challenge': ibid., p158.

383 'a sign of forgiveness': ibid., p148.

383 her relationship with Sally and Elinor was a 'misalliance': ibid., p185.

383 an attempt to go against her true nature: ibid., p107.

383 ' "there *are* no bad. Indifference to the good is all that is needed" ': ibid., p171.

383 ' "a little more carelessly . . . Art can be very subversive" ': ibid., p176.

386 ' "It's gone forever, that funny, young, lost look that I loved" ': du Maurier, ch. 21, p313.

387 'nymphs are not known for their maternal feelings': Brookner, p60.

387 'an eternal agent of reconciliation': ibid., p71.

387 'the last hope of a good outcome . . . by false expectations': ibid., p71.

389 ' "loved – idolized – honored" ': Gilman, p61.

389 'We talk fine things about women . . . very limited beings': ibid., p141.

389 When we say *men, man* . . . – 'the world': ibid., p137.

390 'when we say *women*, we think *female* – the sex': ibid., p137.

390 'feminine civilization', 'the word *woman* . . . only *male* – the sex': ibid., p137.

391 the ' "love-woman" ' Caroline: Bagnold, p96.

391 'a calm, a stoic pleasure in *procession*': ibid., p154.

391 ' "a pipe through which the generations pass" ': ibid., p155.

391 'in a line of women . . . these three women were one': ibid., p264.

391 ‘ "Death is the matter with life" ’: ibid., p45.

391 ‘ "Axed – my babyhood! . . . Axed – my life" ’: ibid., p41.

391 ‘ "How old are you?" ’: ibid., p256.

391 ‘a child in the womb . . . Death recedes’: ibid., p153.

391 ‘body already a little threadbare’: ibid., p154.

391 ‘her own end as endurable’: ibid., p155.

391 ‘She who had once been thirsty and gay . . . her knot of human lives’: ibid., p16.

391 ‘female’, but ‘now what was left . . . neither male nor female’: ibid., p20.

392 ‘the white shirt-front of a man’: ibid., p47.

392 ‘ "I can take nothing of that sort any more" ’: ibid., p47.

392 ‘ "love-woman" ’, ‘ "made to please" ’: ibid., p96.

392 ‘ "older and tougher . . . more male" ’: ibid., p96.

392 ‘ "saying the farewell to sex . . . without mirage, without props" ’: ibid., p175.

392 ‘ "You’re the thing that man sees when he says ‘woman’ " ’: ibid., pp191–2.

392 ‘ "wumen" ’: ‘ "hard-working, faulty . . . in a wheelbarrow" ’: ibid., p191.

392 Bagnold’s own midwife Ethel Raynham Smith: see Anne Sebba’s introduction, ibid., px.

392 she has made her own ‘ "farewell to sex" ’: ibid., p174.

392 ‘ "You’re a drone . . . become a third sex" ’: ibid., p175.

392 ‘ "because I wanted myself for myself" ’: ibid., p129.

392 ‘ "It developed the male in me, the *choosing* streak in me" ’: ibid., p129.

392–3 ‘When you learn that another creature . . . from the very base of the heart . . .’: ibid., p130.

393 ‘with a deep, female pride, she felt herself . . . ticked Time away’: ibid., p264.

394 ‘For Adam was first formed, then Eve . . . she shall be saved by [*sic*] childbearing . . .’: Atwood, p233; and see 1 Timothy 2:13–15.

395 ‘only women who are fruitful and women who are barren’: ibid., p71.

395 ‘ "Nature demands variety, for men" ’: ibid., p249.

396 fundamentalist Islam: the role and influence of Islamic Eve have been outside the scope of this book. For a fictional treatment of some of the religious and social issues involved, see Nawal El Saadawi, Sherif Hetata, trans., *The Innocence of the Devil*, London 1994.

396 'the lowercase . . . generic appellations "poodle," "parrot," "dog," or "bird,"': Le Guin (1995), p332.

396 ' "doesn't exactly seem to fit very well lately" ': ibid., p333.

396 'My words now must be as slow . . . against the winter shining': ibid., p333.

396 rewritten by the divorce court . . . a negligent mother: Byatt (1996), pp517–20.

397 'the original speech of God . . . simply by naming it': ibid., p190.

397 '*one*, as a man and his shadow . . . mind and his brain': ibid., p190.

397 'the languages of men' became opaque, mysterious, idiosyncratic: ibid., p190.

397 'solitude and melancholy': Carter (1982) , p110.

397 'the abode of enforced sterility . . . part of the earth': ibid., p40.

397 the biblically named Beulah, Isaiah's new Israel: see Isaiah 62:4.

397 ' "reactivate the parthenogenesis archetype" ': ibid., p68.

397–8 'the authentic Messiah . . . born of a man': ibid., p69.

398 ' "sexuality is a unity manifested in different structures" ': ibid., p66.

398 'every kitsch excess of the mode of femininity': ibid., p71.

398 'blown up to larger than life-size . . . the murmuring of contented mothers': ibid., p72.

398 'does a change . . . the taste of a fruit?': ibid., p68.

398 'the cock in my head . . . sight of myself': ibid., p75.

398 'seppuku, a ritual . . . upon myself': ibid., p102.

398 'as savage an apprenticeship . . . been devised for me': ibid., p107.

398 'become almost the thing I was': ibid., p107.

398 'blasted his seed' . . . 'Masculinity incarnate': ibid., p104.

398 'My bride will become my child's father': ibid., p136.

399 Masculine and feminine are correlatives . . . the answer to these questions: ibid., pp149–50.

399 'Mother is a figure of speech . . . beyond consciousness': ibid., p184.

399 'The vengeance of the sex is love': ibid., p191.

399 women have been prepared . . . the Genesis account of origins: other interesting fictional treatments include Farmer, Figes, Tennant and Wiggins. See, too, Wandor's Lilith/Eve poems.

AFTERWORD: INTO THE FUTURE

403 'All the mythic versions of women . . . the real conditions of life': Carter (1979), p5.

SELECT BIBLIOGRAPHY

Works and editions consulted:

Peter R. Ackroyd, 'Goddesses, Women and Jezebel', in Cameron and Kuhrt

Aeschylus, Philip Vellacott, trans., *The Oresteian Trilogy: Agamemnon, The Choephori, The Eumenides*, Harmondsworth 1959

Robert Alter, *The Art of Biblical Narrative*, London 1981

Robert Alter, trans. and ed., *Genesis: Translation and Commentary*, New York and London 1996

St Ambrose, Rev. H. De Romestin, M.A., et al., trans., *St Ambrose: Select Works and Letters*, in H. Wace and P. Schaff, gen. eds, *A Select Library of Nicene and Post-Nicene Fathers of the Christian Church*, 2nd series, vol. X, Oxford and New York 1896

Bernhard W. Anderson, *The Living World of the Old Testament*, 4th edition, Harlow 1988

Lucius Apuleius, Robert Graves, trans., Michael Grant, revis., *The Golden Ass*, Harmondsworth 1990

Aristotle, A. L. Peck, trans., *Generation of Animals*, Cambridge, Mass. and London 1942

Margaret Atwood, *The Handmaid's Tale*, London 1987

Erich Auerbach, Willard R. Trask, trans., *Mimesis: The Representation of Reality in Western Literature*, Princeton, New Jersey 1953

Nina Auerbach, *Woman and the Demon: The Life of a Victorian Myth*, Cambridge, Mass. and London 1982

St Augustine, Henry Bettenson, trans., John O'Meara, intro., *Concerning the City of God Against the Pagans*, Harmondsworth 1984

St Augustine, R. S. Pine-Coffin, trans., *Confessions*, Harmondsworth 1961

The Babylonian Talmud:

Rabbi Dr I. Epstein, B.A., Ph.D., D.Lit., gen. ed., *The Babylonian Talmud*, Soncino Press edition:

Rabbi Dr H. Freedman, B.A., Ph.D., trans., *Nedarim*, London 1936

Rabbi Dr H. Freedman, B.A., Ph.D., trans., *Shabbath*, vol. I, London 1938

A. Mishcon and A. Cohen, M.A., Ph.D., trans., *'Abodah Zarah*, London 1935

Maurice Simon, M.A., trans., *Berakoth*, London 1948

Rev. Dr Israel W. Slotki, M.A., Litt.D., trans., *'Erubin*, London 1938

Rev. Dr Israel W. Slotki, M.A., Litt.D., trans., *Niddah*, London 1948

Rev. Dr Israel W. Slotki, M.A., Litt.D., trans., *Yebamoth*, vols I and II, London 1936

Enid Bagnold, *The Squire* [1938], London 1987

Mieke Bal, 'Sexuality, sin and sorrow: the emergence of female character (A reading of Genesis 1–3)', in Susan Rubin Suleiman, ed., *The Female Body in Western Culture*, Cambridge, Mass. and London 1986

Anne Baring and Jules Cashford, *The Myth of the Goddess: Evolution of an Image*, London 1991

James Barr, 'The Authority of Scripture: The Book of Genesis and the Origin of Evil in Jewish and Christian Tradition', in G. R. Evans, ed., *Christian Authority: Essays in Honour of Henry Chadwick*, Oxford 1988

Robert E. Bell, *Women of Classical Mythology: A Biographical Dictionary*, New York and Oxford 1993

Catherine Belsey, *John Milton: Language, Gender, Power*, Oxford 1988

Phyllis Bird, 'Images of Women in the Old Testament', in Ruether

Virginia Blain, Patricia Clements, Isobel Grundy, eds, *The Feminist Companion to Literature in English*, London 1990

Alcuin Blamires, with Karen Pratt and C. W. Marx, eds, *Woman Defamed and Woman Defended: An Anthology of Medieval Texts*, Oxford 1992

Renate Blumenfeld-Kosinski, ed. and trans., Kevin Brownlee, trans., *The Selected Writings of Christine de Pizan*, New York and London 1997

Giovanni Boccaccio, G. H. McWilliam, trans., *The Decameron*, Harmondsworth 1972

Piero Boitani, Anita Weston, trans., *The Shadow of Ulysses: Figures of a Myth*, Oxford 1994

Françoise Borin, Arthur Goldhammer, trans., 'Judging by Images' in Natalie Zemon Davis and Arlette Farge, eds, *Renaissance and Enlightenment Paradoxes*, Georges Duby and Michelle Perrot, gen. eds, *A History of Women in the West*, vol. III, Cambridge, Mass. and London 1993

S. G. F. Brandon, M.A., D.D., *Creation Legends of the Ancient Near East*, London 1963

Anita Brookner, *A Misalliance*, London 1986

Charlotte Brontë, Andrew and Judith Hook, eds, *Shirley* [1849], Harmondsworth 1985

Peter Brown, *Augustine of Hippo: a biography*, London 1967

Peter Brown, 'Late Antiquity', in Veyne (1992)

Peter Brown, *The Body and Society: Men, Women and Sexual Renunciation in Early Christianity*, London and Boston 1990

Elizabeth Barrett Browning, Cora Kaplan, intro., *Aurora Leigh with Other Poems*, London 1978

Elizabeth Barrett Browning, *The Poems of Elizabeth Barrett Browning*, London and New York 1894

A. S. Byatt, *Babel Tower*, London 1996

A. S. Byatt, *Possession: A Romance*, London 1990

A. S. Byatt and Ignês Sodré, Rebecca Swift, ed., *Imagining Characters: Six Conversations about Women Writers*, London 1995

Caroline Walker Bynum, *Holy Feast and Holy Fast: The Religious Significance of Food to Medieval Women*, Berkeley, Los Angeles and London 1988

Averil Cameron and Amélie Kuhrt, *Images of Women in Antiquity*, London 1993

Eva Cantarella, Maureen B. Fant, trans., *Pandora's Daughters: The Role and Status of Women in Greek and Roman Antiquity*, Baltimore and London 1987

Umberto Cassuto, Israel Abrahams, trans., *A Commentary on the Book of Genesis, Part 1: From Adam to Noah*, Jerusalem 1961

Angela Carter, *The Passion of New Eve*, London 1982

Angela Carter, *The Sadeian Woman: An Exercise in Cultural History*, London 1979

Willa Cather, *The Professor's House* [1925], London 1981

Henry Chadwick, *The Early Church*, Harmondsworth 1993

Whitney Chadwick, *Women Artists and the Surrealist Movement*, London 1985

R. H. Charles, D.Litt., D.D., ed., *The Apocrypha and Pseudepigrapha of the Old Testament in English*, vols I and II, Oxford 1913

James H. Charlesworth, ed., *The Old Testament Pseudepigrapha*, vols 1 and 2, London 1983, 1985

Geoffrey Chaucer, 'The Franklin's Tale', in F. N. Robinson, ed., *The Works of Geoffrey Chaucer*, 2nd edition, Boston and Cambridge, Mass. 1961

Elizabeth A. Clark, *Ascetic Piety and Women's Faith*, New York 1986

Gillian Clark, *Women in Late Antiquity: Pagan and Christian Life-styles*, Oxford 1994

St Clement of Alexandria, Henry Chadwick, B.D., trans., *Stromateis, III: On Marriage*, in J. E. L. Oulton, D.D., and Henry Chadwick, B.D., trans.

and eds, *The Library of Christian Classics*, vol. II: *Alexandrian Christianity: Selected Translations of Clement and Origen*, London 1954

Gillian Cloke, *'This Female Man of God': Women and spiritual power in the patristic age, AD 350–450*, London and New York 1995

Shaye J. D. Cohen, 'Menstruants and the Sacred in Judaism and Christianity', in Pomeroy (1991)

Samuel Taylor Coleridge, Ernest Hartley Coleridge, ed., *Complete Poetical Works*, Oxford and New York 1969

Susan M. Coolidge, *What Katy Did* [1872], London 1987

Diane D'Amico, 'Eve, Mary, and Mary Magdalene: Christina Rossetti's Feminine Triptych' in David A. Kent, ed., *The Achievement of Christina Rossetti*, Ithaca and London 1987

Herbert Danby, D.D., trans., *The Mishnah*, Oxford 1933

Natalie Zemon Davis, *Women on the Margins: Three Seventeenth-Century Lives*, Cambridge, Mass. and London 1995

Lesley Dean-Jones, 'The Cultural Construct of the Female Body in Classical Greek Science', in Pomeroy (1991)

Lesley Dean-Jones, 'Medicine: The "Proof" of Anatomy', in Fantham, et al. (1995)

Lesley Dean-Jones, *Women's Bodies in Classical Greek Science*, Oxford 1996

Guillaume de Lorris and Jean de Meun, Frances Horgan, trans. and ed., *The Romance of the Rose*, Oxford and New York 1994

Jacobus de Voragine, William Granger Ryan, trans., *The Golden Legend*, vols 1 and 2, Princeton, New Jersey 1995

Bram Dijkstra, *Idols of Perversity: Fantasies of Feminine Evil in Fin-de-Siècle Culture*, New York and Oxford 1988

Isak Dinesen (Karen Blixen), *Seven Gothic Tales* [1934], Harmondsworth 1963

Mary Douglas, *Purity and Danger: An analysis of the concepts of pollution and taboo* [1966], London and New York 1984

Peter Dronke, *Women Writers of the Middle Ages*, Cambridge 1984

Daphne du Maurier, *Rebecca* [1938], London 1975

Helen Dunmore, *The Raw Garden*, Newcastle upon Tyne 1988

Helen Dunmore, *Zennor in Darkness*, Harmondsworth 1994

George Eliot, Barbara Hardy, ed., *Daniel Deronda*, Harmondsworth 1986

Nawal El Saadawi, Sherif Hetata, trans., *The Innocence of the Devil*, London 1994

Susanna Elm, *'Virgins of God': The Making of Asceticism in Late Antiquity*, Oxford 1994

The Epic of Gilgamesh, N. K. Sandars, trans., Harmondsworth 1972

Louis M. Epstein, L.H.D., D.D., *Sex Laws and Customs in Judaism*, New York 1948

Euripides, Philip Vellacott, trans., *Medea and other plays*, Harmondsworth 1963

J. M. Evans, *Paradise Lost and the Genesis Tradition*, Oxford 1968

Elaine Fantham, Helene Peet Foley, Natalie Boymel Kampen, Sarah B. Pomeroy, and H. A. Shapiro, *Women in the Classical World: Image and Text*, New York and Oxford 1995

Penelope Farmer, *Eve: Her Story*, London 1985

Eva Figes, *The Tree of Knowledge*, London 1990

Anthony Fletcher, *Gender, Sex and Subordination in England 1500–1800*, New Haven and London 1995

Neil Forsyth, *The Old Enemy: Satan and the Combat Myth*, Princeton, New Jersey 1989

David C. Fowler, *The Bible in Middle English Literature*, Seattle and London 1984

Everett Fox, trans. and ed., *The Five Books of Moses*, London 1995

Robin Lane Fox, *Pagans and Christians*, Harmondsworth 1988

Antonia Fraser, *The Weaker Vessel: Woman's lot in seventeenth-century England*, London 1984

Erich Fromm, *You shall be as gods: A radical interpretation of the Old Testament and its tradition*, London 1967

Stella Georgoudi, 'Creating a Myth of Matriarchy', in Pantel

Sandra M. Gilbert and Susan Gubar, *The Madwoman in the Attic: The Woman Writer and the Nineteenth-Century Literary Imagination*, New Haven and London 1984

Sandra M. Gilbert and Susan Gubar, *No Man's Land: The Place of the Woman Writer in the Twentieth Century*, vol. 2, *Sexchanges*, New Haven and London 1989

Charlotte Perkins Gilman, *Herland* [1915], London 1979

Louis Ginzberg, *The Legends of the Jews*, vol. I, Henrietta Szold, trans., Philadelphia 1909; vol. V, Philadelphia 1925

David J. Goldberg and John D. Rayner, *The Jewish People: Their History and Their Religion*, Harmondsworth 1987

The Goodman of Paris: A Treatise on Moral and Domestic Economy by a Citizen of Paris c. 1393, Eileen Power, trans., London 1992

Lyndall Gordon, *Charlotte Brontë: A Passionate Life*, London 1994

Robert Graves, *The Greek Myths*, Harmondsworth 1992

Robert Graves and Raphael Patai, *Hebrew Myths: The Book of Genesis*, London 1964

St Gregory of Nyssa, W. K. Lowther Clarke, B.D., trans. and ed., *The Life of St Macrina*, London 1916

Sarah Grimké, Elizabeth Ann Bartlett, ed., *Letters on the Equality of the Sexes and Other Essays*, New Haven and London 1988

H. Rider Haggard, Daniel Karlin, ed., *She*, Oxford and New York 1991

Sarah Josepha Hale, *Woman's Record*, New York 1853

John Halkett, *Milton and the Idea of Matrimony*, New Haven and London 1970

Edith Hall, *Inventing the Barbarian: Greek Self-Definition through Tragedy*, Oxford 1989

Edith Hall, 'The sociology of Athenian tragedy', in P. E. Easterling, ed., *The Cambridge Companion to Greek Tragedy*, Cambridge 1997

Margaret Patterson Hannay, ed., *Silent But for the Word: Tudor Women as Patrons, Translators, and Writers of Religious Works*, Kent, Ohio 1985

Thomas Hardy, *Tess of the d'Urbervilles: A Pure Woman*, London 1988 (text of 1912 edition)

Jane Ellen Harrison, 'Pandora's Box' in *Journal of Hellenic Studies* 20, 1900, pp99–114

Jane Ellen Harrison, *Prolegomena to the Study of Greek Religion* [1922], Princeton, New Jersey 1991

Susan Haskins, *Mary Magdalen: Myth and Metaphor*, London 1993

Judith Hauptman, 'Images of Women in the Talmud', in Ruether

Richard Hawley and Barbara Levick, eds, *Women in antiquity: New assessments*, London and New York 1995

Nathaniel Hawthorne, Malcolm Bradbury, intro., *The Marble Faun*, London and Vermont 1995

H. R. Hays, *The Dangerous Sex: The Myth of Feminine Evil*, London 1966

Alexander Heidel, *The Babylonian Genesis: The Story of the Creation*, 2nd edition, Chicago, Illinois 1951

Carolyn G. Heilbrun, 'What Was Penelope Unweaving?' in *Hamlet's Mother and other Women: Feminist Essays on Literature*, London 1991

Ernest Hemingway, *The Garden of Eden*, London 1987

Hesiod, M. L. West, trans., *Theogony* and *Works and Days*, Oxford and New York 1988

Christopher Hill, *The English Bible and the Seventeenth-Century Revolution*, London 1993

Richard Holmes, *Coleridge: Early Visions*, London 1989

Homer, E. V. Rieu, trans., *The Iliad*, Harmondsworth 1950

Homer, E. V. Rieu, trans., *The Odyssey*, Harmondsworth 1946

Olwen Hufton, *The Prospect Before Her: A History of Women in Western Europe*, vol. 1, *1500–1800*, London 1995

Laura (Riding) Jackson, Elizabeth Friedmann and Alan J. Clark, eds, *The Word 'Woman' and Other Related Writings*, Manchester 1994

Montague Rhodes James, Litt.D., F.B.A., F.S.A., trans., *The Apocryphal New Testament*, Oxford 1924

Anna Brownell Jameson, *Legends of the Madonna as represented in the Fine Arts*, London 1907

St Jerome, The Hon. W. H. Fremantle, M.A., et al., trans., *St Jerome: Letters and Select Works*, in Henry Wace, D.D., and Philip Schaff, D.D., LL.D., eds, *A Select Library of Nicene and Post-Nicene Fathers of the Christian Church*, 2nd series, vol. VI, Oxford and New York, 1893

St Jerome, F. A. Wright, M.A., trans., *Select Letters of St Jerome*, London and New York 1933

Alexander Jones, gen. ed., *The Jerusalem Bible: Popular Edition*, London 1974

Gabriel Josipovici, *The Book of God: A Response to the Bible*, New Haven and London 1988

John Keats, Nicholas Roe, ed., *Selected Poems*, London and Vermont 1995

Helen King, 'Bound to Bleed: Artemis and Greek Women', in Cameron and Kuhrt (1993)

Helen King, 'Self-help, self-knowledge: in search of the patient in Hippocratic gynaecology', in Hawley and Levick (1995)

Margaret L. King and Albert Rabil, Jr., eds, *Her Immaculate Hand: Selected Works By and About The Women Humanists of Quattrocento Italy*, New York 1983

Christiane Klapisch-Zuber, ed., *Silences of the Middle Ages*, Georges Duby and Michelle Perrot, gen. eds, *A History of Women in the West*, vol. II, Cambridge, Mass. and London 1994

A. F. J. Klijn, *Seth in Jewish, Christian and Gnostic Literature*, Leiden 1977

Ross Shepard Kraemar, *Her Share of the Blessings: Women's Religions among Pagans, Jews, and Christians in the Greco-Roman World*, New York and Oxford 1993

Henry Kraus, 'Eve and Mary: Conflicting Images of Medieval Woman', in Norma Broude and Mary D. Garrard, eds, *Feminism and Art History: Questioning the Litany*, New York 1982

Julia Kristeva, 'Stabat Mater' in Toril Moi, ed., *The Kristeva Reader*, Oxford 1986

Anne Laurence, *Women in England 1500–1760: A Social History*, London 1994

Edmund Leach, *Genesis as Myth and Other Essays*, London 1969

Hermione Lee, *Willa Cather: A life saved up*, London 1989

Mary R. Lefkowitz, *Heroines and Hysterics*, London 1981

Mary R. Lefkowitz, *Women in Greek Myth*, London 1986

Mary R. Lefkowitz and Maureen B. Fant, *Women's Life in Greece and Rome: A source book in translation*, London 1982

Ursula K. Le Guin, 'Is Gender Necessary? Redux', in *Dancing at the Edge of the World: Thoughts on Words, Women, Places*, London 1989

Ursula K. Le Guin, 'She Unnames Them' in Christina Büchmann and Celina Spiegel, eds, *Out of the Garden: Women Writers on the Bible*, London 1995

Gerda Lerner, *The Creation of Feminist Consciousness: From the Middle Ages to Eighteen-seventy*, New York and Oxford 1993

C. S. Lewis, M.A., *A Preface to Paradise Lost* [1942], London 1960

C. S. Lewis, *The Magician's Nephew* [1955], London 1990

Henrietta Leyser, *Medieval Women: A Social History of Women in England 450–1500*, London 1995

Raphael Loewe, *The Position of Women in Judaism*, London 1966

George MacDonald, C. S. Lewis, intro., *Lilith: A Romance*, Grand Rapids, Michigan 1981

Ian Maclean, *The Renaissance Notion of Woman*, Cambridge 1980

Emile Mâle, Dora Nussey, trans., *The Gothic Image: Religious Art in France of the Thirteenth Century*, New York 1972

Thomas Mann, H. T. Lowe-Porter, trans., *Joseph and His Brothers*, Harmondsworth 1978

Dacia Maraini, Dick Kitto and Elspeth Spottiswood, trans., *The Silent Duchess*, London 1992

Carol Mavor, *Pleasures Taken: Performances of Sexuality and Loss in Victorian Photographs*, London 1996

Diane Kelsey McColley, *A Gust for Paradise: Milton's Eden and the Visual Arts*, Urbana and Chicago 1993

Colleen McDannell and Bernhard Lang, *Heaven: A History*, New Haven and London 1990

Carol Meyers, *Discovering Eve: Ancient Israelite Women in Context*, New York and Oxford 1991

Midrash Rabbah: Rabbi Dr H. Freedman, B.A., Ph.D., trans., *Genesis*, vols I and II, London 1939, in Rabbi Dr H. Freedman, B.A., Ph.D., and Maurice Simon, M.A., eds, *Midrash Rabbah*, Soncino Press edition, London

John Milton, Alastair Fowler, ed., *Paradise Lost*, London and New York 1971

John Milton, Ernest Sirluck, intro. and ed., *Complete Prose Works*, vol. II, *1643–1648*, New Haven and London 1959

Lynette R. Muir, *The biblical drama of medieval Europe*, Cambridge 1995

Herbert Musurillo, trans., *The Martyrdom of Saints Perpetua and Felicitas*, in *The Acts of the Christian Martyrs*, Oxford 1972

Lynda Nead, *Myths of Sexuality: Representations of Women in Victorian Britain*, Oxford 1988

Erich Neumann, Ralph Manheim, trans., *Amor and Psyche: The psychic development of the feminine*, London 1956

Lucy Newlyn, Paradise Lost *and the Romantic Reader*, Oxford 1993

Barbara Newman, *Sister of Wisdom: St Hildegard's Theology of the Feminine*, Berkeley, Los Angeles and London 1987

Nel Noddings, *Women and Evil*, Berkeley, Los Angeles and London 1989

Mary Nyquist, 'Gynesis, Genesis, Exegesis, and the Formation of Milton's Eve', in Marjorie Gerber, ed., *Cannibals, Witches, and Divorce: Estranging the Renaissance*, Baltimore and London 1987

Julia O'Faolain and Lauro Martines, eds, *Not in God's Image*, London 1973

Ovid, Mary M. Innes, trans., *The Metamorphoses of Ovid*, Harmondsworth 1955

Ruth Padel, *In and Out of the Mind: Greek Images of the Tragic Self*, Princeton, New Jersey 1992

Ruth Padel, 'Women: Model for Possession by Greek Daemons', in Cameron and Kuhrt

Elaine Pagels, *Adam, Eve, and the Serpent*, London 1988

Elaine Pagels, *The Gnostic Gospels*, Harmondsworth 1990

Elaine Pagels, *The Origin of Satan*, Harmondsworth 1996

Dora and Erwin Panofsky, *Pandora's Box: The Changing Aspects of a Mythical Symbol*, Princeton, New Jersey 1991

Pauline Schmitt Pantel, ed., Arthur Goldhammer, trans., *From Ancient Goddesses to Christian Saints*, Georges Duby and Michelle Perrot, gen. eds, *A History of Women in the West*, vol. I, Cambridge, Mass. and London 1994

Raphael Patai, *The Hebrew Goddess*, 3rd enlarged edition, Detroit, Michigan 1990

Jaroslav Pelikan, *Mary Through the Centuries: Her Place in the History of Culture*, New Haven and London 1996

John A. Phillips, *Eve: The History of an Idea*, San Francisco 1984

Sarah B. Pomeroy, *Goddesses, Whores, Wives and Slaves: Women in Classical Antiquity* [1975], London 1994

Sarah B. Pomeroy, ed., *Women's History and Ancient History*, Chapel Hill and London 1991

James B. Pritchard, ed., *Ancient Near Eastern Texts Relating to the Old Testament*, 3rd edition with Supplement, Princeton, New Jersey 1969

Bernard P. Prusak, 'Woman: Seductive Siren and Source of Sin? Pseudepigraphal Myth and Christian Origins', in Ruether

Philip Pullman, *His Dark Materials*, 1: *Northern Lights*, London 1995 (published as *The Golden Compass*, New York 1996)

Diane Purkiss, *The Witch in History: Early Modern and Twentieth-century Representations*, London and New York 1996

Esther C. Quinn, *The Quest of Seth for the Oil of Life*, Chicago and London 1962

Theodor Reik, *The Creation of Woman*, New York 1960

Michèle Roberts, *The Wild Girl*, London 1984

Gay Robins, *Women in Ancient Egypt*, London 1993

James M. Robinson, gen. ed., *The Nag Hammadi Library in English*, 3rd edition, Leiden, New York, Copenhagen and Cologne 1988

Katharine M. Rogers, *The Troublesome Helpmate: A History of Misogyny in Literature*, Seattle and London 1966

Christina Rossetti, R. W. Crump, ed., *The Complete Poems of Christina Rossetti*, vols I and II, Baton Rouge and London, 1980, 1986

Dante Gabriel Rossetti, William M. Rossetti, ed., *The Poetical Works of Dante Gabriel Rossetti*, London 1891

Alice S. Rossi, ed., *The Feminist Papers: From Adams to de Beauvoir*, New York and London 1973

Aline Rousselle, Felicia Pheasant, trans., *Porneia: On Desire and the Body in Antiquity*, Cambridge, Mass. and Oxford 1993

Rosemary Radford Ruether, ed., *Religion and Sexism: Images of Woman in the Jewish and Christian Traditions*, New York 1974

John Ruskin, LL.D., *Sesame and Lilies*, London 1893

Olive Schreiner, 'Three Dreams in a Desert', in *Dreams*, London 1891

Mary Shelley, M. K. Joseph, ed., *Frankenstein, or The Modern Prometheus*, Oxford and New York 1980

Simon Shepherd, ed., *The Women's Sharp Revenge: Five Women's Pamphlets from the Renaissance*, London 1985

Carol Shields, *The Republic of Love*, London 1992

Giulia Sissa, 'The Sexual Philosophies of Plato and Aristotle', in Pantel

Margaret R. Sommerville, *Sex and Subjection: Attitudes to Women in Early-Modern Society*, London and New York 1995

Muriel Spark, *The Only Problem*, Harmondsworth 1995

Edmund Spenser, A. C. Hamilton, ed., *The Faerie Queene*, London and New York 1980

Elizabeth Cady Stanton, *The Woman's Bible*, Part I, New York 1895

Milton R. Stern, 'A *Marble Faun* Context', in *Contexts for Hawthorne*: The

Marble Faun and the Politics of Openness and Closure in American Literature, Urbana and Chicago 1991

Stanley Stewart, *The Enclosed Garden: The Tradition and the Image in Seventeenth-Century Poetry*, Madison, Milwaukee and London 1966

Lawrence Stone, *The Family, Sex and Marriage in England 1500–1800*, Harmondsworth 1990

Merlin Stone, *When God Was a Woman*, San Diego, New York and London 1976

Leonard Swidler, *Women in Judaism: The Status of Women in Formative Judaism*, Metuchen, New Jersey 1976

Emma Tennant, *Sisters and Strangers*, London 1990

Alfred Tennyson, Christopher Ricks, ed., *Tennyson: A Selected Edition*, Harlow 1989

Tertullian, Rev. S. Thelwall, trans., *On Female Dress*, in *The Writings of Tertullian*, vol. I, in Rev. Alexander Roberts, D.D., and James Donaldson, LL.D., eds, *Ante-Nicene Christian Library*, vol. XI, Edinburgh 1869

Tertullian, Rev. S. Thelwall, trans., *On Exhortation to Chastity, On the Veiling of Virgins*, in *The Writings of Tertullian*, vol. III, in Rev. Alexander Roberts, D.D., and James Donaldson, LL.D., eds, *Ante-Nicene Christian Library*, vol. XVIII, Edinburgh 1870

Keith Thomas, *Religion and the Decline of Magic*, Harmondsworth 1978

J. B. Trapp, 'The Iconography of the Fall of Man', in C. A. Patrides, ed., *Approaches to Paradise Lost*, London 1968

Phyllis Trible, 'Depatriarchalizing in Biblical Interpretation', in Elizabeth Koltun, ed., *The Jewish Woman: New Perspectives*, New York 1976

Phyllis Trible, *God and the Rhetoric of Sexuality*, London 1992

Bruce Vawter, *A Path Through Genesis*, London 1957

Jean-Pierre Vernant, Froma I. Zeitlin, ed., *Mortals and Immortals*, Princeton, New Jersey 1991

Paul Veyne, ed., Arthur Goldhammer, trans., *From Pagan Rome to Byzantium*, Philippe Ariès and Georges Duby, gen. eds, *A History of Private Life*, vol. I, Cambridge, Mass. and London 1992

Virgil, Robert Fitzgerald, trans., *The Aeneid*, Harmondsworth 1985

Peter Walcot, *Hesiod and the Near East*, Cardiff 1966

Michelene Wandor, *Gardens of Eden: selected poems*, London 1990

Marina Warner, *Alone of All Her Sex: The myth and cult of the Virgin Mary* [1976], London 1985

Marina Warner, *From the BEAST to the BLONDE: On Fairy Tales and Their Tellers*, London 1994

Marina Warner, *Monuments and Maidens: The Allegory of the Female Form*, London 1987

Mike Weaver, *Julia Margaret Cameron 1815–1879*, London 1984

Judith Romney Wegner, *Chattel or Person? The Status of Women in the Mishnah*, New York and Oxford 1988

R. J. Zwi Werblowsky and Geoffrey Wigoder, eds in chief, *The Oxford Dictionary of the Jewish Religion*, New York and Oxford 1997

Claus Westermann, John J. Scullion, S.J., trans., *Creation*, London 1974

Claus Westermann, John J. Scullion, S.J., trans., *Genesis 1–11: A Commentary*, London 1984

Marianne Wiggins, *Eveless Eden*, London 1995

Norman Powell Williams, D.D., *The Ideas of the Fall and of Original Sin*, London 1927

John J. Winkler, *The Constraints of Desire: The Anthropology of Sex and Gender in Ancient Greece*, New York and London 1990

Mary Wollstonecraft, Miriam Brody, ed., *Vindication of the Rights of Woman* [1792], Harmondsworth 1985

Linda Woodbridge, *Women and the English Renaissance: Literature and the Nature of Womankind, 1540–1620*, Brighton 1984

Serenity Young, ed., *An Anthology of Sacred Texts By and About Women*, London 1993

Froma I. Zeitlin, 'Signifying difference: the myth of Pandora', in Hawley and Levick

TEXT AND ILLUSTRATION
ACKNOWLEDGEMENTS

The author and publishers are grateful for permission to use text as follows:

'Maiden in the moor lay', The Bodleian Library, Oxford, MS Rawl. D. 913
   (13679), f.Ib;
'I sing of a maiden', and 'Adam lay y-bounden', The British Library, MS
   Sloane 2593, f.10b, f.11b;
'I am Eve, the wife of noble Adam', poem used by permission of the Peters
   Fraser & Dunlop Group Ltd on behalf of Frank O'Connor;
'First Coming', extract by kind permission of Susan Wicks.

PHOTOGRAPHIC SECTIONS

1. Lucas Cranach the Elder, *Fall of Man*, The Courtauld Gallery, London.
2. *Sarcophagus of Junius Bassus*, Vatican Museums and Art Galleries, Rome/
   Alinari.
3. Gislebertus, *The Temptation of Eve*, private photograph.
4. Jean Corbechon, *The Marriage of Adam and Eve*, MS 251, f.16r,
   Fitzwilliam Museum, Cambridge.
5. *Adam digging and Eve spinning with their children, Cain and Abel; Noah's Ark
   at sea*, Flemish, MS 139/1363, f.4v, Musée Condé, Chantilly/Giraudon/
   Bridgeman Art Library, London/New York.
6. Michelangelo, *The Fall of Man and the Expulsion from the Garden of Eden*,
   Vatican Museums and Galleries, Rome/Alinari.
7. Lucas Cranach the Elder, *Eve*, Galleria degli Uffizi, Florence/Scala.
8. *Cleopatra*, photograph Warburg Institute.
9. William Blake, *The Descent of the Angels to One of the Daughters of Men*,
   Rosenwald Collection, photograph © 1998 Board of Trustees, National
   Gallery of Art, Washington.

10. Hans Holbein the Younger, *Allegory of the Old and New Testaments*, National Gallery of Scotland.

11. The Burney Relief, photograph Christie's Images.

12. *Pandora and Epimetheus*, Ashmolean Museum, Oxford.

13. *Conquest of the mother goddess Tiamat by the god Marduk*, British Museum.

14. François Gérard, *Amor and Psyche/Psyche Receiving the First Kiss of Love*, Louvre, Paris, © Photo RMN.

15. Matthias Grünewald, *Annunciation*, Musée Unterlinden, Colmar/Giraudon.

16. Überrheinischer Meister, *The Garden of Paradise*, Stadelsches Kunstinstitut, Frankfurt.

17. *The Creation and Fall of Man*, Moutier-Grandval Bible, Add. MS 10546, f.5v, British Library.

18. Hieronymus Bosch, *The Earthly Paradise*, Museo del Prado, Madrid.

19. Bartolo di Fredi, *Creation of Eve*, Collegiata, San Gimignano/Scala.

20. Masolino da Panicale, *The Temptation of Adam and Eve*, Brancacci Chapel, Santa Maria del Carmine, Florence/Bridgeman Art Library, London/New York.

21. Masaccio (Tommaso di Giovanni), *Adam and Eve banished from Paradise*, Brancacci Chapel, Santa Maria del Carmine, Florence/Scala.

22. Piero della Francesca, *Death and Burial of Adam*, Basilica di S. Francesco, Arezzo/Scala.

23. Jean Cousin the Elder, *Eva Prima Pandora*, Louvre, Paris, © Photo RMN.

24. Hans Baldung Grien, *Eve, the Serpent and Death*, National Gallery of Canada, Ottawa.

25. Pol de Limbourg, *Adam and Eve in the Garden of Eden*, from the *Très riches heures du duc de Berry*, MS 65/1284, f.25v, Musée Condé, Chantilly/Giraudon/Bridgeman Art Library, London/New York.

26. Giovanni di Paolo di Grazia, *The Annunication*, Samuel H. Kress Collection, photograph © 1998 Board of Trustees, National Gallery of Art, Washington.

27. The Master of the Straus Madonna, *Virgin and Child Enthroned with Angels and Saints*, photograph courtesy of Astley Cheetham Art Gallery, Stalybridge, Tameside MBC Leisure Services.

28. Hugo van der Goes, *Adam, Eve and the Serpent*, Kunsthistorisches Museum, Vienna.

29. Berthold Furtmeyer, *Tree of Life and Death*, Archbishop of Salzburg's missal, Clm 15710, fol. 60v, Bayerische Staatsbibliothek, Munich.

30. Rogier van der Weyden, *Mary Magdalene*, Louvre, Paris, © Photo RMN.

31. Dante Gabriel Rossetti, *Mary Magdalene at the Door of Simon the Pharisee*, Fitzwilliam Museum, Cambridge.
32. William Blake, *Satan, Sin and Death: Satan Comes to the Gates of Hell*, from the Butts series of illustrations to Milton's *Paradise Lost*, courtesy of the Huntington Library, Art Collections, and Botanical Gardens, San Marino, California.
33. A mermaid with a fish in her grasp, photograph courtesy of J. C. D. Smith.
34. A mermaid socializing with the devil and a wyvern, photograph courtesy of J. C. D. Smith and the Dean and Chapter of Bristol Cathedral.
35. Rembrandt van Rijn, *Adam and Eve*, Rosenwald Collection, photograph © 1998 Board of Trustees, National Gallery of Art, Washington.
36. Dante Gabriel Rossetti, 'Buy from us with a golden curl', illustration for Christina G. Rossetti, *Goblin Market and Other Poems*, London 1862, private photograph.
37. Agnolo Bronzino, *An Allegory with Venus and Cupid*, © National Gallery, London.
38. The Hon. John Collier, *Lilith*, reproduced by kind permission of the Metropolitan Borough of Sefton Leisure Services Department, Arts and Cultural Services Section, Atkinson Art Gallery, Southport.
39. Kate Carew caricature, photograph courtesy of The Estate of Mary Williams Reed, alias Kate Carew.
40. Tamara de Lempicka, *Adam and Eve*, Christie's Images / © ADAGP, Paris and DACS, London 1998.

CHAPTER ILLUSTRATIONS

The Bodleian Library, University of Oxford:
Intro. and Endpapers. Inset illustration to Genesis 3, Coverdale Bible, Cologne (?), S.Seld.c.9, f.ii recto, bottom (sig.aii recto);
 3. *Eve proffering the forbidden fruit to Adam while the Tempter urges her on*, MS Junius 11, p31;
 4. John Flaxman, engraved by William Blake, *Pandora Opening the Vase*, in *Compositions from the Works, Days and Theogony of Hesiod*, plate 8. Vet A6 b6;
 5. *Penelope*, a detail from the first page of Tacuino's edition of Ovid, Venice, C.8.17.Art.sig.Aiii recto (3rd f. recto);
 6. Joseph Fletcher, *The Historie of the Perfect-Cursed-Blessed Man*, France, 4° P 43. Th (2). Oppos. page 1 (oppos. sig.E1 recto);
 10. From the *Speculum Humanae Salvationis*, B. Richel, Basel, 1476, Douce 277, f.2 recto (left).

Photograph Warburg Institute:

2. Antonio Tempesta, *Three Men Come to Abraham*, Genesis 18:2;

7. Erhard Schön, *Six Old Testament Heroines*;

8. Israhel van Mechenem, *Virgin and Child with Apple*;

9. Albrecht Dürer, *Fall of Man*;

11. Daniel Hopfer, *Eve*;

Afterword. Iobst Aman, *Mother Eve*.

INDEX